EXCAVATIONS AT SALONA, YUGOSLAVIA

EXCAVATIONS AT SALONA, YUGOSLAVIA

(1969–1972)

conducted for

THE DEPARTMENT OF CLASSICS, DOUGLASS COLLEGE,

RUTGERS, THE STATE UNIVERSITY OF NEW JERSEY

by

CHRISTOPH W. CLAIRMONT

with the collaboration of

SUSAN HANDLER AUTH

VICTORINE VON GONZENBACH

Under the auspices of THE SMITHSONIAN INSTITUTION, Washington, D.C. and

THE YUGOSLAV INSTITUTE FOR INTERNATIONAL TECHNICAL COOPERATION, Belgrade.

NOYES PRESS

Park Ridge, New Jersey

Library of Congress Catalog Card Number: 75-29768
ISBN: 0-8155-5040-5

Published in the United States by
NOYES PRESS
Noyes Building
Park Ridge, New Jersey 07656

Library of Congress Cataloging in Publication Data

Clairmont, Christoph W 1924-
Excavations at Salona, Yugoslavia, 1969-1972.

"Under the auspices of the Smithsonian Institution, Washington, D.C. and the Yugoslav Institute for International Technical Cooperation, Belgrade."
Bibliography: p.
Includes index.
1. Salona, Dalmatia. I. Auth, Susan Handler, joint author. II. Gonzenbach, Victorine von, joint author. III. Rutgers University, New Brunswick, N.J. Douglass College. Dept. of Classics. IV. Smithsonian Institution. V. Yugoslav Institute for International Technical Cooperation. VI. Title.
DR396.S63C55 939'.8 75-29768
ISBN 0-8155-5040-5

CONTENTS

Preface vii
List of Figures xi
List of Plates xiii
Abbreviations and Bibliography xv
Note to Reader xvi

Section One—The Excavations, Chronology, and History

I. General Introduction 1
Christoph W. Clairmont
II. The Topography of Salona 11
Christoph W. Clairmont
Excursus I: Panel LXXXVI of the Column of Trajan 26
Excursus II: Caesar, *De Bello Civili* III.9 36
III. The Excavations 38
Christoph W. Clairmont and *Victorine von Gonzenbach*
Introduction 38
The Curia Site 39
The Workshop Area 56
Forum Central Site 63
Forum North Site 67
IV. The Chronological Evidence 83
Victorine von Gonzenbach
Charts 91
V. The History of the Site 106
Christoph W. Clairmont
VI. The Frescoes and Stuccoes 109
Christoph W. Clairmont
The Frescoes 109
Catalogue of Frescoes 116
Stuccoes 124
Catalogue of Stuccoes 125
VII. Inscriptions
Christoph W. Clairmont

Section Two—The Small Finds

VIII. Coins 133
Victorine von Gonzenbach
Catalogue of Coins 136
IX. Roman Glass 145
Susan Handler Auth
Introduction 145
Fine Wares 149
Blue-Green Vessels 156
Non-Vessel Glass 166
Chemical Analyses of Some Glasses from Salona 176
Robert H. Brill

X. Pottery from Closed Deposits 181
Victorine von Gonzenbach
Late Hellenistic Table Wares 184
Early Roman Table Wares 187
Coarse Household Wares 189
Summary 192
Catalogue of Pottery 194
XI. Stone Monuments 209
Christoph W. Clairmont
Sculpture 209
Architectural Fragments 210
Miscellaneous Stone Objects 211
Revetment Plaques 212
XII. Lamps 213
Victorine von Gonzenbach
Hellenistic to Late Republican Lamps 214
Picture Lamps from the First to the Third Century A.D. 216
Firma Lamps, First to Third Century A.D. 219
African Lamps, Fourth to Sixth Century A.D. 220
Lamp from Asia Minor 222
XIII. Metal Objects 223
Christoph W. Clairmont
Bronze Objects 223
Iron Objects 224
Lead 226
XIV. Bone and Ivory 227
Christoph W. Clairmont
Pins, Needles and Other Utensils 227
Disks, Buttons, and Miscellaneous Pieces 228
XV. Clay Objects 229
Christoph W. Clairmont
Architectural Tiles 229
Other Tiles 230
Other Clay Objects 230
XVI. Miscellaneous Finds 231
Christoph W. Clairmont
Stone Mosaic Tesserae 231

Concordances 232
General Index 234
Plates following page 236

PREFACE

Excavations at Salona were made possible by a grant from the Smithsonian Institution, Washington, D.C., under the Foreign Currency Program act. The Principal American Investigator who signs as editor and contributing author of the present report and all those who collaborated with him express their deep appreciation to the authorities of the Smithsonian Institution for making available the grant. We owe sincere thanks for assistance and patience in complex negotiations to Kennedy B. Schmertz, Deputy Director, Foreign Currency Program; Kenneth D. Whitehead, Deputy Director, Foreign Currency Program; Miss Constance Rogers, Grants Technical Assistant; and Mrs. Betty Wingfield, who was most helpful in travel arrangements. We are much indebted also for assistance in various matters to the U.S. Embassy in Belgrade and in particular to Wilfred Declercq, Science Officer; Vladan Barlovac, assistant; and Mrs. Lenka Terzin, of the Fiscal and Budget Office.

The excavations were conducted under the auspices of the Smithsonian Institution in cooperation with the Yugoslav Institute for International Technical Cooperation in Belgrade. We are grateful to this agency and the Archaeological Museum in Split for permission to excavate at Salona. Although the general plan for the Salona excavation called for collaboration between the Yugoslav and the American team, we did not share the excavations proper. Thus, the proceedings in the field and the results obtained were each team's own responsibility and this holds true also for the present final report. Various other tasks have urged my collaborators and myself to make the results of our excavations available as quickly as possible; it is hoped that the report of the excavations of the Yugoslav team will follow soon so as to shed light on the intricate problems of settlement at Salona which we now hope to understand with new perspectives and insights before us. We are deeply grateful to all for their help and continued effort to iron out many of the problems an excavation encounters. In particular we wish to thank the following for their personal interest and goodwill in making the excavations a success: Branimir Gabričević, Principal Yugoslav Investigator; Mladen Nikolanci, Director, Archaeological Museum, Split; Jelko Rapanic and Nenad Cambi, both from the Archaeological Museum, Split; and D. Rendić-Miočević, University of Zagreb, who excavated part-time with the Yugoslav team and discussed many of the problems concerning the history of Salona with the members of the American team.

A grant from the Research Council of Rutgers, The State University of New Jersey, aided the excavation in 1969. We acknowledge this grant with particular thankfulness and extend our appreciation to Charles F. Main, Assistant Director of the Research Council. The grant enabled us to buy some needed equipment more easily obtainable in the U.S. than in Yugoslavia and also contributed towards the transportation and per diem allowance of graduate and undergraduate students from Rutgers University who participated in the excavations.

It is with pleasure that we record here a small grant from the Dean's fund of Douglass College. Our thanks go to Dean Margery S. Foster, who thus contributed to travel needs of participating Douglass students, members of the American team. Dean Foster took also a lively interest in the excavations and, spending three days with us in 1970, expressed her enthusiastic support. The excavations also profited from the cooperation of Dr. Anna Benjamin, chairperson of the Department of Classics, Douglass College. In fact, Dr. Benjamin carries much of the responsibility for instigating the idea of an excavation in conjunction with the program in Archaeology taught by the Department of Classics.

Full scale excavations were conducted during the summers of 1969 and 1970 for six and eight weeks respectively. In 1972, the undersigned returned to Salona for three weeks to clarify certain points in the excavations left unresolved in the previous two campaigns; moreover, extensive conservation work was then carried out in compliance with the laws of the Yugoslav

Republican Institute for the Protection of Cultural Monuments.

The present volume contains a historical-topographical introduction to the site; the description of our excavations; the chronological evidence and conclusions with regard to the history of Salona; and finally, the publication of all small finds, excepting the pottery, which we felt contribute significantly to the overall picture of the site, limited as our excavations were. Pottery published in the present volume includes the stratigraphically dated finds only, as it were some closed deposits all of which date from the Hellenistic period. In a second volume the pottery from Salona from the late Hellenistic period to the sixth century A.D. will be published in a predominantly *typological* sequence. However, the pottery from our excavations is fully evaluated from a *chronological* point of view in the discussion of the history of the site. It is clear, therefore, that the conclusions which we have drawn with regard to the development of the very core of the city, namely the Hellenistic settlement and the Roman Forum, rest to a very large extent on the finds of the coins and of pottery. The significance of both is highly important, if not crucial.

The success of an excavation depends to a large extent on the efficiency, endurance, and continued interest of one's collaborators. The undersigned has had the privilege of finding these qualities present to a high degree in his collaborators, thus lightening the weight of the many tasks which confronted him. I express my sincere appreciation to all of those who worked with us in Salona. The following persons were members of the 1969 American team: Jochen Twele, who drew the plans of the 1969 excavation and supervised various trenches; Mario del Chiaro from the University of California at Santa Barbara, who acted as Field Director's Associate; Mrs. Ann Twele, who was responsible for the inventory and general field organization; the graduate students John Rosser and John McClintock, both from Rutgers University, who supervised trenches; and their assistants Joann Roskoski and Nancy Curriden, undergraduates of Douglass College.

The following persons were members of the 1970 American team: Victorine von Gonzenbach Clairmont, who was in charge of the pottery finds; Susan Handler Auth, in charge of supervising trenches and of studying the glass; Peter Carrington, University of New Castle, England, who supervised the trenches; Jeffrey Greene, who was responsible for drawing the plans of the 1970 excavation and for coordinating both seasons of excavations into the final plans as they appear in this volume; Peter Roselli and the undergraduates Anne Zeloof, Richard Mowery, Robert Scheetz, and James A. Kaufmann, all of who assisted the excavations in many different ways. Mr. Kaufmann was responsible for colored drawings of the frescoes (which, due to high cost, could not be reproduced in this volume) and for most of the drawings of other objects.

With a grant from the Smithsonian Institution, Victorine von Gonzenbach and the undersigned spent several weeks in Split in the winter of 1971-72, in order to study and prepare the finds for final publication. The drawing of the extensive finds of pottery was continued in the summer of 1972, again with the support of the general excavations funds. We wish to express our thanks to the Smithsonian Institution for its continued financial support so that the task before us could be carried to the end.

Susan Handler Auth returned to Split in the summer of 1971 with a grant from the Smithsonian Institution to continue the study of the glass which was begun by her in 1970. She also travelled widely in Yugoslavia itself, visiting museums and sites. We extend our appreciation to the excavators of these sites visited by the authors for permitting us to see their finds and sharing with us problems of dating and of interpretation. Our thanks go to Sheila McNally and the University of Minnesota team, Palace of Diocletian, Split; Edward Ochsenschlager and his colleagues from the excavations at Sirmium; Silvio Skefich and his colleagues from the excavations at Nin;

James Wiseman and his colleagues from the excavations at Stobi; J. Medini from the Archaeological Museum at Zadar.

I owe much gratitude to Susan Handler Auth for having taken upon herself the publication of the Roman glass. She has seen the present report in all its different stages and growth and has contributed greatly to its general improvement.

Victorine von Gonzenbach's task of sorting, cataloguing, drawing and studying the pottery from Salona turned out to be an immense one. Much more pottery was found than could normally be expected, this being largely due to the specific conditions of the site. However the reward for having done this job will be great and appreciated by others who will have to follow her pioneering work if the scientific publication of excavations in Dalmatia is to continue.

Victorine von Gonzenbach's contribution to the present volume is slim if counted by the number of pages, but not otherwise: hers is the careful coordination of the finds of coin and pottery which resulted in determining the general development and history of the site within a chronological framework which derives from archaeological data.

We received much needed assistance in the cleaning and identification of the coins. Our thanks go to Mr. John C. Goyne for the coins found in 1969 and to Herbert Cahn and his collaborators for the coins found in 1970.

We greatly appreciate the time and effort which Dr. Robert H. Brill has given to the analyses of some Roman glass from Salona. His report may be found after the chapter on Roman glass (pp. 176-180).

Professor Dr. Hellmut Sichtermann of the German Archaeological Institute in Rome kindly provided the photographs of details of panel LXXXVI of the column of Trajan in Rome (figs. 7-10); I should like to thank him here for his kindness.

Tomislav Marasović and his staff from the Town Planning Institute of Dalmatia in Split kindly offered their help in various ways while we worked at Salona and permitted the editor of the present report to look through the papers left by E. Dyggve to the Institute for anything of interest with respect to Dyggve's unpublished excavations prior to World War II.

I am greatly indebted to the Research Council of Rutgers University and to its Assistant Director, Professor Charles F. Main, for having awarded me a University Fellowship, a year's leave of absence during 1970-71. It was during this year that the foundations were laid for the present report.

The Research Council has contributed handsomely to the printing costs of the present publication. Our gratitude for this much needed financial support is great indeed.

While in Rome in 1970-71, we enjoyed the hospitality of the American Academy in Rome. Our sincere thanks go to Bartlett Hayes, Director; Frank E. Brown, Director of Classical Studies; and Nina Langobardi, Librarian of the Academy.

Many colleagues in the United States and abroad, on the New Brunswick and Princeton campuses, and at the Institute for Advanced Study in Princeton, have greatly encouraged us by their genuine interest in our work. To all of these go our heartfelt thanks.

Finally, we are greatly indebted to Robert Noyes of the Noyes Press for his acceptance of the present volume for publication. It was a pleasure to work with him and his very efficient staff and, in particular Mrs. Elsie Ehrhardt, who typeset this difficult book; and Mrs. Martha Gillies, who has seen the volume through the press and has saved us from many errors, inconsistencies, and pitfalls. To be sure, for those which remain the undersigned takes full responsibility.

New Brunswick, New Jersey
May 1, 1975

Christoph W. Clairmont
Douglass College
Rutgers, The State University of New Jersey

INDEX OF FIGURES

1 View of southeast angle of platform with arcades. *page* 12
2 Remains of *Capitolium, torcularium,* and portion of drain with pedestal. 12
3 Trench 2, outside *Capitolium.* 14
4 Westernmost wall of *Capitolium.* 14
5 Entrance to Forum central area in Forum enclosure wall. 16
6 Forum central drain with pedestal base. 16
7 Detail of Panel LXXXVI, column of Trajan, Rome. 28
8 Detail of Panel LXXXVI, column of Trajan, Rome. 29
9 Detail of Panel LXXXVI, column of Trajan, Rome. 30
10 Detail of Panel LXXXVI, column of Trajan, Rome. 31
11 Preparation for excavation of curia site, from *Capitolium.* 40
12 Square A3, curia site. 42
13 Square A'4, remains of period I wall, curia site. 42
14 Squares A/B5-6, period I-III walls and apse of curia. 42
15 Squares A/B5-6, period I walls and curia south wall. 43
16 Squares A/A'3-6, period I-III walls and apse of curia. 43
17 Square A'7, curia site, period I wall east. 43
18 Square A'7, curia site, period I wall F and drain b. 44
19 Square A7, curia site, period I, drains c, d. 44
20 Curia after completion of restoration and conservation work. 46
21 Apse of curia; fresco level. 46
22 Curia eastern cross wall and western wall with corner slab. 46
23 Western cross wall of curia with giant corner slab. 48
24 Inscription CIL III. 8817 referring to restoration of the curia. 50
25 Square A'7 of curia site showing portions of pavement and period IV walls. 52
26 Curia site, square A'1. 52
27 Curia site, square A1, remains of drain. 52
28 Curia site, square B3 showing remains of wall with revetment plaque. 54
29 Squares A'6-7 of curia site showing period IV walls behind apse. 55
30 Workshop area in curia site showing remains of glass tank, charcoal pit, and wall A. 56
31 Workshop area showing charcoal pit in course of excavation and wall B. 56
32 Workshop area showing furnace and walls E and F. 57
33 Workshop area showing period IV wall and furnace wall. 58
34 Workshop area; furnace wall with plaster, and wall F. 58
35 Workshop area showing bottom of charcoal pit with lead pipes. 60
36 Workshop area showing south edge of glass tank and adjacent "floor." 60
37 Trench 4 in Forum central site, with walls A-D and Corinthian capital. 64
38 Trench 4 with Corinthian capital and walls C-D. 64

39	Period IV walls E-F, showing reused slabs from Forum drains.	*page* 64
40	Trench 1; Forum and *Capitolium.*	66
41	Trench 2 looking toward Forum central drain with pedestal base.	66
42	Trench 3 looking towards Forum central drain with pedestal base.	68
43	Trench 5 on Forum central site, looking north.	68
44	Trench 5 on Forum central site.	68
45	Forum north site before excavation.	69
46	Forum north site showing period I wall in E5A.	71
47	Period I wall in E4A with period III drain.	71
48	Period III drain and period II wall; north-south wall with remains of plaster.	71
49	W5A in Forum north site showing northern face of east-west main wall.	72
50	E3A in Forum north site with north-south wall.	72
51	W5A in Forum north site showing northern face of east-west main wall.	72
52	Squares W3-5A/C showing portions of Forum north drain and period II-IV walls.	73
53	W3B/C in Forum north site showing period II walls.	73
54	E2-4A of Forum north site showing period III drain.	74
55	E2-3B, Forum north site showing period III and period II walls.	75
56	W5A/AA showing foundation walls for Forum north portico.	76
57	Forum north portico showing upper layers of wall foundation.	76
58	Forum north site, E5AA showing lower layers of foundations for Forum north portico.	76
59	Forum north site, E2B/E3C, showing period IV walls and Forum north drain.	77
60	Fragmentary column in E2C, in context of period IV walls.	78

PLATES

All plans, photographs, and drawings are by the architects (J. Twele, J. Greene), the authors (VvG, SHA, CWC), and the photographer of the Split Museum, Split, unless otherwise specified.

1 Dalmatia. Redrawn after J.J. Wilkes, *Dalmatia* (Harvard University Press, 1969), Fig. 3 (p. 18).

2 Salona bay. Redrawn after J.J. Wilkes, op. cit. Fig. 7 (p. 222).

3 Curia site, period I.

4 Curia site, period IV.

5 Forum north site, period I.

6 The city of ancient Salona. Redrawn, with additions, after E. Dyggve, *Recherches à Salona* I (1928–1933), pl. B (pp. 16–7).

7 Forum of Salona with excavations, 1969–1972.

8 Curia site, periods II–III.

9 Forum north site, period II.

10 Forum north site, period III.

11 Forum north site, period IV.

11 bis Forum central site, Trench 5(E3J/K).

12 Frescoes, catalogue nos. 38, 39, 43, 44, 49.

13 Frescoes, catalogue nos. 50–55.

14 Frescoes, catalogue no. 56.

15 Frescoes, catalogue nos. 57–62.

16 Frescoes, catalogue nos. 63–66, 82.

17 Frescoes, catalogue nos. 67–72.

18 Frescoes, catalogue nos. 73, 74, 79, 80.

19 Frescoes, catalogue no. 76.

20 Frescoes, catalogue no. 77.

21 Frescoes, catalogue nos. 77, 78.

22 Frescoes, catalogue no. 81.

23 Stuccoes, catalogue nos. 1, 2.1–2.3.

24 Stuccoes, catalogue nos. 3.1–3.8, 4.1–4.3.

25 Stuccoes, catalogue no. 4.4.

26 Inscriptions, catalogue nos. 1, 2, 5.

27 Inscriptions, catalogue nos. 6–9.

28 Glass, catalogue nos. 8–12, 14, 15, 24–26, 28, 30, 37.

29 Glass, catalogue nos. 38, 39, 41–52.

30 Glass, catalogue nos. 53–62, 64, 67–70, 72–77, 80, 81, 83, 84.

31 Glass, catalogue nos. 85–90, 93–99, 103, 105, 105a, 106, 107, 107a, 108, 109, 109a, 110–112.

32 Glass, catalogue nos. 1, 4, 12, 18, 22, 25, 26, 35, 38, 41, 42, 61, 67, 70, 72, 77.

33 Glass, catalogue nos. 80, 81, 89, 90, 93, 95–99, 102, 106, 112, 113, 115, 118.

34 Pottery, catalogue nos. P5, P6, P14, P15, P15a, P17, P18, P18a.

35 Pottery, catalogue nos. P22–P24, P31–P39.

36 Pottery, catalogue nos. P42, P44, P53, P57.

37 Pottery, catalogue no. P63.

38 Pottery, catalogue nos. P67, P68, P72, P73, P151.
39 Pottery, catalogue nos. P62, P80, P114a, P122, P123.
40 Stone, catalogue nos. 1–4.
41 Stone, catalogue nos. 11–15.
42 Stone, catalogue nos. 16–21.
43 Stone, catalogue nos. 22–24, 26.
44 Stone, catalogue nos. 28, 29, 31–37.
45 Stone, catalogue nos. 4–8, 10.
46 Stone, catalogue nos. 25, 30.
47 Stone, catalogue nos. 9, 27, 38.
48 Lamps, catalogue nos. 1–5.
49 Lamps, catalogue nos. 9–21.
50 Lamps, catalogue nos. 22–28, 30.
51 Lamps, catalogue nos. 32-36, 38, 39, 41–43.
52 Lamps, catalogue nos. 31, 40.
53 Lamps, catalogue nos. 44, 45, 47–52.
54 Lamp, catalogue no. 46.
55 Bronze, catalogue nos. 1, 2, 8, 19, 20, 23, 24, 28, 29, 32–34.
56 Bronze, catalogue nos. 35, 36, 40–42.
57 Bronze, catalogue nos. 43–45. Lead pipes.
58 Bronze, catalogue nos. 4, 7, 9, 10, 14–18, 21, 22, 25, 30.
59 Bone/Ivory, catalogue nos. 1-16.
60 Bone/Ivory, catalogue nos. 20–30.
61 Clay, catalogue nos. 5–7, 10, 11.
62 Clay, catalogue no. 9.
63 Clay, catalogue nos. 7, 10, 12, 16, 20, 22–24, 26.
64 Clay, catalogue nos. 17, 21, 25.

ABBREVIATIONS AND BIBLIOGRAPHY

Alexander	J. Alexander, *Yugoslavia before the Roman Conquest* (1972).
Alföldy, *Bevölkerung*	G. Alföldy, *Bevölkerung und Gesellschaft der römischen Provinz Dalmatien* (1965).
Aslanapa	O. Aslanapa, "Pottery and Kilns from the Iznik Excavations," *Forschungen zur Kunst Asiens. In memoriam K. Erdmann* (1969).
Braccesi, *Grecità*	L. Braccesi, *Grecità Adriatica. Un Capitolo della Colonizzazione Greca in Occidente* (1971).
Bulić I	Fr. Bulić, "Escavi nella Necropoli Antica Pagana di Salona, detta Hortus Metrodori negli anni 1909 e 1910," *BD* 33 (1910); 3-66, 130-135.
Ceci, *MP*	E. Ceci, *I Monumenti Pagani di Salona* (1962).
Ceci, *MC*	E. Ceci, *I Monumenti Christiani di Salona* (1963).
Davies	O. Davies, *Roman Mines in Europe* (1935).
Dyggve, *Forum*	E. Dyggve, "Le forum de Salone," *RA*, VIe ser., vol. I (1933): 41-57.
Dyggve, *HSC*	E. Dyggve, *History of Salonitan Christianity* (1951).
Dyggve, *Recherches I*	E. Dyggve, *Recherches à Salone I* (with the collaboration of Fr. Weilbach and J. Bronsted, 1928-1933).
Dyggve, *Recherches II*	E. Dyggve, *Recherches à Salone II* (1928-1933).
Egger, *Magdalensberg*	R. Egger, "Ausgrabungen auf dem Magdalensberg 1956 und 1957," *Carinthia* 149 (1959), pp. 3-143.
FS I	R. Egger, W. Gerber, and M. Abramić, *Forschungen in Salona. Die Bauten im Nordwestlichen Teile der Neustadt von Salona* (1917).
FS II	R. Egger, *Der Altchristliche Friedhof von Manastirine nach dem Materiale von Fr. Bulić* (1926).
FS III	E. Dyggve and R. Egger, *Der Altchristliche Friedhof Marusinac* (1939).
Forrer	R. Forrer, *Die römischen Terrasigillata Töpfereien von Heiligenberg-Dinsheim und Ittenweiler im Elsass* (1911).
Grenier	A. Grenier, *Manuel d'Archéologie Gallo-Romaine,* vol. III, *L'Architecture* (1958).
Knorr	R. Knorr and Fr. Sprater, *Die westpfälzischen Sigillata-Töpfereien von Blickweiler und Eschweiler Hof* (1927).
Lehmann-Hartleben, *Hafenlagen*	K. Lehmann-Hartleben, *Die antiken Hafenanlagen des Mittelmeers* (1923).
Liversidge	J. Liversidge, *Britain in the Roman Empire* (1928).
Patsch, *Dalmatien*	C. Patsch, "Archäologisch-epigraphische Untersuchungen zur Geschichte der römischen Provinz Dalmatien," *WMBH* 9 (1904), 171 ff.
Staehelin	F. Staehelin, *Die Schweiz in römischer Zeit* (1947).
Virunum	C. Praschniker and H. Kenner, *Der Bäderbezirk von Virunum* (1947).
Ward-Perkins	J.B. Ward-Perkins, "From Republic to Empire: Reflections

	on the early provincial architecture of the Roman west," *JRS* 60 (1970): 1-19.
Wilkes	J.J. Wilkes, *Dalmatia* (1969).
Wymer	J.E. Wymer, *Marktplatz-Anlagen der Griechen und Römer* (1916).

PERIODICALS

AI	*Archaeologia Iugoslavica,* Belgrade.
BD	*Bullettino di archaeologia e storia dalmata* (also catalogued under *Vjesnik za Arheologiju i Hostoriju Dalmatinsku.*
St Aq	*Studi Aquileiesi*, Aquileia.
WMBH	*Wissenschaftliche Mitteilungen aus Bosnien und der Hercegovina.*

For further, more specialized bibliographies, see Excursus I, Frescoes, Pottery, Coins, Roman Glass, and Lamps. For a general and exhaustive bibliography on Dalmatia up to 1969, see Wilkes, pp. 509-529 and the additions by Šašel in *Gnomon* 44 (1972): 582-589.

NOTE TO READER

The following abbreviations are used throughout:

H.	Height	A	Architecture
W.	Width	Bo	Bone
L.	Length	Bz	Bronze
D.	Diameter or depth	G	Glass
Dim.	Dimensions	G.T.	Glass tank
Th.	Thickness	G.W.	Glass workshop
n. (nn.)	note(s)	Ir	Iron
no. (nos.)	number(s)	Iv	Ivory
ch.	chart(s)	L	Lamp
Trench 1	Trench in Capitolium temple	M	Marble
		P	Pottery
Trench 2	Trench immediately to north of Capitolium	Sc	Sculpture
		St	Stone
Trench 3	Trench to the north of Forum central drain	T	Terracotta
		V	Varia

Provenience of Objects

Reference to the grid plan locations of the curia site consists of one letter and one figure, for instance: A1, B6, or two letters and/or two figures in case of adjacent squares, A/B5, B5-6, B/C3-4, etc. References to the grid plan of the Forum north site consist of two letters and one figure, or combination of letters and figures in case of adjacent squares, for instance: E2B, W3C, E3J/K, etc.

The provenience of objects is recorded in the catalogue by reference to the grid plans; all inventory nos. are found in the Concordances, except for those of the coins, for which see the catalogue of coins and those of the pottery for which see the catalogue of pottery.

I

General Introduction

The ancient city of Salona lies approximately in the middle of the Dalmatian coast between the peninsula of Istria, to the south of Trieste, and the present day Yugoslav-Albanian borderline (**Plate 1**). The coastline has a very irregular, indented formation; due to many small and large islands and many well protected bays it does not lie open to the west but is hidden behind them. Present day Split, Roman Aspalathos, the site of Diocletian's palace, is one of five major modern towns along the coast which are all in the vicinity of ancient forerunners. In the far north lies Rijeka, near ancient Tarsatica; further south comes Zadar, Roman Iader; then Šibenik, whose closest Roman predecessor would be Scardona; finally Dubrovnik (medieval Ragusa), to the north of its Greco-Roman forerunner Epidaurum. Split and Solin—the latter being the modern name for ancient Salona—are only a few kilometers apart. Soon the two will form one large agglomeration, stretching northwards as far as Trogir (Greek Tragurion, Roman Tragurium) and southwards to Stobreč (Greek Epetion, Roman Epetium). Whereas the rapid increase of the population living along the coast is a very recent development, the distribution and number of people settled in Dalmatia during the 19th century, before industry began to move in, can probably yield some comparison with the size of the colonies and *municipia* during the era of Roman occupation.

At the present day, the contours of the ancient city of Salona can be recognized from points situated higher, for instance Klis or Mt. Marijan to the northwest of Split because, as an archaeological zone, it is protected from building and thus appears as an unobstructed green patch amidst the fast growing community of Solin. As modern industrial development expands, the isolation of the site will become more apparent still. The patience with which peasants cultivate their vineyards on the ancient ruins stands in stark contrast to the polluting smoke which emerges from the cement factories nearby and to the incessant flow of traffic which skirts the ancient walls.

In plan, Salona appears as a rectangle with the long axis running from northeast to southwest (**Plate 6**). The rectangle is narrower in its western half; toward the south the city line ran more or less parallel with the shore of the bay of Salona. It would be difficult to find a better, more protected site for a harbour, this certainly being one of the reasons for a settlement here. The same holds true for practically every foundation along the Dalmatian coast—a shore which presents a most inviting configuration for the situating of harbours (**Plate 2**).

The foundation and growth of Salona and some controversial problems concerning the city are intimately bound to the history of Dalmatia at large which has been recently and very carefully discussed by J.J. Wilkes.[1] I shall attempt in the following pages to give a summary of foreign, Greek-Sicilian penetration into Dalmatia and its adjacent islands. Since the area around Salona assumed greater importance in the second and first centuries B.C., it will become necessary to discuss in some detail certain events of major political significance in this period.

The period of Christian Salona has received perhaps more attention than any of its previous phases of pre-Roman and Roman history. We may mention in particular the archaeological excavation and publications by E. Dyggve and R. Egger.[2]

However, the political history of the first three centuries after Christ is not of immediate concern for us, nor can we add much to what is known already.

Greek colonization in central Dalmatia antedates the very active political involvement of Dionysios I of Syracuse in this area by some two hundred years (**Plates 1 and 2**). We hear first of the Cnidians who founded a colony on the island of Korčula (Corcyra nigra), midway between Split and Dubrovnik. Scanty finds as well as literary sources attest to late archaic and classical foundations on the islands of Pharia or Pharos (Hvar), Brattia (Brač), and Melite (Mljet). Greek goods were traded with the native Illyrians who usually lived fairly close to the coast or along navigable rivers such as the Narenta, midway between Split and Dubrovnik.[3] However, the evidence for finds of Greek origin in stratified contexts is extremely scanty. Nor up to now, has fortune been on the side of those who have tried to locate and actually uncover the foremost early Greek settlements. Other problems arise with late fourth century or Hellenistic settlements which, also settled in Roman times, continued to be inhabited in medieval and later days so that it is virtually impossible to get at the earliest levels. Both Tragurion and Epetion fall into this category. The chance discovery in Trogir of a copy of the relief depicting *Kairos,* the original of which is attributed to Lysippos, indicates what treasures may still lie in the earth.[4] The island of Issa (Vis) is better known than any of the other Greek settlements in the central part of Dalmatia largely because in the early fourth century its history is linked to Dionysios I, and recent excavations there have yielded remains of late classical and Hellenistic date.[5]

It is now a commonly accepted view that the citizens of Tragurion, which itself was founded by Issa, established an *emporion* some time in the Hellenistic period to the south of their own city; its name was Σάλων. This emporion lies on the same bay as Tragurion itself; however the distance to the other subcolony of Issa in this area, Epetion, is slightly less than that from Salona to Tragurion.

One can speculate about the reasons which led to the foundation of the emporion. To add a third well-protected harbor to those already in existence at Tragurion and Epetion cannot have been the reason. The main concern of Tragurion must have been the territory between itself and Epetion which, then as now, is very precious ground for cultivation such as is not available immediately to the north of Tragurion nor to the south of Epetion. A gradual infiltration of traders may have made some of this territory available to the colonists, territory which, as far as we know, was under the control of the native Delmatae.

Why did not Issa from the very beginning decide to set up a single subcolony in roughly the center of the general area instead of two subcolonies at both ends of it? This question cannot be answered unless one considers the more basic issue of the relationship between Greeks and native inhabitants. In all their dealings in this territory, the colonists had to reckon with an important factor: how to get along in peaceful terms with the native Illyrians. For Issa, M. Nikolanci recently wrote basing his views on epigraphical studies of Professor Rendić-Miočević, that

> ...les colons n'étaient pas exclusivement des Syracusains, mais que la nouvelle cité comprenait aussi un assez grand nombre d'Illyriens de l'Italie du Sud.... Il est difficile pour le moment d'établir la part de l'élément local illyrien dans cette symbiose gréco-illyrienne, bien qu'elle semble avoir été importante à en juger non seulement d'après le *psephisma* de Lumbarda, mais aussi d'après les trouvailles archéologiques (tombes illyriennes à céramique grecque importée découvertes dans les environs immédiats d'Issa et de Pharos).[6]

If we can believe with Mr. Nikolanci that on the island of Issa Syracusans were settled side by side with Illyrians from southern Italy, then this common enterprise may have had decisive influence upon the ensuing colonizing ventures.

The founding of subcolonies on the mainland may have proceeded more smoothly than one is inclined to think, with the Illyrians from Issa acting as mediators between the Issaean colonists and the native Illyrians on the mainland.

The colonists who settled Tragurion and Epetion must have faced the problem of coexistence with the Illyrians under different conditions than the Issaeans. There was no natural protection such as sea-girt Issa had.[7] On the mainland, the natives overwhelmingly outnumbered the colonists, with their strength being in the immediate hinterland rather than directly on the coast. Thus the foundation of subcolonies on the coast was probably a very daring proposition.

The answer to the question as to why the colonists founded settlements at the edges of the territory rather than in the center—which would have been the logical place to choose for strategic reasons—is that the native Illyrians themselves had a convenient access from the hinterland to the sea in that very key location. This is where the Iader River discharges into the bay of Salona, an area through which anybody going along the coast must pass and one which lies immediately at the foot of the mountains and the pass which leads via present-day Klis to the hinterland.[8]

It is this combination of quick access by the shortest possible route to the hinterland and the excellence of the harbour which was certainly fully recognized by the Illyrians and taken advantage of by them. The growing importance of Salona at the expense of Tragurion and Epetion and the fact that, later, Salona was made capital of the Roman province of Dalmatia shows that first the Greek colonists, then the Romans themselves, became fully aware of its strategic location. With the foundation of an emporion the colonists began penetrating the area where the Illyrians had their harbour.

As for the foundation dates of Tragurion and Epetion, Professor D. Rendić-Miočević is inclined to lower the date to the middle of the third century B.C. in contrast to other earlier authors.[9] He proposes this latter date because he feels that the decree from Lumbarda (on the island of Corcyra nigra), which yields the reference of interest to us here, cannot be dated on epigraphical grounds before the middle of the third century B.C.[10] Rendić-Miočević's dating was most recently challenged by L. Braccesi as being too late.[11] Whatever the reasons proferred by both authors for their respective dating, it is obvious that the final decision rests with archaeologists. In this, as in all similar cases, we need the spadework which will hopefully bring to light traces of the earliest colonization and thus provide its date.

The knowledge that Tragurion was actively involved in the foundation of an emporion near the river mouth of the Iader results from an improved reading of the so-called "Decree of 56 B.C." by Rendić-Miočević.[12] The indirect context of the decree is Caesar's presence in the northern Adriatic (Aquileia). The subject matter of the decree was thought formerly to deal with the legal status and relationship between the mother-colony Issa and the daughter-colony Salona.[13] In substituting for the old reading *πρεσβε[υ]σάντων παγια[.......* the new reading *πρεσβε[υ]σάντων Τραγυρι[νῶν]*—which is what the surviving letters demand—D. Rendić-Miočević proposed that not Issa, but Tragurion, took an active part in the foundation of the emporion. Shortly after a supposed personal visit of Caesar to the original Greek settlements in Dalmatia and shortly before a *conventus civium Romanorum* was established in Salona, the people of Tragurion—not the people of Issa—refer in the decree to the "securing of their priority in legal matters in Salona—on the condition that they themselves as well as Issa uphold *τὴν φιλίαν καὶ τὴν συμμαχίαν τοῦ δῆμου τῶν Ρωμαιῶν*—which was received in so solemn a fashion from the emperor in Aquileia and which had given them the impulse to give due publicity to these important declarations." Thus Rendić-Miočević believes that, beside the native population called by him the Illyrians and Iadastini, there existed at Salona "at the mouth of the Iader also a small emporion" with a community of merchants sent out from Tragurion.[14] Our recent work in Salona permits us to agree with Rendić's reasoning. Before attempting to discuss the date of the foundation of the emporion, it is necessary to consider the evidence for the presence of natives in this area.

Even the latest excavations at Salona have not yielded the slightest remains of any native settlement from the fourth century B.C. onwards. Thus, any finds said to have come from the wider territory of Salona which precede this date must have reached the site as trading goods which were exchanged with the natives; these finds should *not* be interpreted as evidence for a settlement of Greek merchants.[15]

Spadework has not yet given an answer to the question of how early the Delmatae settled near the river mouth of the Iader. If our assumption that the colonists from Issa chose the sites of Tragurion and Epetion because the Delmatae were already present in the Salona area is acceptable, then the Delmatae must obviously have come here prior to the founding of Tragurion and Epetion; as seen previously, a date either in the fourth or third century B.C. has been proposed as foundation date for these two cities on the basis of the decree from Lumbarda.

As for the founding of an emporion by Tragurion in the territory of the Delmatae, the archaeological evidence—scanty as it is—which we ourselves have unearthed, suggests a date in the first half of the second century B.C. An emporion of colonists from Tragurion could have coexisted with the small harbour of the Delmatae specifically mentioned by Strabo.[16] Harbour installations could be very primitive and transitory in such an ideally protected bay. This is certainly one reason for their disappearance, although the general changes due to natural causes such as the silting up of the southeast end of the bay by the river Iader and the drop in level of the coastline should equally strongly be considered.

As we intimated earlier, the principal concern of the natives was to have access to the sea from the hinterland via the shortest possible route, rather than to settle down at the waterfront. However, this was different for the settlers who came from Tragurion. If we are correct in our interpretation of the earliest finds from Salona, the emporion, even if very small, was a settlement in a *strategic* position on a low hillock which, as will be seen, also formed the nucleus of the Roman town of Salona. We wish to emphasize in particular that it would be wise to visualize the emporion on as small a scale as possible.[17]

In 167 B.C., Illyria came under the jurisdiction of the Roman people.[18] After this event, the Roman army was actively involved in wars against the Delmatae of central Dalmatia.[19] The coastal area was in deep trouble by the mid-second century (158/7 B.C.). Polybius relates that in Issa the colonists complained to the Romans about the raids of the Dalmatians which involved their own territory and that of Tragurion and Epetion.[20] Gaius Fannius was sent to investigate "τὰ κατὰ τὴν Ἰλλυρίδα, καὶ μάλιστα τούτων τὰ κατὰ τοὺς Δελματεῖς." It becomes clear from this passage that, beside the mother colony, Tragurion and Epetion were considered alien bodies within Dalmatian lands. There is no reference to the Salona area for reasons by now, obvious.

In 157/6 B.C. the Romans decided to make war against the Delmatae.[21]. Delminium, capital of the Delmatae, was definitely destroyed in 155 B.C.[22]

We hear of Salona again in 119/8 B.C. The reference is in Appian's *Illyrike*[23] and reads as follows, summing up the years from 157-118 B.C.:

> The Dalmatians, another Illyrian tribe, made a raid on the Illyrian subjects of Rome, and when ambassadors were sent to them to remonstrate they were not received. The Romans accordingly sent an army against them, with Marcius Figulus as consul and commander. While Figulus was laying out his camp the Dalmatians overpowered the guard, defeated him, and drove him out of the camp in headlong flight to the plain as far as the river Naro. As the Dalmatians were returning home (for winter was now approaching), Figulus hoped to fall

> upon them unawares, but he found them reassembled from their towns at the news of his approach. Nevertheless, he drove them into the city of Delminium, from which place they first got the name of Delmatenses, which was afterwards changed to Dalmatians. Not being able to make any impression on this strongly defended town by assault, nor to use the engines that he had, on account of the height of the place, he attacked and captured the other towns, which were partially deserted on account of the concentration of forces at Delminium. Then, returning to Delminium, he hurled sticks of wood, two cubits long, covered with flax and smeared with pitch and sulphur, from catapults into the town. These were fanned into flame by the draught, and, flying in the air like torches, whereever they fell caused a conflagration, so that the greater part of the town was burned. This was the end of the war waged by Figulus against the Dalmatians. At a later period, in the consulship of Cecilius Metellus, war was declared against the Dalmatians, although they had been guilty of no offence, because he desired a triumph. They received him as a friend and he wintered among them at the town of Salona, after which he returned to Rome and was awarded a triumph.

The text corroborates our assumption that Delmatae were in Salonitan territory from the very beginning. Their number may indeed have increased considerably with the fall of Delminium, with many Delmatae deciding to seek a new place to live and actually coming to the Salona area.[24] However, one must be cautious about Appian's mentioning of a *polis*. Granted that archaeologists may have completely missed so far the polis of the Delmatae, granted that nobody has discovered the harbour of the Delmatae which Strabo mentions, and granted further that even the emporion was largely levelled to make room for Roman buildings erected during the Imperial period, there simply is no trace of a native Dalmatian settlement or what Appian calls the polis of the Delmatae.

A possible solution for this conflict, in which the literary evidence is not supported so far by the archaeological finds, is to assume that *emporion* and *polis* are one and the same. The finds from the Hellenistic period are clear evidence for the presence of merchants; these finds also testify to their Greek connections. However, objects which would attest beyond doubt the presence of Illyrians are lacking. This, of course, does not mean that Delmatae were altogether absent from the area; in fact, among the pottery in the second to first century B.C. of the emporion settlement are quite a few pieces of handmade coarse ware of typically Illyrian tradition. This, then, would rather simply intimate that "culturally," if not in numbers, the merchant-colonists were predominant, causing Appian to use the term *polis*.[25]

The passage in Appian is of interest for another reason. C. Metellus wished to celebrate a triumph. It so happens that the Delmatae in this part of their territory did not give cause for any attack as they had done elsewhere in 158/7 B.C. Thus Appians tells us that C. Metellus spent the winter among the Delmatae and the triumph was awarded to him for military prowess achieved earlier in the Save valley from where he proceeded eventually to the coast in search for another battleground. The difficulties which this text creates have been interpreted recently in an interesting article by M.G. Morgan.[26] Morgan believes that when Appian says that C. Metellus "wintered among the Delmatae" in 119/8 B.C. in Salona...

> it seems clear that this town, like others along the south Illyrian coast, still contained a Greek element in Metellus' day, this despite steadily increasing pressure from the native Delmatae which culminated in their taking over the town completely in the early part of the first century. It is most plausible to suppose, therefore, that the people of Salona were already under sufficient pressure in 119 to appeal to Rome for help against the Delmatae of the hinterland, and that Metellus used the town as his base of operations and wintered there between campaigns. But if this is what happened, it follows that he undertook

little more than a "police" action against the Delmatae, and yet claimed—and received—a triumph for his efforts.[27]

We agree in principle with Morgan's interpretation of the events, but should like to emphasize that, though Metellus may have actually stayed in the emporion settlement, this was not, as was said earlier, the place where the Delmatae lived. Appian may have used the term "wintering among the Delmatae," because Salona was like an enclave in the territory of the Delmatae which, as time proceeded, the natives were more and more eager to occupy and possibly even to destroy. The presence of C. Metellus served its purpose well because a takeover of Salona by the Delmatae was delayed for more than a generation.

Just when Salona was captured by the Delmatae is difficult to say. More crucial are the questions of whether it was captured for a long period or whether the Delmatae made a punitive invasion and then left, continuing to keep a close watch on the emporion and perhaps limiting some of its freedom and prerogatives. First of all, there is again the problem of the *urbem florentissimam* of Orosius which Cosconius is said to have wrested from the possession of Delmatae in a two-year battle (78-76 B.C.).[28] Topographically and archaeologically speaking the existence of such an *urbs* must be seriously doubted. If it is anywhere, it has not been found, but it is not identical with the Hellenistic emporion which preceded on the same spot the nucleus of Roman Salona. Thus, Cosconius must have dealt with the Delmatae in quite a large area, subdividing them and restoring to the settlers of Salona their freedom of movement and security.

It was this very freedom and security which caused a considerable influx of Italian settlers in the twenty years following the Roman conquest. This led to a change in the composition of the inhabitants of the area with the Roman settlers soon becoming the predominant element beside the original settlers from Tragurion. A *conventus civium Romanorum* may have been founded in 57/6 B.C. at the earliest.[29] Whether or not Caesar visited Salona in 57 B.C., actively concerned about establishing such a *conventus,* we remember the following year as that of the so-called "Decree of 56 B.C."[30] Confirming the rights of the merchant-settlers from Tragurion in the fast growing Roman-Italian community, the decree gives us at the same time a clue to the population of the settlement of Salona and the general area. The masters were the Romans; the merchant-settlers were in the minority; the Delmatae, all around the actual town, no doubt still in the majority, accepted their new masters grudgingly and before long were their open enemies.

Thanks to Caesar's own writing, considerable light is thrown on the conduct of each of the ethnic groups during the ensuing civil war. The Delmatae and the island of Issa, which in itself was of very mixed population, (Syracusans, Illyrians from south Italy, and Romans since the conquest of the island by the latter) sided with Antony. The Romans in Salona, as well as the settlers originally from Tragurion, remained faithful to Caesar despite all attempts of Antony to win the *conventus civium Romanorum* over to his side. Proving unsuccessful, Antony besieged Salona in 48 B.C. It was defended heroically by the Roman citizens. The defense ended in disaster for Antony, who fled with his ships and with a much reduced number of soldiers.[31]

The events of 47 B.C. which Caesar relates about A. Gabinius, who eventually took refuge in Salona after bitter and most devastating fights with the Delmatae, show most clearly how inimical the latter were to the Romans who sided with Caesar.[32] So inimical indeed that only a politically well-organized *conventus* which had the support of the Roman army could survive.[33]

Salona became *Colonia Martia Iulia Salona* after the events of the civil war but before Caesar's death, that is between 47 and 44 B.C. The faithful allegiance of the Roman citizens of Salona to Caesar was most probably the reason for the foundation of the colony. The colonists were enrolled in the voting tribe *Tromentina* which, in subsequent years, existed side by side with a second voting tribe *Sergia*. The existence of the latter led scholars to believe that in addition to a Caesarian colony, a second colony was founded by Octavian, perhaps in 34/3 B.C. but definitely before 27 B.C., thus considerably strengthening the Caesarian colony.

Since we are ill-informed about events in Salona from 47 to 34 B.C., one may surmise that Delmatae once more endangered the city's existence, so that the motives for the founding of a second colony were not exclusively political but military as well. Serious problems arise when modern authors try assiduously to make the status of double colony agree with the topography of the city of Salona and especially with the building of walls. Although both Wilkes and Alföldy express themselves cautiously, realizing the lack of archaeological evidence, it seems to us that they (and others) adhere much too rigidly to the preconceived notion of *spatial* division of the two colonies in the settlement as a whole.[34] As a double colony with two voting tribes, Salona became the provincial capital of Roman Dalmatia.

The period from 33 B.C. to A.D. 9 was full of dangers for the Roman colonists. The Delmatae rebelled against the Romans on several occasions before their pacification in A.D. 9. Roman soldiers were hard pressed against Illyrians, Pannonians, and other tribes along the Danube. Salona was almost captured by Bato early in the first century of our era. The great revolt of the barbarians in A.D. 6 was brought under control three years later and "Roman control was established over the western Balkans, with a frontier line along the river Danube."[35] The attack of Bato was the last time Salona was in danger for a long period to come—namely, until A.D. 169.

Salona steadily grew in size through the arrival of Italian colonists. Issa, which had chosen the wrong side during the civil wars, now became subject to Salona as one of her "most remote parts."[36] Roman colonists settled, too, in Tragurium and Epetium, both cities being now dependencies of Salona. The original emporion, founded by a small number of Greek merchants about 200 B.C. within the territory of the Delmatae, thus grew to become the Roman capital of Dalmatia.

We are ill-informed about the political history of Salona from the reign of Tiberius to that of Diocletian. More than groundwork has been laid for "Bevölkerung und Gesellschaft" in Dalmatia by Geza Alföldy, whose magnum opus bears that very title and which, in conjunction with the same author's *Personennamen*, is and remains the standard work of reference for this aspect of Dalmatia's history. Wilkes's *Dalmatia* deals with specific institutions, notably the Roman army, in greater breadth; moreover, the author's interest in the settlements and their excavation has resulted for the first time in a more comprehensive survey of the Roman-Illyrian civilization in Dalmatia. That it is in no way complete, is not Wilkes's fault. The political history of Imperial Roman Dalmatia cannot be written because of the lack of literary sources for the period concerned, as well as the lack of inscriptional material and archaeological monuments to complement and support the literary sources. To illustrate this difficulty by just one example: though it is perfectly admissible to believe that Trajan passed through Salona on his way to the Danube, we do not know whether or not he in fact did, because this is a point which neither Roman historians nor Trajan himself reveal. The only evidence, questionable and hypothetical as it is, is panel LXXXVI on the column of Trajan which we deal with separately in an excursus.[37]

No miracle will produce the literary testimonies which we need. As for the inscriptions and archaeological monuments, a great miracle would have to occur to reverse the severe delapidation and continuous destruction of the site of Salona since late antiquity.

Notes on Chapter 1

[Abbreviations and Select Bibliography for this chapter will be found on page xv.]

1. See Wilkes pp. 35 ff.

2. See Bibliography, passim.

3. Wilkes, pp. 1 ff. For the age of colonization and Syracuse's expansion into the Adriatic, see the recent work by Braccesi, *Grecità*. The colonies of Issa–Tragurion and Epetion–and pre-Roman Salona are the subject of the last chapter, pp. 191 ff.

The term Illyrians is used here as a general term for the natives who lived along the coast and the immediate hinterland. Literary and epigraphical sources distinguish many differently named peoples. See Wilkes, pp. 1-9.

4. M. Abramić, "Ein neues Kairos-Relief," *OeJh* 21 (1930): 1-8; Lippold, *Griechische Skulptur. Handbuch der Archäologie* (1950), p. 281.

5. B. Gabričević, "Antička Issa. Contribution historico-archéologique au plan de regulation urbanistique de la ville de Vis," *Urbs* 2 (1958): 105-126; idem, *Antički Spomenici Otoka Visa* (1968).

6. M. Nicolanci, "Contacts gréco-illyriens sur la côte est de l'Adriatique," *AI* 5 (1964): 49-60; the quote is from p. 54. Excavations in Issa and finds from these excavations should calm doubts concerning its "colonial foundation by Dionysios I of Syracuse." Wilkes seems overly cautious with regard to this issue in *BJb* 166 (1966): 649, reviewing Alföldy's *Bevölkerung.* For other finds which establish contacts between South Italy (Apulia, Messapia) and Dalmatia see Nicolanci, pp. 53-54.

7. Even so, Issa did not escape the threat of a siege by the Illyrians in 229 B.C. See Polybius II.11.11 f. The arrival of troops under G. Fulvius and Aulus Postumius averted the danger but Issa was placed henceforth under Roman protection.

8. See Alföldy, *Bevölkerung,* pp. 99 f. and the reference in Strabo VII.5.5.: *ἡ τῶν Δαλματέων παραλία καὶ τὸ ἐπίνειον αὐτῶν Σάλων.* Alföldy's wording suggests that this reference has meaning primarily for the mid-second century B.C., when "die Macht der Delmaten in der Umgebung von Salona bedeutend zunahm." However, the reference in Strabo could well include an earlier period, from the moment when the Delmatae were seeking a foothold to the sea at this specific point. Moreover, the passage of Strabo quoted above stands in definite contrast to the preceding one in which are named "Issa, Tragurion, ... Pharos, formerly known as Paros." These sites are mentioned simply as "*ἄλλαι νῆσοι,*" independently from any tribe or nation who ruled them. Strabo knew, of course, that they were colonies and, though Tragurion is not really an island, it may be described as an enclave on Dalmatian territory. Epetion is omitted, but Strabo, speaking of *νῆσοι*, cites three only, to him *γνωριμώταται.* For the origin of the word of the locality Klis (Kleis) see Ceci, *MP*, p. 67, n. 9.

9. "Zur Frage der Datierung des *Psephisma* aus Lumbarda (Syll.[3], 141)," *AI* 6 (1965): 77-80, with reference to earlier discussions of the *psephisma.*

10. Almost a hundred years later than the previously proposed date.

11. Braccesi, *Grecità*, pp. 195-198.

12. D. Rendić-Miočević, "Ricordi aquileiesi nelle epigrafie di Salona," *StAq* 1953, 67-76, with previous literature on the decree. See also M. Nicolanci, (loc. cit. note 6), p. 54; Ceci, *MP*, pp. 34 f.

13. Alföldy, *Bevölkerung,* pp. 99 f., n. 28:, Wilkes pp. 38 f., 220. Wilkes cites the article by D. Rendić-Miočević in his Bibliography (p. 524) but does not fully exploit the new reading when the occasion arises (p. 220).

14. See D. Rendić-Miočević, "I Greci in Adriatico," *Studi Romagnoli* 13 (1962): 39-56, a title to be added to Wilkes' Bibliography. M. Abramić speaks of "Faktoreien" in reference to mainland settlements in "Antike Kopien griechischer Skulpturen in Dalmatien," *Festschrift R. Egger* vol. I (1952), p. 305.

15. There are a number of finds in the Split Museum which fall into this category, although their provenience is disputed. It is an urgent task for the Museum authorities to publish fully in the form of lists the proveniences (if known) of the different categories of objects (especially the small finds) from Salona and vicinity now in the Museum.

16. For the specific period which Strabo refers to, see note 8.

17. The misleading concept of a "Greek Salona" which appears here and there in modern authors should definitely be abandoned in the light of recent excavations. See pp. 00 for Dyggve's insistence on this concept. See also Bulić I, p. 22; Ceci, *MP*, pp. 33 f.; C. Patsch, "Der Kampf um den Donauraum unter Domitian und Trajan," *Sb. Phil.-Hist.Kl.Akad.Wiss,* Wien 217, 1 (1937), pp. 3 ff.; G. Novak, "Das griechische Element in Dalmatiens Stätten," *Carnuntina* 3 (1956): 117-125. Nor can we find any evidence in Polybius (XXXII.18.1 ff.) that "die griechische

Siedlung von Salona wurde von den Delmaten erobert" (so Alföldy, *Bevölkerung*, pp. 99 f.). This would be virtually unnecessary if the Delmatae held the territory near the river mouth of the Iader as Strabo suggests. There is a reference in Polybius to the conquest of Tragurion and Epetion which would indicate that these towns were predominantly settled by Greeks (Syracusans, etc.) rather than by a mixed Greco-Illyrian population.

18. Wilkes, p. 26.

19. Wilkes, pp. 29 ff.

20. Polybius, XXXII.18.1 ff.

21. Polybius, XXXII.19.1 ff.; Appian, *Illyrike* II.11.

22. Wilkes, pp. 31, 89, 179, 183, 188. The city was rebuilt elsewhere; see Wilkes, pp. 271 ff.

23. Appian, *Illyrike* II.11. Translation by H. White from Loeb Classical Library Edition: Appian, *The Illyrian Wars,* vol. II (1912), p. 71.

24. See note 8. It is tempting, but extremely hypothetical, to connect the earliest activity in wall building in Salona with the increase of population from the mid-second century B.C. onward.

25. Among these finds there is only one complete profile, a two-handled cup. For closely related vessels see Alexander, p. 72, fig. 36; p. 127, fig. 74, and pp. 100 f. and map fig. p. 101, with reference to Solin (no. 86). For the stratified pieces of this coarse pottery see the chapter on Pottery.

26. M. Gwyn Morgan, "Lucius Cotta and Metellus. Roman campaigns in Illyria during the late second century," *Athenaeum* 49 (1971): 271-301. I am thankful to the author for an offprint of his article and clarification of some points in correspondence.

27. Morgan, (loc. cit. note 26), pp. 292 f.

28. Orosius, *Hist.* V.23.23: "Cosconius proconsul, sortitus Illyricum, protrita subactaque Dalmatia, Salonas urbem florentissimam post biennium tandem expugnavit et cepit." Eutropius VI.4: "Ad Illyricum missus est C. Cosconius pro consule. Multam partem Dalmatiae subegit, Salonas cepit composito bello Roman post biennium rediit." Note in both texts the plural use of Salona. For the double city see the discussion later. See also Wilkes, p. 35 for Cosconius' warfare.

29. See the quotation from Caesar (note 31). We cannot understand how Suić can derive from Caesar that the *conventus* was founded in 59 B.C.; M. Suić, "Sulle municipalità dell'antica Salona," *BD* 60 (1958): 40. Alföldy, *Bevölkerung,* p. 100 writes of a "reorganization of the Greek colony." But Salona was hardly a colony in the sense that we can speak of reorganization. The *conventus* is very likely the first attempt at political organization proper on Salonitan territory.

30. See note 12.

31. Caesar, *B.C.* III.9. Translation by A.G. Peskett from Loeb Classical Library edition: Caesar, *The Civil Wars* (1951), p. 207.

> On the departure of the Liburnian galleys from Illyricum, M. Octavius comes to Salonae with the ships under his command. There he diverts Issa from its friendship with Caesar, stirring up the Dalmatians and the rest of the Barbarians. Failing to influence the Roman citizen body at Salonae, either by promises or by threatenings of peril, he set himself to besiege the town. Now, the town was strongly protected by the nature of its site and by a hill. But the Roman citizens, rapidly constructing wooden towers, protected themselves with them, and being weak in resistance owing to their small numbers, worn out by constant wounds, betook themselves to the last resource of despair and armed all their grown-up slaves, and cut off the hair of all their women to make catapult ropes. Octavius, having ascertained their sentiments, surrounded the town with five camps and began to press the inhabitants at once by blockade and by siege operations. Prepared to endure everything, they suffered most in the matter of corn supply. To remedy this they sent envoys to Caesar and begged his aid. The rest of their troubles they endured by themselves as well as they could. And after a long interval, when the protracted siege had made the Octavians rather careless, taking advantage of the opportunity afforded by the hour of noon when the enemy had withdrawn, they placed their boys and women on the walls that no particular of their daily routine might be missed by the besiegers, and forming themselves into a band, together with those whom they had just recently liberated, they burst into the nearest camp of Octavius. This being taken by storm, with a similar onset they attacked the second, then the third and fourth, and the remaining one in its turn, and drove the men out of all the camps, and having slain a great number, forced the rest and Octavius himself to fly to the ships. Such was the end of the siege. And now winter approaching, and Octavius, despairing of the siege of the town after receiving such heavy losses, retired to Dyrrachium to Pompeius.

See also the Excursus II.

32. Caesar, *Bell. Alex.* 43. Translation by A.G. Way, from Loeb Classical Library edition: Caesar, *Alexandrian, African and Spanish Wars,* (1955), p. 79.

When Gabinius came to Illyricum in the difficult winter season,—whether it was he thought the province was more abundantly supplied, or whether he set great store by Caesar's winning luck, or whether he trusted his own courage and skill, which had many a time enabled him, when surrounded by the hazards of war, to score great successes by his personal leadership and initiative—anyway he derived no support from the resources of the province, bled white as it partly was, and partly disloyal, nor could supplies be conveyed to him by ship, since stormy weather had interrupted navigation. As a result of these considerable difficulties he was forced to conduct the campaign, not as he wished, but as necessity dictated. And so, as lack of supplies forced him to storm towns or strongholds in very adverse weather, he frequently sustained reverses, and was held by the natives in such contempt that, while retreating on Salona, a coastal town occupied by very gallant and local Roman citizens, he was forced to fight an action on the march. In this battle he lost more than two thousand soldiers, thirty-eight centurions and four tribunes: with what was left of his forces he retired to Salona, where, under the stress of overwhelming difficulties of every kind he fell sick and died within a few months. His chequered fortune while alive and his sudden death inspired Octavius with high hopes of securing possession of the province; luck, however, which is a very potent factor in war, as well as the carefulness of Cornificius and the courage of Vatinius, did not allow Octavius to pursue his successful career much longer.

Both the siege and defense of Salona and Gabinius' defeat are also related in Dio Cassius XLII.11.

33. For additional sources and discussion see Wilkes, pp. 41 f. For a summary of the viewpoints and discussion see Wilkes, pp. 220-224. Among the authors who have contributed in particular to this question see Alföldy, *Bevölkerung,* pp. 101 ff.; R. Syme, "Pollio, Saloninus and Salonae," *CQ* 31 (1937): 39-48; M. Suić; (loc. cit. note 29), pp. 39-42.

34. See Wilkes, pp. 225-226 and Alföldy, *Bevölkerung,* pp. 103 f. Thus Caesar's colony occupies the *urbs vetus* and is divided by a wall from the Augustan colony which settled in the easternmost portion or *urbs orientalis.* Both colonies are connected by a monumental gate, the *Porta Caesarea.* But as of 1971, the town sites had not been sufficiently investigated to permit any such conclusions. There is much reason to doubt that the soil of Salona will ever yield the evidence which would enable us to either reject or accept the theory of spatial division of the colonies. (See our later discussion.) Very improbable are the views held by G. Novak, "Das griechische Element in Dalmatien's Stätten," *Carnuntina* 3 (1956): 117-125; idem, "Isejaska i rimska Salona," *Rad Jugoslavenske Akademije znanosti i umjetnosti* 270 (1949): 67-92. Novak believes that Salona consisted of two parts independent from each other: an Issean-Greek and a Roman, which absorbed the earlier Illyrian. The latter belonged to the voting tribe *Tromentina,* the former to the voting tribe *Sergia.* The Issean-Greek part "war nicht ganz autonom, sondern ist in enger politischer Beziehung zur Mutterstadt Issa geblieben."

We refer to Salona throughout our discussion in the singular Salona, not the plural Salonae. See Ceci, *MP* p. 15, nn. 1 and 2. The problem of "Doppelkolonien" was recently discussed in an interesting monograph by H. Galsterer, *Untersuchungen zum römischen Städtewesen auf der Iberischen Halbinsel* (1971). See especially pp. 12 and 19 with nn. 21, 26, 27, 56.

35. Wilkes, p. 46. The whole period from 35 B.C. to A.D. 9 is admirably dealt with in great detail by Wilkes, pp. 46-77.

36. Wilkes, p. 229. For a different opinion, namely that Issa remained largely autochthonous, see Marin Zaninović, "Decuriones at Salona," *Vestigia, Beiträge zur alten Geschichte,* vol. 17. *Akten des* VI. *internationalen Kongresses für griechische und lateinische Epigraphik* (München, 1972), pp. 499-502. The author also mentions that there is no centuriatio in Issa. For the colony's territory and the *centuriatio* of Salona see Wilkes, pp. 226-230. For the *centuriatio* of Iader see J. Bradford, "A technique for the study of centuriation," *Antiquity* 21, no. 84 (1947): 197-209.

37. For the first to third century see Ceci, *MP*, pp. 50 ff.

II

The Topography of Salona

The present-day visitor to Salona will find numerous relics of the pagan period (**Plates 6 and 7**). The survey of these monuments, some of which are in great danger of disappearing under the lush growth of vegetation, draws heavily on evidence in excavation reports. It should prove useful also for the reader to become acquainted with the topography of the city before we begin with the description of our own excavation (**Plates 3 to 5 and 8 to 11**).

Dyggve has made it clear in his later writings that Salona grew in three steps, first the *urbs vetus,* second the *urbs orientalis* or *urbs nova,* and finally the *urbs occidentalis.*[1] The *urbs vetus* is, basically speaking, of later Hellenistic date. Since vestiges of private houses and remains of possible public buildings are extremely scarce, it is difficult to say at the present to what extent the *urbs vetus* was, in fact, occupied. The entire problem will be dealt with later with reference to our own excavation. The *urbs orientalis* is of early Imperial date; it was mainly settled in the first century A.D. and completely surrounded with a wall in A.D. 170. The *urbs nova* or, more conveniently, the *urbs occidentalis* is later than any of the aforementioned parts. At first, the only building in this area may have been the amphitheater; in A.D. 170, the amphitheater was enclosed by the city wall, the theater itself forming part of the enclosure. The building activity in the *urbs occidentalis* must have been at its height during the late second and third centuries.

We shall now discuss in some detail the remains of the Roman Imperial city (excepting our own excavation) and subsequently the remains of Republican walls and Roman harbour installations.

As one proceeds from Split to Solin and takes the old coastal road to Trogir (not the modern highway which runs along the northern side of the ancient city), one notices among the first vestiges of the Roman city a row of six arcades, running in an east-west direction (**Figure 1 and Plate 6**). The pilasters and arcades are built with smoothly fitting stones. However, there is at present no open passage through the arcades into rooms or possibly one big hall. The opening of each arcade is blocked by stones. The first arcade from the east is adjacent to the southeast corner, from which a solid eastern wall proceeds in a northerly direction.

Only four of the arcades show fully above the ground; farther towards the west, however, the segments of the arcades grow narrow, with the wall gradually disappearing under an artificial rise of the terrain which supports the coastal road. All in all there were twelve arcades, the twelfth stopping at the southwest corner from which a wall runs northward, parallel to the eastern wall mentioned previously. The whole structure is most suitably called a platform. The south wall with the arcades may originally have reached a height of from 6 to 8 meters of which about a third is preserved today above the ground. The length of the platform toward the north is 65 m; the width of the platform is 45 m. The surface of the platform is now cultivated with vines and

Figure 1: View of southeast angle of platform with arcades, looking north.

Figure 2: Forum central area. In foreground remains of Capitolium; beyond torcularium and portion of drain with pedestal.

vegetables; at its north end are two peasant houses, one very close to the northeast corner, the other equally close to the northwest corner. Immediately to the west of the latter is the Roman theater.

Ever since the lengthy description by Cichorius of panel LXXXVI on the column of Trajan,[2] the wall with the arcades has been discussed by other authors and notably by Dyggve.

Dyggve refers to the structure as

> une très grande citerne ou bien un magasin de blé ou d'autres denrées. La situation de cet édifice sur le port rend la seconde hypothèse plus vraisemblable. Si c'était une citerne, il eut été plus rationnel de la disposer de telle sorte qu'elle put mettre à profit les grosses quantités d'eau qui tombaient dans le théâtre, vu que ce dernier édifice est à proximité....La ressemblance de plan avec d'autres magasins romains est très frappante. On a trouvé ici en outre (avant 1823) une grande quantité de *dolia.*[3]

The concept of the cistern, first rejected in favor of the store-rooms, seemed acceptable to Dyggve later.[4] Barrel vaulted structures for *horrea* are not uncommon in the Roman period, serving also as *podia* for platforms.[5] It seems to us that interpreting the structure as store-rooms with a platform above is more acceptable than interpreting it as a cistern. The reason, however, that the platform was built in this location is due in our opinion to the growth of the Roman Forum in the early Imperial period. Because of the recent excavations, we are perhaps in a better position to deal with some topographical aspects of Salona than earlier authors who lacked the evidence now available.

Caesar refers to an "eminence" which was fortified and courageously defended against the attacks of Antony by the Roman settlers, who formed a *conventus.*[6] Even though the great amount of cultivation, modern road-building, and the retreat of the waters in the bay tend to distort the physical aspect of ancient Salona, this eminence can still be seen quite well. The feature of the eminence was undoubtedly much more prominent in antiquity than nowadays; this fact seems the foremost reason that earlier authors never defined the eminence in detailed terms. Standing to the south of the coastal road to Trogir and looking north, it appears that beyond the road the terrain rises gently and then forms a fairly large surface (**Figure 2**). To its north there follows a considerable drop of the ground with the terrain continuing evenly for a distance of 180 meters. Beyond, the terrain rises more steeply, eventually joining the towering cliffs of Mt. Mosor. Both the south and north slopes of the eminence are more marked than those in the east and west. The south slope was, in fact, considered suitable to provide a *cavea* for the Roman theater which takes advantage of the natural setting.[7]

To the east and west the eminence stands out less clearly; but in both directions the terrain is sloping, more so in the east than in the west.

One can hardly doubt that the surface just described, which rises above the surrounding territory, is identical with Caesar's eminence. This is the location of the most ancient settlement of Salona, as our finds definitely prove.[8]

It should have become clear in the meantime that the platform with the arcades previously described is simply an artificial extension to the south of the eminence forming an area which became part of the Roman Forum.

Adjacent to the southwest corner of the platform and immediately to the south of the theater, Dyggve and Weilbach excavated a court-like structure with two porticoes along the east and west sides and in the center of the court a tetrastyle temple.[9] The temple has a deep pronaos and a cella only slightly larger than the pronaos. Corinthian capitals rest on the columns of the pronaos as well as on the pilasters which form the ends of the short antae of the cella. Each portico had four columns crowned with Corinthian capitals.

Dyggve and Weilbach thought that the spaces between the columns were closed by medium-high

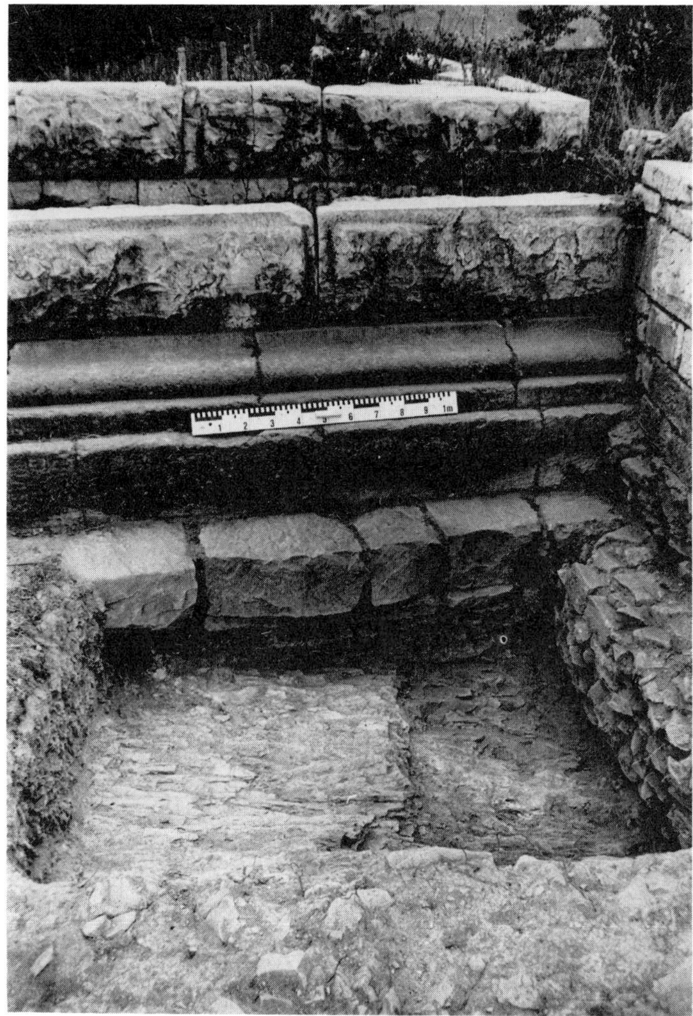

Figure 3 (at left): Trench 2, outside capitolium, looking south.

Figure 4 (below): Capitolium, in foreground westernmost wall, looking east.

screens; between the short antae of the portico the excavators restored gates of the same height as the screens. The roof is pitched. The temple faced north and not, as might be expected, south. Little can be seen at present of this architectural complex which is much overgrown and threatened by the seasonal retreat and rise of the ground water. Staircases and a corridor which connected the court and the tetrastyle temple with the theater to the north are buried underneath the modern coastal road, as is some of the stage building of the theater.

While the temple is dated by Weilbach to the early Imperial period and the theater to the mid-first century,[10] Weilbach did not reach any conclusion as to the date of the enclosing porticoes. However, what Weilbach said concerning the staircases which, leading away from the theater, make "un debouché sur l'emplacement du temple" possible and form at the same time "une liaison entre le théâtre et la colonnade," speaks against a date later than the first century A.D. for the porticoes.[11] J.B. Ward-Perkins refers to the temple as a "peristyle tetrastyle temple" and seems in agreement with the early Imperial dating.[12]

It is unfortunate that the theater is not published in final form, and it is doubtful that it ever will be. The *cavea* was divided into six *cunei* which comprise lower and upper tiers. The latter have completely disappeared along with the upper storeys of the building and the stone seats in the lower tiers. There were altogether three storeys; the supporting piers of the lowermost are the most prominently preserved feature of the theater. Of the stage building there remain now only the foundations. The theater was of respectable size; with the increase of the population in the late second and third centuries A.D. it may have become too small, although the amphitheater, built in the first half of the second century A.D., is not inferior in size to amphitheaters in any other Roman capital city.

Approximately in the middle of the short north side of the platform, at a point where the platform is built against the eminence, Dyggve excavated a second temple which he published in a preliminary article.[13] This is the "tetrastyle situé a l'est du théâtre." One can see at present on the north and west the stylobate with, above it, carefully finished and jointed blocks of stone which form the lowermost portions of the outside wall of the building (**Figure** 3). To the south and east much of the evidence is destroyed. However, remains of steps suggest that the structure was accessible from the south. Most in evidence to the visitor today are three rooms of equal size within the structure, of which the foundation for the dividing short (NS) walls remain extending from the back (EW) wall (**Figure** 4).

The distinction by Dyggve of four building periods, in each of which the building served a different purpose, is highly complex and is difficult to combine with the evidence now visible on the surface. The three rooms (cellae ?) would correspond to Dyggve's period II (late second to third century A.D.) during which he believes they were used as *curia, chalcidicum,* and *secretarium*, replacing shrines of period I (first century A.D.) which were dedicated to Jupiter Optimus Maximum and Divus Claudius, enclosing in between them a tribuna which was on a lower level. A trial trench to bedrock made by ourselves in the westernmost of the three cellae confirmed the initial building period of the building as the first century A.D.[14]

Taking into account the three rooms which were open to the south and which were preceded by a series of steps, and considering furthermore the open space of the platform in front (to the south) of this building, we believe that the term *Capitolium* is the only fitting one for the structure. Its placement on the eminence central to the Forum as a whole, is fitting for a *Capitolium* which, according to Vitruvius, should be situated "in excelsissimo loco."[15]

The remains of structures mentioned so far represent the main building activity during the early Imperial period (ca. A.D. 10-100). Immediately to the north of the theater and the *Capitolium* there extends the natural surface of the eminence (**Figure** 2). Along its western edge runs a street with some of its pavement still preserved, as well as foundations for an enclosure wall along the east side of the street. Some 80 meters to the north of the theater this wall forms a

Figure 5: Forum enclosure wall, western portion, with entrance to Forum central area.

Figure 6: Forum central drain with pedestal base, looking west.

recess and three steps lead up to what must have been a fairly monumental gate which in its turn gave access to what we would like to call the Forum central area as distinct from the South Forum with the *Capitolium*, the artificial platform, the theater, and the tetrastyle temple (**Figure 5**). The enclosure wall continues beyond the gate and terminates in a portico which, in the second and third centuries A.D., closed off the Forum at its north end.

Excavations in the Forum central area by ourselves are discussed fully in this report. However, excavations conducted by Professor L. Crema and others during and immediately after World War II are still unpublished and render the understanding of certain parts of the area somewhat difficult.[16] Some 20 to 40 meters behind the *Capitolium* to the north, the structures date from the middle and late Imperial period. A landmark at the present day is the foundation for a portico-like structure of which large, heavy blocks of stone are preserved for a distance of ca. 20 meters, with a drain running along the south edge (**Figure 6**).

The portico, which ran east-west, was open to the south; its function in this location was to form a division between the South and the Central Forum. Architectural elements such as fluted pilasters which probably belonged to the portico were used subsequently—in the Christian period—for the construction of a *torcularium* or oil press which cannot escape one's attention when one is looking directly to the north from the *Capitolium* (**Figure 2**). Remains of pagan *thermae* adjacent to the *torcularium* and unearthed after World War II by D. Rendić-Miočević await publication. Apart from our own excavations, the reference to the *thermae* concludes the description of those pagan remains which formed the core of public buildings of Roman Imperial Salona; these were built essentially in the area of pre-Roman occupation known as the eminence from Caesar's writing.

Beyond the eminence there is only one additional pagan building: the amphitheater. It is fortunate that Dyggve published the amphitheater so fully.[17] It stands out as the most remarkable and monumental relic of pagan Salona. Its location on the northwest corner of the enlarged city or *urbs nova* is unique as far as other Roman cities are concerned. According to Dyggve, the extension of the wall around the *urbs nova* is to be dated after A.D. 150. He also believes that this partially intact wall which surrounds the western extension of the city was planned in accordance with the construction of the amphitheater which he dates from ca. A.D. 170.

Alföldy is critical of the date assigned to the amphitheater, believing it unlikely to be so late.[18] One would think, indeed, that the amphitheater was enclosed in the circuit of the wall because it was there already when the latter was built. Moreover, the isolated position of the amphitheater previous to the wall building would really not be so astonishing, considering the usage of the building. We can possibly suggest that once the theater adjacent to the Forum was finished (by the third quarter of the first century A.D.), the amphitheater was begun so that it, too, belongs essentially to the early Imperial period or possibly the earliest years of the Antonine emperors.

We now turn to the walls of Salona, still visible or, although investigated by excavators, no longer visible at present. In the mid-nineteenth century, Carrara noted portions of the south wall, now fully destroyed by the building of the railway, but then either covered by marshy ground or water.[19] The south wall is particularly important for situating the port. The remains of this wall were identified by Cichorius with the mole of the Roman port and he was followed by Dyggve.[20] Karl Lehmann-Hartleben however, feeling that two separate walls were needed, interpreted the remains as being identical with the city wall, while the mole was not found.[21] The clue to the problem, in our view, lies in the description of the mole by Cichorius.[22] He writes:

> Die ansehnlichen antiken Substructionen...bilden einen lang-gestreckten Damm aus denselben gewaltigen Riesenblöcken, aus denen die sogenannte Via Munita besteht. Die ganze Anlage dürfte nun aber auch eine ähnliche Bedeutung wie jene Via Munita gehabt haben. Meine im Verein mit Bel angestellte Untersuchung ergab nämlich, dass dieser Steindamm, der zu den Uferbögen ungefähr parallel läuft und mit ihnen durch

> einen kürzeren gleichartigen Querdamm verbunden ist, als ein antiker Molo aufzufassen ist, der einen Teil der Bucht abgrenzte und so einen geschützten Hafen bildete.... Die Höhe unseres Steindammes, die 1.43 m beträgt, wird also im Altertume den Anlageplatz für die Schiffe gebildet haben.[23]

Looking at the plan of Salona it becomes clear that, if we presume with Cichorius the existence of an inner harbour, it was open to and accessible from the west; it lay more or less parallel to the area which stretches from the theater towards the southeast, to the *Basilica iuxta portum*. At the east end, the mole probably came very close to the southeast corner of the central north-south wall (square 7 F).[24] This inner harbour was within easy reach of the area south of the theater.[25] Ships could anchor not only at the inner (northern) face of the mole but probably also at its outer (southern) face, as winds are negligible in this protected corner of the bay. It can reasonably be assumed that the mole fulfilled the role of city wall in this area.[26] Moreover, Cichorius' mole throws important light on the *via munita*, as we shall see later.

The wall which has been preserved best until the present day is the central north-south wall with the *Porta Caesarea*.[27] To the north of the Porta the wall is almost intact, lacking only the uppermost courses of stones. To the south of the Porta the visible height diminishes and eventually the wall disappears under heavy growth into the cultivated fields. The short stretch of wall from the Porta to the original northeast corner of the *urbs vetus* still reveals several phases of construction in its eastern face.

It was suggested that the inception of the wall's construction dates from the Republican period, whereas the Porta, the hexagonal towers of which are not bonded into the wall, dates from the reign of Augustus. Characteristic for the Republican date of some sections of the wall are the very long and massive squared blocks of local modrac stone. The face of the blocks is rusticated.[28] Kähler dates the oldest portions of the wall in connection with historical events from 155 B.C. to Caesar's death. He writes:

> Caesar's Bericht [B.C. III. 9, quoted chapter I, note 31] lässt trotz mancher Unklarheiten erkennen, dass Stadtmauern bestanden, die—weil Türme fehlten oder nur in ungenügender Anzahl vorhanden waren—durch hölzerne Türme verstärkt wurden. Auch eine zweijährige Belagerung im Jahre 78 v. Chr. lässt sich nur erklären, wenn die Stadt schon hinlänglich befestig war. Es ist demnach anzunehmen, dass es sich bei den Mauern der *Urbs vetus,* die in den erhaltenen Teilen ursprünglich nicht durch Türme verstärkt sind, noch um eine späthellenistische Anlage handelt. Es wäre denkbar, dass die Befestigung bereits bestand, als nach der Zerstörung von Delminium im Jahre 155 v. Chr. Salona sich zum Vorort von Dalmatien entwickelte, oder dass sie im Zusammenhang mit diesem Ereignis erbaut wurde.[29]

This interpretation does take into account Caesar's *oppidum* as well as the reference to Σάλων πόλις in both Appian and Strabo which, for another reason, namely the siege of 78-76 B.C., indicates some form of a wall. However, a second-first century B.C. dating of the wall is not so far supported by any Hellenistic remains of domestic architecture, forming part of a settlement on either side of the wall to the north and the south of the Porta Caesarea. We believe that it is due to this lack of evidence that authors, writing after Kähler, have not paid much attention to his dating of the earliest portions of the wall to ca. 150 and 78/6 B.C. respectively.[30] Wilkes believes with others[31] that the earliest portions of the north-south wall date from Caesar's time. The wall was built after the foundation of the conventus, that is after 56 B.C., and despite the fact that the *oppidum* was "et loci natura et colle munitum."[32] Then, with Antony's siege in 48-7 B.C., "celeriter cives Romani ligneis effectibus turribus his sese munierunt."[33]

Considering both datings put forward, one can perhaps reach a middle solution, which would take into account on the one hand the limited size of the emporion, and on the other, the arrival of Roman settlers after the two-year war fought successfully by C. Cosconius, 78-76 B.C. With the settlement suddenly becoming larger and the threats of attack by the Delmatae increasing, a special effort may have gone into protecting the settlement with fortifications. The earliest among these would thus go back immediately to the period after 75 B.C., with additions such as the wooden towers being made when necessary.

As for the west wall of the so-called *urbs vetus*, we have to rely entirely on Dyggve's account. In location 5 D, Dyggve "constatait d'épaisses fondations de murs dans la direction Sud-Nord avec des forts dépots calcaires laissées par les eaux: ces restes de murs pouvaient signifier un aqueduc ou un mur de ville, ou l'un ou l'autre. J'ai plus tard trouvé à cet endroit le mur ouest et la porte principale de la ville grecque même."[34] This important discovery not only definitely delimits the *urbs vetus* to the west but, since tombs belonging to the cemetery were discovered further to the west of the north-south wall, it also gives a *terminus post quem* for the extension of the city into the so-called *urbs occidentalis.*

In conclusion we can say that the area in which the conventus settled corresponds to an area to the west of the Porta Caesarea, the *urbs vetus*, properly speaking. The latter is delimited in the south by the shore and mole, in the west by Dyggve's "Greek" wall, to the north by a stretch of wall (whose visible remains date from a post-pagan stage of rebuilding and reinforcement of the original core), and in the east by Kähler's Republican wall. The shape of the *urbs vetus* is trapezoidal, with the longer axis running north-south.[35] Caesar's *collis*—identical, we believe, with the natural eminence previously described—lies a little off center to the south.

Two approaches to the *urbs vetus* are definitely known. The "Greek gate" in Dyggve's "Greek" (west) wall connects with the major route leading to the northwest, in the direction of Tragurion. The Porta Caesarea in the Republican (east) wall gives access to routes which lead both to Klis and the hinterland, as well as to the south, in the direction of Epetion. Where the north-south wall came close to the shore, we can posit a southeast entrance to the *urbs vetus*. From here, there was a direct communication to the peninsula with the site of Aspalathos, but another route could join the one which departed from the Porta Caesarea and pursued a southern direction along the coast.

It was mentioned earlier that beside Caesar's foundation of a colony in 47 B.C. or shortly thereafter, Augustus is supposed to have founded a second colony, increasing the strength of the first colony with new settlers. Furthermore, the concept of the double colony has been considerably bolstered by the two voting tribes attested for the city, the *Tromentina* and the *Sergia*. Since, rightly or wrongly, the general tendency has been to separate physically the citizen body of each colony, the Augustan colony was relegated to the *urbs nova* or *urbs orientalis*, to the east of the Porta Caesarea, which is said to have served as a connecting link between the two respective settlements.[36]

It is difficult to accept this hypothesis so long as the archaeological evidence from the early Imperial period is so scantily attested for the *urbs nova*. Furthermore, there is general consent that the walls surrounding the *urbs nova* were not built much before A.D. 170.[37] This does leave the *urbs nova* unprotected in an area which is very vulnerable indeed. One could naturally assume that in case of danger from the hinterland, citizens of both colonies could have gathered within the walls of the *urbs vetus*. Thus, the lack of walls surrounding the *urbs orientalis* is in itself not sufficient to discredit entirely the hypothesis of the existence of an Augustan colony in the *urbs nova*.

In addition to the lack of archaeological evidence, however, we can think of two other reasons which suggest that both colonies were at first concentrated together in the *urbs vetus*. The conventus comprised only a small number of citizens,[38] which was increased by the new settlers as a result of the foundation of a colony by Caesar; an addition of new settlers, due to a second foundation of a colony would not augment the population to such an extent as to preclude accomodation within the *urbs vetus*, an area of considerable size. Secondly, we know of only one Forum or administration center.[39] But if one insists on the physical separation of the two colonies, should one not also assume the existence of two administrative centers?

Suggesting then that both colonies were united on the territory of the *urbs vetus*, we would admit the possibility that during the second half of the first century A.D. citizens began to settle to the east of the Porta Caesarea. This was above all the result of an overflow of citizens and, since their number steadily increased, the settlement became the *urbs orientalis* which was surrounded by walls in A.D. 170. The walls around the *urbs orientalis* comprised two new gates, the northeastern *Porta Andetria* and the southeastern gate which led to Aspalathos and directly south along the coast to Epetion.

As indicated earlier, the activity of wall-building also spread to the west of the *urbs vetus*, with the creation of an *urbs occidentalis*. A new gate in the west wall of the *urbs occidentalis* replaced the old *Porta Greca*.[40] If one considers both aggrandizements of the city and especially the completion of the walls, one cannot but come to the conclusion that in Salona building activity in the third quarter of the second century A.D. was at its very height. The city now assumed the oblong, quasi-rectangular shape which we have spoken of in the beginning. While the entire area, composed as it was of three parts "with a wall perimeter of more than 4 kilometers"[41] proved big enough for Imperial times, Christian Salona with its basilicas outside the walls proper extended much beyond the Imperial city.

Also outside the latest stage of wall building in the *urbs occidentalis* there is to the west of the amphitheater the controversial wall in *Hortus Metrodori* called by some "cyclopean wall," by others, "*via munita*."[42]

Excavation began here only in the late nineteenth and early twentieth centuries. Early visitors to Salona, however, were impressed by these very imposing remains which gave rise to different interpretations.[43] The description of the wall as "cyclopean" led to an early dating for it.[44] It was above all Bulić who defended with great enthusiasm the Greek origin of the wall. He did so after having excavated along the wall for 56 meters and towards the north for 23 meters.[45] The excavated area can still be seen at the present day.[46] The wall itself consists of very long and heavy blocks, most of them as long as 4 meters, 1 meter high, and from 80 to 90 centimeters wide. The stones are of the local modrac, have rusticated faces, and are bound with mortar. The wall is a perfect example of *opus quadratum*; it is not cyclopean.

Behind the wall, to the north, are several structures. Beginning in the east, there is a large precinct of rectangular shape, with one of its long sides formed by the wall itself. A rubble wall running from north to south divides off a third of the rectangle in the west and continues as a "revetment" wall (according to Bulić) inside the "Greek" wall, thus forming an eastern space. Within the latter is a smaller rectangle built of very massive long blocks; its corners bear the letters *l*, *m*, *n*, *o* in Bulić's plan. Within the precinct were found several sarcophagi.

At the northwest corner of the precinct just discussed is a small almost square structure of Roman date, built with rubble walls; a crosswall of later date also divides off an eastern half. Further to the west follow several sarcophagi, some in parallel, some in perpendicular position to the main wall. Further west still follows a second precinct with its western end in still unexcavated territory. Within this precinct are half a dozen sarcophagi and rubble walls which serve as substructures for caskets.

Bulić believed that the main wall (cyclopean wall) and the first precinct were built in the third century B.C. Since he considered the wall a defensive wall against attacks from the sea, he called the precincts towers.[48] Except for giving the wall a Greek date, Bulić never committed himself to saying anything about the people who presumably lived "behind the wall." This would have been only logical since a defensive wall ought to have its defenders. Abramić and others who also maintained the Greek origin of the wall were more consistent. They placed the earliest settlement of the Greeks or native Delmatae within the protective power of this very wall.

The crucial question is, of course, whether or not the wall is of third century B.C. date. We admit that to authors writing in the nineteenth or early twentieth century it could seem so. But today, when we have many walls from the Greek and Roman world for comparison, it no longer seems possible to date the wall as early as Bulić and others did. The walls in Lesina, Jelsa, Asseria, Varvaria (Bribir) and Epetium, which Bulić cites for comparison,[49] are either so much different in basic construction from the *Hortus Metrodori* wall that a comparison yields only a negative result, or they are similar, which would simply suggest that they are more or less contemporaneous.

While it is very likely that the walls in Lesina, Jelsa and Epetium are Greco-Illyrian and of the third century B.C., the wall in Asseria is late Republican and if anything contemporary with the wall in *Hortus Metrodori.*[50] One does not have to go very far to find a good comparison for the latter wall. We believe that Kähler's oldest portion of the Republican wall of Salona yields this comparison as well as other architectural details of early Imperial Salona.[51] Moreover, a portion of the wall of Iader was recently assigned a late Republican date and it compares very well with the wall in *Hortus Metrodori.* Quite apart from these comparisons and the structural evidence of the wall itself, Bulić made it very clear that in his excavations in depth along the inside of the wall he has not found "nessuna iscrizione greca ed oltra suppeletila che si potrebbe dire greca."[52] Nor did Professor Gabričević in 1970 come upon any Hellenistic vestiges, such as came to light in excavations on the Forum and in its close proximity.

Bulić believes that, judging from the inscriptions on stelae and sarcophagi, the use of the entire area as a pagan cemetery dates from after the middle of the first century A.D. to the fourth century. Thus, the towers which could no longer serve their original purpose for defense were turned, according to Bulić, into mortuary chapels or the like.[53] The many sarcophagi, with the lids now cast off and showing many other damages, are a vivid testimony to the secondary use of the area. It would be difficult indeed not to accept the Bulić date for the initial phase of the cemetery, based as it is on *inscriptional* evidence. But if we believe that the wall and the precincts along it were erected sometime during the first century B.C., we must try to explain what purpose the area served first. We can think of only one such purpose, namely, that here too, as to the south of the theater district, we deal with some harbour, mole or quay buildings. This latter interpretation was already suggested over a hundred years ago by Wilkinson who was followed by Cichorius.[54]

With regard to this interpretation it is necessary to realize that the total length of the wall is not only 56 meters, but that it continues to the west of *Hortus Metrodori* parallel to the modern shore line.[55] With the ancient shore and the water level having sunk in the past eighteen centuries, the water would have come to the mole in antiquity, and if this interpretation of the *via munita* as mole or quay is accepted, the structures to the north of it could be explained as storehouses and merchants' quarters, or even as having had some function for the Roman legions stationed in Dalmatia.

It is impossible to say whether or not this portion of the port installations was originally connected directly with the mole to the south of the theater. The hypothesis that this was indeed the case is very likely. The reader may be reminded of the port of Claudius in Ostia to be mentioned later[56] and also of the mole in Aquileia,[57] both walls very similar structurally to the wall in *Hortus Metrodori*; their length, too, could provide a comparison for the existence of one continuous mole in Salona.

Finally, we have to come back to the term *via munita.* While some early authors identified the wall itself with a sub-structure for a road (*via*) to which the word *munita* could be applied since it was lined with defensive towers,[58] scholars have spoken more recently of the *via munita* as the road leading from the west gate of the city in the direction of Tragurium and that the road was lined with monumental tombs.[59] But this is not really a fair description, because it brushes aside elegantly the real crux, namely the wall itself. There are other Roman roads lined with monumental tombs but to the best of my knowledge no such massive walls were thought necessary to protect the tombs. In conclusion, we can only say that the term *via munita* does not seem to make any sense if applied to the archaeological remains actually surviving.

Notes on Chapter 2

[Abbreviations and Select Bibliography for this chapter will be found on page xv.]

1. See Dyggve, *Recherches* I, plan B and pp. 12 ff. Both Ceci, *MP* pl. IV (lower) and Wilkes p. 361, fig. 61 have followed Dyggve's plan printing the term *urbs vetus* over one single area and what should really be two different sections of the city, the *urbs vetus* in the center and the *urbs occidentalis* to the west (= left)(**Plate 6**). Cf. also Alföldy, *Bevölkerung,* p. 103, n. 56. It is far from certain that, in the words of Alföldy, "die *urbs occidentalis und urbs antiqua* bildeten aber wohl seit dem Beginn der Kaiserzeit eine Einheit, sie wurden voneinander durch keine Mauern getrennt." Cf. Dyggve, I, p. 14: Dyggve's "Greek" wall could have lasted until the entire *urbs occidentalis* was surrounded by a wall, which is probably not earlier than A.D. 170. See also note 15 for other inconsistencies in the marking of plans.

2. For Cichorius and panel LXXXVI from the column of Trajan see Excursus I.

3. Dyggve, *Recherches* I, p. 25 and also p. 15 with plan B; Ceci, *MP,* p. 138.

4. E. Dyggve, "Forum," p. 55.

5. A. Boethius and J.B. Ward-Perkins, *Etruscan and Roman Architecture* (1971) pp. 173 f.; A. Grenier, *Manuel d'Archéologie Gallo-Romaine,* vol. III, *L'Architecture* (1958), pp. 308-329. The recent study by G. Rickman, *Roman Granaries and Store Buildings* (1971) provides very useful discussion of storage buildings, etc. The section on cryptoporticoes, pp. 144 ff., is of interest for the platform in Salona. The author says (p. 147) that cryptoporticoes not only "serve the obvious and necessary function of substructures" but also "of levelling and confining sites of an irregular nature;" the latter is true for the Salona platform to some extent but the actual extension of the eminence is of greater significance, as we shall demonstrate in our discussion.

6. See chapter 1, note 31.

7. As Dyggve has noticed, see *Recherches* I, p. 14.

8. The eminence was considered to have been vital for the foundation of Salona by others working before us. Foremost among them was Dyggve, who was intimately familiar with the topography of the site and who had situated the Greek acropolis on this eminence. See *Recherches* I, p. 14. See also Wilkes, pp. 224-226 and 358-362; Alföldy, *Bevölkerung,* pp. 103-105. Others have placed the earliest "Greek-Illyrian" settlement next to the so-called *via munita* also referred to as the cyclopean wall. See M. Suić, "Sulla municipalità dell'antica Salona," *BD* 60 (1958): 40; M. Abramić, "La nécropole occidentale de Salone," *BD* 52 (1935-49): 1-18, summary on p. 317. Abramić was rejected by Wilkes, p. 360. See also G. Novak (op. cit. chapter 1, note 34), pp. 81 ff., commented upon by Alföldy, *Bevölkerung,* p. 124, n. 59. Cf. Lehmann-Hartleben, *Hafenanlagen,* pp. 34f. It does not become clear from A.L. Frothingham, *Roman Cities in Northern Italy and Dalmatia* (1910), p. 267, whether or not he places the acropolis near the *via munita* or near the Porta Caesarea. Bulić believed that the oldest city lay to the north of the Porta Caesarea, on the east side of the north-south wall, in what was later the *urbs nova* or *urbs orientalis.* Bulić's main argument for drawing this conclusion was the place of discovery of the "Decree of 56 B.C.," which was a little to the north of the Porta Caesarea. We cannot reject nor accept Bulić's arguments. The study of the finds, especially of the pottery, made in the recent Yugoslav excavations in the *urbs orientalis* along the north-south wall may produce a more final answer, either in support or rejection. With regard to the location of the acropolis by both Abramić and Suić, Bulić never committed himself to placing the latter near the *via munita* as did his two colleagues, although he dated the wall as they did firmly to the third century B.C., taking it for a defense wall against attacks from the sea. Cf. Bulić I, p. 22. For the *via munita* see discussion later in this chapter.

9. For the temple and colonnaded court see Dyggve, *Recherches* II, pp. 13-32 (by F. Weilbach). See especially the figure on p. 25, "periode V."

10. See Dyggve, *Recherches* II, Avant Propos, as against Wilkes, p. 386, who dates the theater erroneously to the second century A.D., an opinion which Dyggve had abandoned when publishing the second volume of *Recherches.* See also B. Gabričević, "Dva Priloga poznavanjn urbanističkog Razvoja Antikne Salone," *BD* 53 (1950-51): 155-161, summary p. 162. A centurion of the cohors I Belgarum was "curagens theatri." This evidence cannot be used as proof for construction of the theater post A.D. 100, the approximate date at which the cohort reached Dalmatia. The term "curagens" can refer to the supervision of repairs carried out at the theater some time after the completion of the building.

11. Dyggve, *Recherches* II, p. 24.

12. A. Boethius and J.B. Ward-Perkins, (op. cit. note 5), p. 366.

13. Dyggve, "Forum," passim.

14. See the discussion following, on pp. 67 f.

15. The article by Dyggve on this building (notes 4 and 13) poses many problems. Confusion is added by the fact that, during World War II, L. Crema returned to the same site. I presume that the plan of the *Capitolium* reproduced by Ceci, *MP*, pl. XVIII.1, was drawn after the completion of Crema's excavations and is otherwise unpublished. Ceci, *MP*, p. 75 comments as follows: "Subito a nord-ovest [for nord-ovest read nord-est] del teatro, il prof. L. Crema (nel 1942-1943) fece sondaggi sul luogo nell'intenzione di scoprire il Capitolium; infatti egli pensò di aver trovata le fondazioni di un tempio a tre celle, dedicato alla triade romana (Iuppiter, Iuno e Mars) . . . ; ma, da allora a tutt'oggi, gli scavi non furono proseguiti"; and, we may add, never published. Ceci's illustration pl. XIX, fig. 1 is not a view over the foundations of the Forum but the *torcularium* (in the foreground) and the *Capitolium* (in the background). Ceci also misnamed as *Capitolium* the structure midway between the theater and the Porta Caesarea, see his pl. IV, fig. 2. What looks on the latter plan like a building with three cellae is a fanciful elaboration of vestiges of stone foundations which Dyggve, *Recherches* I, p. 25 refers to as a drain (running east-west) and which is met by two perpendicular walls and is thus drawn on his plan B. Wilkes omitted Ceci's legend "Capitolium" ? but copied Ceci's building in his plan on p. 361, fig. 16. Our own excavations have confirmed Dyggve's drain which runs in front of a very long porch.

16. The publication of these excavations in the near future would close an important gap in the investigations conducted at Salona. Rather puzzling is also the building complex which Bulić called the *Praetorium*, to the east of the Forum north porch. No remains are visible at present. See the sketchy accounts by Bulić in *BD* 39 (1916): 141; *BD* 44 (1923): 80; and *BD* 47-48 (1924-25): 88; Ceci, *MP*, p. 138.

17. *Recherches* II, pp. 33-150, "L'amphithéatre," par E. Dyggve; Wilkes, pp. 383-386 and fig. 21.

18. Alföldy, *Bevölkerung*, p. 103, n. 56.

19. A.F. Carrara, *Topografia e Scavi di Salona* (1850) passim; Dyggve, *Recherches* I, pp. 17f.

20. C. Cichorius, *Die Reliefs der Trajanssäule* III (1900), p. 75; Dyggve, "Forum," p. 55.

21. Lehmann-Hartleben, p. 169, n. 1. See also Wilkes, p. 360, who accepts a south wall in the "urbs vetus and nova . . . built along the shoreline, but apparently no open quay or harbour buildings."

22. See note 20.

23. Cichorius, (op. cit. note 20), pp. 72 ff., the quote from p. 75. For the "Uferbögen" see pp. 28, 32.

24. For the *Basilica iuxta portum* see plan B in Dyggve, *Recherches* I.

25. Among others who have discussed the port of Salona, we believe that both Bulić and Wilkes place it much too far to the southeast, in a location which is definitely outside the walls of the *urbs vetus*. Bulić, in referring to the property Jankovaća, places it in 8F (see *Recherches* I, plan A) and probably even further to the east. See Bulić, "Ritrovamenti antichi nelle mura perimetrali dell'antica Salona," *BD* 25 (1902): 3-39 and especially p. 10. Wilkes writes, p. 362: "The gate in the southeast corner of the *urbs nova* was the only exit which led towards the harbour." This places the harbour in 8F-9F.

26. The strength of the city wall had to lie in the north against attackers from the hinterland. Consider the number of square towers along the north wall (Dyggve, *Recherches* I, plan B) as compared with the complete lack of towers in the south, except one (no. 92). All the wedge-shaped towers are from the post-pagan period. Moreover, for at least 200 years, from ca. 30 B.C. to A.D. 170, the *urbs orientalis* lacked walls altogether. Before the extension of the *urbs vetus,* tower no. 92 formed its southwest corner. This is where the mole could have ended in the Republican period before being extended farther to the west during the first century A.D.

27. H. Kähler, "Die Porta Caesarea in Salona," *BD* 51 (1930-34): 1-51. As far as we can see, Kähler's dating remained unchallenged. See also Wilkes, pp. 224 f.; Alföldy, *Bevölkerung,* pp. 103 f.

28. See especially Kähler (op. cit. note 27), pl. IV.1 (eastern face) and pl. IV.2 (western face).

29. Ibid., p. 31.

30. Lehmann-Hartleben, p. 34, n. 5, who admits a mid-Hellenistic date for the wall, saying: "Aber die dort aufgedeckte vorrömische Mauer weist im Gebrauch von Mörtel nicht auf griechischen Ursprung und kann kaum älter sein als das 2. Jahrh."

31. Wilkes, pp. 224 f. and 362, also *BJb* 166 (1966): 651, where he is rightly very cautious about the dating of the walls for the lack of archaeological evidence. Alföldy, *Bevölkerung,* p. 104; cf. also M. Suić, "Richerche archeologico-topografiche sull'antica Jader," *Zbornik* 2 (1956-57): 13-48, summary pp. 49 f., accepting Kähler's dating.

32. Caesar, *B.C.* III. 9 (see Chapter 1, n. 31).

33. See foregoing note.

34. Dyggve, *Recherches* II, p. 138, n. 4 and fig. 71, p. 140.

35. For the *conventus* and the settlement in the *urbs vetus* see Wilkes, pp. 224 f. and especially n. 6 on p. 224; Alföldy, *Bevölkerung,* p. 104. I find Wilkes a little too cautious as regards the identification of Caesar's colony with the *urbs vetus.* One has very little choice for situating the *conventus* and the colony. If one excludes the area just described, there remains that which is to the north of the Porta Caesarea, where Bulić located the Greek acropolis and where, in later times, some modern authors settled the Augustan colony or, at any rate, the portion of citizens who belonged to the voting tribe *Sergia.*

36. Wilkes, pp. 224 f., n. 6, finds it "hardly credible" with reference to the two "settlements being established at so nearly the same time and existing without substantial change into late antiquity." However, on p. 225, Wilkes states: "... the new city on the west [for "west" read "east"] was certainly in existence during the first century, probably as part of the colonial foundation." As against Wilkes, Alföldy, *Bevölkerung,* pp. 103 f., is very firm about the double colony.

37. Kähler, (op. cit. note 27) p. 39, pls. VIII-IX:; Wilkes, pp. 224 f.; Alföldy, *Bevölkerung,* pp. 104 f.

38. Caesar, *B.C.* III.9, "paucitas hominum." This is against C. Daicovici's claim of "grande numero di Italici (Romani) stabiliti a Salona" in "Gli Italici nella Provincia Dalmatia," *Ephemeris Dacoromana* 5 (1932): 93, with reference to the pre-Augustan period.

39. Beside the Forum on the eminence, there is a second square, but hardly another Forum, within the *urbs vetus,* to the west of the Porta Caesarea and thus marked in Dyggve, *Recherches* I, plan B. Ceci, *MP,* pl. IV, fig. 2 follows Dyggve; Wilkes p. 361, fig. 61 records the excavation but omits the legend "Forum." See also Dyggve, *Recherches* I, p. 21; Kähler (op. cit. note 27) p. 14; Egger, *FS* I, p. 14, fig. 2a and pp. 16 f. for the plan of the partly excavated area, especially what he calls "Platz" inside the Porta Caesarea. Definitely wrongly situated is the main Roman Forum by Wilkes, p. 361, fig. 61, to the southeast of the platform and to the north of the *Basilica iuxta portum.*

40. We do not know what happened to the west wall of the *urbs vetus,* or whether or not it was partly demolished in order to create one unified area. Alföldy's view, *Bevölkerung,* p. 103, n. 56 that "*urbs occidentalis* und *urbs antiqua* bildeten aber wohl seit dem Beginn der Kaiserzeit eine Einheit, sie wurden voneinander durch keine Mauern getrennt," does not take into account Dyggve's research near the *Porta Graeca* and the existence of a cemetery to the west of it.

41. Wilkes, p. 225.

42. The term is attested in an inscription, *CIL* III.2072, but there has been some problem how to relate the term to the wall, if at all. (See the discussion following.) The designation *Hortus Metrodori* for the area was deduced from *CIL* III.2207, but the denomination is not absolutely certain, according to Bulić.

43. A.L. Frothingham, (op cit. note 8) calls it "via munita" and says that it is the "oldest known Dalmatian road." For other early visitors see Dyggve, *Recherches* I, p. 20. It is to be kept in mind that only Wilkinson thought that the wall had to do with port installations, long before Cichorius, who seems not to have been familiar with Wilkinson's hypothesis.

44. The wall is not polygonal but very clearly *opus quadratum.* F. Lanza's "mura ciclopiche regolari" is a misnomer; see his *Origine primitive di Salona Dalmatica* (1889), p. 17 (fig.).

45. Bulić I, pp. 3-82.

46. The site was cleaned completely from all overgrowth in 1970. Professor Gabričević not only examined some portions along the wall anew, but also opened several test pits in a field to the northwest of Bulić's excavations, behind the depth line of 23 m.

47. See Bulić I, pl. IV.1 and pl. XIII.

48. Bulić I, p. 22.

49. Bulić I, pl. IV.2-IX.

50. See M. Suić (op. cit. note 31), pp. 24 and 49. Suić also calls the walls of Asseria and Varvaria (Bribir) Republication first century. For comparisons from outside Yugoslavia see G. Lugli, *La tecnica edilizia Romana* (1937) pl. 47.3 (Via Appia) and pl. 48.2 (Palestrina).

51. See Dyggve, *Recherches* II, pp. 13 ff., figs. 2, 12 and 14, all from the southern temple and the colonned court. For recently excavated comparative material, see p. 00.

52. Bulić I, p. 22. The only Greek inscription found dates, according to Bulić, from the third-fourth century A.D. (p. 22, n. 2).

53. Bulić I, p. 22; Dyggve, *Recherches* I, p. 22 "édifices funéraires ou tours de défense ?"

54. See Excursus I.

55. Excavation would be necessary to determine its total extension towards the west. Even though similar stretches of wall are said to have been seen in the Kaštela region and close to Trogir, the wall cannot have gone as far as the latter city, as has been suggested by some. The disappearance of the wall is due, according to Suić, to reuse of stones when the wall surrounding the *urbs occidentalis* was built. See Suić, "Sulla municipalità dell'antica Salona," *BD* 60 (1958): 11-38, summary pp. 39-42.

56. See pp. 26 ff. For comparison see O. Testaguzza, *Portus. Illustrazione dei porti di Claudio e Traiano e della città di Porto a Fiumicino* (1970), plates preceding p. 105. For the plans see plates following p. 148. See also figs. 86-88 and 90 and the plan pp. 105 f.

57. There is no final publication of the port of Aquileia. For pictures of the wall see G. Brusin, *Aquileia. Guida storica e artistica,* pp. 8 f., fig. 6. A. Calderini, *Aquileia Romana* (1930), pp. XCII-XCIII and especially p. XCIII, n. 1. Cf. also G. Brusin, "Strutture murarie della Romana Aquileia," *Carnuntina* 3 (1956): 34-39, illustrating other Aquileian walls, Republican (pl. IV) and later ones.

58. See Bulić I, pp. 16 ff. for a summary of opinions and his own views. His interpretation of *munita* is connected with the nature of the "marshy terrain" (see the sketch in Bulić I, p. 11, fig. 2, indicating the marshy terrain) but the road itself started within the town of Salona and then passed along the cyclopean wall. The major reason for Bulić's hypothesis was that *CIL* III. 2072, in which the *via munita* is mentioned, was found ca. 1200 meters to the east of *Hortus Metrodori.*

59. Wilkes p. 224, n. 6. Dygvve, *Recherches* I, p. 22; more questionable is Alföldy's interpretation *Bevölkerung,* p. 104, n. 59: "Der Name *via munita* deutet nicht Befestigungen, sondern diese monumentalen Bauten an der Nordseite der Strasse an." Does Wilkes *BJb* 166 (1966): 651, really mean that the road in question leads to Andetrium? This is not what he claims on p. 453 of his monograph, nor is it in accord with his calling the northeast gate of Salona *Porta Andetria.*

EXCURSUS I:

Panel LXXXVI of the Column of Trajan

The description of the pagan remains of Salona would be incomplete if we omitted a reference to a series of reliefs on the column of Trajan. The interpretation and identification of cities which are represented in these reliefs have led to numerous conflicting views and scholars are far from having reached agreement.[1]

One of the panels under consideration—Cichorius' panel LXXXVI—was thought to depict a view of Salona. Thus it would seem natural that we take up the discussion once more, especially since we feel that new evidence is now available to give preference to the identification of the city with Salona as compared with any of the other cities which have also been proposed.

The *Fasti Ostienses* inform us that Trajan left Rome for the second Dacian campaign on June 4, 105. The route which he followed from the capital and the port from which he sailed with the smaller part of his army are unfortunately not mentioned in the *Fasti*.[2] Panels LXXIX ff. of the column prove not very helpful in clarifying the emperor's route to the Balkan peninsula. However, a majority of scholars have accepted the identification of panel LXXIX with the city of Ancona.[3] This interpretation has not remained unchallenged, but, after weighing the arguments for and against the identification, it seems to us that the only minor obstacle against the proposed identification with Ancona is the arch in the left foreground of the panel. This arch does not correspond in important details to the arch which we know was erected by Trajan in Ancona and which was dedicated in A.D. 115, two years after the column itself was finished. However, since all the other evidence in the panel favors the identification with Ancona, we have to ask if there is any means to explain the obstacle. S. Stucchi's theory that, prior to Trajan's arch another, earlier one stood in the same location, seems to us valid if not provable. Moreover, since the basic design and composition for panel LXXIX was probably conceived several years before the dedication of Trajan's arch, it would seem only natural that the responsible artist incorporated in his composition the arch which he saw at the time, not one which was to be erected in the future. It is then this earlier arch which the sculptor represented in panel LXXIX, not Trajan's arch.[4]

Degrassi proposed to identify the crucial arch in LXXIX with an arch erected in Brundisium by Augustus. But we lack ancient references to the decorative details of this arch, and only its foundations were found in modern times. Furthermore, since it is unknown whether or not the arch was still standing when Trajan is supposed to have come through Brundisium, the proposed identification is very hazardous. Thus, no conclusive evidence can be deduced from the arch as to which of the two cities is represented in the panel.

For those who wish to see in panel LXXIX a representation of the city of Brundisium, there arise several difficulties.[5] Not only is the general topography of this latter city much less known than that of Ancona, but it is different in specific details. There is in Ancona a temple situated on a fairly high elevation, with a statue of Venus within the building and a steep zigzag path leading to the hill and temple, which one might call key elements well attested in literary sources for the ancient topography and also attested by actual remains. There are no tangible clues that Brundisium's topography ever included details so specific as those just mentioned. Even if Brundisium had an *arx* elevated some 20 meters above the city, the specific details in panel LXXIX fit so well the given situation in Ancona, that venturing to propose any other identification is really a tour de force. In the case of Ancona, the sculptor has chosen a most satisfactory point from which to view the city. It would be difficult, however, to claim that this same view is one that also fits the rendering of Brundisium, because there are hardly two cities with such a degree of topographical identity.[6]

"Reality," "invention," "schematism" are terms by which scholars have characterized the artistic concept which lies behind some of the representations on the column of Trajan. It is noteworthy that the panels under consideration (LXXIX to LXXXVI) contrast strongly with the majority of the other panels in giving tangible clues to specific details which make it possible, in the case of panel LXXIX, to identify the city with Ancona. In the words of K. Lehmann-Hartleben, "die starke und sicherlich realistisch gemeinte Ausgestaltung der Architekturen in den ersten Bildern der Reihe [that is panels LXXIX ff.] scheint hier dafür zu sprechen, dass tatsächlich historische Grundlagen ziemlich ernsthaft benutzt sind."[7]

Even though we fully subscribe to this statement, it soon becomes evident when analyzing the panels that the first and last—panels LXXIX and LXXXVI—are even more specific than the intervening panels. What is especially lacking in the latter are city-views with multiple buildings as they occur in LXXIX and LXXXVI. We have a colonnaded court with a temple inside (LXXXI); an isolated arch with people streaming through it to take part in a sacrificial rite which involves several altars and victims (LXXXIII to LXXXIV); another sacrifice on two altars with a towerlike fortification in the background (LXXXV). With such meagre evidence, the identification of panels LXXX through LXXXV with any known ancient city through which Trajan may have come is certainly very difficult, if it is not mere guess work. This is at least one reason for the widely differing proposals for Trajan's actual route to the Balkans. Least acceptable among these proposals is that Trajan left Ancona, sailed through the Adriatic and eventually reached Byzantium (supposedly depicted in LXXXVI!) having passed earlier through Corinth and the Piraeus.[8]

Degrassi and others who followed the identification of panel LXXIX with Brundisium have Trajan cross the Adriatic from the latter city and land at Dyrrhachium, from whence he followed well-known routes to reach Naissus, close to his future battlefields. Even if the identification of panel LXXIX with Brundisium were acceptable, the proposed route beyond encounters difficulties in panels LXXX to LXXXV. Stucchi correctly noted that if panel LXXXVI is equated with Dyrrhachium as Degrassi proposed, it is hard to know to which localities panels LXXX to LXXXV refer. Since the route proposed by Degrassi from Brundisium to Dyrrhachium is direct and across the sea, no other localities could have been visited by Trajan. The route over land begins with LXXXVII, so that LXXXVI represents the last port of landing. Moreover, the identification of LXXXVI with Dyrrhachium is very problematical as N. Turcan saw because, in her words, "nous ne savons rien de la topographie de Durazzo."[9] Thus the lack of tangible clues for specific details in the topography of Brundisium not only excludes the possibility of identifying LXXIX with this city, but the assumption of a direct route from Brundisium to Dyrrhachium conflicts with the sequence of panels LXXX to LXXXV, and, last but not least, tangible clues do not exist for equating LXXXVI with the city of Dyrrhachium. With so much negative evidence at hand, the proposed route via Brundisium has lost any basis.

S. Stucchi was the major spokesman for a northern route with departure in Ancona, stops at some ports in the northernmost Adriatic—Ravenna, Aquileia—and disembarkation at Tergeste. From Aquileia onwards, Trajan himself may have followed the land route, meeting with his praetorians in Tergeste. In Stucchi's view panel LXXXVI represents Tergeste, the last port before the land route to Dacia.[10] The suggested route poses several problems. First of all, could Trajan, whose presence in Dacia was urgently needed, follow a route which definitely implies a detour from other, more direct routes? Stucchi feels that Tergeste would have been an ideal meeting place with other Roman troops who, arriving from the northern part of the empire, were about to participate in the battle against the Dacians. Such a meeting of troops, however, could have taken place much nearer the actual battlefields in the midst of the Balkans. Stucchi's northern Adriatic route is difficult also to bring into accord with the localities depicted in panels LXXX to LXXXV. Stucchi suggests for LXXX identification with Ravenna, for LXXXI with Aquileia, for LXXXII with the port of Aquileia, for LXXXIII and LXXXIV the departure from Aquileia, and for LXXXV Timavo, near present-day Monfalcone/Duino. As we noted previously, details on these panels are

Figure 7: Detail of Panel LXXXVI, column of Trajan, Rome.

not specific enough to yield any tangible clues for the identification with any of the above sites as known to us from excavations. It is different with panel LXXXVI, which renders a city-view with multiple buildings.

Can the city be Tergeste? It should prove helpful here and for the subsequent discussion to give a more detailed description of what can actually be seen on panel LXXXVI.

The emperor with some praetorians following him and carrying *signa* approaches the city from the left. They are disembarking from a ship which has drawn close along the side of an arcaded quay which, together with the representation of water, fills the lowermost stripe in the relief panel. The emperor stands on the arcaded quay in front of an altar about to make a sacrifice (**Figure 7**). Opposite the emperor, to the right of the altar, a huge ox is slaughtered by a *victimarius* (**Figure 8**). Behind the latter figure and further to the right stands a mixed group of citizens: males, females, and children. They welcome the emperor and watch as he sacrifices. All of these figures stand in front of an elaborate architectural background which contains the following elements and buildings from left to right (**Figure 9**): a city wall forming a corner behind the last praetorian and continuing

Figure 8: Detail of Panel LXXXVI, column of Trajan, Rome.

into the background of the relief is interrupted by an arched gateway visible above the head of the second praetorian from the left. A railing, in diagonal position outside the wall to the left, belongs to a ship whose position suggests that the arcaded quay forms a projection of the mainland, to the left and right of which there was additional harbour space for the anchoring of ships. Behind the gateway and railing there appears a massive wall with three arches; possibly it is meant to continue towards the right; a moulding, running first horizontal, then vertical, seems to indicate that the wall terminates to the left behind the railing.

Within the wall there comes first a portico-like structure (**Figure** 7) of which we see one corner supported by a Corinthian column with two more columns to the left and at least five columns to the right of the corner column respectively. There is some indication of entablature and a roof covering a narrow portion of the portico; the center space which the portico encloses is open to the sky; two trees grow within this enclosed space. This precinct is connected with a theater by means of a single arched doorway.

The theater is by far the largest building in the panel (**Figures** 7 and 8).[11] The outer wall of the *cavea* is in three storeys, with the lowermost storey taller than the other two. The sculptor gives us a glimpse into the *cavea* with six *cunei*. The facade is detailed, with a large central arched door framed by pilasters; to the left and right are rectangular doors also framed by columns which carry an entablature. There follows a plain band, several mouldings, and finally a row of eight arched windows; pillars form the corners; this storey is surmounted by a decorated cornice. On the top of the *cavea* there possibly runs an *ambulacrium*, covered by a roof (?). A second archway corresponding to the one at the left of the theater follows on the right; this archway is closely connected with a rectangular door further to the right with three rectangular windows

Figure 9: Panel LXXXVI, column of Trajan, Rome. Detail.

above. This structure is difficult to interpret. However, a clue to its understanding might come from the roof, which first runs horizontally, then slants slightly upward to the right. Perhaps this indicates that the arcaded portion with two windows above is to be seen frontally, the rectangular doorway with the one window above in side view. We could have, therefore, one end or corner of a stoa to which the arched doorway gives access from the short side, while the long side, which disappears behind the small temple, is accessible by rectangular doors, one of which happens to be shown.

Figure 10: Detail of Panel LXXXVI, column of Trajan, Rome.

Two more structures complete the description of the city (**Figures 8 and 10**). First, a prostyle, tetrastyle temple; the pediment bears no decoration, although the roof structure is rendered in detail. Secondly, a curious structure with two columns, probably forming a porch; the solid wall and an entrance to the building are not shown: a feature which also characterizes the tetrastyle temple. There is a rather low second storey above the columns with two windows. The roof seems flat above the center of the building; or could the building be hypaethral?[12]

On the extreme right side of the panel we have another ship (**Figure 8**) and a recession of the city wall into the background, similar to the design seen earlier on the left of the panel.

Viewing the panel as a whole, one can say that the sculptor distinguished between two parts in the depiction of the city. On one hand is the harbour with the arcaded mole, on the other the city proper. Sacrifice is made by the emperor before he enters the city, which is depicted in the background. The city wall not only serves the purpose of enclosure but leads the eye from the foreground to the background of the panel. If one compares both ends of the wall near the water, one receives the impression that distance is greater in the left half of the relief than it is in the right. Distance from the spectator is corroborated also by the scale of the warriors who follow Trajan. The figures of citizens on the right (**Figure** 8) are among the tallest; they must be thought of as being closest to the viewer. Thus the harbour mole is receding in the left half of the panel. If the interpretation of the railing mentioned earlier as belonging to a ship is correct, then the harbour has a continuation to the left.

Stucchi has taken great pains to convince his readers that panel LXXXVI depicts Tergeste.[13] From the harbour of the city, the spectator faces the hill of S. Giusto, at the foot and on the slopes of which was built the ancient city. The difficulties in identifying the buildings are minor, according to Stucchi. The remains of the Roman theater of Tergeste proves identical with the theater on the relief in major features, both architectural and decorative, except for the number of *cunei*. The portico enclosing a court corresponds to the precinct of the goddess Bona Dea and her small temple, 180 meters to the east of the theater. For the tetrastyle temple and the building next to it, Stucchi is unable to find suitable candidates among the ancient monuments in Tergeste, but he notes the nonclassical features of the two-storied building which suggest to him that "ci troviamo in ambiente romanizzato, come appunto potrebbe essere stata la regione di Trieste." Finally, with regard to the walls, Stucchi believes that the relief panel could suggest a solution for what the course of the walls was like in antiquity.[14] Although to draw such an inference from a rendering in the relief to a feature in the ancient topography seems to us to be somewhat audacious, the point shows how far Stucchi has gone in identifying LXXXVI with Tergeste.

Stucchi was familiar with the fact that a great many scholars adhere to a travel route for Trajan which, after departure from Ancona, included such important Dalmatian cities as Iader, Scardona, Burnum, Asseria, and especially Salona. Cichorius, who gave a lengthy description of panel LXXXVI, proposed identification with Salona. His main reasons were the theater and the arcaded wall which runs continuously along the lowermost portion of the relief. This arcaded wall, to which we have assigned the term quay or mole, represented for Cichorius a specific detail of the topography of Salona which he believed he could still identify in his own day with the arcades which support the platform and which we discussed in great detail earlier. The identification is no longer acceptable because the platform with the six (originally twelve) arcades is short, whereas the quay with many low arcades suggests continuity over some distance as in other slabs of the column (LXXIX, LXXXI).[15] Such continuity is necessary if ships are supposed to dock along the mole. Moreover, the scanty remains of the mole in Salona which face the theater and Forum district and which Cichorius was among the first to investigate do not give any hint as to exactly what the mole looked like when intact.

What then remains in panel LXXXVI to suggest that the city is indeed identical with Salona? The theater is definitely of primary importance. Like the temple of Venus with the statue of the goddess within it in the Ancona panel (LXXIX), the theater is a specific and salient feature in Salona's topography, thus yielding a tangible clue to its identification.[16] The theater, which was very close to the harbour mole, impressed itself most strongly on the mind of the sculptor responsible for the carving of the slab. The precinct with the portico which, in reality, is to the south of the theater, is moved in the relief to the left of the theater.[17] The *Capitolium* is correctly situated to the right (east) of the theater. Noteworthy are the arched gateways on both sides of the theater. The one on the left could be identified tentatively with the "liaison entre le théâtre et la colonnade" as attested by the excavations.[18] The one on the right with the adjacent doorway and the windows in the upper storey could hint at the portico which was situated behind the theater, that is to the north.[19] Finally, there is the small building to the right (east) of the *Capitolium*. This is hardly a religious building. Although the area immediately to the east of the *Capitolium* was never investigated, the curia now excavated by us corresponds to the general location of the building in the relief. To be sure, the curia is in reality not immediately adjacent to the tetrastyle temple, but is some 40 meters to the east, so that the panel could depict yet another building between temple and curia not identified by excavation. However, the curious architecture of this building indicates a secular use, and it is thus tentatively suggested here that the sculptor recorded in his relief the impression of a building which, in fact, is identical with the curia.

The religious and public center of Roman Salona presented itself as a closely knit unity to the mind of the artist, as it probably did to anyone who saw the city from the harbour side. This is the view we get in the relief panel. Much more archaeological evidence is presently available to identify panel LXXXVI with Salona rather than with any other city proposed as candidate. And what makes Salona's candidacy particularly attractive is that two buildings—theater and *Capitolium*—can be fully accounted for by actual remains, whereas the remaining structures have found their near-identity in excavations as well, something which cannot be said of Tergeste.

Moreover, there is the whole problem of Trajan's route. Whereas sailing to the N. Adriatic and visiting Tergeste would have taken Trajan out of his way, a stop at Salona would have provided the starting point for a direct, well-known route to Sirmium and the Danube river.[20] The Adriatic crossing from Ancona to middle Dalmatia is short and safe. Lastly accounting for the intervening slabs LXXX to LXXXV, we have no other choice than to assume, as other scholars have done before us, that Trajan sailed from Ancona to Iader, which was his first stop in Dalmatia. He then proceeded, possibly via Scardona, Burnum, and Asseria and, alternating the overland with the sea route, the last leg was achieved by sea and brought Trajan to Salona. From here begins the trip inland which is the subject matter of LXXXVII and the following panels.

Notes on Excursus I

1. Select Bibliography and Abbreviations for Excursus I:

Bulić 1915	F. Bulić, "La Dalmatia nei bassorilievi sulla colonna Trajana con speciale riguardo all' opera di C. Cichorius 'Die Reliefs . . .' ", *BD* 38 (1915): 91-127.
Benndorf-Niemann	O. Benndorf and G. Niemann, *Das Monument von Adamklissi. Tropaeum Traiani* (1895).
Bendinelli	G. Bendinelli, *La Colonna Traiana* (1936).
Cichorius	C. Cichorius, *Die Reliefs der Trajanssäule* I-III (1896-1900). For slab LXXXVI see vol. III (1900), pp. 59-76, pl. 63, nos. 225-228.
Degrassi I	A. Degrassi, "La via seguita da Traiano nel 105 per recarsi nella Dacia," *Rend. Pont. Accad. Romana Archeologia* 22 (1946/7): 167-183.
Degrassi II	A. Degrassi, "Aquileia e Trieste nelle scene della colonna Traiana?", *Rend. Accad. Archeol. Lettere, Belle Arti*, Napoli, 36 (1961): 139-150.
EAA	*Enciclopedia dell' arte antica* vol. II (1959), s.v. Colonna di Traiano, pp. 756-760 (L. Rocchetti).
Florescu	F.B. Florescu, *Die Trajanssäule* (1969).
Garzetti	A. Garzetti, *L'impero da Tiberio agli Antonini* (1961).
Stuart Jones	H. Stuart Jones, "The historical interpretation of the reliefs on Trajan's column," *PBSR* 5 (1910): 435-459.
Loewy	E. Loewy, "Apollodor und die Reliefs der Trajanssäule," *Strena Buliciana* (1924), pp. 73-76.
Lehmann-Hartleben	K. Lehmann-Hartleben, *Die Trajanssäule* (1926).
Patsch	C. Patsch, "Der Kampf um den Donauraum unter Domitian und Trajan," *Sb. Akad. Wien, Phil-hist. Kl.* 217, 1, 1937.
Petersen	E. Petersen, *Trajans Dakische Kriege nach den Säulenreliefs erzählt.* Vol. II: *Der zweite Krieg* (1903).

Picard I	Ch. Picard, "Brundisium. Notes de Topographie et d'Histoire," *REL* 35 (1957): 285-303.
Picard II	Ch. Picard, "Pouzzoles et le passage portuaire," *Latomus* 18 (1959): 23-51.
RE (1965)	*RE* Suppl. X (1965), M.U. Traianus (B. Hanslik-W.H. Gross).
Romanelli	P. Romanelli, *La Colonna Traiana* (1942).
Rossi	L. Rossi, *Trajan's column and the Dacian wars* (1971).
E. Strong	E. Strong, *Roman sculpture from Augustus to Constantine* (1907). See especially pp. 166-213.
Stucchi I	S. Stucchi, "Il coronamento dell'arco Romano nel porto di Ancona," *Rend. Accad. Archeol., Lettera, Belle Arti,* Napoli, 32 (1957): 149-164.
Stucchi II	S. Stucchi, "Contributo alle conoscenza della Topografia dell'arte e della storia nella colonna Traiana," *Accad. Scienze, Lettere, Arti di Udine,* ser. VII, vol. I (1960), pp. 7-102.
Stucchi III	S. Stucchi, "Intorno al viaggio di Traiano nel 105 D.C.," *RM* 72 (1965): 142-170.
Turcan	M. Turcan-Déléani, "Les monuments representés sur la colonne Trajana. Schématisme et Réalisme." *Mél. Ec. Franc. Rome* 70 (1958): 149-176.
Vidman	L. Vidman, *Fasti Ostienses* (1957).

2. See Vidman passim.

3. The following authors have opted for Ancona for panel LXXIX: Bendinelli, Cichorius, Benndorf-Niemann, (Garzetti), *EAA* (L. Rocchetti), Patsch, Romanelli, Rossi, Petersen, E. Strong, Stucchi I-III, Turcan.

4. Stucchi I, pp. 158-159.

5. The following authors have opted for Brundisium: Degrassi I-II, Garzetti ("preferably B., rather than Ancona"), Picard I-II, *RE* (1965), Vidman.

6. The importance of the temple of Venus, the statue of the goddess, the hill behind the harbour, and the steep zigzag path was naturally played down by all those who prefer to identify the locality in the panel with another city. In addition to the temple, etc., the crescent-shaped inner harbour still corresponds to its present-day configuration and is excellently suggested in the relief by the position of the ships, the half circle of the port, and other buildings behind the ships. The views juxtaposed by Turcan-Déléani (figs. 1 and 2) are very suggestive indeed.

7. Lehmann-Hartleben, p. 30. See also Turcan, passim. She raises the fundamental problem of the impact of artistic-representational schemes upon renderings of city views, which are different from renderings which are based on the experience of viewing a site personally and reproducing one's impression thereafter.

8. For slab LXXXVI the following cities have been proposed; *Salona:* Bulić 1915, Cichorius, Dyggve, Stuart Jones, Turcan; *Dyrrhachium:* Degrassi I-II, Garzetti, Picard I-II, *RE* (1965); *Tergeste:* Stucchi I-III and prior to him Kandler (1866); *Byzantium:* Benndorf-Niemann; *unnamed city:* Florescu, Romanelli, Rossi. Lehmann-Hartleben does not seem to have committed himself to any specific city, either for panel LXXIX or LXXXVI.

9. Turcan, p. 171. For Degrassi I, p. 177, n. 42 the route via Brindisi, etc. is "più brève e più commodo" and the "Via Appia ben tenuta e ricca di città." See also note 20 below.

10. Stucchi was preceded in this identification by Kandler who as early as 1866 proposed for panel LXXXVI Tergeste. See Stucchi II, p. 67.

11. Stucchi II, pp. 58, 66 also noted the rendering of a rocky surface above the archway which connects the portico with the theater; he proposes to identify this rock with the colle S. Giusto behind the theater in Tergeste.

12. Cichorius III, p. 60 describes the building as follows: "Ein Haus, das an der Vorderseite im unteren Stockwerk zwei Säulen, im oberen zwei kleine Fenster hat; das mit Ziegeln gedeckte Dach steigt von zwei Seiten nach der Mitte zu in die Höhe."

13. Stucchi II passim, and especially his figures 8 ff.

14. Stucchi II, p. 97 ". . . vediamo quale nuovo aspetto alla conoscenza della topografia anche di quest' antica città ci può venir dato dalla sua veduta sulla colonna."

15. This was already seen by Dyggve, *Recherches* I, p. 15. For the platform see pp. 11 ff. For the wall with arcades see Cichorius III, pp. 72 ff. However misconceived some of the arguments are, the discussion by Cichorius still makes stimulating reading. For the mole of the port of Salona see Cichorius III, p. 75 and our discussion of the *via munita.* The wall with three arcades to the left of the colonnaded court, behind the city-gate (cf. our description above) comes closest to the platform with the arcades. Beyond this similarity it is difficult to guess the function of the wall in the relief.

16. As for Stucchi's main argument (Stucchi II, pp. 71 f.) against equation of the city on the slab with Salona—

namely that Salona's theater is to be dated post-Trajanic and thus cannot be represented on the column, citing as evidence the article by B. Gabričević—it is doomed, because the theater does in fact date from the first century A.D. (See note 10, chapter II.) In addition to the date, Stucchi notes that details in the rendering of the theater on the slab do not correspond to the actual architecture of the theater in Salona, except for the number of *cunei*. But approximation is all we can really expect. Stucchi's notion of the topography of Salona is ill-conceived when he denies, for instance, the hilly territory of the inhabited city. Salona is *not at all* a "città che è tutto piano." Both Stucchi and Degrassi took very little issue in their writings with the more commonly accepted view that part of the army, led by Trajan himself, landed on the Dalmatian coast at either Zadar or Salona, with Ancona as port of departure.

17. Dyggve, *Recherches* II, pp. 15 f. does not seem to have clearly visualized on slab LXXXVI the colonnaded court with the trees (instead of the temple) within. But when he wrote *Recherches* I he had not yet excavated the temple to the east of the theater, published in *RA*.(See Dyggve, "Forum.") Thus he thought that the temple within the colonnade "a été complètement supprimé et qu'on a seulement reproduit *un autre* [italics ours] tétrastyle situé à l'est du théâtre." This "autre tétrastyle" was Dyggve's more recently found temple. The earlier temple had been omitted indeed, but not the colonnade! Maybe Dyggve did not want to accept the tree-filled court as having anything to do with or being essentially the same structure as the temple within the colonnaded precinct.

18. Dyggve, *Recherches* II, p. 24.

19. See the plan on our Plate 7.

20. Degrassi concedes (Degrassi I, p. 177, n. 42) that the route via Ancona-Salona to Moesia is about 100 kilometers shorter than the Brindisi route, but "sulle strade montagnose e inospitali della Balcania," which may not be conforming entirely to the truth!

EXCURSUS II:

Caesar, *De Bello Civili* III. 9.

In a paper read in October 1970, at a symposium held to celebrate the 100th anniversary of the Split Museum, Professor D. Rendić-Miočević proposed a new interpretation for Caesar's *De Bello Civili* III. 9. Mr. Rendić, Jr. kindly put at my disposal a copy translated into French of Professor Rendić's Serbo-Croatian paper.

The author reiterates (pp. 1-5) his conclusion arrived at earlier (see Chapter I, note 14) that Issaeans (Greeks) came to Salona from Tragurion. While he considers the presence of Delmatae in Salona very likely, he believes that they were even reinforced by Delmatae who came here after the destruction of Delminium in 155 B.C. This assumption finds support, according to Rendić-Miočević, in writers like Appian and Strabo. Furthermore, he feels that the plural form of Salona, Σαλῶναι, is the result of the presence of "plusieurs noyaux ethniques," not yet gathered in an *oppidum* but in a port settlement, ἐπίνειον. The plural Σαλῶναι "doit être comprise comme appelation d'un territoire collectif, par laquelle il faut aussi sous-entendre la communauté ethnique dalmate et romaine—et peut-être même la grecque (isséenne) vivant sur ce territoire."

Taking issue first with these general assumptions, we can only repeat briefly what has been discussed at some length earlier, namely that the Issaeans (Greeks) from Tragurion represent the commercial interests in a small, settled community within the territory of Delmatae who were not, so to speak, their co-residents. Turning now to the new interpretation by Professor Rendić of Caesar's *B.C.* III. 9, the author proposes the involvement of three different groups of people in the conflict which centers around Salona: the Delmatae, the Issaeans in Salona, and the members of the *conventus*, the Roman settlers. Once Antony arrived with his boats, Rendić-Miočević believes that he faced "une Salone pluraliste." The reference to Delmatae and "other barbarians" in and around Salona whom Antony was successful in inciting to rebellion against Caesar confirms our own assumption of their presence in the general area.

But what about the reference to Issa and Issaeans respectively. Until now, modern commentators took it to refer to the island Issa; the word occurs in the accusative singular, "Issam." Rendić believes, however, that Caesar has in mind *not* the island but instead Issaeans in Salona. He supports his new interpretation in a lengthy statement as follows (pp. 9-10):

> Octave n'a pas pu non plus, de Salona (qu'il n'avait pas en mains) inciter à la revolte et à la desobéissance toute la population du vaste territoire dalmate, ni même, à partir de lieux aussi éloignés, agir sur les habitants de la lointaine Issa, pour qu'ils renoncent à l'amitié et à la protection de César. Il est beaucoup plus facile et simple d'expliquer la mention de Dalmates et Isséens dans le 'contexte' salonitain mentionné ci-dessus, surtout quand dans le texte lui-même, est clairement exprimé que toute cette action s'est deroulée *là (ibi)*—ce qui veut dire sur le territoire de Salone et non de là (*inde*) ou quelque chose de semblable. Cela ressort aussi du rythme et de la construction du texte qui, après Dalmates et Issa, passe logiquement à "conventus." L'action se développa progressivement: d'abord ce sont les Dalmates qui se révoltent, puis les Isséens (ceux qui vivaient sur le territoire de Salone) qui sont acquis à la cause et alors s'accomplit l'essai de conquête pacifique du "conventus," c'est-à-dire des citoyens romains. Il serait assez incompréhensible que César—qui connaissait bien les conditions existant dans cette ville complexe—ignorât les Dalmates ou Isséens salonitains, ne parlât que des citoyens romains salonitains, et des Dalmates et Isséens comme d'un élément inexistant sur le territoire de Salone. Le "conventus" s'y confronte si directement avec les Dalmates mentionnés ci-dessus et les Isséens, qu'il ne peut y avoir d'autre alternative syntaxique.

In this writer's opinion, Rendić's hypothesis is doomed a priori because, grammatically, it is not permissible to read into and translate "Issam" to mean "Issaeans residing in Salona." Surely Caesar means the island Issa. Since Delmatae were in the general territory around Salona from at least the beginning of the Hellenistic period, *ibi* refers to Delmatae in this territory; and the "other barbarians" aroused by Antony probably refer to Delmatae and other tribes residing beyond a more narrowly limited territory around Salona. There is no evidence in Caesar that, after the rebellion of the Delmatae, "les Isséens (ceux qui vivaient sur le territoire de Salona) sont acquis à la cause." What we know conclusively is that the island Issa severed its friendly ties with Caesar and was won over by Antony. Now, if Rendić's assumption of a "Salona pluraliste" were correct, it could mean that Issaeans in Salona left the city together with the Delmatae because the conventus of Roman settlers courageously resisted all temptations of Antony to give itself up to him. Since the conventus seems to have been dominant in Salona at this time and defended itself successfully in the ensuing battle, the Delmatae, who were induced to rebellion, would break their ties with the conventus and avoid the settlement proper. While it is understandable that the Delmatae should turn against the conventus, it could well be that the Issaeans in Salona followed the example of their mother-island and made friends with Antony, too. However, this would presuppose not only a fairly large community of Issaeans in Salona—and we really know next to nothing about the size of this community—but it would also mean that the Issaeans renounced their political status within the conventus which was clarified and settled in the "Decree of 56 B.C.," as Rendić himself has shown. This political settlement would make it unnecessary to refer specifically to "Issaeans in Salona" because they were part of the conventus.

Whereas Issa's influence upon the settlements on the coast was important during the Hellenistic age, it fell into the status of political dependency from Salona after the conventus defended itself successfully for Caesar's cause against Antony and Pompey who, after defeat, withdrew from the political scene in this part of the Adriatic. From this shift of political dominance one must conclude that Issa, the island, did defect from Caesar thus making a political mistake by joining the losing side. However, the Issaeans in Salona who decided to stick with the conventus according to our view did not have to regret their decision. Caesar's passage dwells on the disloyalty of the mother-island Issa, not that of the Issaeans in Salona. For if Issa does not mean the island of Issa, as suggested by Rendić-Miočević, what other passage is there, by any other historian which informs us of the defection of the island from Caesar, the defection so clearly in evidence in ensuing history?

III
The Excavations

INTRODUCTION

The choice of the site for our excavation of 1969 and 1970 was determined by the work of our predecessors, foremost among them E. Dyggve. We proposed to tackle one major task: the search for the Hellenistic settlement. We have discussed earlier the opinions of several authors with regard to the location of the Hellenistic acropolis or settlement. Of all the excavators preceeding us, Dyggve seemed most enthusiastic concerning the existence of Hellenistic levels and the possibility of uncovering them. In 1933, when working on the temple just behind the theater, (**Figure 4**), he wrote in reference to the virgin soil that "il n'a encore jamais été atteint et sur lequel reposent les plus anciennes couches grecques, datant de la fondation de la factorerie Σαλώνη."[1] In 1928, Dyggve expressed both enthusiasm and optimism about spade work in Salona by comparing it with Pompeii, saying:

> ces deux villes ont cela de commun que leurs terrains ont été exempt de ces habitations ultérieures qui rendent ailleurs très difficile ou impossible des recherches approfondies .... Mais Salona a encore un avantage très important pour la recherche archéologique moderne scientifique: les pièces decouvertes sont taillées dans un pierre si excellente que la grande majorité des trouvailles ... ont conservé leur forme et leur aspect comme si elles étaient d'hier.[2]

The comparison between Salona and Pompeii is far from being a happy one. While the latter site was covered by the eruption of Mt. Vesuvius with a thick layer of protective pumice stone and ashes, Salona, on the contrary, became a valuable source for building material from the late Roman period onward throughout medieval and later times.

When Salona became a center of Christianity shortly after A.D. 300, the Roman Forum served other purposes. A *torcularium* made up of reused building elements from the Forum can still be seen in fairly good preservation to the north of the *Capitolium* adjacent to the Forum central drain (**Figure 2**).[3] The *torcularium* and finds of pottery and coins on the entire "eminence" are proof for the continuation of life in this sector of the city through the fourth to sixth centuries A.D.[4] However, there can be little doubt that, with the growth and dominance of the Christian community, the center of town had shifted and was concentrated around the major Christian basilicae to the northeast of the Porta Caesarea.[5]

After A.D. 612, the year in which the Vandals sacked the city, the large scale looting of Roman and Christian Salona began.[6] Masonry blocks from the buildings and city walls were taken far afield: to Klis, to the Kaštela region along the bay, to Trogir, and, of course to Split.[7] Stone-breaking in situ is proven by numerous stone-beds or *gomile*, often referred to hereafter, which render excavation a difficult task, since they destroy not only profiles but walls, floors, and artifacts. In summary then, we can hardly see any validity in a comparison between Salona and Pompeii; one is confronted with two entirely different forms of preservation on the two respective sites.

With regard to the depth of the Hellenistic levels Dyggve was also over-optimistic.[8] It is now difficult to understand why he did not venture to probe the depth of the debris accumulated, for instance, to the north of the *Capitolium* and penetrate those pre-Roman levels, the existence of which he firmly assumed. It soon became evident to us when we started work in 1969 that virgin soil is much closer to the surface than anyone anticipated. All that we could discover were scant traces of one Hellenistic building period with few accompanying finds.[9]

Excavation in the Roman levels proved more rewarding. We have gained certain insights with respect to building activity on the Forum which are an improvement on those of our predecessors. Special attention was given to the small finds, and in particular to the pottery, the study and publication of which were much neglected by former generations of excavators. This is not to say that there were no small finds from Salona prior to our excavation. G. Alföldy sums up the situation very well when he says:

> Es möge hier nur darauf hingewiesen werden, dass die Provinzhauptstadt Salona trotz der grossen Tradition ihrer Erforschung heute noch immer nicht genügend bekannt ist: obwohl die Ausdehnung der Stadt schon längst festgestellt ist, wurden in ihrem Innern nur einzelne Gebäude freigelegt. Systematisch ausgegrabene Fundplätze stehen der Forschung in Dalmatien kaum zur Verfügung .... Als besonders misslich erweist sich die Lage im Falle des Kleinmaterials. Die für die wirtschaftgeschichtlichen Studien so bedeutenden Fundtypen, wie Keramik, Glas, Fibeln u.s.w., wurden bis zur letzten Zeit fast vollständig ausser acht gelassen.[10]

THE CURIA SITE

There were several reasons which prompted as choice for excavation in 1969 the site to the east of the *torcularium*—henceforth called the curia site. First, the surface level of the area lay considerably higher (+7.65 meters elevation) than the area to the north of the theater and the *Capitolium* (+6.40 meters), simply because it had not been previously excavated. (**Figure 11**). Second, measurements taken of the elevation of slabs of the Forum central drain (**Figure 6**) indicated a gradual slope towards the east and we could surmise, therefore, that the drain ran in that direction. This drain could have continued far beyond the curia site, namely to a point where major drains from other parts of the *urbs orientalis* or *urbs nova* met before their eventual discharge into the river Iader. Moreover, mention was made earlier of the arcaded wall which supports a platform; the latter, or Forum south area, is really an artificial extension of the eminence, or Forum central area.

The east wall of the platform is still clearly visible as it runs from the arcaded wall straight north, theoretically at least, as far as the point where the rocky plateau, the eminence, begins to rise, with the wall butting against this natural formation of the terrain (**Figure 1**). The fact that historical sources speak of some sort of defense wall around the eminence made us go one step further in our assumptions. Could the east wall of the platform have been aligned with a wall that bordered the east side of the eminence? Did this wall play the role of defense wall during the Hellenistic-Republican period and continue, even if rebuilt, to make a Forum enclosure in the Imperial period? If this assumption were proven correct, the Forum enclosure and any preserved remains of the earlier Hellenistic defense wall would have to intersect with the Forum central

Figure 11: View from Capitolium towards northeast, with curia site in preparation for excavation.

drain. This intersection ought to be situated in square A3 on the curia site. Evidently then, the area chosen for excavation could bring to light remains of buildings along the drain, possibly an entrance to the Roman Forum at the point of intersection of the east enclosure with the drain, and lastly, remains of additional buildings outside the east enclosure.

The curia site measures circa 45 by 25 meters, with the long axis running east-west. The site shows a mild eastward slope in the first 18 meters from the west; then, with the slope becoming more marked in squares A/C4-7, the terrain falls off abruptly about 10 meters beyond square A/C7. The southward slope of the terrain is less pronounced.[11] The site has been cultivated but never excavated. Heavily overgrown with grass and weeds, the curia site is surrounded by privately owned vineyards to the south, east, and north. On the north side the boundary consists of a low stone wall which continues to the northwest into a *gomila* or stone mound.

The topsoil on the curia site has an average depth of 0.80 to 0.90 meters. It clearly shows many traces of vine roots which go very deep into the topsoil. Its dark brown earth is thoroughly mixed with crushed mortar and carbonized matter; fragments of pottery and glass, mosaic tesserae, and bones turn up in small quantities at 0.40 meters below the surface level and increasingly from a depth of 0.70 to 0.80 meters. Several squares were completely disturbed to bedrock by looters.

At an early stage of the excavation it became evident that the terrain had been disturbed almost throughout by looters. They looked not only for metal and building stones but also for material for lime kilns. Thus all marble was broken up and smashed. All these activities resulted in many huge stone heaps *(gomile)* above ground or used as fill for the many trenches dug down to bedrock by the looters. A further result was the destruction of any once coherent stratification in the majority of the squares excavated.

The excavation proceeded by the squares of the grid plan to which we refer throughout the text (A1, A2, etc.). An unforeseen complication was encountered in the ground below topsoil, which turned out to be destruction debris possibly carted from some distance and thoroughly levelled to prepare the ground for succeeding building periods. Therefore, any occasional mention of layers (I, II, etc., counted from bedrock upwards) does *not* refer to any natural stratification but indicates steps in excavating. One layer represents a summary of several layers, the contents of which proved eventually to be of one rather than different historical periods.

This concludes the description of the curia site prior to excavation. There will now follow a discussion of the building periods on the curia site. These will be treated in chronological order, with the earliest period I, first.

The structural remains of the excavations as a whole make it possible to speak of a total of four building periods. The small finds provide the absolute chronology for each individual period as follows:

Period I	late Hellenistic-Republican/Augustan age.
Period II	first century A.D.
Period III	second and third centuries A.D.
Period IV	fourth to sixth century A.D.

PERIOD I (Plate 3)

The earliest, Hellenistic, structural remains on the curia site consist of a series of walls and drains. Both are preserved in their foundations only. The building material is a yellowish limestone and no mortar is used for the joining of the stones. The blocks are joined in a fairly compact manner; big and small rectangular stones form the edges of the walls; in the case of bigger stones, two rows side by side make up the total width of the wall; in the case of smaller stones the core of the wall is made up of a fill with still smaller stones, but each course is usually different in composition from the next following. It is also common to find one oblong stone placed sidewise interrupting the continuity of stones placed in a lengthwise fashion. The stones are fairly thin.

The uniform levelling of the limestone walls down to the lowermost courses speaks for systematic destruction. This is supported by the levelling of the general debris, which contains many small stones and fragments of tiles and which shows, furthermore, signs of heavy conflagration especially in squares A'/A/B6-7. The destruction and levelling of period I remains suggests that this was done primarily in view of the building program at the beginning of period II.

The lowermost courses of a wall, one or two stones high, are preserved in square A3 (**Figure 12**) forming a corner and continuing to the north and, in a more fragmentary state of preservation, also to the west. Very scanty remains of the north-south portion of the wall in A3 are preserved in A'3, suggesting that this wall continued originally to the south (**Figure 13**). Squares A3-4 are a particularly disturbed area, but A4 contains an eastern continuation of the limestone wall for a distance of 2.30 meters. Further east still, the wall continues in square A6, disappearing eventually under the main structure of the next building period (**Figure 14**). The wall is 0.45 meters wide and we refer to it as wall A.

Drain *a* runs parallel to wall A along a short portion of its length (**Figures 14, 15, and 16**). The covering slabs of the drain are not preserved; its sidewalls are built with small stones. Like wall A, drain *a* was also covered up by the later building period.

To the south of drain *a* are the foundations of another wall B (**Figure 14**). It is 7 meters long and 0.40 meters wide. A later disturbance destroyed the middle section and some of the stones were lifted out of their original position. The easternmost portion of wall B was destroyed by a *gomila* which cut deeply into the entire wall system in square A6. Two isolated stones in square A'4 may have belonged to wall B; however, four additional stones somewhat to the south

Figure 12: Square A3, curia site.

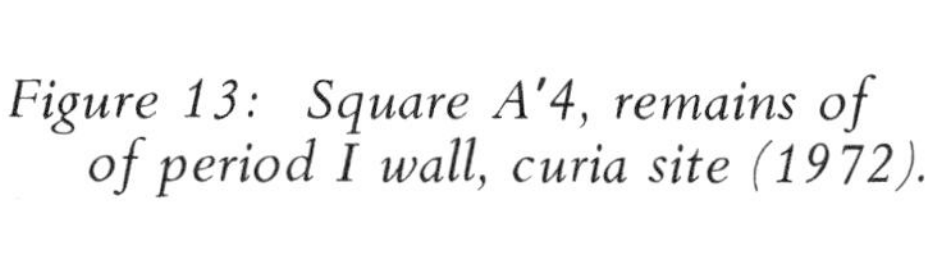

Figure 13: Square A'4, remains of of period I wall, curia site (1972).

Figure 14: Squares A/B5-6, period I–III walls and apse of curia looking northeast (1969).

Figure 15: Squares A/B5-6, curia site, remains of period I walls in foreground, curia south wall in background (1969).

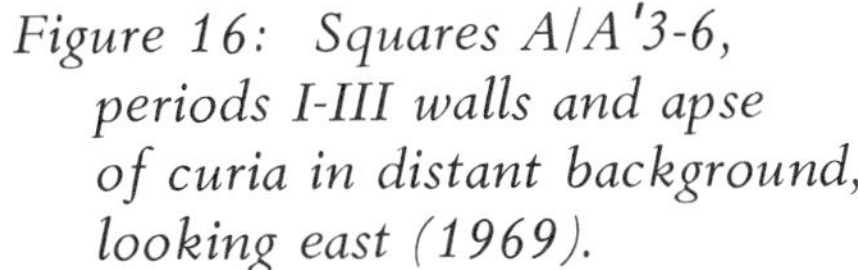

Figure 16: Squares A/A'3-6, periods I-III walls and apse of curia in distant background, looking east (1969).

cannot be placed in any specific context.

A third wall C is to the south of wall B. It forms a perfect right angle in square A4-5, running southward and disappearing beneath walls of period II (**Figure 16**).

The scanty remains of walls in squares A/A'6-7 do not, unfortunately, aid in clarifying the walls discussed so far. A few oblong limestone slabs, three courses high and 0.50 meters wide, came to light in square A6. This wall E runs southwest to northeast. If wall B is prolonged in an eastward direction it could have joined, when intact, wall E, thus forming an obtuse angle (**Figure 17**).

Figure 17: Square A'7, curia site, period I wall east (1970).

Another wall F in A/A'7 runs parallel to E (**Figure 18**). Instead of oblong slabs set parallel to each other in the width of the wall, rectangular slabs measuring the whole width of the wall (0.55 meters, slightly wider than other period I walls) formed a major course. Irregularities in this course were corrected by smaller stones.

Both at the north and south end of wall F there are drains (*b-d*). The southerly drain *b* runs in a northwest direction at first (**Figure 18**), then turns northeast somewhat beyond wall F, thus running parallel to it. Drain *c* comes from the northeast and originates in the general area to the north of the curia site. Drain *d*, to the north of wall F, takes an eastward course and represents, in fact, the confluence of drains *a-c* (**Figure 19**).

Except for a few isolated stones in square C7 no other structural remains of period I were found on the curia site.

Figure 18: Square A'7, curia site, period I wall F and drain b in left foreground (1970).

The floor level of period I is not preserved in any location on the curia site. This is due to the general levelling of period I remains at the beginning of the next building period. However, this layer of debris was sealed off by pavement slabs in squares A'/A/B7 in the course of the building activities of period II; this is the only area on the curia site of which it can be said that it has remained undisturbed by any later form of building activity or looting.

Walls A–D are unfortunately too fragmentary to give us any clue about the type of construction or building to which they may have belonged. Considering the fact that drain *a* runs between walls A and B, this may suggest that we have here a street which ran in an eastward direction from the settlement on the eminence (**Figures 15 and 16**). Walls C and D could have belonged to adjacent structures, as did wall E which we believe was closely related to wall C.

Although drain *a* is not in line with the Forum central drain of period II/III, it is clear that the builders of the later drain still considered the same general area the most efficient one for the disposal of water. As for the north-south portions of the period I walls in squares A/A'3 (**Figures 12 and 13**), it is most important to note that the general direction of this wall seems to have been taken into account by the builders of the platform which we discussed earlier. Moreover, three facts, namely the meeting point of north-south and east-west walls in square A3, the likely presence of a drain, and the transition in square A3 from the even surface of the eminence to its eastern slope, could indicate that this square was of strategic importance. It would not seem too farfetched to say that there was in square A3 an entrance from the east to the "acropolis" of the Hellenistic settlement.

PERIODS II AND III (Plate 8)

The building which we have named the curia was first built early in the first century A.D. and existed for about three hundred years. We propose to discuss the evidence for the building's name in the conclusion of our description. We distinguish two building periods of the curia.

In order to prepare the site for the building, the remains of period I were completely levelled. Among the latter is a previously described drain which, even though rebuilt, coexists with the curia. The origin of the drain, then as now, is in the central area of the eminence, with the waters being evacuated towards the east. The drain of period II passes inside the curia close to its southwest corner running parallel to the south wall. Just inside the curia, the drain is deviated slightly to the northeast for a short distance, continuing henceforth in a straight course (**Figure 16**). At the point of the second "bend" there is a stump-like secondary arm, probably a safety device permitting a sudden onrush of water to regulate its winding course thus avoiding an overflow. The drain is paved throughout. Although the greater portion of the drain inside the curia is no longer preserved, it ran, in principle, straight east. This is suggested primarily by the northern edge of the drain which continues for about 4 meters in square A5 beyond the point of redirection which occurred in period III to be described later. During period II the drain may have been connected in square A5 with the period I drain. Two pavement slabs in square A5 very likely belong to this linking portion between the old and the new drain but since the whole area in A5 is completely disturbed, it is difficult to understand all of the details.

The curia is a rectangular building with an apse built onto the east wall (**Figures 14 and 20**). The measurements of the building are not exactly known because of the poor preservation of the west wall. However, the length of the interior of the curia measured between 15 and 16 meters; the width of the building is 13.20 meters at the east end but becomes narrower towards the west, namely 12.70 meters, at a distance of about 10 meters from the east wall. The diameter of the apse is 5 meters; its depth is 2.50 meters (**Figure 21**). From the curve of the apse to the northwest and southeast corners the distances are 4.10 and 4.20 meters respectively. The width of the apse is a little over a third of the total length of the east wall. The foundation for the east wall is built of rubble set in mortar mixed with pebbles. The footing inside reaches a width of 0.55 meters in its northern portion; in the central portion it is only 0.35 meters wide. Still narrower is the footing in the northern portion on the outside of the east wall. Immediately beyond the apse to the south, foundation and wall itself have been completely destroyed by a *gomila* for a distance of 2.10 meters. Then, towards the southeast corner, the foundation becomes narrower, the footing being only 0.20 meters wide on the inside, somewhat larger on the outside.

The wall proper is 0.55 meters wide. Wall and apse are built of small masonry blocks set in mortar. A fill of earth and rubble forms the core of the wall and the apse. The curved masonry of the apse is bonded perfectly into the east wall. The highest portion of elevation of the apse as presently preserved is at +6.013 meters. This is probably very close to the ancient floor of the apse, since we encountered a mass of grayish mortar spread layer-wise over the rubble and earth

Figure 20: Curia after completion of restoration and conservation work with western cross wall, looking east towards east wall of curia (1972).

Figure 21: Apse of curia looking southwest with southeast corner of curia in center of picture close to upper edge. The light-colored fresco level is clearly visible adjacent to corner, underneath dark-colored surface soil (1969).

Figure 22: Curia eastern cross wall (left, after restoration) and western wall with giant corner slab (1972).

core. This might indicate either the lowermost portion of the actual floor or the bedding for a more elaborate floor which could have been a mosaic.

The south wall of the curia (**Figure 16**) is impressive for both its preservation and for its solid construction of small mortared masonry with an earth and rubble fill. The foundations, 1 meter wide, are preserved from the southeast corner for a distance of 10 meters. Of the wall proper there remains a length of 1 meter only at the easternmost portion of the curia. It is 0.55 meters wide. In square A'4 the remains of the foundation have been disturbed; however, the wall does not seem to have run straight west but rather deviated a little from its former course, returning to the latter in square A'4 West as can be seen from a single course of stones of the wall which is preserved together with the foundation. Close to this area should be located the southwest corner of the curia, deducing from the scanty remains of the west wall of the curia. These remains, belonging more likely to period III, follow nevertheless an earlier course which was established in period II.

The north wall of the curia during period II is preserved only in its rubble foundation in squares B5 East and B6 West at an elevation of +5.138 and +5.133 meters (**Figure 14**). Its continuation farther west is surely identical with the course of the north wall which belongs to period III.

In the center of square B5 a short portion of a cross wall 0.55-0.60 meters wide and 3.80 meters long, runs north-south (**Figure 22**). The lowermost course of masonry rests on clay soil at +5.185 meters; four courses of carefully fitted and mortared rubble masonry are preserved to a height of 0.665 meters. At its north end this wall is bonded into the rubble foundation of the curia north wall. We call the wall just described the east cross wall to distinguish it from a period III cross wall immediately to the west. The east cross wall might well have been needed for support of the curia roof. Particularly noteworthy is the fact that this wall does not run parallel to the curia east wall but deviates slightly to the east.

Beside giving some support to the curia roof, the east cross wall might have divided the building into two principal rooms, a supposition which we could infer from the later, period III west cross wall. But too little is preserved of the east cross wall of period II to insist firmly on this supposition.

The general slope to the east of the terrain of the curia site could be easily seen prior to the excavation, as mentioned earlier. There is no evidence for any pavement inside the curia for period II. The floor consisted of a mixture of packed earth with clay, which was primarily the result of the levelling of the period I remains in preparation for the building of the curia. Due to the slope of the terrain one could surmise, however, that the floor levels to the east and west of the period II cross wall were slightly different, the difference being bridged over by one or two steps between the two respective rooms. The apse, the seat of the tribunal, naturally lay higher than the floor level of the east room, for which we have some indication in the footing along the east wall which was probably just covered with the earth/clay floor.

The end of the first phase of the curia's existence is indicated in a destruction layer, 0.10 to 0.15 meters thick, which is a deposit of charcoal suggesting a major conflagration. This layer is most clearly visible in the southeast corner of the curia; it is less well preserved in other sections of the building. Though probably attesting the burning of the entire interior of the curia building, the fire has possibly destroyed the southeast section more thoroughly. Inscriptional testimony refers to the restoration of this building at one time; this would corroborate the data gathered from the excavation itself.

The course of the drain underwent a major change in building period III. In square A'4 East, its former eastward course was changed to a course straight south, with the drain disappearing underneath the south wall (**Figure 16**). Since the terrain to the south of the south wall is not available for excavation, one can only surmise what the farther course of the drain could have been. The most likely supposition is that it ran along the outside of the curia south wall eventually joining the drainage system to the east of the curia which belongs to period I and which could well have been used over many centuries.

The very scanty remains of the curia west wall belong most likely to period III, as indicated earlier. It appears that only the core of the foundation of this wall is left intact; this is a very coarse, mortared rubble wall preserved in two courses of irregular height. It is preserved for a length of 4.40 meters but at the midpoint of the curia building the original setting is not intact. What was in period III a gap of 0.90 meters in the wall was filled in the subsequent building period IV by four oblong stones (elevation +6.253 meters), one of modrac, two of yellowish stone, and the fourth of whitish marble. A fifth stone rests partially on top of one of the four stones. For a possible identification of the gap with the entrance to the curia from the west, it is important to visualize that it lies in the axis of the apse, a location which can hardly be called accidental.

Figure 23: Curia western cross wall with giant corner slab, looking north (1972).

In square B4 West the north wall was destroyed down to the rubble foundation by a *gomila*. Further east, the foundation and the wall, 0.55 meters wide, are preserved. (**Figure 23**). In square B5 West the course of the north wall is interrupted as it passes over into the westernmost cross wall. Especially noteworthy is a slab of gigantic proportions which forms the uppermost course of the foundations at the outside corner (**Figures 22 and 23**). The foundation of the cross wall is built of rubble and has a length of 8.50 meters (**Figure 20**). For the footing fairly regular large and small stones were used. The wall itself is preserved in one to two layers in its northern part; only one layer remains towards the center of the curia. The length of the wall is 7.70 meters including a gap measuring about 1.16 meters, although damage to the masonry has obscured its original width. However, the gap is roughly in the center of the cross wall as well as in the axis of the apse and also the gap which we noted in the west wall.

The alignment of the western entrance, the opening in the west cross wall, and the center of the apse cannot be accidental. We believe that the opening in the west cross wall of period III indicates the location of a door, which was possibly the only door connecting the two principal rooms of the curia, the apsidal east room, and the west room. Since the eastern portion of the curia north wall is preserved in B5 West in its rubble foundation only, it is difficult to know how it was related to the much better preserved western portion. Judging from the gigantic slab used in the foundation of the corner, one could surmise that there was an entrance here to the curia east room also from the north. Whether or not this entrance succeeded an earlier one in the same place is difficult to say. However, it is possible that the earlier east cross wall specifically served the purpose of a cross wall; when it was replaced by the later west cross wall, it came to lie under the presumed entrance and was completely buried. The new cross wall, more massively built than the old wall, served the same purpose of dividing the curia into two main rooms and of supporting the roof. In the course of rebuilding it was also found that an additional entrance to the curia was necessary. This entrance led into the curia east room from the north.

The floor level of phase 2 of the curia building (period III) is to be situated, generally speaking, directly under the destruction layer of the curia which is characterized as a fairly thick fresco layer. There are only a few small areas where this layer and the floor level of phase 2 have not been disturbed. The latter, 7 centimeters thick and mostly of clay, is again best preserved in the southeast corner of the curia which was more extensively damaged than the rest of the building in the conflagration mentioned previously, and where the restoration of the floor might have been a primary concern, whereas it is very possible that the phase 1 floor (period II) continued in use elsewhere in the building.

From the fresco layer we can gain some insights of the interior decoration of the curia. The fresco layer varies in thickness from 0.25 to 0.50 meters depending on its location; it is thickest in the curia east room, 0 to 3 meters away from the east and south walls (**Figures 14 and 21**). Yellowish in color, this layer is rather loose in composition due to its strongly decomposed, gritty material (lime, sand, and mortar). This layer was full of fresco fragments. Only relatively small fragments could be recovered, since any larger panels which may have fallen from the sidewalls and perhaps also from the ceiling (?) slowly decomposed through the centuries. However, fragments survive in sufficient quantities to give a general idea of the decoration of the curia. The specific level of the fresco layer suggests that it belongs only to phase 2 (period III) of the building.

A considerable number of stucco mouldings turned up in the fresco layer, especially along the south wall and at the northern end of the apse. Chunk-like fragments of so-called *sedra* which came to light plentifully in the fresco layer, especially in the center of the east room and along the south wall of the curia, provide important information about the roof structure of the building. This yellowish-brown, very porous stone was generally used for roofing and vaulting. It can still be seen in the vaults of the palace of Diocletian, especially in the fully excavated northern half of the basement apartments of the emperor.

Elements for the reconstruction and decoration of the building other than frescoes, the stuccoes, and the elements of *sedra* are the mosaic stones which were found, though not very plentifully, throughout the fresco layer.

The use of reed matting for making the stucco adhere and better protect the wall-paintings which were painted onto the stucco is fully discussed later. This specific evidence does suggest a building whose interior structure relied heavily on the use of timber. It is not possible to determine the exact form of roof which covered the building. It is obvious that the answer cannot be found in the depiction of a building on relief panel LXXXVI of the column of Trajan, which we should like to identify with the curia. We can only keep the suggested identification in mind.

The *sedra,* fresco decorations, stucco mouldings, and mosaic tesserae are all precious evidence for the decorative and structural details of the curia. Besides the apse, which in a curia served as tribunal, and the inscriptional evidence to be discussed, it is the interior decoration together with the architectural layout which finds parallels in other Roman curiae.

In Yugoslavia itself three sites have to be considered for comparison with the curia at Salona. Doclea near Titograd has a Forum measuring approximately 80 by 75+ meters.[12] To the east of the Forum square is a basilica "deren gut erhaltene Fundamente eine einschiffige Halle von ungefähr 13 m Breite zeigen."[13] At the north end of the basilica is a room more wide (13 meters) than long (10 meters), with an apse opposite the entrance from the basilica; a secondary entrance is in the west wall; a window gives on to the Forum.[14]

In Delminium the rectangular Forum is closed off at the south side by a rectangular building with two large and three very small rooms. Room B, the smaller of the two big rooms, 8 by 7.75 meters, without an apse, is thought to have been the curia.[15]

In Aequum the curia was a square of 10.50 meters, accessible by a central stairway.[16]

As for Fora in the Roman provinces it is not always easy to identify the curiae among the remaining administrative buildings.[17]

At the southeast corner of the Forum of Cambudunum (Kempten, Germany) is a structure 20.90 meters long, 13.50 meters wide, but narrowing to 10.40 meters near the apse which itself is 3.70 meters deep; its width is almost that of the entire back wall.[18] This is most likely a curia. Similar structures, always in the range of approximately 9 to 12 meters, some with apses, some without, and usually at the sides of Fora or adjacent to basilicae are known from Octodurus (Martigny, Switzerland),[19] Calleva (Silchester, England),[20] Sufetula (Sbeitla, Tunisia),[21] Timgad,[22] Thuburbo Majus,[23] Jemila,[24] Sabratha[25] (all in North Africa), and from Virunum[26] and Magdalensberg (both in Austria).[27]

Supplementary evidence for the identification of the building discussed is the fragmentary inscription *CIL* III. 8817 (**Figure 24**).[28] Bulić dated it to the late first century A.D.; Dyggve supported this dating "au point de vue technique et paléographique."[29] The inscription reads:

CURIAMINC(**HOATAM?**)
SUAPECUNIAR(**ESTITUIT**)
curiam inc(hoatam ?)
sua pecunia r(estituit)

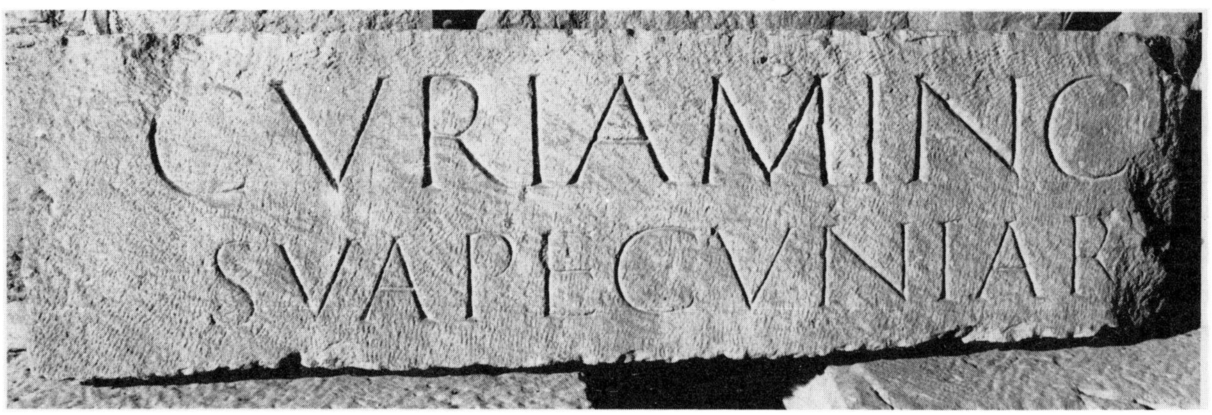

Figure 24: CIL III. 8817, inscription referring to restoration of the curia.

The inscription was found one hundred meters to the east of the Forum and Bulić situated the curia accordingly on the map of the ancient town.[30] This location corresponds exactly to the site where we excavated the apsidal building. The inscription was "une trouvaille isolée" according to Dyggve.[31] He thus disagreed with Bulić and thought "il ne convient pas avec Bulić de situer la curia ... au lieu de la trouvaille, juste sur la limite de la vieille et de la nouvelle ville. Comme preuve que les trouvailles isoleés peuvent être faites à distance considérable du lieu de leur provenance, on peut signaler un bloc du théâtre, avec inscription découvert en 1929, à l'est du théâtre."[32] Dyggve's idea was correct for the latter inscription but he has been proved definitely wrong for the inscription referring to the curia about which we may now say that it was found in situ, confirming Bulić's location of this public building.

A major argument in favor of the identification of the building is, last but not least, its location in the planning of the Roman Forum which was initiated in the Early Imperial period, our period II (**Plate 7**). Anyone who wished to go to the curia from the west would probably use a path along the Forum central drain which led directly to the curia west entrance (**Figure 6**). In front of the curia there may have been a "piazetta," judging from the very scanty remains of pavement slabs discovered in square A3. Moreover, if the evidence of earlier, period I walls is considered as well as the artificial platform to the south of the *Capitolium* which was built in the early Imperial period, it becomes evident that the curia is built in relation to the eastern side of the Forum and is accessible immediately from the latter. The entrance to the curia came to lie above what may have been in the Hellenistic period one of the entrances to the eminence from the east. Thus, what was a strategic point in the pre-Imperial period, continued to be a point of major interest throughout the Imperial period.

PERIODS II AND III OUTSIDE THE CURIA (Plate 8)

In squares A/A'/B7, period I was sealed off completely by a heavy and large pavement, the slabs of which formed a square measuring approximately 5.50 by 13 meters (**Figures 25 and 26**). The laying of these slabs is contemporary with the building of the curia. This is most clearly seen by the remains of slabs in back of the apse which are placed on the footing of the apse wall, whereas the courses of masonry of the apse itself are laid on the pavement. The pavement immediately to the east and southeast of the apse is not entirely preserved due to later wall building and other disturbances.

Two walls start from the north section of the apse and curia east wall respectively, one of them running northeast, the other due east. Both walls are bonded into the foundation of the apse and the east wall of the curia respectively. Their structure is identical with that of the walls of the curia. It is noteworthy that no traces of pavement slabs were found within the small area bounded by these walls, nor in that to the north which is formed by the curia east wall, a very massive wall running east in squares B6-7, and the continuation of the northeast wall which started at the apse proper. The absence of any pavement in both the very small and larger rooms might suggest that they formed an adjunct structure of the curia.

Square A1 (Plate 8)

In square A1 was discovered a short portion of the drain which forms the continuation of the Forum central drain (**Figure 27**). Its poor preservation is probably due to another destructive *gomila* which filled most of the eastern section of square A1. All along the south edge of the preserved portion of the drain and extending further to the west where the drain has disappeared was found at +6.116 meters solidly packed earth mixed with yellowish clay and small stones showing traces of conflagration. To the north of the drain the conflagration level is 7 centimeters higher. Within this conflagration level (+6.116 to +5.98 meters), stones increased in number and clay became more dense until bedrock was reached. Bedrock appeared at +6.06 meters in the center of square A1. The bedrock slopes gradually from the south towards the center; further north it descends abruptly to +5.091 meters. No pavement slabs from the area south or north of the drain could be recovered in square A1. It can, however, be surmised that the solidly packed earth mixed with clay and small stones served as foundation for a pavement.

Even if we do not at present have the connecting link between the two portions of the drain preserved in square A1 and the curia building respectively, the assumption that both belong to one and the same drain is certainly permissible. And, if we are correct with our assumption, it follows that a first deviation of the Forum central drain must have occurred in square A2 to make it join up with what is preserved of the drain in A3 East, just outside the presumed curia west wall.

Square A3 (Plate 8)

Two very fragmentary slabs of modrac stone, identical in thickness to the pavement slabs to the east of the curia were found at the south edge of square A3 with elevations of +6.343 and

Figure 25: Curia site, square A'7, portions of pavement in situ and period IV walls behind apse, looking south (1970).

Figure 26: Curia site, square A'1, portions of pavement in situ with period IV walls behind apse, looking southeast (1970).

Figure 27: Curia site, square A1, remains of drain in situ (1969).

+6.289 meters. The thickness of these slabs (0.13 to 0.15 meters) also corresponds to the average thickness of slabs resting on the Forum central drain. It is very likely that they represent the remains of the pavement in front of the curia, forming a small "piazzetta" near its presumed western entrance.

Square C1 (Plate 8)

Square C1 was only partially excavated. Remains of a rubble wall built with fairly large stones set in mortar probably formed the southern corner of a room belonging perhaps to a larger complex of buildings (baths ?) to the north of the *torcularium* (**Figure 11**). The wall forms a right angle roughly in the center of square C1, running north-south and east-west. Its original widths were 0.50 and 0.40 meters respectively. Along the south face of the east-west portion and along the east face of the north-south portion, the wall was subsequently reinforced by a 0.35 meter wide wall built with chips of stone set in mortar, forming a dense, very hard mass. This wall is unique among the walls found in the excavations especially for its quality of impregnability. The total width of the wall amounts to 0.90 meters (east-west) and 0.70 meters (north-south).

Along the south face of the wall lay numerous stones of all sizes—probably remains of the upper portions of the collapsed wall. Bedrock was reached in square C1 at +5.362 meters. Compared with the respective level in square A1 this indicates a gradual rise of the bedrock from south to north.

In square C1 were found a considerable quantity of mosaic tesserae clusters, mostly white with some black, still adhering to their concrete setting. In an extension trench of square C1 to the northwest a small coherent portion of this mosaic floor came to light. The fragment measures 1.20 meters (north), 0.80 meters (south), and 0.60 meters (east), and was broken with a very irregular edge at the west side. The mosaic had a black design on white. The white background between the frame and the wall was set in either diagonal or horizontal rows. A frame of four rows of black tesserae enclosed a double meander in black upon white. The meander is set with two tesserae. Since the northwest extension of square C1 is at the very foot of the *gomila* which first skirts the Forum central area along its east side and then crosses it for the entire width, further excavation in this area became impossible. The mosaic had a very definite slant towards the north. This slant may well have been due to the crushing weight of the *gomila* heaped upon this room, the center of which ought to have been to the northwest, judging from the mosaic decoration which we found. Although the mosaic, which could not be saved, is not connected with the wall proper, it dates, on technical grounds, at the earliest from the third century A.D. This might be the period in which the existing walls were reinforced and the mosaic decoration added. Reinforcement and mosaic could suggest that the room served as a *frigidarium,* belonging to the complex of baths further to the west which was excavated after World War II by Professor Rendić-Miočević.

Square B3 (Plate 8)

In square B3 Northeast a short portion of a north-south wall came to light (**Figure 28**). A *gomila* determines its present southern limit; the excavation of the wall to the north was not pursued. The wall is 0.70 meters wide and carefully built upon a rubble foundation with small masonry set in mortar mixed with pebbles, the foundation being of the same width as the wall. A thick layer of mortar mixed with numerous tiny fragments of crushed tiles covers the two courses of masonry above the rubble foundation on the west face of the wall. Upon this mortar were still preserved some revetment plaques with a thickness varying between 9 and 11 millimeters, of greenish-gray and greenish-blue marble. The revetment plaques have presumably covered the

Figure 28: Curia site, square B3, remains of wall with revetment plaque (1969).

lowermost portion of the wall to a height which cannot, of course, be determined. However, they reached to the floor, the level of which was also visible in the north profile of the trench further west. The connection of this wall, probably of period III, with the curia building is not clear, since the northwest corner of the curia is not preserved. But our wall must have come very close to this very corner, continuing, as it were, the general direction of the presumed west wall with which, however, it is not in complete alignment.

Period IV (Plate 4)

Evidence for the occupation of the curia site into late antiquity is well attested by coins and pottery and some structural remains. Wherever the latter can be grasped, they have a very ephemeral character. Evidence from the curia site as well as from the Forum North and Forum Central sites shows that the eminence cannot have played any longer the role in the life of the town which it played during the earlier periods.

We are not in a position to date precisely the period IV walls. However, pottery and coins (see the charts following this chapter), suggest a general date from the early fourth to the sixth century A.D. It proved impossible to subdivide this long span of time, simply because the evidence is much too scarce.

Period IV Within the Curia

The surface soil reached a depth of 0.60 to 0.80 meters within the curia. It was much disturbed by long periods of cultivation. The destruction level of period III within the curia is clearly indicated by the thick fresco layer and also here and there by a thin layer of charcoal. *Gomile* in squares B3-4, in square A'3 (over the southwest corner of the curia), and in squares

B/C6 and A6 have penetrated the surface soil causing destruction in this and the period I–III levels. The *gomile* are difficult to date. Some may date from the fifth and sixth century A.D. (see coin no. 70), others are probably much later and are to be connected with the periods when the cultivation of the soil began. It is safe to say that the floors of period IV were disturbed throughout, only patches of them being preserved here and there. Noteworthy among period IV structures within the curia is a deep pit in square A'5, built against the north face of the curia south wall, which has also cut through wall C of period I.

It is difficult to assert which portions of the curia continued to be in use during period IV; as the evidence stands, it points to the western rather than to the eastern room.

Period IV Outside the Curia

Several walls of this phase run eastward from the curia building in squares A/A'7 (**Figures 25, 26, and 29**). One wall in square A7, 2.60 meters long, consists of three courses of square masonry around an earth, rubble, and loose mortar fill. The wall now ends abruptly where the large paved area covers the drains of period I. Remains of very poorly built walls, making use of large slabs, among which is a reused one with a moulding (part of a threshold ?), run both to southwest and northeast. The southwest wall probably joined another which had been built against the southeast corner of the curia and which also rests on pavement slabs. This wall in square A'6 West has yielded to the pressure of a *gomila* and now leans heavily to the north. Another rubble wall in square B4 runs southward from the north wall. That so little of the wall is preserved here is once more due to a *gomila* which has damaged not only this section of the curia but also two massive walls which run to the east beyond the northeast corner of the curia and which will be discussed later together with the workshop area.

Figure 29: Curia site, squares A'6-7, period IV walls behind apse, looking northeast (1972).

Evidence for period IV floors outside the curia is not altogether absent, but usually the mortar was in such an advanced stage of decomposition that it is rather hazardous to come to any firm conclusion. The best evidence for late floors comes from the area to the west of the curia. In square A3 remains of a late floor exist at an elevation of +6.43 meters. In square A1 a much disturbed burial which extends from +6.32 to +6.55 meters was lying just above the level of the drain slabs. There is, of course, no way of ascertaining its date.

Some interesting finds came to light in the corridor which was formed by walls A and B. These are fully described in connection with the workshop area, following this section. This corridor was full of debris from the period IV habitation level. Among the finds in the debris are a lamp, a marble bowl, the fragments of a portable altar, a sherd with the painting of a fish, and the stem of a glass goblet.[33] One coin comes from the upper level of the corridor (no. 59); two coins were found near the very bottom of the corridor, at a level of circa +4.71 meters (nos. 86, 41). No. 41 can be firmly dated to the decade A.D. 330-340. No. 59 is badly corroded but dates very likely from the period of Constantine's sons. The third coin (no. 86) is hopelessly corroded.

The objects (excepting the coins) just mentioned are admittedly few, but they do seem to have some Christian connotation. Their discovery in the debris in proximity to the curia could throw some light on the uses of the building or part of it after A.D. 314. One cannot exclude entirely the possibility that the apsidal building of the curia was then used for the purpose of Christian worship as a small basilica. In Salona there is no lack of basilicas. From the middle of the fourth century A.D. onwards, and throughout the fifth and sixth centuries, basilicas rose in great number in all parts of the city. Perhaps the curia was turned for some decades after A.D. 314 into a place of worship, until other basilicas were ready to take over in areas at some distance from the heathen center of Salona.

THE WORKSHOP AREA (Plates 4 and 8)

The workshop area covers the southeastern portion of square C6, a much larger portion of square C7, and some of squares D6-7. The area is vaguely determined by several fragmentary walls; we cannot speak in terms of a well-defined structural complex.

Wall A, immediately to the north of the curia northeast corner, is 1.15 meters wide; it is built with small squared masonry around a rubble fill.

Wall B runs parallel to wall A (**Figures 30 and 31**). It has a maximum width of 1.20 meters; originally it was only 0.90 meters wide but it was reinforced at some time by the addition of the width of two stones of squared masonry to the south face of the original wall. The original wall is built with squared mortared masonry around a rubble core. Both walls resemble the curia walls in building technique.

Figure 30: Curia site, workshop area. In middle foreground remains of glass tank, charcoal pit, and wall A, looking south (1969).

Figure 31: Curia site, workshop area. Charcoal pit in course of excavation; at left, wall B (1969).

The most likely explanation for the sequence of walls is that wall B—without the addition—was built first. The reinforcing of wall B and the building of wall A might well have been dictated by the activities concentrated to the north of wall B (in square C7). It would be hardly credible that the contiguity of the curia north wall with wall A represents the original arrangement; such tight quarters bespeak a later transformation.

The corridor (0.60 meters wide) between walls A and B was full of rubble and earth. Before the building of wall A and the reinforcing of wall B there was here a wide enough passage to lead possibly from the area to the east of the curia to its northern entrance. But with the transformation just described the passage became very narrow; it was blocked in a later period to the east by wall C, running north-south (**Plate 4 and Figure 30**, left edge). This wall is not only roughly and poorly built but it is also of irregular width. Since it is built in part on a level of conflagration, it should be of a later date than the period of use of the workshop; the lack of mortar for the binding of the masonry corroborates this. The northward continuation of wall C was destroyed by a *gomila* which extends into square D7.

To the west of the workshop area square C6 to the north of the curia was filled below the surface soil with a large *gomila*; this *gomila* (visible at the right edge of **Figure 30** and in **Figure 31**) caused the destruction of the curia north wall and walls A and B. In the profile at the east edge of square C6, a thick layer of carbon starting at circa 1.10 meters below the surface level thins out gradually at a depth of 1.50 meters and is clearly the western extension of the heavily carbonized layer in the center of the workshop area. Its horizontal extension northwards from the *gomila* continues for 0.90 meters, while traces of a less heavily carbonized layer extend still further north for about 0.60 meters.

Remains of the rubble foundation for a wall D were found in square C6 on a thin layer of clay above bedrock. The foundations are little over 1 meter wide. Wall D runs southwest-northeast; therefore, it did not run strictly perpendicular to either wall A and B, nor to wall E which will be discussed shortly. The irregular rubble foundation of wall D is very similar to that of the north wall of the curia. This fact and the fact that the carbonized layer does not occur to the west of wall D suggests that it was in existence when the workshop was in use. Thus, we may surmise with fair certainty that wall D indicated the western limit of the workshop area.

Figure 32: Curia site, workshop area. Furnace, looking north, with wall F (period IV) in foreground, wall E (period III) in background (1970).

Wall E in square D7 is preserved for a distance of 1.70 meters (**Figure 32**, in background). Beyond its eastern terminal point it is destroyed down to the very foundations by a *gomila.* Wall E has two courses of foundations built of squared, mortared masonry; the wall proper is built with squared, mortared masonry around a rubble fill.

In square C7 there is also a short portion of a mortared rubble wall F (**Figure 32**, right middle ground; **Figures 33 and 34**). It rests partly on the accumulation of debris in the northern half of the workshop area, as does wall G further to the west; only two courses of this latter wall are preserved. It is fairly obvious that whereas wall E could have delimited the workshop area towards the north, walls F and G are of later date.

Figure 33: Curia site, workshop area. Period IV wall F and, to the right, furnace wall with whitish plaster adhering (1970).

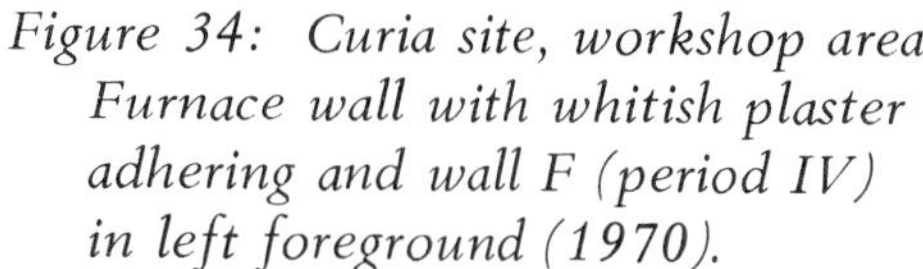

Figure 34: Curia site, workshop area. Furnace wall with whitish plaster adhering and wall F (period IV) in left foreground (1970).

In summary, walls A, B, D, and E are contemporary and determine the workshop area towards the south, west, and north side. Wall C is of later date but its general direction could indicate that of an earlier wall, situated further to the east, which would have been the eastern wall of the workshop area. Walls F and G date from a period when the workshop was no longer in use.

The elevation of wall B is +5.792 meters. In excavating to the lowermost foundations of this wall it was noticed that the clay level above bedrock was of considerable depth. Some of the depth can be explained by the fact that, in order to lay the foundation course for wall B on bedrock, some clay had to be removed and was dumped towards the north, in what became the actual workshop. A similar procedure is in evidence for the building of the furnace, when clay was moved from the spot where the furnace was to be erected to the center of the workshop area.

At a level of +5.792 meters the layer of conflagration in squares C6-7 also begins. The area covered by the conflagration measures circa 2 by 4 meters. Its northern and southern limits are indicated by wall B on the one hand and by the furnace on the other (**Figures 30, 31 and 33** show heavy traces of conflagration.) The quantity of glass fragments and of glass slag recovered from the conflagration level suggested to us that the area may have served as a glass workshop. A large number of tiles, quantities of coarse pottery, large and small pieces of charcoal, balls of cobalt and other coloring stuff, scraps of ivory and bone, as well as some bronze tools were found here, thus supporting our surmise of the existence of a workshop.

Since the layer of burning is of considerable depth, it is doubtful whether one could interpret it as a destruction-conflagration level. It seems rather an area of deposit of waste materials which accumulated for some period. This interpretation is supported by the discovery of a very simply constructed pit with slabs of modrac stone (**Figure 31**). The top of the pit, at a distance of 1.40 meters to the north of wall B, is at an elevation of +5.51 meters. One of the slabs, 0.49 by 0.53 meters, was found in a vertical position at the south side; a second slab, measuring 0.73 by 0.46 meters, was lying at a slant of circa 45° at the north side of the pit; a third slab, not found in situ but close enough to the last described stone so that it probably represents the east side of the pit, measures 0.38 by 0.295 meters. The material from within the pit consisted entirely of charcoal. The bottom of the pit was found at +4.94 meters, consisting of three small flat pavement stones with very irregular edges. On top of these stones lay a lead pipe consisting of two pieces, one large bent piece with one arm 0.34 meters long, the other 0.33 meters, with a diameter of 7 centimeters; the second smaller piece was 0.22 meters long (**Figure 35**). The lead pipes had no practical function in the pit but must be considered as discarded pieces originally serving some plumbing installation. That the two pieces were saved is due entirely to their being hidden at the bottom of the charcoal pit; other similar pipes, if found, would be considered too valuable not to be removed by treasure hunters.

Under the lead pipes and stones the charcoal level continues for a few centimeters and passes gradually into dense yellowish clay (**Figure 30**). The natural clay above bedrock did not yield any finds throughout the entire workshop area, except one which has some significance for the date of the initial stage of the workshop.

In summary we can say that the pit originally formed a square of 0.70 by 0.80 meters with a depth of from 0.55 to 0.60 meters. It probably had, within the area of deposit of waste, the function of a combustion pit, the existence of which near the furnace is not surprising.[34]

The significance of the heavily burnt area became more meaningful still with the excavation to the north of what we believe served as a tank for the preparing and melting of glass batch. The area immediately to the south of wall F (**Figures 32 and 33**) showed many signs of destruction from a level of +5.80 to +5.417 meters. In this layer of circa 0.40 meters were found great quantities of broken tiles of various sizes mixed with concrete, lime, glass fragments, completely crushed brick, and lumps of clay. Traces of burning were noted and became more dense just above the scant remains of a surface preserved in a much decomposed state. This surface consists of very irregularly broken tiles which had been set in a mixture of clay and mortar (**Figure 36**, close-up of tank, and **Figure 30**). The irregular, rounded edge of this surface towards the south is hardly original. Along the north side of the surface runs a row of closely fitted rectangular stones which formed a straight line, 1.40 meters long. While some of these stones are only 7 centimeters long, the largest do not exceed 12 centimeters and their height varies between 8 and 10 centimeters. These stones were covered thickly with glass slag on the inside (north side). We take the stones found in situ to represent the uppermost portion of the long side of a tank-like structure in which the batch of glass was prepared and melted.[35] From between the edge of the tank and wall F, that is, presumably from within the tank itself, came many fragments of tiles, individual stones with glass slag adhering; very great quantities of glass slag as well as many fragments of glass; also some pottery, among which was a fairly well preserved amphora neck.[36] As the excavation of the presumed tank proceeded, the finds became more scarce, but hardly any clay layer was encountered as was the case in the central area of the workshop and the pit structure.

Due to its poor preservation it is not possible to come to any definite conclusion with regard to the construction of the glass tank. Some of the small stones from within the tank probably came

Figure 35: Curia site, workshop area. Bottom of charcoal pit with lead pipes (1969).

Figure 36: Curia site, workshop area. South edge of glass tank and adjacent "floor" (1969).

from the remaining edges of the tank, now destroyed. However, not nearly enough stones were found to suggest that the entire tank was stone-made, which could be a possibility, although one would prefer a hollowed-out, single stone, like a trough, for this purpose rather than a container of many stones. But it is interesting to note that tanks in modern glass furnaces are made of many unmortared blocks which are fused together by the molten batch. Among the fragmentary terracotta tiles none was found with glass slag adhering, a condition which one might expect if the actual container or tank was made of this material. It could be mere coincidence that the tiles do not show any remains of glass slag. Furthermore, the quantity of such tiles suggest that they come from the roof structure over the workshop area, and that they are possibly also connected with the structure of the furnace. This is certain for at least one very special tile (clay objects, no. 21).

There is some indication from the surface or working floor around the row of stones covered with glass slag that these did not continue further toward the west. At the westernmost stone there may have been one of the tank's corners; towards the east, the row of stones could have continued but, since the actual length of the stone edge is already 1.40 meters, it hardly extended much further to the east. The tank was probably of rectangular shape; dimensions of 1.50 by 0.80 meters would be ample for the purpose of preparing the batch and melting the glass. Furthermore, the suggested size finds support in the dimensions of the furnace which seem to have been taken into account when structuring the tank. Only the discovery in recent excavations of quite similar installations of glassworks leads us to speak in terms of a glass tank with regard to the remains discovered in Salona.[37]

As compared with the deep layer of clay below the area of conflagration in squares C6-7, no such layer was encountered below the glass tank and in the general area to the north of it. The reason for the absence of clay is explained by the remains in square C7 North of an oval-shaped furnace which was accessible from square D7 South. The furnace wall consists of an inner mantle of whitish mortar, 4 centimeters thick, with a maximum height of 0.70 meters, resting against a solid wall of baked clay of reddish-brown color (**Figure 33 and 34**). The further one moves from the inner mantle towards the outside, the more does the resistance of the clay yield. Thus it is clear that the furnace was literally sunk into a space from which the clay had been removed, creating a hollow in which to place the furnace. Once the oval shape of the furnace was determined, mortar was plastered against the clay which gradually became hard baked and assumed a reddish-brown color due to the heat which developed within the furnace. The furnace mantle as preserved is now a rather irregular oval, flattened in the original center section, this being probably due to the pressure and crushing weight of the soil above. It is a fair guess that close to half of the furnace is preserved and that its dimensions were circa 2 by 2.50 meters. Both ends of the furnace wall as discovered probably continued to curve for a short distance; they may have run into a corridor-like opening which was to the north. This opening is identical with the stoking hole which was accessible from a point close to the north wall (wall E) of the workshop area (**Figure 32**).

The height of the furnace probably did not exceed 1.20 to 1.50 meters; with the present maximum height of 0.70 meters, only about half of the total height is preserved. The north-south profile at the western edge in C/D7, running tangential to the curvilinear part of the furnace, reveals four different layers of great interest. Below the top soil of 0.70 to 0.75 meters, there comes as the first layer the period IV habitation level: wall G, in which square masonry was reused, consisting of only two preserved courses (**Figure 32**). As noted earlier, this wall runs parallel to wall F, but the latter projects further to the south. The second layer 0.15 to 0.20 meters thick, represents the final stage in the destruction of period III. The third layer, 0.15 meters thick, has the predominant red-brown color of iron slag which was found plentifully in squares C/D7. The fourth layer, ±0.70 meters, represents a mixture of light brown earth, with crushed mortar and sand, showing less traces of conflagration than layer 2; it yielded quite a few tile fragments, pieces of charcoal, and pottery. This layer is a typical debris layer of period III which had accumulated for some time during the use of the workshop.

There is little doubt in our view that furnace and glass tank are related to each other, but that the furnace was not built with the intention of serving in glassmaking. The furnace was rather reused for this purpose. This explains why the glass tank is placed about eighty percent within the curvilinear wall of the furnace in an elevated position above the bottom of the furnace, the stoking hole, and hot box.

It is very likely that two phases of activity in the workshop have to be distinguished. The furnace served in the first place as a foundry for the smelting of metals. This is strongly suggested by the quantity of iron slag found in squares C/D7 and adjacent quarters (B6-7). Many of the individual pieces were identical in size, resembling small round cakes or buns with a slightly concave bottom and rounded top. Besides iron, a number of bronze objects were also found. Destroyed and fragmented so that it is impossible to recognize their original shape, these fragments may have belonged to large vessels (cauldrons and the like). As mentioned earlier, it does not come as a surprise that the majority of the utensils discovered in the excavations come, very appropriately, from the workshop area.[38]

On the basis of comparison with excavated smelting and other furnaces, we must try to visualize how our furnace may have looked when intact. The curvilinear remains of the mortared wall against clay can be compared with the type of bowl-furnaces which are embedded in the ground, not projecting above it.[39] There is good reason, however, to believe that our furnace represented a version in which elements from two types, the bowl- and the shaft-furnace, were combined.[40] Our furnace was not exactly free-standing as are most shaft-furnaces, nor was it entirely embedded in the clay as are the bowl-furnaces; only about 0.50 meters of the presently preserved 0.70 meters of mortared wall is plastered against the clay bed.[41] Thus at least 0.80 meters projected above the ground, if we assume a total original height of 1.20 to 1.50 meters. Moreover, it is very likely that the furnace was free-standing to the north, at the stoking hole side, where a quantity of iron slag was recovered.

We have no idea whether bellows were in use with this furnace; if so, they could only have been used from the area to the north of the curvilinear part of the furnace.[42] It is not excluded, however, that stoking hole and blast hole were identical; the ground level of the latter was simply of clay, like the hot box, and was only a few inches above bedrock.[43]

The diameters of furnaces vary greatly, ranging from less than 1 meter to 3.50 meters.[44] The height of the furnace depends largely on the size of the hot box. Pottery kilns tend to have greater height since pots are usually stacked on shelves, one above the other. Dome-shaped roofs with a central escape for the smoke are fairly common.[45] The roof could be a structure of bricks, but a roof of clay is more likely.[46]

Combining the evidence from the finds made within the furnace area with the comparative material from smelting and pottery kilns, we can tentatively come to the following conclusions. The roof over the smelting furnace was probably dome-shaped; a hole in the apex of the dome served as an escape for the smoke, and we should like to assign to it one of the chinmey-like terracotta tiles.[47] Other tiles, some wood, and above all clay, were probably the essential elements in the roof structure.

With the installation of the glass tank, the purpose of the furnace enters its second stage. Since the glass tank is at a higher level within the furnace than its hot box, the latter continued to be used as firing area. However, the firing area probably became narrower, and was concentrated underneath the tank itself. To support the working floor around the tank a pillar-like structure underneath may have taken up much of the space which was formerly the hot box of the smelting furnace. Because of the scanty evidence which is available, any reconstruction must naturally remain very hypothetical. The dome-shaped roof over the smelting furnace may have been completely abandoned when the area was set up for the manufacture of glass.

All the evidence found suggests that the general date of the workshop area is contemporary with period II-III of the curia site (early first century A.D. to late third century A.D.). Though the workshop area as such could have been used for a long period, it is unlikely that the life-span of the active use of the furnace proper exceeds one or two generations. An exceptional find from the center of the workshop may give us a general lead. When digging through the layer of conflagration and the deep deposit of clay, a one-handled local Illyrian bowl or drinking cup was found just above bedrock.[48] Professor Marović from Split feels that the latest possible date for this vase is the first century B.C. The cup may have lain abandoned for some time before being buried in the clay deposit. However, since the dumping of the clay in the central area of the workshop is to be connected with the building of walls A and B adjacent to the curia north wall on the one hand, and the preparing of the hollow for the furnace on the other, it is our feeling that the initial stage of the building of the workshop dates from the early to middle first century A.D. It may have been at first a place for the smelting of metals. This activity may have soon necessitated the reinforcing of wall B and the building of wall A, which may have occured late in the first century A.D.

The evidence from the glass finds indicates that the workshop area was in active reuse, with the glass tank related to the earlier furnace, by the mid-third century and the following decades. In the meantime, that is from the late first to the mid-third century A.D., the furnace itself may not have played an active role, but the workshop as such was in use throughout this period.

FORUM CENTRAL SITE (Plate 7)

Five trenches were dug in the area between the Capitolium and the *gomila* which separates the Forum central and the Forum north sites. Trench 1 within the Capitolium was dug in order to gather data for the construction of this temple. Trenches 2 and 3, directly outside the Capitolium to the north and directly adjacent to the Forum central drain respectively, were dug primarily in an attempt to establish the depth of the bedrock close to the center of the eminence.[49] Trench 4, excavated in 1969, was of exploratory nature to aid in choosing a major site of excavation for the year following.[50] Finally, trench 5 was dug with the intention of establishing the sequence of levels in the Forum central area. We begin with trench 4, by far the largest of the five trenches.

Trench 4 (Plate 7)

Trench 4, 1.50 meters wide and 19 meters long, runs roughly parallel with the *gomila* to the east. This trench is to the north of the Baths excavated in 1945/46 but never published. The trench yielded four mortared rubble walls built on bedrock and preserved in the lowermost one to three courses of stones. The walls appear at ±0.90 meters below the present-day surface level. Their direction parallels the central Forum drain and major walls of the Baths which are still visible above ground.

Wall A, built of mortared squared masonry around a rubble core, is 0.60 meters wide (**Figure 37**, in middle ground). Bedrock has an uneven formation and is encountered at a depth of ±1.50 to 1.60 meters from the surface of the soil. To the south of wall A are the remains of two floors. The first floor rests upon a rubble foundation 0.25 to 0.35 meters thick laid directly upon bedrock. This floor, which consists of small dark stones embedded in a herringbone pattern into a concrete foundation, is not physically connected with the south face of wall A but must be contemporary with it. Above the floor just described were found traces of mortar used in a second

Figure 37: Forum central site. Trench 4, looking north, with walls A-D and Corinthian capital (1969).

Figure 38: Forum central site. Trench 4, Corinthian capital and walls C-D just beyond (1969).

Figure 39: Forum central site. Period IV walls E-F, showing reused slabs from Forum drains (1969).

floor, against the south face of wall A. The thickness of both floors, including the concrete foundation for the earlier floor, does not exceed 0.30 meters.

To the north of Wall A, in an area 4.60 meters wide, remains of the later (second) floor contemporary with the floor to the south of wall A were found, but no evidence of the earlier herringbone patterned floor. Most characteristic among the finds in this area were fragments of frescoes, presumably fallen from walls A and B (see Chapter VI).

Wall B (0.60 meters wide) is preserved only in the lowermost course. Of particular interest here is the layer of plaster, 4 to 5 centimeters thick, irregularly preserved, which covers the south face of the wall.

In the area between walls B and C, 3.70 meters wide, were found many more fragments of frescoes above a thin layer of conflagration. No traces of a floor could be noticed here. Close to wall C a Corinthian capital of good workmanship which probably dates from the late second or third century A.D.[51] was found, lying upside down (**Figure 38**). This capital may have been removed from the Capitolium or theater area in a much later period when the Forum began to be pillaged and was eventually abandoned here.

In wall C (maximum width 0.60 meters) chips of stone fill some of the gaps in the mortared rubble. Nothing but carbonized soil was found between walls C and D.

Wall D is substantially wider than walls A, B, and C. The wall, 1.05 meters wide, is preserved in two to three courses of mortared rubble resting on the clay above bedrock (**Figure 38**).

Besides the fresco fragments, a number of mosaic tesserae in white, blue, and green stone were scattered throughout trench 4. All small finds come from a layer 0.60 to 0.90 meters below the surface level. There is little doubt that the building or buildings represented by the remains just described belong to period III of the Forum north and the curia site, that is the period of the second and third centuries A.D.

Extensions of the long trench at its south and towards both the east and west revealed a much disturbed area (**Figure 39**). The short sections of two walls E and F built with squared, mortared masonry around a rubble core precede period IV in date. Wall E, more than 0.60 meters wide, runs parallel with walls A to D; wall F, 0.50 meters wide, runs perpendicular to them towards the south. There were scant remains of a later building period (period IV) with reuse of building stones from the Forum. To these stones belong portions of the Forum drain (in two sections) and slabs, probably from architraves, one of them still preserving the mouldings of an Ionic frieze (0.50 meters long, 0.40 meters wide, 0.31 meters thick). Three very massive stones set in a row come most likely from the foundations of walls such as were found in the porch building on the Forum north site. The reused stones rest on rubble foundations.

In this eastern extension of trench 4, a coin of Divus Claudius Gothicus (coin no. 33) was found near the reused slabs. This coin might be contemporary with the period IV building activity. Other finds, such as mosaic tesserae, fragments of glass, fragments of roof tiles and of revetment plaques, as well as three hypocaust tiles, date from period III.[52]

Trench 1 (Plate 7)

Trench 1, in squares E5-6 U'/V', was dug within the foundations of the westernmost of the three cellae of the Capitolium (**Figures 4 and 40**). The trench reached a depth of ±0.60 meters when bedrock was reached (at +5.92 meters). The trench was filled with a mixture of loose rubble and earth, representing a layer of 0.40 to 0.50 meters; this was followed by a layer of clay above bedrock. The rubble layer, which can be considered a sealed deposit, yielded fragments of pottery, several lids, one iron nail, and tiny fragments of glass (see chart 1). The trench also exposed the lowermost foundations of the west and the north (back) wall of the temple as well as the dividing wall between the western and the middle cella. The foundations of these three walls

Figure 40: Forum, Capitolium, trench 1, looking west (1970).

consist of rubble fairly regularly heaped in several courses; in the case of the north (back) wall, however, the rubble foundation is not continuous. It is present mostly near the northeast and northwest corners of the cella, but not in the center where the foundation is a densely packed mixture of clay and earth with very many tiny stones. For the evaluation of the sealed deposit see pp. 85, 91.

Trench 2 (Plate 7)

This trench, in squares E5X'Y'Z', extends to the north from the moulded podium substructure of the Capitolium (average elevation before excavation +6.30 meters). Large slabs with roughly cut sides, circa 0.20 meters thick, a second course of very thin plaque-like slabs below, and the natural clay layer above bedrock, 0.10 to 0.15 meters thick, (**Figure 3**) serve as the lowermost foundations for the temple north wall and in particular the moulded slabs of the podium. Except for period IV walls running east-west in the middle and at the north end of the trench (**Figure 41**), only remains of three fragmentary pavement slabs came to light. The trench itself contained earth mixed with building debris and small finds ranging from middle Augustan to late Augustan times.

Figure 41: Forum central site Trench 2, looking north towards Forum central drain with pedestal base (1970).

Trench 3 (Plate 7)

Trench 3 (**Figure 42**), in squares E2W/X, was dug between the Forum central drain and one of the walls to the north of it which was uncovered in the 1945/46 excavations. The trench is circa ±0.60 meters deep at its north end, and somewhat less near the Forum central drain (average elevation before excavation +6.46 meters). The foundation for the drain, consisting of two courses of rubble mixed with earth, was exposed. In the trench itself the layer below the surface soil consisted of earth mixed with fragments of pottery, tiles, and a number of other small finds. There follows the clay layer above bedrock, first mixed with mortar, very probably the remains of decomposed period III-IV floors, then dense and pure clay immediately above bedrock (+5.88 meters). Bedrock slopes towards the north forming a sudden fold near the north end of the trench, where it reaches an elevation of +5.76 meters. The small finds range predominantly through periods II-IV. As in trench 4, fragments of fresco painting, mostly painted plain red, occur.

Trench 5 (Plates 7 and 11 bis)

Trench 5 or squares E3J/K are adjacent to the southeastern extension of trench 4. The reused slabs mentioned above form the south edge of the squares (**Figure 43**). The slabs rest here on reused unmortared squared masonry, four to five courses or circa 0.60 meters deep (the elevation of the uppermost course is at +7.104 meters, the reused slabs at +7.150 meters). The profile of the west side of the excavated square reveals surface soil some 0.25 to 0.30 meters thick followed by a *gomila* which filled the inside of the trench to some 0.80 meters to the east of the west edge.

Both the east and north sides of the excavated squares are formed by walls built with squared mortared masonry (**Figure 44**) reaching a height of ±1.60 meters (the maximum elevation of the northeast corner is at +7.362 meters). The rubble foundation for the walls is placed immediately above bedrock; its elevation in the center west of the square is +5.486 meters.

The profile underneath a displaced (reused) slab within the squares close to the south edge (slab elevation at +7.126 meters) reveals the following layers (**Figure 43**): top soil (0.25 meters); a layer of earth mixed with stones and sherds (0.30 meters); a slightly darker earth layer also mixed with stones and sherds (0.15 meters); a lightly carbonized layer containing a few stones and small finds (0.25 meters); a floor level of very dense pink mortar containing small fragments of crushed tile (0.10 meters); a layer of earth mixed with clay (0.25 meters); and a pure clay level above bedrock (±0.10 meters). The floor was completely crushed by the *gomila* and was partially preserved in the remainder of the squares. In the center of the squares bedrock was reached at an elevation of +5.754 meters. This is some 0.26 meters higher than the elevation at the west edge of the excavation. It is very possible that the difference is explained by the intentional removal of bedrock in this area; additional investigation further to the west would be needed in order to ascertain this possibility.

Small finds range over all periods (I-IV). It was not possible to single out those objects which might have been connected with period I underneath the pink mortar floor level. For the finds from E3J/K see chart 1.

FORUM NORTH SITE (Plates 5, 9, 10, and 11)

The Forum north site presented itself as a rectangle, measuring about 35 meters east-west by 20 meters north-south. It was delimited on the north by a short stretch of a wall and low mounds of stones completely covered by underbrush, clearly indicating the *gomila* heaped on top of an existing but hidden structure. The terrain immediately north of the latter is considerably

Figure 42: Forum central site, Trench 3, looking south towards Forum central drain with pedestal base (1970).

Figure 43: Forum central site. Trench 5 (E3J/K), looking north (1970).

Figure 44: Forum central site. Trench 5.

lower than the Forum north site itself. It is this considerable drop of terrain towards the north which was emphasized in chapter II in our discussion of Caesar's reference to a *collis* or "eminence". To the west the rectangle is bordered by a modern road which follows the course of the ancient road along the western Forum enclosure and eventually leads to the Porta Caesarea. To the south, there is the westernmost extension of the *gomila* which we encountered already in square C1. Finally, to the east (**Figure 45**), there is a low, modern wall enclosing a considerable amount of building debris from the Forum and forming still another *gomila* (highest elevation +7.41 meters) which separates privately owned and cultivated fields.

The Forum north site seems to have been abandoned for cultivation some time ago. It used to be a vineyard, like the fields to the north and east, where a large fig tree is a dominating feature. In the northeast corner of the site there are the remains of a stone trough with traces of the chemicals used for spraying grapes.

Figure 45: Forum north site before excavation, looking east, with remains of gomila in background, drain in foreground and middleground (1969).

The most prominant feature prior to excavation consisted of a row of drain slabs still in situ, running east-west in the northern third of the site.[53] The slabs are best preserved in the central section from W2A to E2A (**Figure 45**). In W3-5A some drain slabs are missing; others preserved have a considerably chipped surface with only 2 to 3 centimeters of the drain cavity itself intact; this is probably the result of ploughing. In E3-4A, no slabs are preserved; the excavations provided the reason for their absence.

The depth of the cultivated soil on the Forum north site is identical to that of the curia site. Bedrock falls off sharply in the northern half of the site; in its southern half there are some deep pockets. The layer of yellow clay on bedrock is 0.10 to 0.20 meters thick. We shall now describe the remains on the Forum north site by periods (I-IV) which correlate to those on the curia site.

Period I (Plate 5)

The earliest remains on the Forum north site consist of a short portion of an east-west wall in E4-5A (**Figure 46**). Two to five courses of stones are preserved with the lowermost course laid directly upon bedrock which sloped towards the north as indicated earlier. Most of the slabs are oblong, many close to 1 meter long, 0.15 meters thick, and approximately 0.60 meters wide. Smaller stones are used for the filling of gaps or when the large slabs suffered damage; thus the wall must have been kept in constant repair. The quality of the stone is similar to the yellowish limestone which is attested for period I on the curia site; it is decidedly different from the more commonly used grayish modrac, the principal building material during Imperial times also on the Forum north site. No mortar was used in the building of the wall.

Some of the upper courses of the north face of the wall in E4A were destroyed at some later date by the construction of a drain which flows off in a northern direction (**Figure 47**).

The south face of the wall is much battered. A dozen or so stones lying to the south of the wall itself probably belonged to those courses of stones (in E5A) where a deep gap now exists. If the wall was destroyed on purpose for the sake of extracting valuable building material, it must have been attacked from the south and the slabs still in situ could not escape damage. However, the large and only slightly damaged slab which is at an elevation of +5.404 meters, about 1 meter above bedrock to the north, suggests the approximate width of the earliest wall at this point (**Figure 46**).

In E3-4A there is a seam between the period I wall and a differently structured wall which forms its continuation (**Figure 48**). There is no evidence on the entire Forum north site of any other wall which is contemporary with this easternmost portion just described and which we should like to call the main east-west wall on this site.

To period I also belongs a pit in W1C in which many crushed amphorae were found. This pit presented itself as a deep pocket in the bedrock formation but it is not entirely excluded that some of the bedrock was cut away to provide more room for a storage facility. The elevation at the bottom of the pit is +4.004 meters. A second pit turned up farther to the west, in W5D, with an elevation at the bottom of +4.743 meters. The use of the first pit in period I is attested by the dating of the amphorae.

Period II (Plate 9)

The continuation of the period I wall in E3A is slightly recessed in relation to the earlier wall (**Figure 48**). The building material used is greyish modrac. Larger slabs of stone were used primarily for the lowermost foundation courses which sit on bedrock; above these follow courses built with squared masonry. Mortar is used throughout. The junction of the earlier wall with the period II wall is clearly visible by the difference in building technique. From this junction a perpendicular wall (A) runs northward in square E3A, 0.60 meters wide with a maximum preserved height of 0.73 meters; its mortared masonry encloses a rubble fill. The plastered west face (0.15 meters thick) is particularly well preserved (**Figures 49 and 50**). The east face may never have been plastered.

Further to the west there is a slight differentiation in the structure and appearance of the main east-west wall. Fairly low, oblong stones, presenting a very rusticated face (in E2-3A) pass into more regular structured courses in which stones have smaller dimensions and are rectangular rather than oblong. This is best exemplified by a portion of wall in square W2A. The top of the wall is preserved only in square E1A. The foundations for a second perpendicular north wall (B) are found here. Wall B, also 0.60 meters wide, has been largely destroyed by a *gomila* which fills the northeast corner of square E1A. There is no evidence that wall B was ever plastered like wall A. The distance between centers of walls A and B is 6.60 meters.

In its westernmost portion (W5A) the structure of the main east-west wall is markedly

Figure 46: Forum north site. Period I wall in E5A, looking south (1970).

Figure 47: Forum north site. Period I wall in E4A with period III drain to right. Period I wall seen from north (1970).

Figure 48: Forum north site. Period III drain (to left) and portions of period II wall in E3-4A. Close to lower edge of photo north-south wall with remains of plaster surface in E3A (1970).

Figure 49: Forum north site. W5A. Northern face of east-west main wall (1970).

Figure 50: Forum north site. E3A with north-south wall, looking north. Bedrock is visible below scale and rubble of a gomila (1970).

Figure 51: Forum north site. W5A. Northern face of east-west main wall (1970).

inferior in construction in comparison with the portions discussed earlier. Many smaller stones of irregular dimensions may not, of course, represent original (period II) portions but may rather point to some later repair in period III (**Figure 51**).

The terminal point of the main east-west wall was found in W5A; however, the wall may have been continued in period II further to the west.

The south face of the main east-west wall of period II is no longer preserved due to its transformation in period III.

In addition to walls A and B two more walls (C, D) to the south are also preserved (**Figures 52 and 53**). Built with small mortared masonry, these walls closely resemble and relate to the north face of the main east-west wall in their careful structure; the width of the footing and the walls themselves are also similar to those of the walls of the curia in period II. In W3B wall C runs off the main east-west wall for a distance of 5 meters. Since the south face of the main east-west wall is not the original one of period II, the junction between it and wall C is not preserved.

Wall D runs east-west and is bonded into wall C. Wall D is slightly wider (0.70 meters) than wall C (0.55 to 0.60 meters); it is, however, narrower than the main east-west wall. Wall D is preserved from W2C to W5C, with the best-preserved portion being in W3-4C. The wall suffered heavily from the building activity of period III and was completely destroyed in W5C.

Figure 52: Forum north site. Squares W3-5A/C looking north with portions of Forum north drain in background, period II-IV walls in foreground (1972).

Figure 53: Forum north site. W3B/C. Period II walls with scale on bedrock (1970).

To the south of wall D and parallel with it runs an originally covered drain; it was paved throughout; its depth is only one course of squared mortared masonry (**Figure 52**, left foreground). It is remarkably well preserved, especially in W5C and W3C. Its eastward continuation was destroyed by the building activity of period III. A single slab which covered the drain in W5C is preserved at an elevation of +5.419 meters.

Period III (Plate 10)

Period III is characterized by the erection of a monumental structure of unquestionably public character in the northernmost portion of the site. Only preserved in its foundations, the structural remains belong to a portico, the main long facade of which faces the south. Since the foundations for the north wall of the portico rest on the terrain immediately to the north of our site which lies considerably lower than the Forum north site, the back wall of the portico is like an enclosure wall of the eminence to the north. The erection of the portico can be assigned to the second and early third century A.D.

The north face of the main east-west wall remained unaltered during the period III activity. However, the now visible south face was added in this period; an addition responsible also for other fundamental changes.

The drain slabs of the main east-west wall are now continuously preserved for a distance of 12 meters from E2A/B to W2A/B; in antiquity they must have extended as far as W5A/B. The reason for their termination in E2A/B could be determined by the examination of the top of the wall preserved in E3-4A/B (**Figure 54.**) Here the drain was laid underground with the water most probably conducted through clay pipes within the wall and being eventually diverted to the north in E4A. The pipes were apparently embedded on top of the main east-west wall into a shallow cavity, 0.37 meters wide. At the point where the drain is diverted to the north, two large slabs form the base for the drain which in its further course had to cut through the already existing period I wall as mentioned earlier. The level of the drain falls rapidly to the north with a difference in level of 0.32 meters in the short distance of 1.20 meters (**Figure 48**). The inside face of the drain consists of small squared mortared masonry; rubble set in mortar forms the actual width of the very irregular wall which is widest (0.60 meters) at the north edge of the trench. The bottom of the drain maintains the same width even though the sides of the walls are inclined towards each other.

Figure 54: Forum north site. E2-4A. Period III drain to right; scale rests on original portion of period II main east-west wall. Adjacent to scale on left is added portion of period III wall (1970).

The period II wall was widened for the purpose of placing large drain slabs. These very massive slabs rest for about 40 percent of their width on the widened portion of the main east-west wall. The junction between the original south face of the period II wall and the added portion is clearly seen in the illustration (**Figure 54**) accompanying the description. We have not attempted to investigate more thoroughly the south face of the original period II wall at any point along the drain slabs. However, in square E3B (**Figure 55**), a short portion of the original face was laid bare.

Figure 55: Forum north site. E2-3B, looking north. Period III wall with E2B drain above to the left in picture. In center, period II main east-west wall and remains of part added to wall during period III (1970).

The difference in structure between the original (period II) south face and the added width is clearly visible here. As for the face and structure of the added wall, the further it proceeds eastward (E4B), the poorer its foundations become; it seems that the builders took into account the fact that the drain was placed underground with the result that the wall had to carry much less weight. In the west trenches the quality of the added width is considerably better (**Figure 52**). This becomes especially apparent in square W3B where squared masonry of small dimensions set in mortar forms a solid substructure for the drain slabs, one of which protrudes beyond the wall for 0.25 meters, while a slab further to the west sits flush on the foundation. In square W5B, the last of the drain slabs also protrudes beyond the wall upon which it rests.

The north face of the main east-west wall gradually receded in its westward course; this is first visible in W2A and again in W5A, where the recess from the eastern portions is greatest and where the foundations, therefore, become least wide. Because of the placing of the heavy drain slabs, the builders decided to widen also the north face of the main east-west wall in W5A. Two courses of stones are preserved from the bedrock up, placed in front of the original face of the wall. The face of the added masonry is in perfect alignment with the face of the wall in E1-3A. The workmanship of both the added width and the main east-west wall itself in W5A is definitely inferior to the rest of the wall, which suggests some major rebuilding of just this portion of the wall even before the drain slabs were placed upon it (**Figure 51**).

Some slabs in W5B/C were already visible on the surface of the Forum north site prior to excavation. These slabs had a northern continuation in W5A at a lower level. If not quite as massive as their companion slabs further south, they were still of remarkable size. They also continued into W5AA which trench produced eventually the inside (northwest) corner of the portico (**Figure 56**). The foundations for the portico are preserved in W5A/AA in two-four

Figure 56: Forum north site. W5A/AA. Foundation walls for Forum north portico, period III (1970).

Figure 58: Forum north site. E5AA. Lower layers (above bedrock) of foundations for Forum north portico, period III. Remains of period I main east-west wall at right edge (1970).

Figure 57: Forum north site. E5AA. Forum north portico, upper layers of wall foundation, period III (1970).

courses of slabs. One can presume that the foundations for the back wall of the porch are equally well, if not better preserved, since some slabs, which ought to belong to this wall, have been laid bare underneath the thick overgrowth of shrubbery and the many smaller stones which had been placed upon them. The inside northeast corner of the portico was found in E6AA (**Figure 57**). Due to the accumulation of a *gomila* in E6B/C, held in check by a recently built wall, excavation in this sector became difficult. We could ascertain, however, that the short east wall of the portico (**Figure 58**) continues, in fact, beyond the south face of the period I portion of the main east-west wall into E6B, as is also the case in W5-6B/C.

We pointed out earlier that the back wall of the portico is also an enclosure wall at the north edge of the eminence or Forum per se. The enclosure at the west edge of the Forum terminates with the short west wall of the portico. Future excavation can determine to how great a distance the short east wall of the portico continues beyond the main east-west wall to the south.

The evidence for preserved walls of period III outside the portico is scanty. Built against the additional south face of the main east-west wall is wall E in square E2B, running to the south (**Figure 59**, wall with scale on top). Its width is 0.65 to 0.70 meters; the preserved length is 2.30 meters. Its foundations are built of large rubble, the wall itself of square mortared masonry. It so happens that the east face of this wall coincides with the termination of the drain slabs, and this can hardly be mere coincidence.

Figure 59: Forum north site. E2B/E3C. Period IV walls to the south of main east-west wall with Forum north drain (1970).

Contemporary with the portico building are five enormous slabs in W2B/C (**Figure 52**). In W2B they rest on a fairly rough rubble foundation; in W3B the upper courses of period II wall D were knocked down, while the lower courses served as foundation for the slabs. These slabs are much too big and too heavy to have belonged to the pavement in front of the portico. One can form an idea of the kind of pavement used on the Forum north site and elsewhere by directing one's attention to the street pavement which runs along the outside of the west enclosure of the Forum. Some interpretation other than floor pavement must be sought for the five slabs just discussed.

Period IV (Plate 11)

The latest stage of building activity, period IV, brings us to the fourth century A.D.; scanty remains of walls from this phase came to light. We have no complete plan of individual buildings. The surface level of the period IV walls is at ±6 meters. Remains of floors in an advanced state

Figure 60: Forum north site. Fragmentary column in E2C in period IV walls context (1970).

of decomposition were found in squares E1-2C at +6.317 meters. In square E2C was found a column drum of yellowish marble (**Figure 60**); it seems to have been buried underneath the late floors and may have belonged to the portico of some other building on the Forum which fell into decay after A.D. 300.[54]

All of the late walls adhere to the basic direction of the major walls of earlier building periods. North-south walls, running closely parallel to earlier walls, were found in squares W5B and W3-4B/C (**Figure 52**). Both north-south and east-west walls occur in squares E1-W1-2C/D, E2B/F, and in E3-4C/D (**Figure 59**). All of the late walls have in common a haphazard, poor construction. They are built in part of reused squared masonry or simply of rubble set in earth and very poor-quality mortar. The foundation for the walls consists very often simply of the debris which is the result of the collapse of the previous period III buildings.

Summary of the Excavations

The earliest stage of building activity on the Forum north site is preserved in E4-5A with the remains of the impressive, strongly built wall. This wall could have continued for some distance towards the east to a point where it may have met at an angle with a north-south wall which we believe formed the east enclosure wall of the eminence in the Hellenistic-Republican period and continued to form an enclosure of the Roman Forum during the Imperial period. We derive support for this hypothesis not only from scanty remains of a north-south wall on the curia site in square A3, but also from the general configuration of the terrain and the border lines of the privately owned fields to the east of square E6A. Here, in order to clean ground for cultivation, small stones have been heaped upon what would seem to be an artifical elevation, that is, a wall existing previously. If our assumption is correct, this division can only have been the continuation towards the east of the wall preserved in E4-5A. All future excavations in the Forum area of Salona must concentrate on the plots adjacent to this hypothetical eastern enclosure wall, to the east of the Forum.

We feel that the earliest wall also continued from E4A towards the west, fulfilling the same purpose as in the east: namely of surrounding the eminence which comprised the Salona settlement during the Hellenistic-Republican period.

The core of the main east-west wall was built in period II in continuation of the wall of period I in E4A. Against the south face of this wall was built a rectangular room, approximately 6.50 meters by 5.20 meters deep (walls C and D). There could have followed to the east more rooms, since wall D continues beyond wall C towards the east; but this must remain a hypothesis for lack of evidence.

In front of wall D ran a drain covered with slabs. The drain evacuated its waters towards the west. It may have continued for some distance towards the east beyond what is presently preserved. Thus, considering what was said about the possibility of rooms and taking into account the drain and, of course, the main east-west wall, one might surmise that there was here during period II an oblong structure subdivided into rooms.

Built against the north face of the main east-west wall are two perpendicular walls (A,B) with a space of 6.60 meters between. Since, as was pointed out earlier, the terrain to the north is on a considerably lower level, we have here a basement-like room if, as is likely, walls A and B were met by a perpendicular wall towards the north.

In period III the main east-west wall was widened and a drain placed on top. The addition of massively built north, east, and west walls resulted in a portico-shaped building. Both the east and west wall continue to the south beyond the main east-west wall.

Five slabs survive in W2B/C. They run southward from the main east-west wall. These slabs indicate the period III floor level in front of the portico but they hardly belonged to the general Forum pavement. They probably fulfilled here a special purpose which we can no longer determine. However, the slabs may have formed a substructure for rostra (?) or some fairly large pedestal. The closest comparison in Yugoslavia itself comes from the Forum of Delminium where a similar series of slabs were found.[55] Needless to say, many fora have yielded, usually in great number, bases for dedicatory monuments; these could be placed rather haphazardly on the public squares.

The drain slabs terminate in E2A and the surface drain goes underground. It is worthwhile mentioning that, from the point where the row of slabs in W2B depart to the south, there is an equal distance of from 9.60 to 9.70 meters to the western enclosure wall on the one hand and the termination of the drain slabs in E2A on the other. We believe that some significance should be attached to this symmetry. Moreover, the distance from the termination of the open drain to the east wall of the portico is slightly longer, namely 10.70 meters. We have, in other words, two equal parts and a third slightly longer part. The termination of the surface drain would indicate a rectangular room closed by four walls. Adjacent to this room, to the west, there would have been the open portion of the portico, about twice the length of the eastern, closed room, with the open drain in front of the portico. It is possible that the fragmentary column from E2C belonged to the open portico. Other architectural elements that can be safely attributed to this building are not available. However, many architectural fragments published in the section "Monuments in Stone" were extracted from the *gomila* in E2D/E and thus must have belonged to structures in the vicinity such as the portico; the date of these fragments, the late second and third century A.D., also fits the date of the portico.

During period IV, in the fourth and the following centuries, building activity took place exclusively in front of the period III portico. But the general pillaging of the site and the poor workmanship of the walls do not give much of a clue for a reconstruction of any buildings.

Notes on Chapter 3

[Abbreviations and Select Bibliography will be found on page xv.]

1. Dyggve, *Forum,* p. 57.
2. Dyggve, *Recherches* I, p. 31.
3. For the *torcularium* see D. Rendić-Miočević, "Nuoveau pressoir à Salone, au nord du Forum," *BD* 55 (1953): 205-212.
4. See FS I, pp. 7 ff.; Ceci, MC, p. 65.
5. See FS I, pp. 23 ff.; FS III, passim.
6. There is no evidence for squatters in the Forum area after A.D. 614. Coins of the eighteenth to twentieth

centuries and occasional fragments of modern pottery simply attest that farmers cultivated the ground during at least the past two hundred years.

7. See the article by C. Fiskovic̀, "Démolition et enlèvement des monuments de Solin," *BD* 53 (1950-51): 197-206. Cf. also Dyggve, *Recherches* I, pp. 28 f.

8. Cf. his quote about the virgin soil above.

9. See the discussion later on in this chapter on period I on the curia site.

10. Alföldy, *Bevölkerung,* p. 18. The effort to remedy this general situation is very considerable, as is attested by browsing through any Yugoslav archaeological periodical. Increased excavation activity by both Yugoslav and Yugoslav-American teams is a noteworthy development. The main national Yugoslav interest has so far been directed towards the prehistoric and native Illyrian periods. Christian Salona has fared slightly better with regard to small finds, but the yield is nonetheless minimal. See FS III, passim. For objects in the Split Museum see the installments of Bulic̀ in *BD*, starting with vol. 14. The objects published are rarely drawn and there is an almost total lack of photographs. The inscriptions are more completely published than anything else.

11. Curia northwest corner (0/18) +7.76 m; southwest corner (0/0) +7.37 m; northwest corner (38/18) +6.59 m; southwest corner (38/0) +6.44 m. Eastward slope northwest to northeast corners: 1.17 m; southwest to southeast corners: 0.97 m; southward slope, northwest to southwest corners: 0.39 m; northeast to southeast corners: 0.15 m.

12. P. Sticcoti, Doclea. *Die römische Stadt Doclea in Montenegro. Schriften Balkankommission, Antiq. Abt.* 6 (1913): 106-138 and especially p. 127, figs. 57-74; Wymer, p. 50, fig. 22 (the reproduction of the plan omits the subsidiary western entrance and the eastern window is not too clear); Wilkes p. 371, fig. 18.

13. Wymer, p. 50.

14. Wilkes also omits the door in the west wall.

15. Patsch, *Dalmatien,* p. 177, fig. 3; Wymer, pp. 48 f., fig. 21; Wilkes p. 371, fig. 18 (letters designating the rooms are lacking).

16. E. Reisch, "Colonia Claudia Aquum," *OeJh,* 16 (1913): Beibl. 135-144, fig. 36. Wilkes p. 369, fig. 18 (p. 370). Wilkes says "Two stairways entered the central room." According to Reisch, there is only one, flanked by two small rooms, which Wilkes may have mistakenly conceived as staircases.

17. Cf. the general remarks in A. Boethius-J.B. Ward-Perkins, *Etruscan and Roman architecture* (1970), p. 311.

18. Wymer, pp. 54-58, fig. 25 (p. 55); *Germania Romana*^{2} II, pl. X, fig. 2.

19. Staehelin, p. 160, fig. 23; Grenier, pp. 380 ff., figs. 120-121.

20. Wymer, pp. 41-45, figs. 17-18.

21. Ibid., pp. 32-34, fig. 13; see also p. 77.

22. E. Boeswillwald, R. Cagnat, and A. Ballu, *Timgad. Une cité Africaine* (1905), pp. 32-37; Wymer, pp. 25-29, figs. 10-11; R. Cagnat-V. Chapot, *Manuel d'Architecture Romaine* I (1916), p. 122, fig. 58.

23. A. Merlin, *Le Forum de Thuburbo Majus* (1922), pp. 34 f. On p. 34, Merlin refers to other curiae in Tipasa and Mdaourouch.

24. L. Crema, *Archittetura Romana,* in *Enciclopedia Classica* III, vol. XII.1, p. 375.

25. Ibid., p. 584.

26. A. Schober, *Die Römerzeit in Österreich* (1953), p. 65, fig. 11; Ward-Perkins, pp. 1-19; *Virunum,* fig. 13.

27. R. Egger, "Die Ausgrabungen .... 1953," *Carinthia* 146 (1956): 24 f.

28. CIL III, ed. O. Hirschfeld; Bulic̀, *BD* 11 (1888): 65, no. 26; Dyggve, *Forum,* pp. 56 f.

29. See notes 28 and 30.

30. Bulic̀ I, pl. II.

31. Dyggve, *Forum,* p. 56, n. 3.

32. Ibid.

33. For the bowl and altar see stone monuments, nos. 29 and 30. For the glass, see glass, no. 106; inv. nos. of the pottery are 69P52-53.

34. An interesting parallel for our charcoal pit comes from Emona, the Roman predecessor of Ljubljana. W. Schmid, "Emona," *JAK* 7 (1913): 61-188; see pp. 107-109, fig. 37, showing the better of the two furnaces. The smelting pits are virtually identical to our pit in general shape and measurements, if more regularly built, but also using stones of varying thickness. The smelting pits have three sides only and the interior was filled with "Asche und verbrannten aufrechtstehenden Stücken von Nadelholz." The pits were erected above a layer of clay, 3 to 4 cm thick, which covered virgin soil. Nearby were found fragments of pottery, charcoal, bones, ashes and iron slag.

Schmid concludes that "die Grössenverhältnisse der beiden Öfen schliessen ihre Verwendung als Hochöfen aus; sie waren Schmelzofen, geeignet für den Handwerksbetrieb, für das Einschmelzen von Metallbruch."

35. The word tank is used here for convenience rather than for a clear concept of its actual construction.

36. Inv. 69T3.

37. See especially G.D. Weinberg, "Roman Glass Factories in Galilee," *Bull. Museum Haaretz Tel Aviv* 10 (1968): 49-50, pl. 7. From the Jalamet el Asafna excavations comes "a furnace floor showing indentations to receive" rectangular tanks in which the "glass was melted"; see pl. 7, 1. The date of this installation is the third quarter of the fourth century A.D. The finds from Somelaria, dating from about a thousand years later are described thus: "The furnace has now been completely excavated and proves to have a deep firing chamber adjacent to the rectangular tank, as well as vents on the rear and on the side of the furnace opposite the firing chamber"; see pl. 7, 2.

Elsewhere G.D. Weinberg describes in "Glass manufacture in Hellenistic Rhodes," *Arch. Delt.* 24 (1969), p. 149, pl. 85 a-d, and pl. 86a, "Clay receptacles," of the size of 0.18 m by 0.155 m by 0.036 m, with a "coating of glass"; the author produces modern parallels (pl. 86b). The receptacles "were used to hold small amounts of glass within the furnace—the colors to be used for decorating beads." Remains of metal rods, of pigments on pottery sherds, of bronze fragments, and of lead characterize the working area in Rhodes just as they do in Salona.

Two glass kilns, one for the making of glass ingots, were described by G.T. Scanlon in "Fustat Expedition: Preliminary Report 1965, Part II," *JARCE* 6 (1967): 65 ff., especially pp. 75-80. The kiln at W (XXI-1/2) "was hewn into the gabal . . . its sides built up by brick to a height of flooring since disappeared, and the interior plastered with what appears to be ground sandstone, giving it an ivory tint." (Cf. pl. 9b and fig. 8.) Some basic remarks on glass furnaces are available in the article on "A medieval Glass-Factory at Corinth," by G.R. Davidson (Mrs. G.D. Weinberg) in *AJA* 44 (1940): 297-324. Cf. also vol. V of R.J. Forbes, *Studies in Ancient Technology* (1957), pp. 110 ff., pp. 119-120 for furnaces specifically. Somewhat reminiscent of glass tanks are the installations for the purpose of dyeing at Isthmia as described, depicted, and compared with other similar ancient and modern dye-works in Israel by Ch. Kardara, *AJA* 65 (1961): 216-266, pls. 79-82.

38. See among the published objects, metal nos. 7, 37, and 45; among unpublished objects inv. nos. 69Bz2-5 and V1-2.

39. See Davies, p. 42, fig. 1. The following literature has proved most useful in preparing the account of the Salona furnace: L. Beck, *Die Geschichte des Eisens*[2] I (1890-91), passim; H. Blümner, *Technologie und Terminologie der Gewerbe und Künste bei Griechen und Römern* (1875) I, pp. 65 f.; pp. 23 ff.; IV, pp. 217 ff.; R.J. Forbes, *Metallurgy in Antiquity* (1950), pp. 388 ff.; see also for a revised version of this account vol. IX of Forbes' *Studies in Ancient Technology* (1964). Cf. further E. Pasalić, "Production of Roman Mines and Iron-works in West Bosnia," *AI* 6 (1965): 81-88. The author does not, unfortunately, give us the badly needed precise information on smelting furnaces. H. Blank, "Archäologische Funde und Grabungen in Norditalien 1959-1967," *AA* 1968, p. 509, fig. 76, furnace in Marzobotto, for which see also G.V. Gentili, "Problemi e testimonianze della città etrusca de Marzobotto," *St. Etr.* 36 (1968): 116-117, with little really relevant information; Egger, *Magdalensberg,* pp. 3 ff. and 38 ff. For more recent evidence see the very interesting article on a number of smelting furnaces in the Jura mountains of Switzerland by P.-L. Pelet, "Sidérurgie antique au pied du Jura vaudois," *Helvetia Archaeologia* 1 (1970): 86 ff. The furnaces date from the late iron age to the sixth century A.D. The furnaces are mostly oval in shape, some juxtaposed. Abandoned furnaces were used as bases for more recent or superimposed furnaces. Of particular interest for us with regard to the charcoal pit is Pelet's remark that "les forgerons jetaient alterativement charbon du bois et minerai dans le gueulard." This working process is similarly described as a result of the study of copper smelting processes as revealed in the Timna explorations. See *Pal. Expl. Q.* 103 (1971): 2, summarized after *Archaeologia Austriaca* 47 (1970): 91 ff. (not available in Princeton): "The smelting charge of ores, fluxes and charcoal, prepared at the neighbouring crushing and grinding workshops, was poured onto the burning charcoal heap inside the furnace."

40. Davies, pp. 44 f., figs. 1 (upper), 10, and 11. The description of the prehistoric furnace in Sanskimost is somewhat reminiscent of our findings. See F. Fiala, "Das Flachgräberfeld und die prähistorische Ansiedlung in Sanskimost," *WMBH* 6 (1899): 62-128, especially p. 123, fig. 180. Davies calls the furnace "hardly different from a bowl furnace."

41. Walls of furnaces are usually just of clay. In her article on the glass factory in Corinth, Mrs. Weinberg says of the wall of the furnace that it was "thickly plastered inside and out."

42. Cf. Egger, *Magdalensberg,* p. 40, about the use of bellows and the marks which they left around the furnaces.

43. For a furnace entirely embedded in clay ground see F. von Kenner, "Forschungen in Vindobona," *JAK* 3 (1909): 82 f., figs. 42 A and B. These furnaces have apparently escaped the attention of Davies. For replacing a simple clay floor with a double tile layer see Forrer, p. 42, furnace no. X.

44. Smelting furnaces: in Carnuntum, M. von Groller, *Der Römische Limes* 6 (1905): 143-151, diam. 3.40 m, 2.20 m, and 2.30 m respectively. In Magdalensberg see Egger, *Magdalensberg*, pp. 38 ff., circular shape, diam. 0.60-0.70 m and a few of them larger; cf. Beilagen II, VIII, and IX, also figs. 44 and 52. See note 39 for the furnace in Marzobotto. In Immurium-Morsham (Austria) see R. Fleischer, "Immurium-Morsham, Die Grabungen 1966 and 1967," *OeJh* Beibl. 48 (1966-67): 175 f. See also Davies, passim. The variety in size and shape of kilns is very remarkable as becomes clear from the references to pottery furnaces. In Colchester, M.R. Hull, *Colchester* (1958), pp. 248 ff.; idem, *Germania* 18 (1934), p. 32, diam: 7 feet; in the Nene valley, England, Liversidge, p. 192 f., figs. 88-89, diam. ca. 4 feet. Forrer, pp. 32 ff., furnace no. II, diam. 2.50 m (figs. 9-12). In Iznik, Turkey, Aslanapa, pp. 143 ff., figs. 1-5, diam. 3 m (nos. II-III). In Lyons, France, M. Leglay, "Information archéologiques," *Gallia* 26 (1968): 270 ff., rectangular furnace; idem, *Gallia* 24 (1966): 491, figs. 5 f., furnace no. 2, diam. 1.25 to 1.335 m, found together with other less preserved furnaces of circular, oval, and pear-shaped forms. In Acquincum, Hungary, B. Buzsinszky, *Das grosse Töpferviertel in Aquincum* (1932), figs. 38 ff.; oval and circular furnaces. In Blickweiler and Eschweiler Hof, Germany, Knorr, pp. 112 ff., diam. 2.73 m, see fig. 40 for a reconstruction of the kiln. Of uniformly large diameter, that is from 2.50 to 3.50 m, are Roman kilns discovered in the Canton Zurich. See the report by W. Drack in *Neue Zürcher Zeitung* of July 29, 1970. Diameters varying between 0.90 and 1.70 m are attested for kilns in Augusta Raurica, see R.M. Swoboda, "Der Töpfereibezirk am Südostrand von Augusta Raurica," *Helvetia Archaeologia* 2 (1971): 7-21. Very useful for comparison with ancient kilns are the studies by R. Hampe and A. Winter, *Bei Töpfern und Töpferinnen in Kreta, Messenien und Zypern* (1962) and, idem, *Bei Töpfern und Zieglern in Süditalien, Sizilien und Griechenland* (1965). In the latter work Hampe gives on p. 223, nn. 13-14 (with reference to *BSA* 61 (1956): 64 ff., useful additional lists of pottery kilns. A kiln in Sutri, Italy, of semicircular shape, is called by the author the stoking area; we would apply the latter term to the rectangular corridor (2.60 by 0.85 m) which leads to the semicircle. It is difficult to see the practicality of the rectangular kiln with the dimensions just quoted. See G.D. Duncan, "A Roman Pottery near Sutri," *PBSR* 32 (1964): 38-88, esp. pp. 40 f., figs. 2 f., pls. 14-16.

45. For the central chimney see the Corinthian pinakes figured in *BSA* 56 (1961), pl. 7 a-c. The brick-lined kilns in Iznik are 2 m high. Kiln no. III has a dome-shaped roof, presumably a brick structure, with a central vent hole; so has no. II, unless the drawing implies that there was a large opening in the roof about two-thirds the diameter of 3 m of the kiln; cf. Aslanapa, p. 146. The roof over the Blickweiler-Eschweiler Hof reconstructed kiln is dome-shaped with a central escape for smoke; cf. Knorr, fig. 40. Many more parallels for dome-shaped roofs from ancient and modern times could be cited.

46. A "domed clay roof with ventilation holes" is attested for the kilns in the Nene valley area. See Liversidge, figs. 88-89.

47. See clay objects, cat. no. 21.

48. In square C6.

49. Trenches 1-3 and 5 were dug in 1970.

50. At the same time that trench 4 was dug, a very small sounding was made on the Forum north site, in a location which corresponds to E1A/E2B of the 1970 grid plan (Plates 9 and 10). This latter sounding will not be described when we deal with the Forum north site, since it was incorporated into the full scale excavation of that area. The disappointing results in excavating trench 4 were the major reason for the decision to excavate the Forum north site, which seemed much more promising from the finds of pottery made in a relatively small area. During the 1969 sounding there was found also the Republican coin of C. Serveilius (coin list no. 2).

51. Yellowish marble. H. 0.55 m, D. at base 0.45 m. A rectangular cavity in the center of the base is 3.5 cm by 6 cm. The entire trench 4 was filled in again at the end of the 1969 season and the capital consequently buried, rather than being taken to the Split Archaeological Museum which already has many similar architectural fragments.

52. See clay objects, cat. no. 16.

53. The level of the drain is at +6.376 m in E2A.

54. The column lies at a slant from +6.186 m to +5.902 m. The shaft is tapering; it has a rounded and stepped moulding at the top. L. 1.61 m; D. 0.56 m; D. of central cavity 9 cm.

55. Patsch, *Dalmatien*, p. 177, fig. 3; Wymer, fig. 21.

IV

The Chronological Evidence

As has already been pointed out, it was not possible in any of the excavated areas to read off a sequence of building periods from an undisturbed stratification; in extremely rare instances stratified layers could be observed, but these extended only over very restricted areas. This destruction of almost all artificial floors and other levels has made it impossible throughout the entire excavated terrain to establish a secure relationship between walls and corresponding floor levels. The only important and helpful exception is the street or piazza pavement to the east of the curia which sealed off the remains of period I (**Plate 8**).

Consequently, only a very small percentage of the finds could be connected securely with a specific building phase on the basis of their location alone, without taking into account also their intrinsic absolute dates. This represents the main problem for establishing the absolute dates for the excavated structural remains. The one exception is the street pavement east of the curia noted above, which provides the *terminus ante quem* for period I. In this area the thoroughness with which the various looters proceeded is best demonstrated by the pottery and coins of the fifth and sixth centuries A.D. found directly on top of the street pavement which was laid early in the first century A.D. Thus, the activities of the stone and metal robbers were stopped only by the presence of the pavement, whereas elsewhere they were able to continue right down to bedrock. (Cf. charts 13-14. Charts will be found on pages 91 to 105.)

It follows that the majority of the small finds, coming from thoroughly disturbed contexts, provides no *direct* evidence for establishing the absolute chronology of the individual building phases observed. For this reason the bulk of the pottery from the 1969-70 excavation will be published in typological arrangement in a separate volume. This future publication will include, however, all necessary references to those stratified pottery finds or to such finds otherwise connected with building periods which are published in the charts and in the pottery catalogue of the present volume.

However great the restrictions in using the small finds as dating evidence, they do indicate in their totality the duration of the settlement. Fortunately, the earliest and latest finds are numerous enough to establish beyond doubt the beginning and end of the settlement. Furthermore, as the early and late finds are evenly distributed within the excavated areas, they attest to continuous habitation of the eminence of Salona from the first half of the second century B.C. to the sixth century A.D.

Within this time span a sequence of at least four building periods (I-IV) is sufficiently established by the superimposition of structural remains. Only for period I do we have satisfactory dating evidence from a large closed deposit, as noted above. To determine as closely as possible under the given circumstances the absolute dates for periods II-IV, other less accurate auxiliary means have to be brought into play, yielding less stringent results. We tried to isolate as many complexes of small finds as possible which, although coming from secondary locations such as fills, drains, etc., had nevertheless a clear physical relationship to walls and, at the same time, belonged within restricted time periods. The comparison of several such complexes in conjunction with the distribution pattern of coins and certain types of pottery sheds some light on the building history of certain areas.

The facts already stated have made it desirable for us to present the chronological evidence in the form of charts. At the same time these tables make it possible to check our conclusions and, if necessary, to correct the interpretation here proposed in the light of later excavations and of the results of the work carried out by the Yugoslav team during 1969-71 to the north of the Porta Caesarea. Furthermore, charts provide the reader with some idea of what pottery fabrics and types were found associated with each other, a possibility which is precluded by typological presentation of the material. It was attempted to isolate some promising find complexes excavated during the 1970 season. The results obtained in the examination of these complexes were then checked against some coins found in 1969 in stratified location inside the curia (see charts 8 & 10). These coins provide the necessary basis for correlating the corresponding building periods in the Forum north and the curia sites.

The primary dating evidence rests with the coins, of which most are listed in the charts as well as being fully catalogued. The pottery mentioned in the tables is chosen exclusively because it provides some sort of dating evidence. It goes without saying that relying on pottery for the purpose of dating can be open to error. The presence or absence of certain types of imported wares, the dates of which have been established in areas outside of Dalmatia, can always be the result of specific patterns of trade rather than being indicative chronologically. We do believe, however, that the inclusion of a large spectrum of such internally dated pottery, including at times household wares as well, counterbalances possible sources of error. It is evident, moreover, that the broader dates proposed for periods III and IV reflect the less advanced state of knowledge of later Roman pottery in the Mediterranean as compared with that of earlier centuries.

Period I

(For the structural remains see **Plates 3, 5 and 8.**)

Primary evidence of the dating of the oldest settlement is provided by the finds from the area to the east of the curia sealed off by the street pavement of period II. Although these finds clearly come from levelled-out destruction debris used as fill, there is no reason to doubt their contemporaneity with the few earliest structural remains found in situ in this area. All of the pottery is extremely fragmentary and almost no joins were possible. Many pieces show traces of burning at their broken edges. The sherds of heavy amphorae were found nearest to bedrock, as could be expected when debris is unloaded and levelled out. In only one instance it is possible that pottery was found in situ, thus indicating some kind of floor level. In B7 a large handmade storage jar was found lying on its side. It was crushed but otherwise complete and its mouth was covered with a plate of gray ware P59, P114. All of the pottery from this sealed off deposit is described later, in the chapter on pottery (Figs. A-G).

Finds indicating the beginning of period I include the following groups: late Hellenistic black glaze ware; gray relief ware, a variant of "Megarian" bowls but different in shape and make; and a fragment of one "Megarian" bowl. While no single element among these groups points to a date earlier than the late third or the second century B.C., it is difficult to determine a more specific date on the basis of the pottery alone (see chart 2).

Nor is the testimony of the few coins very helpful. Of three identifiable coins, the earliest are two Roman asses of the second century B.C. (C. 4-5); they were found in close proximity to each other. While there is no way to determine whether these coins reached Salona soon after being minted, this possibility cannot be excluded and would then corroborate nicely the date of the earliest pottery. Taking also into account the types represented by the coarse pottery, one might be inclined to suggest a date in the first half of the second century B.C. for the beginning of period I: that is, for the earliest settlement.

The *terminus ad quem* of period I is indicated by the third identifiable coin, an as (of series I or II) from Nemausus (C. 12), and by the finds of Italian terra sigillata. All of the sigillata stamps are rectangular. While types of Haltern Service II are well represented, Service I is attested by some plates. These finds would suggest a late Augustan date for the end of period I. The absence of stamps *in planta pedis* corroborates this dating. Although sigillata and other fine wares came to Salona as imports from the same Italian centers of production during period I and II, typically Tiberian wares, such as fine Nigra ware, are not among the remains of period I. This finding is supported by the evidence of non-Italian fine wares which are related to Italian terra sigillata. Only two examples each of Eastern sigillata AII and Eastern sigillata B ware came to light (P 74-77, Fig. D).

The latest lamps found in this complex from below the pavement are late Augustan. Considering also the evidence of the coarse wares, one might be inclined to say that period I comes to a close in the first years of the first century A.D., sometime around ±10 A.D.

A small complex of pottery from a sealed deposit in the Forum central site confirms this date. Trench I was dug into the core of the foundation of the Capitolium which was built during period II. The core of the foundation was mortared rubble and included some coarse pottery, mostly amphorae and lids found with some mortar still adhering. These vessels must have been used and discarded prior to the building of this platform. The only series of pottery types upon which to base a judgment are the series of amphorae among which none can be dated later than the first century B.C. (chart 1 and Figs. F and G2).

Farther to the north in the Forum central site, period I is well attested by numerous pottery finds in trench 5 (see chart 1). Although no continuous floor level and no walls of period I were preserved, the bulk of the earliest pottery comes from the earth just above bedrock. The presence in this lot of pottery of some earlier ceramic groups identical with those in the sealed levels (period I) to the east of the curia and in roughly the same numeric proportions to each other, may be taken as sufficient evidence for the presence of period I on the Forum central site (see charts 1 and 2).

The rich pottery finds from this square provide a welcome support for the conclusions drawn from the evidence gathered in trenches 2 and 3 near the Capitolium. There bedrock was almost immediately reached. While in trench 3 (see chart 10) the very meager finds consisted of pottery of six centuries mixed together, trench 2 (see chart 1) entirely lacks pottery of the second to the sixth century A.D. This indicates that the terrain has been extensively levelled since the occupation of the eminence.

On the Forum north site, period I is amply attested by finds from disturbed levels and, with one possible exception, not in their original location. Accordingly, all of the pottery is in very fragmentary condition with almost no joins being possible. Nevertheless, the presence of a period I wall in E4-5A precludes the assumption that these finds were dumped here from any great distance. They are evenly distributed within the areas examined to the south of the main east-west wall (see chart 2). Furthermore, the homogeneous group of crushed but complete amphorae from a deep pocket in the bedrock in W1C, can perhaps be interpreted as remains of period I in situ. The amphorae can be assigned to the latter part of the first century B.C., that is, to the end of period I. It is also possible, of course, that intact amphorae were used to fill up an undesirable pit in preparation for the building activity at the beginning of period II (Fig. G3).

The pre-Imperial coins from the Forum north site, although listed in Table 2 for reasons of consistency within the table, cannot be taken as evidence for period I. (See page 92.)

The distribution of period I pottery on the Forum north site shows some significant features which can be gleaned from chart 2. It is far less numerous to the north than to the south of the main east-west wall of period I-II. To the north of this wall the period I finds were more heavily concentrated in square E5AA than in the squares excavated further to the west. Nevertheless, two sample complexes from directly above bedrock in square E5A and W5A include none of this earliest pottery (cf. Table 4). This is the more surprising since the concentration of early pottery in proximity to the period I section of the main east-west wall in E5A/AA supports the attribution of this wall to period I on other grounds. This apparent inconsistency is probably due to the fact that the entire ground to the north of the main east-west wall is fill which was brought in after period I (for discussion of this context see the following section of period II). This explains the disturbance of any "earliest level" in E5A/AA as well as in all the corresponding squares further west, while the additional scattering of the earliest pottery throughout that fill might possibly be connected with the building of the heavy enclosure wall of period III to the north and east of E5A/AA.

The rarity of early finds in the areas examined to the north of the main east-west wall is probably also to be explained by the configuration of the terrain which slopes steeply to the north. If the period I portion of the east-west wall marked a northern boundary of the earliest settlement on the eminence, this slope lay outside it.

Period II

(For the structural remains see **Plates 7, 8, and 9**)

The curia. Direct evidence for the beginning of period II is very scanty and limited to the curia site. But what there is, leads to the assumption that rebuilding of the settlement followed immediately upon the destruction of the earlier one. A few coins from undisturbed locations (see charts 8 and 10) provide our main evidence, namely a Quadrans of Augustus (C. 10) from the destruction debris of period I-II in square A/A'5; coins of Tiberius found on top of a partly demolished wall of period I in destruction debris of period I-II in square A1 (C. 15) and found in the destruction debris of period I-II in square B5 (C. 16-17).

Since the ground immediately above the street pavement to the east of the curia is thoroughly disturbed, there is no way to determine the time gap, if any, between the latest finds from below the pavement (period I) and the earliest finds of period II above these slabs. These slabs represent the only preserved "floor" level, which marks the beginning of period II on the entire curia site.

Forum central site. The few finds from trench 2 (see chart 1) which come from the level of the lowermost step of the podium can be expected to be contemporary with or earlier than the erection of the Capitolium. The latest among the chronologically indicative finds are a few pieces of Italian sigillata with shapes of Haltern Service I and II; there is one rectangular stamp: DASI (see chart 1). The middle to late Augustan date of this small complex would correspond to the latest finds of period I from underneath the pavement to the east of the curia. The unstratified finds from the lower levels in square E3J/K (see chart 1) do not show any apparent gap present in the sequence of pottery types between the end of the first century B.C. and the first half of the first century A.D.

Forum north site. Broader, even though not more direct, evidence for the absolute dates of the beginning as well as the end of period II comes from the fill to the north of the main east-west wall (see charts 3-6 and 11). As mentioned above this fill must have been dumped here before the portico of period III was erected; its specific function was to strengthen the foundation for the heavy structure. The composition of the fill, namely building stones, tiles, mortar, charcoal and vast amounts of pottery, as well as its distribution with, occasionally, a clearly discernible direction of fall after dumping, leave no doubt that it represents destruction debris. Accordingly, the pottery and coins were more or less evenly distributed in the fill, with later types sometimes occurring close to bedrock and earlier ones higher up. The pottery itself often showed burnt edges and signs of rolling and was extremely fragmentary throughout. This fill clearly represents the debris of building period II in the Forum north site. The wholesale demolition of period II structures is demonstrated by the levelling of all period II walls to a common height and by the alteration of the main east-west wall in order to accomodate the portico and drain of period III on top of it.

The presence of structural remains to the south of the main east-west wall makes the very large amount of pottery included in the fill to the north of the above wall less surprising. Examples of period I pottery in the upper levels of the fill (see chart 2) also support the conclusion that, along with the debris of period II from south of the main east-west wall, a shovel full of debris of period I from a deeper layer was also picked up occasionally and dumped onto the sloping ground to the north.

It is for this very reason that the datable content of the fill taken by itself could be expected to provide less accurate indication for the beginning of period II than for its duration and its end. However, the scarcity of period I pottery on the one hand and the comparison of the coins from the fill (see chart 3:1) with that of coins from the sealed off period I deposit to the east of the curia on the other (chart 9), make up sufficiently for this difficulty.

The earliest coins from the fill are a group of Republican silver coins (see chart 3:1). According to the currency pattern securely established for Italy as well as for the region to the north of the Alps, none of these earliest four coins from the fill is likely to have reached Salona earlier than the first half of the first century A.D. The validity of this rule for Salona is in our view supported by the small complex of coins in the period I deposit to the east of the curia. Among the three pre-Augustan coins found in that area (C. 1, 4, and 5) there are no Republican denarii or quinarii. In contrast to this picture, the four Republican silver coins from the fill are not accompanied by any other pre-Augustan coins. The only Augustan coin in the fill (C. 11) was issued in 11/12 A.D. and may well have reached Salona a couple of years later. Thus it seems safest to assume that the Republican silver coins from the fill (C. 2, 7, 8, and 9) reached Salona at the beginning of Tiberius' reign at the earliest.

In the light of the evidence from the period I deposit to the east of the curia a cautious approach seems in order in evaluating the two Augustan terra sigillata stamps from the fill (cf. charts 5 and 15, *Hilarus* and *Anemo*). Whether found in situ or dumped with the period II debris, they might also represent remains of period I. The earliest well datable sigillata stamps *in planta pedis* from the fill are those by Gellius and C. Murrius, both potters active from the reign of Tiberius. Since furthermore examples of terra sigillata of Haltern Service I are very rare in the fill as compared with the great amount of late Augustan/Tiberian types, the evidence of the Italian terra sigillata concurs with the belief that the beginning of period II in the Forum north site is to be dated sometime during the reign of Tiberius (for other early groups of fine pottery from the fill see chart 6).

The only three pre-second century A.D. coins from the disturbed levels south of the main east-west wall (charts 3:2 and 3) corroborate this conclusion, as do the Italian terra sigillata stamps from this area (see chart 5).

The contemporaneity of the beginning of period II—in the reign of Tiberius—in the three main areas explored (curia, Forum central, and Forum north site) has been determined by evaluating the evidence for each area independently. We may therefore say in conclusion that during period II an overall rebuilding of the previous settlement was taking place.

The duration of period II is not indicated by any remains from stratigraphical contexts. The pavement of the portico of period III was entirely removed in late antiquity. Although some slabs indicated a floor level of period III—the drain slabs resting upon the period II main east-west wall—the earlier walls sealed off by these slabs did not yield any significant finds.

The *terminus ad quem* for period II has, therefore, to be determined from the latest datable finds in the fill of period II (see chart 6). The latest coins (see chart 3:1) from this fill, however, cannot be taken as decisive evidence. The bulk of the pottery found is pre-Flavian, as will become apparent by the full publication of the material later. The second half of the first century A.D. is sufficiently well represented by pottery and lamps, however, to contradict the *terminus ad quem* after the middle of the first century A.D. advocated by the coins (cf. chart 3 and 6). The end of period II, therefore, has to be determined exclusively from the latest pottery items in what otherwise appears as an uninterrupted sequence of types. In examining the Italian sigillata, the absence of "three letter stamps" so characteristic for the potters active during the second half of the first century A.D. is surprising indeed. It is, of course, possible to assess this as a mere coincidence in our rather small number of post-Augustan sigillata stamps. However, this interpretation is somewhat unlikely in the view of the fact that the elsewhere extremely popular post-Claudian shapes corresponding to the Gaulish types Dragendorff 35 and 36 with barbotine decoration are represented in the Salona excavations of 1969-70 by only one or two specimens. Given the presence of undoubtedly later Flavian pottery in the fill, the absence of later Italian sigillata does not seem to be conclusive.

Positive evidence for the duration of period II throughout the entire first century A.D. is definitely available in the large group of Eastern sigillata B ware, part of which is undoubtedly post-Claudian. Chronologically significant are the fragments of a sigillata flask with relief decoration imported from La Graufesenque in southern Gaul. Rare items at any site, they can be securely assigned to Neronian or early Flavian times. On the other hand, sigillata chiara of type A which made its appearance as a traded commodity all over the Mediterranean sometime in the first half of the second century A.D., is completely absent from the fill, while it is attested in the area to the south of the main east-west wall (see chart 6).

Unfortunately, the numerous but fragmentary Firma lamps present in the fill can only demonstrate the presence of post-Neronian products. Period II may then probably have lasted into the first quarter of the second century A.D.

Period III

(For the structural remains see **Plates 7, 8, and 10**)

Throughout the area examined, floor levels and other occupation strata were neither securely related to a structure of building period III nor preserved to any meaningful extent. Therefore, we have no means of determining directly and precisely the duration of this period in terms of absolute chronology.

For this reason, too, the surprisingly rare coins of the second century A.D.—only one or two, both from the curia site (C. 28 and perhaps C. 28a, see chart 8)—are of little help in assessing the *terminus post quem* for the beginning of period III. But in the curia site as well as in the Forum north site, there is reason to believe that the building activity started immediately after the end of period II.

On the Forum north site, it very much looks as if the demolition of the period II buildings was done deliberately in order to accomodate the new buildings and the enclosure wall, both of which belong to a new Forum concept. This view is supported by the lack of any specific gap in the sequence of pottery from the disturbed levels I-IV to the south of the main east-west wall of period II (chart 11). On the basis of the *terminus ad quem* previously suggested, the beginning of period III might perhaps be dated to the second quarter of the second century A.D.

Remains of frescoes in the curia attest to a redecoration, including a first (?) application of wall-paintings to the interior after the building or part of it had been damaged by fire. From a stylistic point of view the frescoes most probably date from the early Antonine period. Since an extensive remodelling of the building itself is attested, it is reasonable to assume that the frescoes are to be connected with this new period of the curia. It must be emphasized, however, that this remodelling may well have been prompted by the necessity of repairing the damage caused by fire and that it may well have been restricted to the curia.

The positing of the heavy drain slabs of modrac in the Forum central site, which were later partly reused (in period IV, in trench 4) and which were also found in square A1 is undoubtedly contemporary with the corresponding drain of period III in the Forum north site. Thus they would indicate a new building activity in this central area of the Forum which also extended to the curia site sometime before or around the middle of the second century A.D. On the basis of this evidence the rebuilding of the curia is most likely to be contemporary with period III on the Forum north site. We are thus entitled to speak of one and the same building period III for the entire area examined.

For determining the duration of period III it might be helpful to take into account the contrast in numeric proportion between the finds belonging to the second and third centuries with those of the preceding and following centuries, or periods II and IV respectively. The marked decline in the number of small finds from the Forum north site during period III could be partly explained on the basis of the new functions assumed by this area during that time. The Forum north site seems to have become public space during this period as part of the extension of the Forum of period II. Furthermore, since we feel quite certain that the open space to the south of the portico was paved, it is legitimate to assume that few of the small objects, once lost on that pavement, were not picked up again in antiquity. This would represent a satisfactory explanation for the relative scarcity of coins as well as of pottery and lamps. Moreover, it is undeniable that coins of the second half of the second and first half of the third centuries A.D. are extremely rare throughout the entire area (see charts 3, 8, 9, and 14). Lastly, the pottery series from the disturbed levels of the workshop area (chart 13) and from trench 5 (chart 2), which bordered the Forum area on the east side, seem to point towards a general decrease of finds during period III. However, it would seem futile at the present state of our knowledge to speculate about the reason for this general pattern of "recession."

The end of period III can be inferred almost exclusively from the coins found on the Forum north site. From Diocletian onwards they represent a continuous and large series throughout the fourth century A.D. This indicates a sudden change in the social function of the Forum north site in the beginning of the fourth century A.D. These coins are fairly evenly distributed among the main areas of excavation, the Forum north and the curia site (see table 15 and the coin list).

Only one homogeneous complex of small finds could be isolated in this whole excavated area. It might perhaps suggest some sort of damage or deliberate alteration in at least a restricted area of the Forum north site at the end of the third century A.D. Outside the west enclosure wall of the Forum there came to light in squares W6-7B a mass of heavily burnt debris evidently dumped here pell-mell. Among pottery and lamps of the second and third centuries A.D.—with typically fourth century A.D. material apparently absent—there is one coin of Aurelian (C 34; for finds from W6-7B see chart 7). Inside the enclosure wall in W5A which is roughly opposite W6B, a continuous layer of charcoal about ±0.30 meters thick could be noticed in which two coins of Gallienus and Tacitus respectively were found (C. 31 and C. 35; see chart 3). These two coins together with the charcoal debris could not have been deposited in W5A without lifting the pavement slabs of the portico. The area inside and outside of the enclosure wall then contained the only coins of the later third century A.D. from the entire Forum north site. In our opinion this evidence could possibly point to some alteration or other activity near the western entrance to the portico of period III at about 300 A.D. or shortly thereafter. This interpretation could also explain some of the irregularities visible in the westernmost end of the main east-west wall.

Period IV

(For the structural remains see **Plates 4, 7, and 11**)

The beginning of period IV is clearly indicated by the impressive coin series of the fourth century A.D. These coins are evenly distributed exclusively in the excavated area to the south of the period III portico, namely squares W2-5B/D and E2-3B/E (cf. chart 15). This distribution is exactly matched by the concentration of pottery from the fourth to the sixth century A.D. in this same area and, of course, by the architectural remains. The apparently total absence of securely identifiable coins of the fifth century is indeed puzzling. The fifth century A.D. coins, however, might well be among the illegible late Roman coins from this area (see coin list C. 78 ff.). As pottery and lamps of the fifth and sixth centuries are well represented, together with coins of Justinian, this explanation of the lacuna seems likely enough.

The end of continuous settlement in the entire excavated area came some time after the reign of Justinian, in the latter part of the sixth century A.D. as suggested by the concurring testimony of coins, pottery, and lamps.

A possible answer to the question of when the massive dismantling of the monumental buildings in the Forum north site began might be found in the distribution pattern of coins and pottery from the fourth to the sixth century. In the squares excavated inside the portico of period III, namely between W5A/AA and E5A/AA, only two coins of the fourth century were found (C. 48 and 49, see chart 15) and two fragments of sigillata chiara D; no other material of the fourth and the following centuries came to light except two illegible coins (C. 83 and 84).

This suggests that at least until the later sixth century the massive pavement of the portico must have remained untouched in situ. Otherwise, more later material would inevitably have been deposited in the area south of the open portion of the portico drain. On the other hand, the finds from inside the underground drain of period III in square E4A/B (see chart 12) date mainly from the fourth and fifth centuries and thus suggest that already during period IV the drain system of the previous period fell into disuse or decay. That the massive tunneling and looting began on the whole only after the close of period IV is, in our opinion, further indicated by the many underground *gomile* inside as well as outside the portico. Inside, the *gomile* cannot be earlier for the reasons stated above. Outside, they are incompatible with the existence of dwellings during period IV, humble as they may have been. This last point is emphasized by the remains of the column in square E2C.

Summary of Chronology

Period I	(200)-150 B.C.	to	± A.D. 10
Period II	± A.D. 10	to	± A.D. 100-125
Period III	± A.D. 100-125	to	± A.D. 300
Period IV	± A.D. 300	to	A.D. 612

CHART 1: POTTERY FROM THE FORUM CENTRAL SITE (see Plate 7)

PE refers to pottery from the curia and Forum central sites; PN refers to pottery from the Forum north site.

		Trench 5	Trench 1 (under Capitolium)	Trench 2	Trench 3
Second and first century B.C. including time of Augustus	Late Hellenistic black glaze	Beaker, PE 47 Handle, PE 48 Cup, PE 45 Bowl, PE 50 Bowl, PE 51			Patera, PE 31
	Campana B and imitation (?)	Mastos, PE 37 Bowl, PE 52 Cup (?), PE 53			Mastos (?), PE 30
	Gray relief ware, "Megarian" bowl	Bowl, PE 35			
	Gray ware, plain	PE 38 PE 39 PE 40 PE 41	P 115-115a, Fig. F		
	Lamp, black slip, "Warzenlampe"	L 2, Pl. 48.			
	Various fine ware	Beaker, PE 63 Unguentarium, probably Ha 30, PE 62			
	Pitchers, jugs	PE 74-77	P 116, Fig. F	PE 19-21	
	Handmade	Jug, PE 167			
	Cooking ware	"Pompeiian red plate," PE 70 Cooking pot, PE 69	Cooking pot, (P 118, Fig. F)	Cooking pot, "à mandorla," PE 7 Casserole with horizontal rim, PE 5	
	Mortarium, "Reibschale"		P 119, Fig. F		
	"Honeyjar" lids	PE 72-73	P 120-124, 151-158, Fig. F		
	Dolia	PE 78	P 117, Fig. F		
	Amphorae	Greco-Italian type, PE 159-161, 163	P 130-143, all of Greco-Italian type, Fig. G	Dressel I B, PE 21	PE 34
First century A.D.	Italian Terra Sigillata	Plate, PE 54 Plate, PE 55		Plate, Ha Service I, PE 13 Cup, Ha 8, rectangular stamp: DASI, *P 73, Fig. D	
	Eastern Terra Sigillata A II (or imitations)			Plate, Ha Service II, PE 15	

CHART 1: (continued)

		Trench 5	Trench 1 (under Capitolium)	Trench 2	Trench 3
First century A.D.	Eastern Terra Sigillata B	Bowl, PE 55a		Cup, PE 16 Plate, Ha Service II, rouletted rim, PE 18	
	Fine Nigra ware	Black slip, barbotine, PE 63 With rouletting, PE 64			
Second and third century A.D.	Eastern Terra Sigillata 2nd cent. A.D.				Cup, PE 32
	Eastern Terra Sigillata Chiara, type A ca. A.D. 150-250	Bowl La6/Hs 34(?), PE 80 Bowl La23/Hs 6 or 28(?), PE 83 Bowl, Hs 99, Severan prototype (?), PE 82			Bowl Hs 9B, PE 33
	Coarse cooking ware, 2nd & 3rd cent. A.D.	2 frr. of bottoms, PE 81, 84			
	Terra Sigillata Chiara, type B				
	Coarse cooking ware, 2nd & 3rd cent. A.D.	Casserole La 10A/ Hs 23B, PE 87 Casserole, Hs 23B, PE 85 Lid, Hs 196, PE 86			
Fourth to sixth century A.D.	Terra Sigillata Chiara, type C	2 frr. of bottoms, PE 81, 84			
	Coin				no. 61a
	Terra Sigillata Chiara, type D	PE 79			
	Coin	no. 78			

CHART 2: FORUM NORTH SITE

Distribution of Hellenistic Pottery, Lamps, Glass, and Coins of the Roman Republic*

	A In sealed fill of periods I and II in W5A to E5AA	B In disturbed layers to the south of main east-west wall, periods I-IV	C East of curia, period I
COINS	no. 2, 110/108 B.C. (E1A I) no. 7, 47/46 B.C. (E4A I) no. 8, ad 32/31 B.C. (E1A I)	no. 6, 77 B.C. (E2B/3C)	nos. 1, 4, 5, 12
GLASS	G8 (E3-4A)	G9 (E2D) G7.7 (W2B/C), not catalogued	
LAMPS	L5 (E5A I) L8 (W2A I)		L3, 4, 6, 7
POTTERY Late Hellenistic black glaze	PN569 (E5A I)	PN761 (E2B/3C) Patera PN760 (E2D) PN767 (E2F) PN763 (W3B) PN762 (W4B/C) Stray find PN69.921	20 frr., see Fig. A and Pl. 34
Campana B and imitations	Mastos PN738 (E5AA) PN570 (W5A II) Beaker PN571 (W5A I) PN566 (E5A II)	Patera (E1C/D)	4 frr., see Fig. A
Gray relief ware, "Megarian bowls"	PN736 (E5AA)	PN750 (W2B/3C) PN758 (E2F)	17 frr., see Fig. B and Pl. 35
Eastern sigillata A I	Large plate PN4090 (E5A I) Small plate PN4062 (E2A)	PN141 (E3A/B)	2 frr., see Fig. D

*For specifications of finds from Trench 5 see Chart 1.

CHART 3: DISTRIBUTION OF COINS FROM FORUM NORTH SITE

1. Coins found in the fill to the north of the main east-west wall, excluding coins from the fourth to sixth century A.D. for which see Chart 15.

Location	Coin No.		Time of Issue
E1A I	2	D	110/108 B.C., C. Serveilius
W5A I	9	D	90/80 B.C., anonymous, Rome
E4A I	7	Qui	47/46 B.C., M. [Porcius] Cato, Rome
E1A I	8	D	32/31 B.C., Antony
E2A I	11	Ae	A.D. 10/12, Augustus
E5AA I	21	Ae	A.D. 41/52, Claudius
E5A	22	Ae	post A.D. 41, Claudius

2. Coins found in the destruction level of period I/II immediately to the south of the main east-west wall.

Location	Coin No.	Time of Issue
E2B/3C	6	c. 77 B.C., Rome, Q.C. Metellus pius
W2B/3C	13	A.D. 22, Tiberius

3. Other pre-fourth century A.D. coins from Forum north site.

Location	Coin No.	Time of Issue
W2C, in destruction level of periods I-IV	18	A.D. 39/40, Caligula

4. Coins of third century A.D., all found immediately to the north and south of the main east-west wall (nos. 29, 30, 35) and in fill against second century A.D. Forum west enclosure wall (no. 34).

Location	Coin No.	Time of Issue
E4A/B II	29	A.D. 218/222, Elagabal
W5A II	30	A.D. 260/268, Gallienus
W5A II	35	A.D. 275/276, Tacitus
W7B II	34	A.D. 270/275, Aurelian

CHART 4: FORUM NORTH SITE

Pottery (Fine and Handmade Wares) from Selected Complexes Found on Bedrock to the North (Complex A & B) and Immediately South (Complex C) of the Main East-West Wall of Period II.

	A	B	C
	E5A	W5A	E3-4A/B
Hellenistic wares: Campana groups, gray relief ware "Megarian bowls," eastern sigillata A I			
Italian sigillata	not inventoried: Plate Ha 2a, service II Plate, shape undetermined Plate, shape undetermined	Small cup Ha 10 (?) PN371	Cup Ha 12, PN132 Cup Ha 15, PN133 Plate Ha 1, service SI, PN134
Early Italian (?) sigillata with heavy dipping marks			Plate (foot), PN140 Small plate, PN141
Eastern sigillata B		Fine cup, PN40101 Fine cup, PN40102	Fine cups PN135-136
Wares in natural color of clay, eggshell and related wares	not inventoried: Cup, Ha 40A	Cup Ha 40/41, PN537 Inkwell, Lindenhof figs. 3, 6, PN539	Republican beaker with "décor clouté" (Moevs form I) PN137, *Gallia*, suppl. 14 (1961), 103, fig. 69; Ampurias I, figs. 225, 251, 262; *Gallia* 14 (1956); fig. 221; Athens, Agora F24.
Fine Nigra ware from Po valley	not inventoried: Cup (?) with rouletting; Cup or beaker with incised decor; Cup or beaker, black slip, barbotine decor		
South Gaulish import (?)		Cup Hofheim 22 with large barbotine scales, brownish slip (EV224)* PN536	
Unguentarium			Foot of Ha 30, PN138
Handmade ware			Cooking pot with "Griffknubbe," PN139

*EV = Vindonissa (see Abbreviations); Hofheim = E. Ritterling, *Das frührömische Lager bei Hofheim im Taunus, Nassauische Annalen* 40 (1913).

CHART 5: FORUM NORTH SITE

All Sigillata Stamps of Period I–II from the Fill to the North of the Main East-West Wall and, in parentheses, to the south of the same wall.

	Time of Augustus	Time of Tiberius (planta pedis + manus)	Time of Claudius (planta pedis + manus)	
Hilarus *O.-C. 796	1 (0)			
Anemo O.-C. 75	1 (0)			
Gellius O.-C. 736-737		2 (2)		
Murrius**		1 (0)		
Comm(unis) O.-C. 466			1 (0)	?
Lyro [not in O.-C.]			1 (0)	
Patro(clus)(?) O.-C. 1230			1 (0)	
Viator O.-C. 2283			0 (1)	?
Illegible remains			3 (1)	
Total identified	2	5	4	
Total illegible			4	

*O.-C. = Oxé-Comfort.
**Potter from Arezzo; all other potters from Po valley.

CHART 6: FORUM NORTH SITE

Pre-fourth century A.D. pottery from (A) fill of period I/II to the north, (B) from to the south of the main east-west wall, and (C), for comparison, period I pottery from beneath period II pavement to the east of curia. Reference is to number of pieces found.

		A	B	C
2nd and 1st cent. B.C. through Augustan times	Megarian bowls	--	--	1
	Late Hellenistic black glaze	2	6	20
	Campana B and imitations	4	1	(3)
	Gray relief ware, "Megarian" bowls	1	2	17
	Eastern Sigillata A I	2	1?	2
	Lamps, Campana A	--	--	1*
	Lamps, types: "Warzenlampe," "Vogelkopf," Dressel 3	2	--	4
	Vitreous glazed relief ware	4	--	1
	Italian Sigillata, stamps, rectangular	2	--	3
	Eastern Sigillata B (early, pre-Flavian)	47	--	2
	"Pompeijanische Platten"	20+	--	--
Through 1st cent. A.D.	Italian Sigillata, stamps: planta pedis	9	4	
	Fine Nigra ware (Tibero/Claudian)	many	few	
	South Gaulish marbled T S (Claudio/Neronian)	1	--	
	South Gaulish relief T S (Neronian/Vespasian)	1	--	
	Firma lamps, Loeschcke IX, stamp Modesti (Flavian)	--	1	
2nd and 3rd cent. A.D.	Firma lamps, Loeschcke IX, stamp Communis (Flavian-Trajan)	3	--	
	Various Sigillata:			
	Eastern Sigillata B (Flavian & later)	4	2+	
	Eastern Sigillata (2nd cent. A.D.)	1	5	
	Cypriote T S (?), 2nd cent. A.D.	2	2	
	Sigillata Chiara, type A (2nd cent.:Severan incl.)	--	6	
	Sigillata Chiara, type Degenerate A	--	2	
	Picture lamps (2nd and 3rd cent. A.D.)		(2+)**	
	Lamps Loeschcke X (2nd cent. A.D. and later)		1(2)***	

*L 1, found in 1969, is not from a closed deposit.
**These lamps are especially difficult to identify when in small fragments. The pieces listed come mainly from the third century A.D. fill in W6B (see chart 7), from outside the Forum enclosure west wall.
***1 from E2E, 1 from fill in W6B (see previous note).

CHART 7: FORUM NORTH SITE

Coins, Pottery and Lamps from Fill Against Forum Enclosure West Wall in W6-7B'

	Lamps and Coins	Sigillata	Miscellaneous Fine Ware	Coarse Household Ware
First Century A.D.			Small flask, PN 124 "Honeyjar" lids PN 127, 128	Handmade bowl with graphite finish PN 140
Second Century A.D.	1: L 27, type Agora 181-182 2: L 39, type Loeschcke 10 3: L 28	Sigillata Chiara, type A Dish Hs 31, PN 119 4: Dish Hs 32, PN 112 5: Dish Hs 33, PN 111 Type: Degenerate A 6: Dish Hs 6A (?), PN 2000	9: Small "barrel,"* PN 121 (white clay, brown slip) Lid for PN 121, PN 126 10: Jug**, PN 123 123	Casserole Hs 23A/La 10B ("a striscie"), PN 115 11: Casserole Hs 197, PN 116 Lid, Hs 19, PN 120 12: Lid Hs 196, PN 130
Third and Fourth Centuries A.D.	Coins no. 83 no. 84 late Roman illegible: nos. 85-86	Type C 7: Large bowl, Hs 46, PN 118 8: Bowl Hs 53, PN 117		

1 Arabic numerals followed by : refer to the drawings on the opposite page.
* Type: Behn 1297/98; F. Behn, *Römische Keramik, Kataloge des Römisch-Germanischen Central-Museums,* 2, 1910.
** Type: Gose 388/89;(E. Gose, Gefässtypen der römischen Keramik im Rheinland, *BJb,* Beiheft 1, 1950); Behn 731.1113.

CHART 7

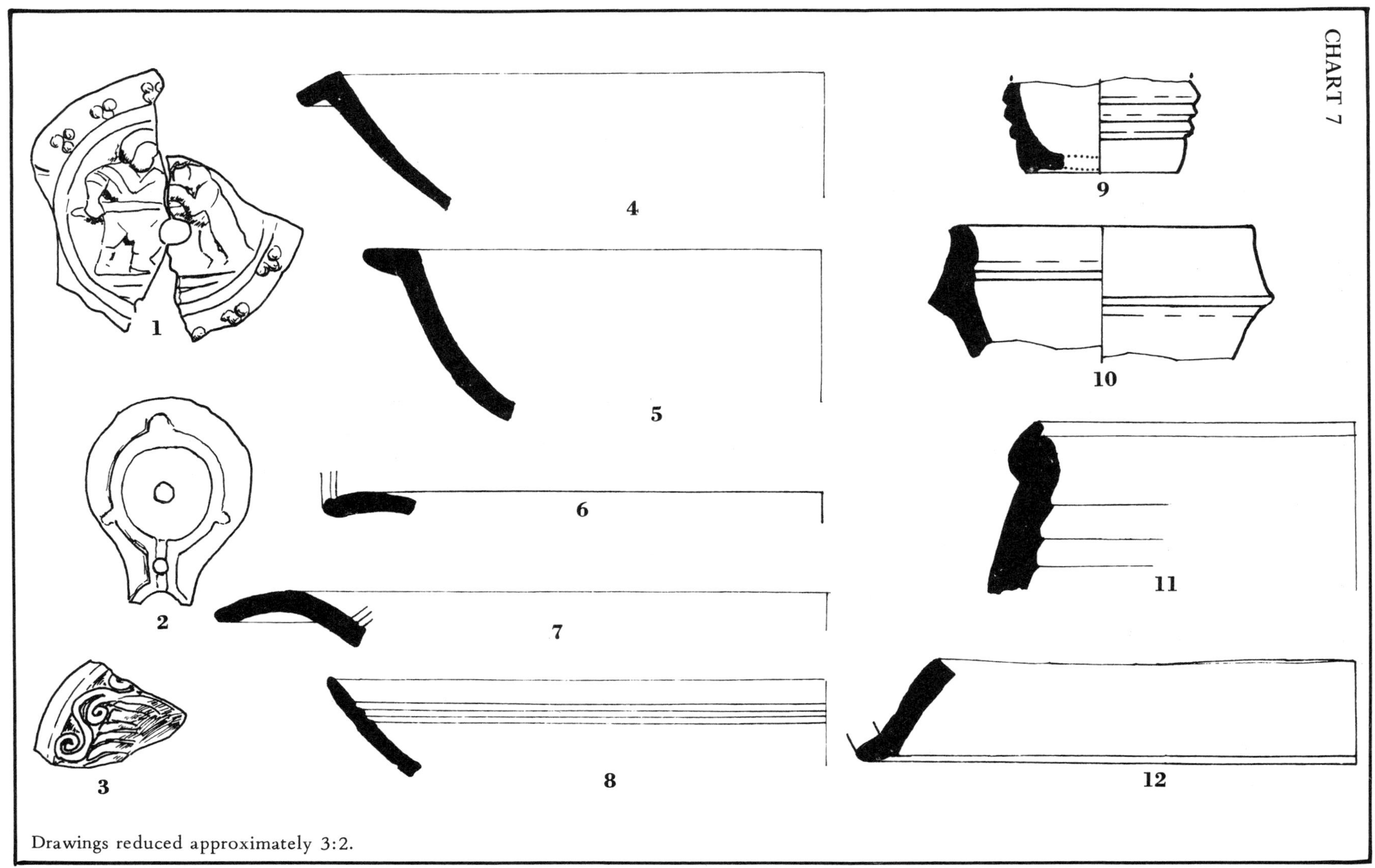

Drawings reduced approximately 3:2.

CHART 8: COINS FROM INSIDE THE CURIA

Chronological Sequence

Coin No.	Time of Issue	Location	Building Period and Layer
3	c. 109 B.C.	A5	III, from fresco layer
10	c. 5 B.C., Augustus	A/A'5	II, from just below burnt layer
16	Tiberius	B5	II, below fresco layer
17	Tiberius	B5	II, below fresco layer
24	Vespasian	A6	II, immediately below fresco layer
25	Vespasian	A6	II, immediately below fresco layer
28	Trajan	B6	III, from fresco layer
28a	lst or 2nd cent. A.D.	A/A'6	II, from burnt layer
36	Probus	A5-6	III, from fresco layer
43	Constantine	A/B6	IV, below top soil
60	Constantine	B3-4	III, from fresco layer
47a	Constantius II	A/A'5-6	III, from fresco layer
57	Constans	B3-4	III
56	Constans	B6	III
87	Undetermined, 4th/6th cent. A.D.	B3-4	II

By Sequence of Building Periods

Coin No.	Time of Issue	Building Period
10	Augustus	II
16	Tiberius	II
17	Tiberius	II
24	Vespasian	II
25	Vespasian	II
28a	1st or 2nd cent. A.D.	II
57	Constans	II
87	Undetermined	II
3	109 B.C.	III
28	Trajan	III
36	Probus	III
60	Constantine	III
47a	Constantius II	III
56	Constans	III
43	Constantine	IV

CHART 9: COINS FROM IMMEDIATELY OUTSIDE THE CURIA

Location	Coin No.	Building Period	Time of Issue
A/B6-7, northeast of apse, under pavement slabs:			
-0.60 m	1	I	Hellenistic, small bronze
-0.65 m	4	I	2nd cent. B.C., Roman As
-0.65 m	5	I	2nd cent. B.C., Roman As
-0.65 m	12	I	28/15 or 15/2 B.C., Nemausus, As
on pavement slabs:	69	III	A.D. 380-390
	79	III	Late Roman
above pavement slabs:	80	III	Late Roman
+1.10 m	26	IV	lst cent. A.D., As
A7, east of apse:	42	III	A.D. 326(?), Constantine
	44	IV	A.D. 324/335, Constantine
	58	IV	A.D. 340/350, sons of Constantine I
	47	IV	A.D. 346/350, Constantius II
A'6, southeast of apse, in rubble:	71	IV	5th century A.D. (?)
A3, adjacent to hypothetical west wall of curia, in destruction level of period I:	15	II	A.D. 22- Tiberius
	20	II	A.D. 41/52, Claudius

CHART 10: COINS FROM CORRESPONDING BUILDING PERIODS INSIDE AND OUTSIDE OF CURIA AND RESULTING CHRONOLOGY

INSIDE				OUTSIDE		
Coin No.	Time of Issue	Building Period		Building Period	Time of Issue	Coin No.
		I	*1st and 2nd cent. B.C.*	I	Hellenistic	1
				I	2nd c. B.C. Roman	4
				I	2nd c. B.C. Roman	5
				I	15/2 B.C. Nemausus	12
10	Augustus c. 5 B.C.	II	*1st cent. A.D.*			
16	Tiberius	II		II	Tiberius	15
17	Tiberius	II		II	Claudius	20
25	Vespasian	II				
24	Vespasian	II				
28a	lst or 2nd c.	II				
3	109 B.C.	III	*(2nd, 3rd and) 4th cent. A.D.*			
28	Trajan	III				
36	Probus	III				
				III	Constantine	42
47a	Constantius II	III				
56	Constans	III				
57	Constans	III				
60	Sons of Constantine	III				
				III	A.D. 380/390	69
				III	Late Roman	79
				III	Late Roman	80
43	Constantine	IV		IV	Constantine	44
				IV	Constantine or sons	58
				IV	Constantius II	47
				IV	5th century A.D.(?)	71

CHART 11: FORUM NORTH SITE

Pottery from Two Selected Complexes Found on Bedrock to the South of the Main East-West Wall

		A	B
		From W5B/C, in Connection with Period II Walls	From W4C, Together with Structural Remains of Walls of Periods II-IV
To the end of 1st cent. A.D.	Lamp	Picture lamp A, Loeschcke I	
	Eastern Sigillata B(ESB)	Cup, PN 101 PN 100a	
	Italian Terra Sigillata	Cup Ha 15, stamp in planta pedis: GELLI, PN 421	
	Tableware in Natural Color of Clay	Beaker with shoulder set off from body, PN 102	"Aco" beaker, PN 99
	Handmade Ware	Small handle of cup (?), PN 104	Beaker with graphite finish
2nd and 3rd cent. A.D.	Sigillata Chiara, Type A Ware	Foot of bowl, probably Hs 8 or 9, La 1/2, PN 106	Casserole Hs 23A/La 10B "a striscie," PN 2097 Casserole Hs 23B/La 10A (both in dark red fabric, burnt ?), PN 2095
2nd cent. A.D. and later	Coarse Household Ware		Large bowl with grooved rim, PN 2104 Jug, PN 2102 Cooking pot, PN 2103 Amphora, PN 2106
4th cent. A.D. and later	Coins		Roll of undetermined coins in cloth purse
	Sigillata Chiara, Type D Ware		Bottom of vessel with hollowed base, PN 2098 Dish Hs 87 or 104, PN 2096
	Late Roman C Ware		Dish Hs 3, PN 2099 Dish Hs 2, PN 2100

CHART 12: FORUM NORTH SITE

Finds from Inside the Drain Underneath the Porch (E4A/B) Built in Period III*

1st cent. A.D.	2nd cent. A.D.	4th-6th cent. A.D.
3 tiny frr. of Italian Terra Sigillata (not inventoried)	Fragment of Sigillata Chiara. Type: A/AD; Form: La 54/Hs 61A	4 frr. of Sigillata Chiara, Type D 1: Hs 14/17 ?, PN 2111 2: Hs 14/17 ?, PN 2109 3: Hs 70 ?, PN 2110 4: Hs 61B, PN 2108 Fr. of lamp with dark olive green glaze (not inventoried)
	5: Two-handled casserole, PN 2112, Cp. *Diadora* 4, 1968, 201, pls. II/III; Agora J 55-56	

*Arabic numerals followed by : refer to the drawings below. Drawings reduced approximately 3:2.

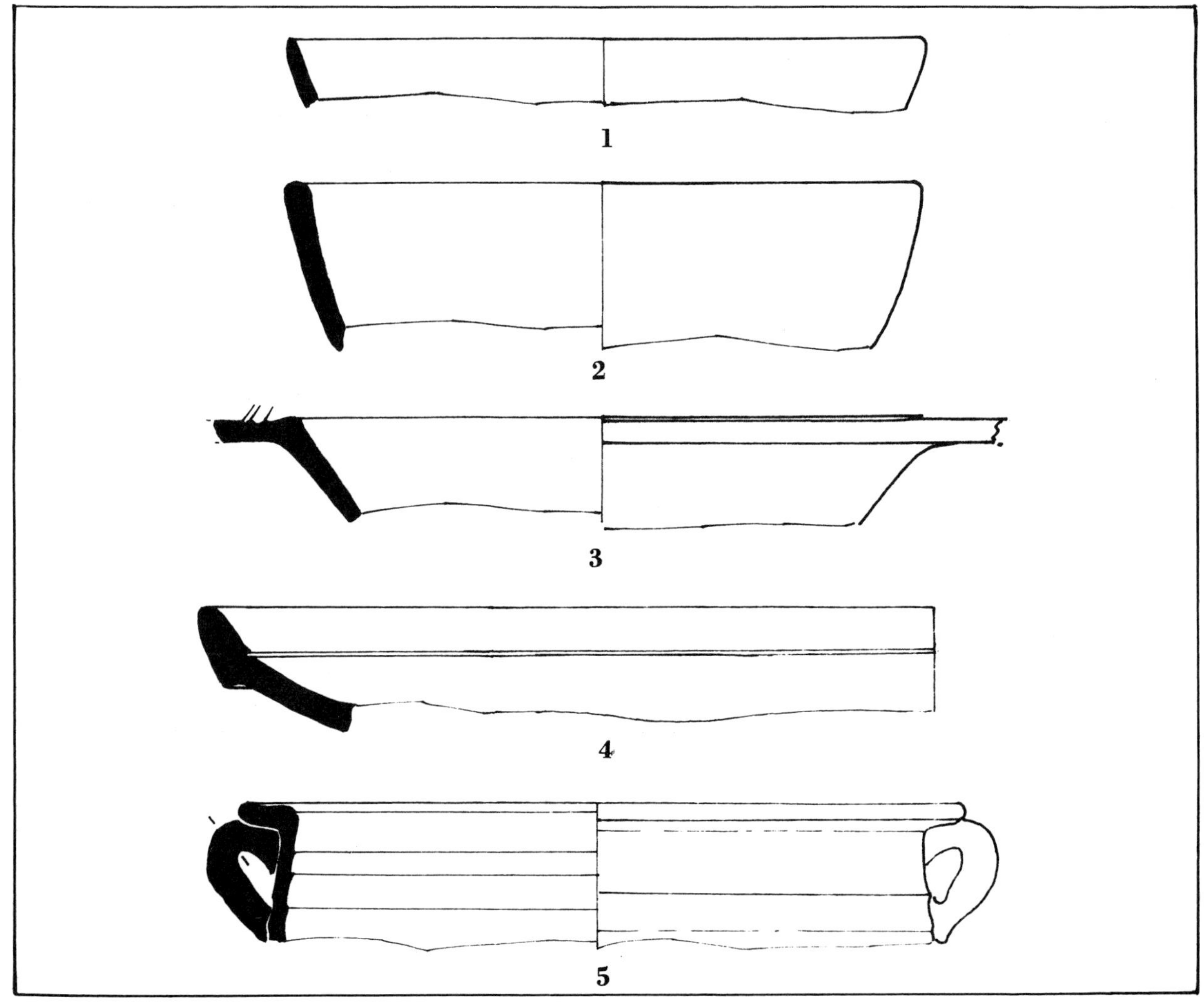

CHART 13: CURIA SITE AND GLASS WORKSHOP

Coins and Pottery from the Disturbed Levels I-IV

Period	Coin No.	Late Hellenistic Black Glaze	Campana B and Imitation	Handmade Ware	Sigillata Chiara, Type C	Late Roman C Ware	Later Roman Coarse Cooking Ware
2nd and 1st cent. B.C.		PE 69.1106 PE 69.1107	Patera, PE 69.92C Patera La 5, PE 69.92B	PE 69.694 PE 69.691 PE 69.693			
1st cent. A.D.	19 (Claudius) 23 (Vespasian)			PE 69.692			
A.D. 100-250							Large casseroles PE 69.2089-2090
Late 3rd and 4th cent. A.D.	30 (Gallienus) 37 (Diocletian)				Large dish Hs 50/La 40, PE 69.2070		
5th cent. A.D.						Bowl Hs 3, PE 69.2070	

CHART 14: COINS FROM THE NORTH AND WEST OF CURIA

(from Squares in Disturbed Condition)

Location	Coin No.	Time of Issue
D7	32 63	Gallienus 4th cent. A.D., Valentinianus I(?)
C6-7 (G.W., from furnace level)	19 23 31 37	Claudius Vespasian Gallienus Diocletian
C6-7	86	Undetermined (4th/6th cent. A.D.)
A1 (in topsoil and destruction level of period III)	62 85 88	Valentinianus I and Valens Undetermined (4th/6th cent. A.D.) Undetermined (4th/6th cent. A.D.)

COINS FROM THE DISTURBED TRENCHES ON THE FORUM CENTRAL SITE

Location	Coin No.	Time of Issue
Trench 3	61a	Valens I
Trench 4	33	Divus Claudius Gothicus
Trench 5	78	Late Roman (4th/6th cent. A.D.)

CHART 15: DISTRIBUTION OF COINS AND SIGILLATA STAMPS IN THE FORUM NORTH SITE

			100 B.C.	50 B.C. / 27 B.C.	Augustus	A.D. 14 / Tiberius	Caius	Claudius / A.D. 54	1st cent. / A.D. 100	2nd cent. / A.D. 200	3rd cent. / A.D. 300	4th cent. / A.D. 400	Probably 4th cent. / A.D. 500	5th cent. A.D.	6th cent. A.D.	5th-6th (?) cent. A.D.	
Outside of portico of period III		W7B									33						W7B
		W6B														83, 84	W6B
Fill of periods II & III to the north of main east-west wall		W5A/AA	9	▭ Anemo		⬭⬭ Communis ? ⬭ ?					30, 35	48					W5A/AA
		W2A										49					W2A
	Gomila in N	E1A		8												95	E1A
		E2A			11												E2A
		E3A				⬭ Patro(clus)?											E3A
	Gomila in N	E4A	7			⬭ Gellius ⬭ C. Murrius			27			46, 60c				89	E4A
		E5A/AA		▭ Hilarus		⬭ Lyro		21, 22				53					E5A/AA
Disturbed level, walls of periods II-IV		W5B/4C				⬭⬭ Gellius(?) ?						45, 54, 60a	92		74a	82, 91	W5B/C4
		W2B/2C				13 ⬭ Viato	18					55	93				W2B/2C
		E2B/3C	6									64, 66			76, 77		E2B/3C
		E4A/B									29						E4A/B
Disturbed level, walls of period IV		E5B/4C										68					E5B/4C
		E2D										52, 61, 65	81				E2D
		E3D															E3D
		E2E										60b	90		72		E2E
		E2F			[14]							40, 50, 51			73, 74		E2F
		W2-4C/D									38		94				W2-4C/D

[ ] coin used as pendant

⬭ = *planta pedis*

V

The History of the Site

We do not have any literary sources which suggest a date for the first settlement at Salona. Modern authors have spoken with confidence of a Hellenistic Salona which would have been settled by colonists of other Greek cities in the general area, notably Tragurion and Epetion and possibly also the island of Issa.

Our excavations on the "eminence," which we believe to be identical with Caesar's *collis*, suggest that it was settled sometime in the first half of the second century B.C. at the earliest. Finds from the last two centuries before the turn of the millenium are very scarce because of the general destruction and levelling that occurred when a new building period was initiated in early Imperial times. However, these finds—notably pottery and glass—fully confirm the suggested date of the beginning of the settlement.

During our period I, which covers a time span of over 150 years, the settlers had probably occupied the eminence to its full extent, a rectangle of approximately 120 by 75 meters. All of the historical events which center around Salona in the period from circa 155 B.C. to the end of the Augustan period are not in any way reflected in the excavations proper. It is certain that the number of settlers grew very slowly in the first hundred years. After 70 B.C., with the arrival of Roman colonists, this number must have increased more rapidly. In this case the historical sources are far more eloquent than the archaeological finds which are definitely not a witness of the increase of the population.

The successes of Tiberius in the Illyrian wars of A.D. 6 to 9 mark the beginning of a new era for Salona. Period II covers roughly the first century A.D., continuing into the reign of the emperor Trajan. The southern part of the eminence now became part of the Forum. An artificial platform was built against the south edge of the eminence with the sole purpose of enlarging the area towards the south, bringing it into closer proximity with the harbor.[1] A *Capitolium* was built where platform and eminence meet; this area played the role of the city center, surrounded by a theater with a second temple in its vicinity, a newly built curia on the eastern side of the eminence and, to the north of the *Capitolium*, an open square possibly adorned with a portico-like building. At the extreme north edge of the eminence there may have been another portico-like building containing merchants' shops. It is also suggested by the excavations that the area to the north of the curia was designated as one in which artists and artisans worked. Thus, the fact that Salona had become the capital of the Roman province of Dalmatia is fully reflected in the general building activity during period II. The finds, among which there are many imports, complement this picture.

In period III, roughly the second and third centuries A.D., the Forum of period II was further enlarged. The Forum by now comprised the total extension of the eminence and the platform. At the north edge of the eminence a monumental portico was built. It is likely that the entire Forum space—especially, of course, the eminence—was then surrounded by enclosure walls, possibly lined with shops. Through the center of the Forum ran a drain, probably along the main east-west artery through the city center. The curia had suffered some destruction towards the end of the first century A.D. and was rebuilt and redecorated during period III. The most remarkable features in this redecoration were the frescoes and stuccoes, fragments of which were found in the excavations. The workshop north of the curia continued in use and glass was made here probably late in period III. Considering the increase of the population of Salona during period III as reflected primarily in the inscriptional material, the number of finds from period III is surprisingly small and proportionately smaller than the finds from period II or from one single century. The lack of finds is probably explained by the fact that the area, parts of which we excavated, was public and paved throughout. Thus, great quantities of objects could not really get lost; and when the pavement was removed by looters, it was certainly swept clean first, especially of any objects of value.

When Salona became a Christian city in A.D. 314, the Roman Forum as such could not survive. This post-Roman era is our period IV. The scanty remains of structures have a very ephemeral character. It is very likely that the eminence was again used primarily as a residential quarter. Some of the larger Roman public buildings were transformed, but it is difficult to say what they were used for. The curia or part of it may have served as a primitive basilica for Christian worship. Finds cover the entire period IV, that is the fourth, fifth, and sixth centuries A.D., but tend to thin out considerably in the latter century. We know that Salona was probably attacked by the Vandals in A.D. 612 and that the destruction of the city continued thereafter.

We have attempted to distinguish three parts which constituted the city center of Salona during period III. It would be difficult to find any two Roman Fora which are alike in the distribution of individual buildings. However, a general concept which we might call the "threefold ensemble"—firstly a temple standing within a court, with or without porticoes, secondly, a Forum square surrounded by porticoes and shops and, thirdly, additional structures such as basilicas, porticoes, administrative buildings—is attested in a great many city plans, forming a tightly knit, closed unity.[2] That this threefold ensemble is also present in Imperial Salona has become clear from the previous summary description. The temple area on the platform and south edge of the eminence, the theater with its own temple precinct, the central and north Forum sites, and the curia illustrate Salona's role as capital of Dalmatia. It is interesting to note that, so far, remains of a basilica in Salona have not yet been found. Such a building belongs, strictly speaking, to the threefold ensemble. But even with the buildings presently known, only the Forum of another Roman city in Dalmatia, Iader, is comparable in size and grandeur to that of Salona.

Finally, one may ask whether Diocletian, who was born in Salona, took with him to Aspalathos some inspiration from the platform with arcades. The impressive and dominating seaside facade of Diocletian's palace also has a storey of arcades with an *ambulatio* from which the emperor could view the bay and the nearby islands. This facade is, of course, much more grandiose than anything which could be seen in Salona itself; in all its provinciality Salona's architecture is only a dim reflection of the greatness of Roman art and architecture during the Imperial period which celebrates its last Dalmatian triumph in Diocletian's palace at Split.

Notes on Chapter 5

1. The relationship of the city to the harbour can best be visualized on panel LXXXVI of the column of Trajan if indeed our identification of the city represented on the panel with Salona holds its ground (see Excursus I). Needless to say, the representation on the panel does not reflect in precise detail the reality of the ancient topog-graphy; but all we can surmise is that the artist was impressed by the close proximity of the harbour to the *nucleus*

of the town; this led him to represent the defilé and sacrifice made by Trajan and his troops, as they disembark from the ships, in sight of the city.

2. Ward-Perkins speaks of a "forum-basilica complex ... with perhaps a temple in symmetrical relationship"; see pp. 7, 10, 17. But it seems to this writer that one ought to speak of all three elements together, as equals, as I have attempted to do by referring to the "threefold ensemble." A list of city centers in which the three elements are physically closely together follows:

Zadar: Temple within court (in part cryptoporticus)–forum square–basilica at south side of forum. Ward-Perkins, fig. 10, pp. 11, 13.

Virunum: Capitolium–forum square–basilica. Ward-Perkins, fig. 13.

Augst: Temple within court–forum square–basilica with curia attached. Staehelin, p. 600, fig. 188; Ward-Perkins, fig. 2.

Leusonna: Temple–forum square (not enclosed)–exedra and basilica. Staehelin, p. 619, fig. 197; Ward-Perkins, fig. 8.

Velleia: Basilica–forum square–temple. Ward-Perkins, fig. 4.

Herdonia: Basilica–forum square–temple. Ward-Perkins, fig. 5.

Alesia: Temple within court–curia, basilica, court–forum square. Grenier, pp. 342-46, fig. 101.

Augusta Bagiennorum: Temple within court–basilica–forum square with another temple at northern end. Grenier, p. 384, fig. 122; Ward-Perkins, fig. 3.

Lugdunum Convenarum: Temple within court–forum square with shops on west side. Grenier, pp. 327-341, figs. 95-99; Ward-Perkins, fig. 7.

Arelate: Temple within court–longitudinal court with apsidal ends–forum square (cryptoporticus). Grenier, pp. 291-303, figs. 76-81; Ward-Perkins, fig. 9.

Timgad: Basilica–forum square–temple, curia, and other administrative buildings. Wymer, pp. 25-29, figs. 10-11. Ward-Perkins (p. 11) refers to several cities which made use of a cryptoporticus in connection with fora, such as Conimbriga, Portugal (fig. 10), Aosta, and Narbo Durocortorum and Baganum, both in France. Of great interest is the general discussion in Ward-Perkins' article with regard to the genesis of city center architecture in the European provinces: "Cisalpine Gaul, if anywhere, was the school in which the architects of the early Imperial European provinces learned their craft." See p. 5, also pp. 13, 19.

VI

Frescoes and Stuccoes

THE FRESCOES (Plates 12 to 22)

Excavation within the curia yielded a rich harvest of frescoes. As was mentioned earlier, remains of frescoes were found in great quantity all along the east wall of the curia together with fragments of stucco decoration. While excavating the curia in a westward direction, it was found that the fresco level continued throughout the eastern room to the cross wall. Finds of frescoes were plentiful in A'4-5 along the south wall, at a distance of 0 to 3 meters from the wall. Here came to light frescoes with a surprising variety of decoration. Finally, fragments decorated in a style different from that of the bulk of the frescoes (which we shall refer to as the arabesque style) came to light exclusively within the curia east room, in A/B5 and A6. The fresco level existed also in the curia west room but it was much thinner than that in the curia east room and was composed primarily of crushed mortar and sand and an occasional fragment with remains of some of the basic colors. One must conclude from this that the walls and ceiling of the curia west room were not left rough but could not have been decorated as profusely as the walls and ceiling of the curia east room; stuccoes, too, were preponderantly found in the eastern half of the curia.

The fresco fragments are usually preserved with some of the mortar backing adhering to the stucco surface. The thickness of the mortar rarely exceeds 4 centimeters but as much as 7 centimers has been noted in a couple of examples. The mortar is medium-rough, composed of sand, lime, and very small fragments of crushed tile; it forms one single layer rather than several layers which would be distinguished by the composition of the mortar.[1] The painted surface is a fine, well-polished and smooth texture of stucco. That the paintings were executed *al fresco* (excepting nos. 63 and 75) becomes clear from the basic (ground) colors and the way these colors have been soaked up by the thin layer of the stucco. The technical quality of the frescoes is very good throughout; the quality of the plaster and colors of these provincial wall-paintings compare very favorably with wall-paintings from major sites in Italy.

There are many fragments of wall-paintings and stuccoes in which the mortar shows reed imprints (see **Plate 25**, which illustrates a stucco fragment, 4.4). In the majority of such fragments the plaster has an average thickness of 3 centimeters. A thickness of plaster of 5 centimeters showing reed imprints is exceptional. Reed imprints on mortar have often been noted in finds of frescoes from other sites but have not usually been given much attention.[2] The problem with the Salona frescoes is that the thickness of the mortar usually preserved is not great enough for the reed imprints to have survived. However, even if there are less fragments with reed imprints than without, their mere existence suggests that had the preservation been perfect, the mortar should reveal reed imprints throughout. Even when the mortar is thicker than 4 centimeters and reed imprints are lacking, we cannot conclude that reed matting was not used in the structure of the walls. It may be that a certain irregularity of the stone wall caused the mortar to be spread unevenly, thus varying its thickness.[3]

Whenever reed imprints show on mortar, authors are reminded of Vitruvius and his reference to the preparation of walls for paintings in construction which relies heavily on the use of wood (*opus craticium,* German: Fachbauwerk). Vitruvius writes:[4]

> But if plastering is required on timber partitions, owing to their uprights and cross-pieces, cracks are bound to appear in it. For when they are coated with clay they must take up moisture; and when dry they shrink and cause cracks in the plaster. Hence the following precautions must be taken. When the whole wall has been smeared with clay, reeds are to be fixed right along with broad-headed nails. When a second layer of clay is put on, if the first coat has been set with horizontal reeds, the second must be set with the reeds vertical; according to the previous instructions, coats of sand and marble and indeed the complete coat of stucco may then be laid on. The double unbroken rows of reeds fixed crosswise on the walls will prevent any flaking off and the occurrence of cracks.

The imprints of reeds on mortar prove helpful in most cases in giving the fresco fragments their correct orientation, especially if these imprints run diagonally to the design on the obverse. Since, according to Vitruvius, the reed matting is placed either horizontally or vertically, the imprints of reeds on the mortar suggest only two possible positions for the painted design; it is usually not too difficult to decide on the correct position of the pieces.[5] Naturally enough there remain doubtful cases.

Since reed matting was used not only for walls but for plastered ceilings (or vaults) as well, reed imprints on flat fragments cannot tell us anything about the specific provenience of the fresco fragments. Some pieces which are for the most part flat have a slightly upturned edge and thus clearly belong to the bottom of walls where they form the transition to the floor.[6] Other fragments are curved; unfortunately they lack reed imprints.[7] These fragments could belong to a vaulted ceiling but it is also possible that, within the curia, there were arched or domed niches and/or windows to which these curved fragments could be assigned. Finally, they might come from the transition between the wall and a flat ceiling. Needless to say, the flat fresco fragments with reed imprints could come from a horizontal ceiling if it is correct to assume that reed matting formed part of its structure as it did for vaults according to Vitruvius.

Two background colors, red and ochre, are predominant in our frescoes which are dependent on Pompeiian wall-decoration of the Second to the Fourth style. For the socle portion of the walls horizontal bands must have been common; the wealth of color combination in bands and stripes is remarkable with several colors alternating. It is possible that occasionally a naturalistic motive, even if highly stylized, decorated the socle portion.[8] To this portion of the wall we assign also the surfaces with splashed decoration.[9]

One or two surface colors with one or possibly more parallel stripes suggest that the fragments come rather from vertical panels, placed above the socle portion of the wall. Fragments in which stripes form corners leave little doubt about the existence of such panels; however, details about their size, especially their height, escape us. There is no clear evidence that any of the flower and related motives decorated the center of the panels; however, in one or two instances it is not unlikely that they did.[10]

Finally, above the vertical panels may have come low friezes with some design between stripes. We would place some of the fruit and flower motives in these friezes.[11] A palmette flower frieze which can give us an idea of the continuity of a design is attested in several beautifully preserved fragments.[12] One could surmise also small picture-size panels enclosed by stripes and bands and alternating with the continuous friezes above the middle portion of the wall.

There is no evidence for any architectural decoration, such as columns, architraves, cornices, etc. Human figures are lacking completely.[13]

In a more rarely attested style of decoration than that discussed, namely the arabesque style, the decoration is painted in black, dark-brown, or dark-red on a light-colored surface. Yellow for a small leaf or blob and green for plant design occurs very occasionally; these colors play a totally subordinate role. The frescoes in the arabesque style are markedly different from the wall-painting fragments in which very bright colors are juxtaposed. For the sake of distinguishing the two styles of painting, we shall use the terms "panel" or "Pompeiian" (omitting any specification as to whether they are Second, Third, or Fourth style), and "arabesque" style.

The frescoes found are too fragmentary to permit reconstruction of the overall wall decoration. The greater the variety of the motives (especially in the curia east room), the greater the difficulty in visualizing the composition of the walls in detail. Relying heavily on comparative material from other finds in Dalmatia and adjacent Roman provinces, we can gain some valuable insights.

Judging from the finding spots of our fresco fragments, the lower-middle portion of the walls of the curia east room was decorated with panels divided by stripes and bands in imitation of Pompeiian walls. The numerous stucco fragments also found within the curia east room strongly suggest that these belonged to cornices which ran not only horizontally along the uppermost third of the painted walls but also were used for accentuating recesses, such as niches, windows, and especially the east wall apse or tribunal. If stucco cornices indicate that the paintings did not cover the entire height of the wall but only two-thirds of it, we may assume whitewashed or lightly colored walls above, lacking any specific design.

As was mentioned earlier, we can recognize in the frescoes two distinct styles or principles of decoration. Comparative material from the northeastern and western provinces of the Empire shows that both these styles originated ultimately in Italy but flourished elsewhere as well.

The larger group of fresco fragments is clearly inspired by Pompeiian wall-painting prototypes of the Second to the Fourth style. After the destruction of Pompeii in A.D. 79, essential features of these styles lingered on in Italy and the provinces until the close of the first century and witnessed a strong revival in the Antonine period. It has become customary to speak of *panneaux* decoration, hence our reference to panel style.

From ca. A.D. 100 to 150/60, a classicizing mode draws heavily on the Third Pompeiian style. There is a preference for light or white-ground walls with dark brown or black linear design instead of the intense colors, such as red, black, and yellow, which are characteristic of the Second and Fourth style tradition.[14] The "philhellenic" or arabesque style, as we prefer to call this style in reference to Salona, is long-lived; it continues into the second half of the century when decorators begin to turn away from the linear concept of rendering objects to a more naturalistic depiction.

In the fragments painted in the arabesque style the decoration consists of garlands of flowers, with the buds or the blossoms rendered in a highly stylized manner; the abstract concept is illustrated by the exclusion of natural colors for the plant motives. These are mere silhouettes, arabesques in dark on a white ground. Flowers in the panel style decoration were also stylized but an attempt was made to characterize certain plant species by distinct and varied colors. Moreover, in the arabesque style the design does not seem to be limited to a specific division of the wall or ceiling. It covers large surfaces freely, even if it is arranged in geometric forms, such as triangles, hexagons, etc. The continuity of the design is given much more importance because of its unlimited form. This is a system of decoration which is eminently suitable for ceilings. The linearity of the style has already been noted; the flower motifs are conceived without corporeity. It is in this detail as well as in the preference for the light ground that the arabesque style is reminiscent of Third style concepts. The immediate predecessors of the arabesque style in Salona are paintings attributed to the "philhellenic" style of the first half of the second century A.D.

The excavation of the curia provides only a very wide datable context for the frescoes. The total absence of fresco fragments in its first building phase (period II) and the casual finds in the destruction layer of the second building phase (period III), indicate the latter half of the first century, the period of the Flavian emperors, as the period when the curia was possibly first decorated with wall-paintings. The *terminus ante* for the decoration is period IV, the initial date for which is most likely the early fourth century A.D. It is within this period of from 200 to 225 years that the curia was decorated with frescoes; we are not in a position to date the fresco level more precisely. Though it could obviously be possible that the panel style precedes the arabesque style and that the curia was decorated in successive stages, we favor dating both groups of frescoes in the Antonine period despite their distinct styles and systems of decoration. Whereas the succession in the case of the four Pompeiian styles is, stylistically speaking, fairly clear-cut, this is no longer true for the Middle Imperial period. The panel style in the tradition of the Second and Fourth Pompeiian style is continuously in existence after A.D. 79. The classicizing style makes a strong come-back early in the second century. From then on both styles are used side by side, as many finds from the provinces attest.[15] One can visualize certain preferences for a system of decoration which characterize a major trend in a specific period. But one must also recognize that overlappings are numerous, especially from the second century onwards. And while fashion in highly creative centers changes fairly rapidly, it may take a couple of generations in more remote areas before an accepted form of decoration is replaced by another.

As noted earlier, the panel style had a strong revival in the Antonine period. The fact that all our plant motifs tend to be conceived as abstract rather than natural forms, with the colors completely out of tune with nature, points to their Antonine date. The frescoes painted in the arabesque style can be compared with wall-paintings from Ostia, dated ca. A.D. 160 to 170 and to paintings in the tomb of Clodius Hermus, contemporary with them.[16] Our impression is that in the arabesque style in Salona are found elements seen also in catacomb paintings from the mid-second century onwards.[17] Wall-paintings in the *vigna* Codini and Hadrian's villa in Tivoli provide further comparisons.[18] Away from Rome, in the Balkan provinces, A. Frova has noted the "style columbarium" in Bulgaria.[19] Numerous examples of paintings on white-ground come from Pannonia and date from the mid-second to as late as the fourth century A.D.[20] Finds from as far north as Trier have reminded archaeologists of the catacomb paintings.[21]

Inscriptions could provide a possible source for dating. Among our fresco fragments are two with letters; two letters are preserved entirely, one letter partially. Unfortunately this is not enough for dating purposes. If we are correct in assuming the existence of niches in the curia, one of our inscriptions could have labelled a specific person or object which was painted within the niche; alternately inscriptions could have fulfilled the same objective in a panel decoration.[22]

From the location of the fallen frescoes it becomes clear that frescoes in the panel style decorated the south wall of the curia in particular. As for the remaining walls, they may have been decorated in the lowermost third with plain colored surfaces divided by stripes with horizontal bands and stripes below. It would be tempting to relegate the frescoes of the arabesque style, found plentifully in the center of the east room of the curia, to the ceiling. Just as the walls were probably not decorated to their full height, so it is possible that only some parts of the curia ceiling were decorated with frescoes. A vaulted ceiling seems excluded since all fragments of the arabesque style are flat. Those fragments of the arabesque style which were covered subsequently by a thin layer of mortar do present a problem. However, we do not believe that the dating of the frescoes is affected in any way by the evidence of this additional layer of mortar.

It could affect the chronology if there were any hint that these fragments were intended for redecoration in the panel style. This style of decoration would then clearly follow the arabesque style. But no such evidence of redecoration is available. We are led to believe, therefore, that either an altogether different decoration was planned and never executed, or that the layer of mortar was added to erase the fresco decoration.

In summary, we would like to suggest that the curia was only decorated once: namely in the second half of the second century. The panel style on the walls was combined with the arabesque style which may have decorated the ceiling. A first curia building of early Imperial date may have been partly destroyed (destruction layer, period II); only the rebuilt curia was decorated with frescoes, probably not immediately but many decades later. A possible hint at a still later (third century?) renewal of the decoration within the curia, never actually executed, is gathered from the additional mortar on some fresco fragments of the arabesque style.[23]

The reference to some major sites in Dalmatia in which wall-paintings were discovered as well as to frescoes found in the adjacent provinces can give us not only some idea of possible connections between the provinces themselves but also of the relationship between the provinces and the original, creative centers of Roman painting. The latter art was received enthusiastically in the Roman empire. It was transformed and adapted mostly by local talent and cast some splendor of Imperial art into the sober setting of Roman provincial life.

Authoritative statements with regard to Roman wall-painting in Dalmatia are premature, considering that much material excavated earlier is lost or still awaits publication. But from what is known so far, we may say that Dalmatia stands behind northeastern and western provinces in artistic scope and accomplishment. It has been said that the provinces did not pay much attention to the notion of architecture, all important in Pompeiian wall-painting itself.[24] This statement is very true for Dalmatia, where few of the exquisite spatial renderings or detailed pictures of architectural compositions occur. We catch here and there an impressionistic flavor in the rendering of human figures[25] or of subject matter which deals with plants and fruits.[26] But evidence for the survival of architectural painting in imitation of the Second to Fourth style is much scarcer in Dalmatia than in other provinces.[27] One feels a good deal more distant from the Italian prototypes in viewing Roman wall-paintings in Dalmatia as compared with those discovered in other provinces which, geographically speaking, are much further away from the source of inspiration.

We will now list frescoes from the province of Dalmatia and Roman sites within the present-day confines of Yugoslavia and will refer to those sites on which Roman wall-paintings have been found and published in great enough quantities (even if they have not been well illustrated) to tell us something about the nature of the decoration. Places where occasional fragments are mentioned summarily together with other small finds will here be disregarded. The sites, in order from north to south, are as follows:

> *Emona* (Ljubljana).[28] The usual division of the walls is found and panel decoration seems to have been predominant, using basic colors such as black, red, and green; panels are separated by stripes of contrasting colors. Figures are painted (Bacchants, putti) within the panels. Floral and plant motifs are scarce: ... "grüner Zweig, graurote Blumen" are mentioned;[29] elsewhere the author speaks of "weisse herabhängende stilisierte Blätter."[30] A decoration of red splashes on a gray background or on a white surface occurs. The authors note that practically all houses in the city were decorated with wall-paintings over a long period and that they were replaced at least twice over 200 to 250 years.[31] Of interest to us is the combination of wall-paintings with stucco decoration for cornices. Wall-paintings and especially mosaics have come to light in recent excavations and await publication.[32]

Poetovio.[33] For the socle decoration "incrustation" has been noted as well as geometric patterns. Above follow *panneaux* painted black and divided by red stripes. A later decoration is essentially naturalistic, with storks, waterbirds, and waterplants. In the temple of *Vicus Fortunae* the walls were painted yellow, and stucco cornices were decorated with plant ornaments. The latest decoration dates from the third and fourth centuries A.D.

Istria, peninsula of.[34] Wall-paintings in the architectural style with yellow, red, and green surfaces. Painted walls are combined with stucco cornices. Noteworthy is the reference to a narrow frieze with lions hunting animals.[35] A continuous frieze with leaves and plants along a painted wooden fence suggests the rendering of a garden.

Pola.[36] The lowermost portion of a wall (0.86 meters high) is painted red and divided into panels by vertical, horizontal, and diagonal stripes. Above follow orthostate-like panels, painted orange-yellow and divided by red bands. Vegetal, ornamental, and figurative decoration in white, yellow, and red on black occurs on a wall which also has a red-painted socle.

Islands near Pula (Brioni, etc.).[37] Strong influence from Pompeiian wall-paintings of the Second and Fourth styles was noted. The color reproduction of the wall-paintings are among the best published among Yugoslav frescoes and make a detailed description superfluous.

Majdan, near Varcar Vakuf.[38] The lower portion of the walls have vertical red stripes. Above are yellow vertical bands with red stripes and vegetal motifs enclosed by red curvilinear designs (lines). Panels are light yellow with irregular gray stripes.

Clambetae (Cvijina Gradina).[39] The interior of the temple was painted with Pompeiian red.

Zadar.[40] Very fragmentary remains of excellent quality are Flavian in date; gray-blue color is used for human figures on a yellow or Pompeiian red background. Stucco cornices were also found. Full publication of the frescoes is expected.

Sirmium.[41] Walls and ceilings of buildings were decorated, the date being the middle of the fourth century. There are fragments which imitate marbles. White-ground panels are decorated with dark red flowers and green leaves surrounded by black bands with white astragal patterns. Yellow surfaces are bordered by red, black, and white bands and white dots; additional decoration consists of fan-like flowers with white petals and green and red sepals; stems with cherry fruit also occur. Lastly, a circular red medallion painted on white-ground has a black and white dotted border, as well as a second pink border, and heart-shaped green leaves.

Domavia (near the Drina valley).[42] The excavators found fragments of white, red, and green frescoes near an apse of a building which may have served as a foundry at one time.

Ilidze (near Sarajevo).[43] The Roman buildings were lavishly decorated with wall-paintings. Panels painted with basic colors of red, yellow, green, and black are divided by stripes and bands. Scarce fragments with remains of leafage, geometric ornaments, and a fragment depicting a bowl with fruit have been noted.

Delminium.[44] Two rooms, one large (basilica?), the other small (senate house?) adjacent to the Forum were decorated with Pompeiian red walls above limestone orthostates.

Salona. Wall-paintings were found here prior to our excavations; only a few of these date from the pagan era.[45] To the latter belonged the paintings in the baths.[46] Evidence for fresco painting was very probably found elsewhere in buildings dating from the Imperial period. Due to their poor preservation they were not specifically mentioned and thus fell into oblivion as is unfortunately also true for so many groups of small finds unearthed on our site.

Split. Fragments of frescoes were found in recent excavations by the Town-Planning Institute of Dalmatia and the University of Minnesota in the palace of Diocletian. Fragments "show white and black ornaments and a completely different decoration, executed in shades of red and yellow."[47]

Valley of the Lasva.[48] In a Roman house the lowermost portion of the wall was painted white and was decorated with vertical red bands.

Stolac (Bregava valley, near Narona).[49] Wall-paintings decorated private houses but only very general references are given.

Frescoes from the Roman provinces of Noricum and Pannonia can also serve as comparative material for our finds. Not only are the Roman sites in both these provinces well known from investigations conducted over many decades, but the frescoes have also been given due attention in excavation reports and separate articles and monographs.

Of the greatest interest are wall-paintings discovered in *Magdalensberg* (near Klagenfurt, Austria).[50] Dating from the forties of the first century B.C., they are good examples of the Second style in a provincial city. The division of the walls into three different portions is attested here in particularly close imitation of Italian prototypes (black painted socle, orthostate panels with figures, lastly horizontal bands). In the Magdalensberg paintings, as in our fragments from Salona, we note the lack of architectural detail in the horizontal bands and stripes which really play the role of mouldings and cornices. The representation in the orthostates of figures of deities[51]—Venus, Minerva, Mercury (?), Mars (?)—and the signature of the artist (probably of Greek origin) are the outstanding features of these frescoes.[52]

In *Virunum* also the harvest of frescoes was very rich.[53] Especially interesting and of high quality are the plant, fruit, and bird designs in the best tradition of Pompeii. Paintings here begin in the middle of the first century A.D.; the first period comprises the entire second and third centuries. Numerous stuccoes rich in detailed ornamentation were found. It is difficult to find anything in Yugoslavia comparable in quality and variety to the Virunum frescoes.

Plant motifs decorating a black painted socle with geometric patterns in various colors above were found in *Vindobona* (Vienna).[54] The panels were separated from each other by "ornamental verzierte Pilaster." Remains of human figures painted in yellow on a bluish-black surface occur also.

In *Carnuntum* dancing figures are rendered sketchily on light surfaces above black socles, and decorated stucco friezes serve for cornices. The decoration is believed to be primarily of second century date. Later, in the third century, the division of walls and the choice of colors becomes more haphazard.[55]

In Pannonia, civic buildings such as the governor's palace in Aquincum and numerous private villas were decorated profusely with wall-paintings. Thanks to E. Thomas's monograph on the Roman villas in Pannonia[56] we are better informed about these frescoes than about those in other regions.[57] Not only can the dependency on the Pompeiian predecessors be grasped very well but also how the styles, notably the Second and Fourth style, undergo a transformation in the province. Combinations of frescoes with stucco friezes are very common.[58] The frescoes in Pannonia range over some two hundred years, from the late first into the third century. This allows us to witness in Pannonia a development which is particularly instructive for comparison with Salona where a similar succession and/or simultaneity of styles can be observed. Walls decorated in the tradition of the Second and Fourth styles, using one or two primary colors and a combination of several colors in stripes or patterns, have to be distinguished from light painted walls decorated with one or two dark colors; thus, the ornaments appear like dark silhouettes on a light background, a style reminiscent of certain trends in the Third style. Floral motifs in Pannonian frescoes are also frequent; the variety of these and the vigor of colors is well worth noting.

Roman painting in the provinces discussed may be said to have adhered fairly strictly to the principles of wall division into socle, panels, and horizontal upper friezes followed by stucco cornices. But otherwise great freedom is enjoyed in decorative effects and in the choice of motifs. For the final result a great deal certainly depended on the artists at work. Thus, regions in which Roman penetration was strong have yielded wall-paintings which are more closely connected to their Italian prototypes, probably because they were painted by Italian artists.[59] Appreciation of decorative art by the local inhabitants of a provincial town is no doubt responsible for the quality of the achievements in this and other fields of art.

CATALOGUE OF FRESCOES[60]

1. Plain surfaces
   α. *Single color*
      A. Pompeiian red
         1. The abundance of fragments decorated in so-called Pompeiian red does not come as a surprise. The red is fairly uniform in tone; slightly different shades may be due to differences in preservation. Fragments come from many locations within and without the curia and from the Forum but their greatest concentration is in the curia itself. The majority of the fragments shows no reed imprints. From A'A4-6 come five fragments all slightly curved and forming a surface of ca. 18 by 18 cm. Curved fresco fragments are rarely found in the Salona excavations. One fragment is interesting because it most likely comes from near the base of the wall, as is indicated by the upturned edge which forms the transition between the wall and the floor. The red color stops just above the curvature. With this latter fragment and the curved fragments mentioned earlier, we gain some precious indications about the decoration of the lowermost section of the walls and possibly the transition from wall to ceiling, or even the decoration of niches in the curia.
      B. Ochre
         2. Not quite as abundant as plain red but definitely very plentiful are fragments painted with the ochre also well-known from Pompeii. Finds come primarily from within the curia. A large number of fragments show reed marks. One fragment which lacks reed marks is slightly curved.
      C. Blue
         3. (From A4-5 and the Forum central site.) There are two shades of blue: a light blue and a greenish-blue. The former occurs more frequently. In the majority of fragments the blue is not painted directly onto the plain stucco surface but onto Pompeiian red and very rarely on white. Whenever the blue flakes off, the basic red is clearly visible. Fragments occur with and without reed imprints. Blue is much less frequent than red or ochre. However, it is found more often than all the remaining plain colors. Furthermore, it forms the background for some important plant designs.
      D. Dark brown
         4. This color does not ever seem to have been painted directly onto the stucco but onto white as indicated by the fragments. These come from the curia; others come from the

Forum at large. Some have reed imprints, while others lack them. In one fragment the dark brown is superimposed on blue, and this in its turn overlays Pompeiian red. The fragment shows a slight curvature. Could these fragments hint at redecoration, the dark brown indicating a second stage of painting? As was noted earlier, blue is very frequently painted over basic red. If we eliminate the possibility of redecoration, it would be somewhat difficult to explain why two different colors were needed as basic background.

E. White

5. There are relatively few fragments, none of which show any reed imprints. Finds come only from the south wall of the curia and from the Forum in general.

β. Two colors

F. White and blue

6. Two fragments (maximum dimensions 7.3 by 7 cm) are perhaps too small to be claimed for this group. However, the bigger fragment should make it clear that we are dealing here not simply with bands but with larger surfaces. Both colors are painted on basic Pompeiian red. Blue usually is, but none of the plain white fragments have the Pompeiian red foundation. Reed imprints are on the larger of the two fragments.

G. Black and blue

7. Both colors are superimposed on basic red. Six fragments come from A'5, the largest measuring 8 by 7 cm. No reed imprints.

H. Ochre and dark red-brown

8. From A5. Basic ochre underlies the dark red-brown which alternates with ochre as a surface color.

2. **Surfaces with striped design**

α. One surface color, one stripe color

A. Red with white stripes

9. Numerous fragments were found in different locations within the curia, especially along the south wall, in A'4-5. The largest fragment measures 18 by 6 cm. Reed imprints were noticed on only one fragment. The width of the white stripes varies between 3 and 4.5 cm, with red surfaces in between as narrow as 4 cm. The width of stripes and surfaces is not consistently uniform. However, when viewed from a distance these slight variations may not have been easily perceived by the naked eye. On two fragments corners formed by white stripes are preserved, revealing the following patterns:

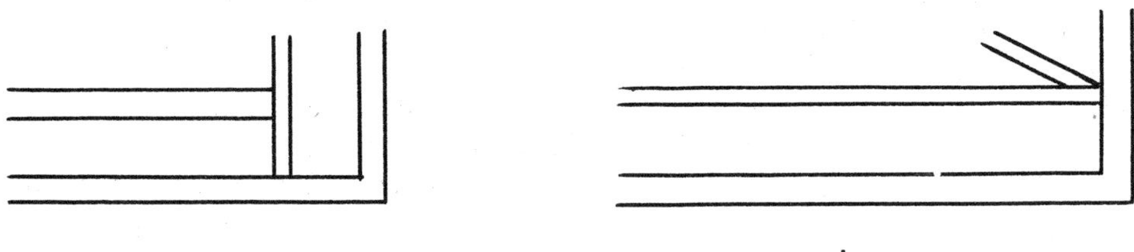

In (b) the diagonal stripe going inward from the frame is noteworthy. It is the only fragment showing this diagonal design. In (a), we may note vertical reed imprints in the present position of the design. Occasionally a white stripe is framed by a thin black line on either side.

B. White with red stripes.

10. From A4-5. This group of fragments is identical with the foregoing except for the inversion of colors. No two parallel red lines are preserved to indicate the width of the white surfaces. In one fragment from A5 some dark red occurs as shading in the red stripe itself. No reed imprints.

C. Black with white stripes

11. Fragments are painted black on basic red or directly onto the surface of the stucco. Though fairly large panels in black with white stripes could be visualized, one fragment reveals some blue surface in continuation of the black. Reed imprints lacking.

D. Ochre with brown stripes

12. Fragments are scarce. In one, the mortar is preserved to a thickness of 7 cm. About 5 cm below the decorated surface a horizontal line is visible running through the mortar forming as it were two layers, 5 and 2 cm respectively. The mortar in both layers is identical. The possibility of redecoration is unlikely because there are no traces of color along the line as could be expected if redecoration were the case. Thus, one can only conclude that a surface prepared to be painted and indicated by the line which runs through the mortar was covered for some reason with another layer of mortar and was eventually painted. No reed imprints. The fragments are too small to inform us about the extension of the ochre surfaces.

E. Brick color with white stripe

13. Only one fragment from B6. The white stripe is 1.5 cm wide and forms a corner. The brick color is an interesting change from the usual Pompeiian red. No reed imprints.

β. *One surface color, two stripe colors*

G. Red with white and blue stripes

14. Numerous fragments from within the curia and the Forum. The most frequent pattern shows white stripes, 5 to 6 cm wide, framing blue stripes, 1.8 to 2.2 cm wide. The red surfaces are contiguous with the white stripes and are themselves crossed by white stripes. Most fragments lack reed imprints. In two fragments from the Forum the stripes form a corner enclosing a central panel. A single fragment, about 9.5 cm square has one faint reed imprint and shows a rather pronounced blue painted curvature at one edge. At the transition from the vertical to the curve is a horizontal white stripe; the vertical portion is painted red. It is possible that we have here a fragment from the uppermost portion of the wall or from a niche rather than the transition piece from wall to floor, in which both the white band and the painted curvature would be more difficult to explain. Still another fragment may point to redecoration: a red surface is decorated with a narrow blue stripe; above follows a red and a white stripe respectively; but both have been painted over with light blue color in a secondary (?) stage of decoration.

H. Red with blue and yellow stripes

15. The stripes are contiguous and are framed by red surfaces. Only one fragment from the curia, with reed imprints.

I. Red with blue and black stripes

16. Large fragment measuring ca. 40 by 28 cm and three smaller fragments from the Forum. Six fragments from A'/A5, the largest measuring 8 by 7 cm. The red underlies the stripe colors. The blue stripes are narrow, 5 mm, and occur in pairs framing black. Another blue and black stripe, 3.2 and 5.1 cm wide respectively, is contiguous. No reed imprints.

K. Red with white and black stripes

17. White stripes frame a black band, with red serving as the basic color and for the surfaces. Two fragments from A4-5. No reed imprints. From B6 comes a closely related fragment with basic red and white stripes enclosing a black band. The lower edge of the red surface has a concave curvature indicating that here we have a fragment from the bottom or top of the wall joining with the white-painted portion above the floor or ceiling. No reed imprints. Other identical fragments lack the curvature and the reed imprints, nor did the red color serve as basic background in these fragments.

L. Yellow with blue and white stripes.

18. Only one fragment from the curia. The blue stripe is 4.4 cm wide, the adjoining white only 4 mm. Yellow surfaces frame both stripes. No reed imprints.

M. Yellow with white and dark brown stripes

19. From A'4-5. The dark brown stripe, 2.8 cm wide, is enclosed by white stripes (3 and 4 mm respectively). These in turn are framed by yellow surfaces. No reed imprints. Perhaps all colors were painted over a light red surface, traces of which are apparent; redecoration is less likely.

N. White with red and brown stripes

20. From A'5. The red stripe, 6.5 mm wide, and the brown stripe, 4 mm wide, are contiguous and are framed by white surfaces. No reed imprints.

O. White with red and black stripes

21. From A'5. The red stripe (3 mm) and the black stripe (2.5 mm) are not contiguous. There is some lighted red shading in the red stripe but it is rather faint. No reed imprints.

γ. *One surface color, three stripe colors*

P. Red with blue, black, and white stripes

22. Red underlies all three colors. On one fragment, ca. 12 by 10 cm, white stripes (3 mm) frame a blue stripe (3.5 cm). Red follows above, black below. In another fragment the color succession is as follows: black-white(5 mm)-black(3.2 cm)-blue, the latter being a thin stripe partly on the preceding black, partly on the following red. Finally, there comes a white stripe (4 mm). A second fragment illustrates yet another variety, with red underlying all colors, and probably forming some surface design which cannot be reconstructed from what remains. Fragments come from several locations inside the curia. Reed imprints are occasionally preserved.

Q. Yellow with white, red, and blue stripes

23. One fragment from A'6, ca. 7.5 by 5.6 cm. The fragment is interesting because the white and slightly wider red stripes run perpendicular to the blue stripe. The latter is probably to be placed vertically. The contingent white and red stripes may have divided what was basically a yellow panel. No reed imprints.

R. Yellow with white and blue stripes and brown blobs

24. From A5. Fragment measures ca. 5.2 by 4.5 cm. The white stripe meets the blue stripe at a corner, thus forming a frame enclosing yellow. Outside the frame, the yellow color continues but is partly covered by brown blobs. No reed imprints.

S. White with blue-green, black, and red stripes

25. From curia. Few fragments. The largest of four fragments measures 13.5 by 11 cm. A blue stripe runs over a white surface, 7.3 cm wide. Above follows black, below a red band. No reed imprints.

T. White with red, blue, and yellow stripes

26. From the curia. While the width of the yellow stripe cannot be determined, the red and blue stripes are 5 mm wide. White surfaces between the stripes. No reed imprints.

U. Red with blue, yellow, and white stripes

27. Several fragments, the largest measuring 10 by 6.8 cm. From both the curia and the Forum. Red underlies the three colors. The white stripes are 3 to 4 mm wide, dividing yellow from blue stripes (2.5 to 3.5 cm). Red surfaces extend beyond. In one fragment the reed imprints run diagonally to the general direction of the stripes. In another fragment the stripes are curvilinear, the yellow stripes running concentrically, the blue and white adjacent. Reed imprints are preserved on the last mentioned fragment.

V. Red with white, yellow, and gray-green stripes

28. Two fragments from A6. The red differs from the usual Pompeiian red and is rather of the brick color mentioned earlier, though it is of a very light tone. All stripes are painted onto the brick-colored background. White stripes, 2.5 to 3 mm wide, alternate with broader gray-green and yellow stripes. Reed imprints preserved in one fragment.

δ. *One surface color and multiple stripe colors*

29. From A6. Surface of fragment is painted ochre. Stripe colors alternate as follows (from top to bottom): white, yellow, red, green-black, gray, whitish-gray enclosing a white band, gray-green, and turquoise.

ε. *Two surface colors, one stripe color*

A. Red and green with white stripe

30. Small fragment from A5. Basic red underlies the green surface as well as the white stripe (5 mm). No reed imprints.

B. Red and black with white stripe

31. Larger fragment from A5. White stripe is 6 mm wide and divides red from black. Red also underlies black surface. No reed imprints. In a second fragment, the white stripe is painted over the black surface and the black adjoins the red. No reed imprints.

C. Red and blue with white stripe

32. From A4-5. Four fragments, the largest 14 by 12 cm. Contrary to expectation, red is not used as basic color. The white stripe is irregularly drawn, in one fragment becoming perceptibly wider. In still another fragment, there are two tones of red, one lighter, the other darker. This fragment has reed imprints.

D. Yellow and green with white stripe

33. From A5. Basic red. The white stripe divides the yellow from the light green surface. No reed imprints.

E. Yellow and black with white stripe

34. From A5. Basic red. White stripe, 1 cm wide, divides black from the yellow surface. No reed imprints.

F. Yellow and dark brown with white stripe

35. From A5. Basic yellow. White stripe divides yellow from dark brown surface. No reed imprints.

G. Red and white with black stripe

36. From near apse of curia. Black stripe is 1.3 cm wide and curvilinear. No reed imprints.

ζ. *Two surface colors, two stripe colors*

H. Red and white with blue and red stripes

37. One fragment 15 by 10 cm. The succession of colors is as follows: a white surface is crossed by adjoining narrow red and blue stripes. Below the white follows a red surface. No reed imprints.

3. Other Non-Vegetal Design*

(*Only solid black surfaces are rendered black in the outline drawings on the plates.)

38. (**Plate 12.**) From A5. Triangular shaped light red colored surface is framed by white stripe. An irregularly wide gray-blue band is contingent with the triangle and also framed by white on its lower side. Above and below green and yellow surfaces respectively.

39. (**Plate 12.**) Four fragments. Yellow background. Portion of "horn of consecration" design in dark red resting upon dark brown horizontal band. As the remaining fragments are smaller than the one illustrated, the complete design is not known. Vertical reed imprints.

40. From Forum. Numerous fragments. A stylized feather or like pattern is painted with wide and narrow brushstrokes in gray-green upon a white surface. The pattern is slightly diagonal and some feathers criss-cross. In two large fragments the following stripes and surfaces come above the feather pattern: (a) red, dark gray-green, green, and red; (b) red, black, white, and red. Reed imprints are preserved on some fragments.

41. From Forum and curia. Splashed decoration. White background. Splashes in red and green are more numerous than those in brown but all are thinly spread. No reed imprints.

42. From curia. Splashed decoration. Pink background. Sparsely spread splashes in dark rose, green, and dark gray with one big blob in dark rose. No reed imprints.

43. (**Plate 12.**) Brick-colored surface with blue-green rhomboid pattern outlined in white and a crossbar in white near one of the corners of the rhomb. If geometric design is placed hroizontally, reed imprints run vertically. A related fragment shows a blue horizontal stripe ca. 1.5 cm below the corner of the rhomb. Reed imprints run vertically to the horizontal line.

44. (**Plate 12.**) From A6. Brick colored background. Curvilinear design is painted in light blue with superimposed narrow white stripe. Another curvilinear design in shades of ivory, ivory-yellow, and yellow is adjacent. The curves almost touch and may have formed large circles. Reed imprints run vertically in position given to fragment on the plate.
45. From A6. Brick-colored background. The curvilinear design is painted in shades of gray-blue and light blue. In the lower right corner a yellow surface touches the curvilinear design and a dark red band crosses it. To the left is the rounded end of a scroll (?) painted white and gray-blue. Reed imprints run vertically in present position of fragment.
46. From A5-6. Brick-colored surface with remains of two gray curvilinear designs. In one of them a white line runs in the center, then along the edge of one of the curves. Reed imprints run horizontally in present position of fragment.
47. From A6. Basic black background, white horizontal stripe. Above, scanty remains of circular design of concentric circles in brown, beige, and ivory.
48. From A4-5. Three fragments. Green surface is painted on basic yellow. "Ox-hide" design is painted brown with two dark brown extremities at either side of fragment.
49. (**Plate 12.**) From curia. A cloud or rock formation is painted in dark red on a pink background. No reed imprints.

4. **Painted Inscriptions**

50. (**Plate 13.**) From A'4-5. Light blue-green and gray surface. In upper left corner remains of two letters. The first probably a V, the second an M. Further below, a portion of a rectangle, perhaps a frame, painted yellow-brown and brown to suggest shading, perhaps for a three-dimensional effect. In the lower right corner, connected to the rectangle, a white patch surrounded by a yellow-brown band. No reed imprints. A second fragment also from A'4-5 has the blue-green and gray surfaces but neither decoration nor reed imprints.
51. (**Plate 13.**) From A5-6. In the upper right corner of partially preserved white field is painted the Greek letter X (chi) or the Roman numeral X (ten). The edge of the field is painted gray. Outside the field a brown painted surface with darker brown shading and two horizontal yellow stripes of different width, as well as a short diagonal yellow stripe at the extreme right edge. The brown may suggest a specific material such as wood, different from the stone or ivory field containing the letter. No reed imprints.

5. **Fruit and Floral Design**

52. (**Plate 13.**) From A6. Brick-colored background. Four berries, painted in shades of white and cream to light brown against a dark background. Above, a leaf in light blue-green with details added in white. No reed imprints. Compare for this design Drack, *WM* 73, fig. 52, pl. IV (from Comugny) and pl. IX (from Vindonissa); see also Thomas, *Villen*, pl. 56; continuous tendrils with grapes, cf. Barbet-Allag, "Techniques" p. 1017, fig. 39 (Pompeii I.6.15).
53. (**Plate 13.**) From A'5-6. Light green background. Scanty remains of brick-colored stalk with two yellow berries. In the lower right corner of fragment a small hole (not drawn on plate), perhaps a compass hole for a circle not on this fragment. A groove visible on the fragment is probably compass-drawn as suggested by its regularity. Reed imprints run vertically with the fragment in its present position.
54. (**Plate 13.**) From A6. A vine leaf is rather cursorily painted in dark gray-green on the deep yellow background. Six grapes without stalks are painted in light green on the leaf and the yellow surface. In the grapes green color is used possibly for shading. No reed imprints and thus position of fragment unknown.
55. (**Plate 13.**) From A5. Light green surface. Yellow oval outlined by dark red with two white-painted stalks (?) or leaves. Possibly a very stylized fruit (?). No reed imprints.
56. (**Plate 14.**) From A'/A5-6. Palmette and flower frieze. Numerous fragments. Surface color is brick-red. Different tones of blues: light blue, green-blue, and gray-blue are

used. The orange-yellow which serves for the framing of the palmettes, flowers, and horizontal stripes is consistent in tone. The friezes form narrow bands above blue or blue-green surfaces often divided from the friezes by white stripes. In the most complete fragment, palmettes alternate with flowers rendered upside down. In two fragments, the flowers seem to be of a different kind; in the better preserved painting, small petals cling narrowly to the center circles, which are painted orange-yellow and brick red respectively. Much white is used in the rendering of the other flower, too fragmentary to be adequately described. Most fragments show reed imprints running vertically to the horizontal frieze. The thickness of the mortar does not exceed 3 cm. For a related design cf. C. Praschniker-H. Kenner, *Virunum* p. 173, nos. 7125 f; Barbet-Allag, "Techniques," 1006 ff., fig. 33, no. 1 (Pompeii VI.16.15).

57. **(Plate 15.)** From A6. Flower frieze. Several fragments. Dark gray background. Volutes enclose rudimentary flower petals seen in side-view with the tip of the pistil (which has itself been omitted from the painting) above them. Enough of the flowers is preserved to suggest a frieze. Yellow color is used for the design and for a horizontal band below which the petals and tip of the pistil are painted in an inverse position. Reed imprints run vertically to the frieze.
58. **(Plate 15.)** From A6. Two fragments. Yellow background. Remains of a petaled flower and scanty traces of two petals probably belonging to a second identical flower. In between the flowers, heart-shaped buds with a dot above. Leaf-design (?) below the fully preserved flower. Buds, petals, leaves, and dots are painted in ivory color, with the center of the flower in blue-green. It is likely that the design was continuous. The fragment is very definitely curved. The reed imprints run vertically to the horizontal frieze.
59. **(Plate 15.)** From A4-5. Brick-colored surface. Abstract palmette design painted gray-blue. In present position of fragment the reed imprints run diagonally; thus the original position of the design must have been different from the one shown on the plate. For the design cf. Drack, *WM* p. 105, fig. 102.
60. **(Plate 15.)** From B6. Basic yellow background. In the uppermost red painted frieze a dark red bud sits on a white stalk, with a second vertical stalk to the right. A white blob to the left. Below, alternate stripes of white, ivory, gray, ivory, white and gray.
61. **(Plate 15.)** From A'5-6. Black background. Stylized flower painted as a green circle on a light yellow colored stalk with two red berries, one on either side but not connected with the stalk. A few black dots on each berry. On the right edge of the fragment, remains of yellow petals (?). No reed imprints. Cf. Drack, *WM* pl. IX (left), berries with dots, dated to the Flavian period.
62. **(Plate 15.)** From A/B6. Pink served as basic background color over which the black surface was painted. Individual leaves, scrolls, etc. in red, white, and yellow-brown may belong to a fruit or flower composition.
63. **(Plate 16.)** From A6. Brick-colored surface with flower (?) or feather (?) design. The colors were applied in several stages, overlapping one another. On the brick color some light gray came first; then a dark gray-red; eventually there followed a light gray for the rendering of detail. Reed imprints preserved. Thickness of mortar 3 cm. The layers of colors indicate that this fragment could not have been painted *al fresco*.
64. **(Plate 16.)** From A6. Several fragments. Dark green background. Flame-like leaves(?), painted in two tones: light green and ivory-yellow. It is difficult to place this fragment. If the design is placed vertically, the reed marks run horizontally. Perhaps the more correct position is with the reed imprints running vertically; then the leaf design runs horizontally as shown in plate. Cf. Drack, *WM* p. 87, fig. 75; C. Praschniker-H. Kenner, *Virunum* p. 204, fig. 198, no. 8315.
65. **(Plate 16.)** From A5. Fragment with acanthus flower. Black surface on basic red. A horizontal band painted in shades of light blue to gray-blue with crescent-shaped details painted white and red probably serves as the base for an acanthus plant of which the

left hand scroll is preserved. It is painted gray-green with shading in light brown with white for highlights and red dots. No reed imprints. Cf. Drack, *WM* p. 93, fig. 87.

66. **(Plate 16.)** From A'4-5. Four fragments. Black color is painted on basic red. Patches of green may represent plant design and leaves. Another small fragment with what looks like an acanthus plant should be connected with this one. Finally, a third fragment has below the plant design a white stripe (7 mm) followed by a red surface which could indicate a portion of a wall. Reed imprints on two fragments. For the general concept of the plant design cf. Drack, *WM* p. 57, pl. 16 (center), dated from A.D. 150-175.
67. **(Plate 17.)** From A5. Deep yellow-brown surface. Foliage painted in shades of light green and gray with two highlights; flowers on high stalks which are painted red-brown grow out of leaves. Reed imprints run horizontally.
68. **(Plate 17.)** From A5. Deep yellow surface. Horizontal red stripe and contingent thinner white stripe. Vertical white stripe indicates perhaps division of panels with plants and flowers painted white with some green and light green. No reed imprints.
69. **(Plate 17.)** From A5. Brick-colored surface. Curvilinear band in gray and grayish-white enclosing flower motif in grayish-white. In present position of fragment reed imprints run vertically; thickness of mortar 2.7 cm.
70. **(Plate 17.)** From near front of apse (A6). White background. Highly stylized flower (?) design in brick color with some gray for curvilinear designs. No reed imprints.
71. **(Plate 17.)** From A6. Two fragments. Brick-colored surface with abstract flower (?) design, painted in white with gray-blue shading along curvilinear fronds (?), gray-blue blobs on white circles and drop-shaped forms. Reed imprints probably give fragment correct position on plate.
72. **(Plate 17.)** From A6. Brick-colored background. Oblong, gray-blue surface is bordered by white band with two scrolls coming out of band and a rudimentary leaf design painted in white on gray-blue. An ivory-colored light blue surface at left. In present position of fragment reed imprints run vertically.
73. **(Plate 18.)** From A6. Colors identical to fragment already described (above no. 59).
A Decoration of parallel stripes and two rows of circles; the larger circles rest on one of
& the stripes, the smaller circles immediately above the larger ones. The original position
B of the design was probably diagonal as suggested by the reed imprints. Closely related in composition is another fragment with the stripes and circles painted white on a black background. Reed imprints run parallel to the circles and stripes so that either the present position or a vertical one is possible.
74. **(Plate 18.)** From A6. Black surface background. Ivory-colored horizontal band; above, continuous white drop-like design with circles at a slightly higher level, probably forming a continuous row. The pattern is somewhat reminiscent of the previous fragment (73). Noteworthy is the fragment which was painted with pink as basic color over the stucco before applying black or white. Cf. Drack, *WM* p. 86, fig. 71; p. 120, fig. 123; p. 125, fig. 127.
75. **(Plate 18.)** From A4-5. Brick-colored surface. White painted frame forming angle with white painted tendril (?) attached to frame. Within frame a thickly painted blue band, enclosing a white surface. No reed imprints. The blue color, applied in a creamy manner, was certainly painted *al fresco.*

CATALOGUE OF THE WHITE-GROUND FRESCOES IN ARABESQUE STYLE*

(*Solid black surfaces are rendered black, or dark-dark brown with hatching.)

Joining proved to be easier with fragments painted in the white-ground arabesque style than with the other fresco paintings. But even so it is somewhat difficult to imagine the overall decoration. Many fairly large fragments are decorated with stripes only. These are usually dark brown or red, 5.6 mm or 2.8 to 3.2 cm wide. Parallel dark brown bands, 7 mm wide and 1 cm apart, occur in one fragment. Only about 15% of the fragments show reed imprints.

76. (**Plate 19.**) In the first panel with arabesque motifs a black horizontal band forms the lower border; above, in the white field, there is a dark brown painted garland with small flowers not actually attached to the garland but certainly meant to be connected with it. There follows a narrow dark brown band with low blossoms, the left hand one suggesting a calyx shape, the right hand one a pelta. Further above flowers and small leaves (?), resting on a narrow black band, alternate, the flowers about three times the size of those in the garland below. Finally, there is a wide, diagonal, dark brown band with grain-shaped yellow blobs on one side and short red lines on the other. The arabesque plant design is swiftly executed; in one of the flowers of the garland the brush was dripped, leaving small blobs; a much larger blob is seen further to the right.
77. (**Plates 20 and 21.**) Three closely related fragments have a main frieze framed by two horizontal bands; garlands with small flowers are attached and stylized buds and leaves grow from both bands. The design color is a uniform dark brown. One of the three fragments lacks the second band. Some 5.5 and 7 cm away from the frieze comes another stripe; it, too, has stylized buds, small flowers and cone- or circle-shaped blobs attached to it. The design is much less crowded than in the frieze. Lighter brown appears here beside the dark brown.
78. (**Plate 21.**) In two more fragments a dark brown frieze quite similar to the one just described runs diagonally above horizontal bands in which alternating colors are dark brown, white (general surface ground), and red. From the diagonal frieze in the smaller of the two fragments runs a horizontal brown stripe with leaves (?) and a garland or simple scallop design below. Judging from yet another fragment, there was more white below the red band. The red bands are fairly regular in width; where protrusions are shown, one wonders whether or not some specific detail is meant.
79. (**Plate 18.**) This fragment is unique. Possibly a flower on a high stalk with leaves growing out from the bottom of the stalk was intended. Such flowers could have been arranged frieze-like, as the point of another bottom leaf to the right seems to indicate. Below the horizontal stripe there might have been a scallop pattern enclosing small flowers. The color is brick red.
80. (**Plate 18.**) Among the white-ground frescoes in the arabesque style one fragment is different from the others in that green color is probably meant to render foliage, whereas brown and black leaves with a grain-shaped yellow patch on top of the black is used for two flowers; they are reminiscent of crocuses.
81. (**Plate 20.**) The small size of the fragment makes identification of the composition impossible. The predominant colors are black, brown, and dark red with a single red oval blob (the larger polygonal blob in the drawing stands for a cavity in the surface).
82. (**Plate 16.**) The leaves of half a flower rest on the upper of two horizontal bands. Around the flower there are concentric half circles in brown and brick red respectively, the same colors which also occur in the flower. This may have been a continuous frieze. All circular lines are compass-drawn.

STUCCOES (Plates 23 to 25)

Numerous fragments of stuccoes were collected along with the frescoes. Their heaviest concentration was in A/A'4-6 and A/B6. This concurs in general with the most prolific finding spots for frescoes.[61]

The individual fragments do not exceed 20 by 14 cm; most of them are in the 8 by 10 cm range. The mortar is the same as that which serves as background for the frescoes with a highly polished, very fine layer of plaster laid over the coarse mortar. Only a few stuccoes reveal additional painting in plain colors; some blue and red can be seen on sloping edges, contrasting with adjacent surfaces. Otherwise, the natural color of the plaster is an off-white or ivory color. The mortar of some fragments shows the reed imprints; if the latter are present, the mortar is of an average thickness of 3 to 3.5 cm; some stucco fragments have a thicker layer of mortar, 4 to 5 cm, but lack reed imprints.

Most surprising is the diversity of the mouldings, as will be seen from the catalogue and the drawings. The majority of the fragments belonged to cornices. According to Vitruvius, cornices in the interior of buildings have a primarily practical function. Other mouldings may be connected with the apse in the east wall and with those niches and windows which we believe existed in the long and short walls of the curia. These mouldings would have served primarily as frames, forming a transition between the actual recesses and the walls, and, secondarily, as decoration for the apse and the niches.

Finally, there is enough evidence to suggest that plain surfaces were framed by stucco mouldings perhaps dividing these larger surfaces into rows of successive panels in imitation of marble slabs.[62] These pseudo-marble panels could easily replace the more expensive marble revetments commonly found in Roman palaces. Revetments of colored marble are known in Salona, but they were used only for small surfaces.[63]

In Dalmatia the combined use of frescoes and stuccoes is known from Roman villas in Istria.[64] In the same villas the finding of "costly species of marbles from thin revetment panels" is recorded as well as "profilierte Leisten aus weissen Marmor."[65] The reference to the latter is especially interesting; many of our stucco mouldings are very likely cheap versions of the more fancy profiled marble mouldings. In Emona stucco cornices were combined with painted walls according to early excavation reports.[66]

Evidence of rich stucco decoration comes from Domavia,[67] where stuccoes decorated the baths. Many stuccoes were adorned with additional reliefs consisting of plant motifs: ivy and laurel leaves and flower buds; as in Salona, there are corner pieces from panels. The stuccoes are believed to come from either walls or ceilings. A combination of stuccoes and frescoes is attested for Ilidze;[68] some of the mouldings are of sandstone, others of plaster.

Outside the province of Dalmatia, the combined use of frescoes and stuccoes is plentifully attested in Pannonia and Noricum. Few stuccoes seem to have been plain; most were decorated with geometric, figurative, and plant design.[69] Some of the latter were subsequently painted. An unusual find of black stucco from a ceiling comes from the Magdalensberg, where the common white mouldings were also found.[70]

CATALOGUE OF STUCCOES

1. (**Plate 23.**) Flat surface with sloping edge. Several fragments from various locations: B6, A6, and A'4-5. The largest fragment measures 18 cm by 13.2. The width of the sloping edges varies considerably, from 1.3 to 2.6 cm. Some corner fragments are instructive: the edges of different sides never have the same width; variations are as follows: 1.5 and 1.6 cm; 1.3 and 1.9 cm; 2.3 and 2.6 cm. As can be seen in the fragment illustrated, the stucco continues horizontally beyond the sloping frame. This is attested in more than one fragment. Reed imprints occur occasionally; an entirely flat reverse lacking imprints was also noted; this would suggest a well-prepared background upon which the mortar was laid because the breakage of the mortar in the frescoes was found to be always very irregular except when reed imprints were preserved.

2. (**Plate 23.**) Fragments come from various locations: B6, A6, and A5. The surfaces are flat with grooves; some fragments with reed imprints. The largest fragment (2,1) measures 10 by 10.5 cm. Grooves run perpendicular to each other, sometimes joining at right angles, with slopes of different or equal size width. One fragment (2,2) has a grooved surface passing over into a sloping edge; this fragment clearly belongs to a recessed panel rather than to the group of fragments in which the surfaces are all raised. Another recessed panel (2,3) is more complicated. The surface has a shallow triangular groove; it then passes into a concave edge with two very shallow rounded grooves. Beyond the edge the fragment continues flat.
3. (**Plate 24.**) Fragments with concave or convex profile or a combination of both. Many fragments were found: from A/B6, A'/A5-6. Quite apart from the fact that the correct positioning of these fragments could not be determined due to lack of reed imprints or other evidence, the drawings reveal the great diversity mentioned earlier. In 3,1 the concave surfaces remind one of the fluting of columns. Most of the other profiles are less regular, with a concave profile passing into a long or short slope (3,3 and 3,2 respectively). Other profiles resemble a wavy line (3,6-8) with much less emphasis on the bulging or concave elements. So far as we can judge from the preservation of the fragments considered, their general depth is minimal, with a maximum of 1.4 cm.
4. (**Plates 24 and 25.**) The profiles in this group of fragments reveal much greater depth, starting at 1.4 cm and reaching up to 5.2 cm. The mouldings fulfill the notion of cornices to a greater extent than the previous examples. In this group concave surfaces alternate with convex and flat ones. The profile of two mouldings, each of which was found in only a few fragments, is very complex (4,4). Narrow convex surfaces alternate with concave; the top of the fragment is indicated in one of these mouldings by a 5 cm wide, horizontal unsmoothed surface continuing into a vertical unsmoothed edge of which 1 cm is preserved. The horizontal part, if fitted above eye level against the wall, could not be seen and therefore did not have to be polished as was the visible part of the moulding. The vertical edge should indicate the wall itself which rose above the cornice. Likewise, at the bottom of the fragment, there is a narrow horizontal unsmoothed surface, 9 mm wide, with a tiny bit of a vertical edge following.

   The positioning of this moulding is not easy since no horizontal edge remains to give us any clue. But there can be little doubt that it also was used as a cornice fulfilling the function to which Vitruvius so specifically alludes.

Notes on Chapter 6

The following abbreviations are used in this chapter:

Barbet-Allag	A. Barbet-Cl. Allag, "Techniques de préparation des parois dans la peinture murale Romaine," *MélEcoleFrançaise Rome, Antiquité* 84, 2, 1972, 937-1069.
Blanchet	A. Blanchet, *Etude sur la décoration des édifices de la Gaule Romaine* (1913).
Drack	W. Drack, *Die Römische Wandmalerei der Schweiz* (1950).
Frova	A. Frova, *Pittura Romana in Bulgaria* (1943).
Gnirs	A. Gnirs, "Forschungen über antiken Villenbau in Istrien," *OeJh* 18 (1915): Beibl. 99-164.
JAK	*Jahrbuch für Altertumskunde.*
Malta	*Missione archeologica Italiana a Malta. Rapporto preliminare delle campagne.* 1967 (1968); 1968 (1969).
Parlasca	K. Parlasca, *Römische Wandmalereien in Augsburg* (1956).
Schmid	W. Schmid, "Emona," *JAK* 7 (1913): 61 ff.
Thomas	E. Thomas, *Römische Villen in Pannonien* (1964).
Wirth I	F. Wirth, *Römische Wandmalerei vom Untergang Pompeijs bis ans Ende des dritten Jahrhunderts* (1934).

Wirth II F. Wirth, *Römische Wandmalerei vom Untergang Pompeijs bis ans Ende des dritten Jahrhunderts* (1934).

1. For problems relating to layered mortar see Drack p. 10. Drack holds the view that layered mortar is typical for "Stadt Rom." See, however, A. Gnirs, "Forschungen über antiken Villenbau in Istrien," *OeJh* 18 (1915): Beibl. 99-164, who noticed this layered mortar for Istria as well. See also most recently in Barbet-Allag the table following p. 1069. We have noted exceptions to the general rule of al fresco painting in the catalogue, below nos. 63 and 65.

2. I have noted the following occurrences; *Magdalensberg:* The reed imprints are very ably discussed by A. Scherbatin in *Carinthia* 151 (1961): 49 ff.; *Vindobona: JAK* 3 (1909): 88. Abramić, referring to the plaster, says: ". . . hie und da sind noch Reste eines Strohgeflechtes zu bemerken," but omits detailed discussion; *Pannonia:* Numerous examples in Roman villas referred to by Thomas, pp. 276, 396; *Malta* 1967 (1968), p. 81, pl. 37, 3; 1968 (1969), pp. 162 f.; *Zliten* (N. Africa): S. Aurigemma, *L'Italia in Africa Tripolitana,* vol. I.2, *Le pitture d'età Romana* (1967) p. 37. Reed imprints have been preserved on mortar of wall-paintings found in Bolsena, as I could verify during a visit in 1971 to the French Archaeological School in Rome, where the wall-paintings are presently kept for study and publication. These fragments are now mentioned together with other occurrences of reed imprints in Barbet-Allag, p. 945, fig. 4 and pp. 940 ff., fig. 1 (Zliten), fig. 2 (Strasbourg). In speaking of frescoes in Trier, P. Steiner, *Trierer Zeitschrift* 11 (1927): 54 ff. refers to "Lehmfachwerkwände" and claims that "die Fläche dieser Lehmwände wurden in der üblichen Weise . . . durch die Strichelung gerauht, damit der Verputz besser hafte." The marks of "Strichelung" could also be the reed imprints rather than just a pattern of "Rauhung" of surfaces. Blanchet, pp. 54 f. claims that "des stries très nettes" on mortar are due to "briques à surface striées." A similar explanation is given by Parlasca, p. 12, pl. 8,1: ". . . auf der Rückseite zeigt die Mehrzahl der Bruchstücke noch die Abdrücke senkrecht gestellter Hohlziegel (tubuli) an denen der Bewurf haftete." Already in prehistoric times the imprint of rounded or split beams have been noted on mortar. See W. Radinsky, "Der prähistorische Pfahlbau von Ripac," *WMBH* 5 (1897): 61, figs. 23-25. For general remarks and comments on Vitruvius see M.E. Blake, *Ancient Roman constructions in Italy from the prehistoric period to Augustus* (1947), pp. 69, 309-321.

3. Thus the Italian excavators in Malta refer to the "spessore complessivo dell intonaco" as varying from 2 to 6 cm, "in quanto si adatta all'irregolarità del muro"; see *Malta* 1967 (1968) p. 75. See also M. v. Groller, "Grabungen in der Zivilstadt Carnuntum," *Der römische Limes* VII (1907): 122 ff., where it is said that a first layer of rough mortar had to even out all the irregularities, cavities and protrusions created by the *opus incertum* building technique. Only then could the finer plaster be applied and the frescoes be painted. Cf. also H. Schwalb, "Römische Villa bei Pula," *Schriften Balkankommission,* Ant. Abt. 2 (1905): 35 ff., noting that for rubble walls decorated with frescoes a much thicker layer of mortar is needed than for timber construction, "da . . . der Bruchstein viel hygrokospischer ist als Holz und die für die Ausführung der Freskenmalerei so notwendige Feuchtigkeit vom Stein viel leichter entzogen werden konnte, finden wir hier die ganze Verputzschichte viel dicker als bei den Fachwerkwänden."

4. Vitruvius VII.3.11. Translation by F. Granger, Loeb. ed. (1934). Cf. with this passage VII.3.1f. in reference to vaults and II.8.20 in reference to opus craticium. See also C. Fensterbusch, *Vitruv. Zehn Bücher über Architektur* (1964), passim.

5. See catalogue nos. 39, 43, 56, 58, 67, 73.

6. See catalogue nos. 1, 14 (?), 17.

7. See catalogue nos. 1, 4, 14, 17.

8. See in particular catalogue no. 40.

9. Catalogue nos. 41, 42 (?).

10. Catalogue nos. 69, 71, 72.

11. Catalogue nos. 60, 68, 73, 74.

12. Catalogue nos. 56, 57.

13. This was already noted for Salona and other sites by Frova, p. 24.

14. Wirth I, pp. 92 ff.

15. In her interesting article "Peinture du second style 'schématique' en Gaule et dans l'Empire Romain," *Gallia* 26 (1968): 145-176, A. Barbet speaks of this linear, bodiless style of fresco painting as "peintures du Second style schématique," which announce the Third style: "Ainsi on peut supposer avec vraisemblance qu'au début du règne d'Auguste, alors que le Second style allait vers son raffinement final, un Second style schématique existait qui annonce déjà certaines caractères du Troisième style." Her examples in Thera, Delos, Ensérune, Masada—to mention

some of the sites—date from before or are contemporary with Augustus. For decorative "ensembles" see Barbet-Allag, fig. 29 a-c with "schematic vegetal motives." For the simultaneity of the styles see also *Malta* 1967 (1968), 77 ff., pls. 45-48.

16. See A. Barbet (op. cit. note 15), p. 175 with reference to Drack. E. Thomas p. 375, has the white-ground frescoes begin in mid-century, and discovers in them ". . . einen späteren Ausklang der weissgrundigen Wandgemälde der Vespasianzeit"; thus she contests the initial date for the style given by L. Nagy as the period after Septimius Severus.

17. Good examples are paintings on the ceiling of the *hypogeum* of the family of the Aurelii which date from the early third century. See E. Nash, *Topographical Dictionary,* s.v. Sepulcrum Aureliorum; G. Wilpert, "Le pitture dell'ipogeo di Aurelio Felicissimo," *Mem. Pont. Acc.,* ser. III,1, part 2 (1923-24), pp. 1-43, pls. 1-24.

18. A. Strong, "Forgotten fragments of ancient wall-paintings in Rome," *PBSR* 7 (1914): 114-123. Wirth I, pp. 118 ff. and 125 ff.; pp. 99 ff. for the "Flaviergalerie" and the catacomb of Domitilla, etc. See also Wirth II, p. 104, fig. 47; p. 122, fig. 58 (Ostia), and p. 142, pls. 24 and 34 (tomb of Clodius Hermes).

19. Frova, pp. 21 ff.; idem, "Peinture romaine en Bulgarie," *Cahiers d'art* 29 (1934): 25-40, 247-259.

20. Thomas, p. 40, pl. 2; p. 79, pls. 58-73; p. 101, where the author claims the *al secco* technique for the black on white style which is certainly also to be considered for the Salona white-ground frescoes of the arabesque style. The white color has a pasty quality quite different from the yellow, red, or black colors used for large surfaces. See also Thomas, pp. 176 and 376.

21. S. Steiner (op. cit. note 2), pp. 60 ff., fig. 15.

22. See catalogue nos. 50 and 51. An interesting inscription is found on a fragment from Otford, Kent, in the British Museum; see Hinks, *Catalogue of the Greek, Etruscan .... Paintings and Mosaics . . .* (1963), p. 56, no. 84(b); see also the Fayoum portrait, ibid. p. 58, no. 86. A painted inscription with two letters (fragmentary) comes from Virunum: *Virunum,* p. 189, fig. 173,3. In contrast to painted inscriptions, graffiti are very numerous on wall-paintings but are hardly ever contemporary with the paintings.

23. The possibility that the curia was used as a primitive church after the death of Diocletian and with the change-over from pagan to Christian Salona is not entirely excluded. For other than arabesque style fragments suggesting redecoration see nos. 4 and 14.

24. Parlasca, p. 28.

25. In the frescoes from Zadar; see note 40.

26. See catalogue no. 52.

27. Cf. certain frescoes from Virunum or Commugny, Switzerland (Drack, pls. 3 and 5, and p. 73, figs. 44-47.

28. Schmid, 61 ff., especially 92, 100, 113, 130 ff.; *RGK* 6 (1910-11): 79; Nagy, *RM* 41 (1926): 81, 118.

29. Schmid, p. 92.

30. Ibid., p. 133.

31. Nagy, *RM* 41 (1926): 118.

32. These were kindly shown to us in the summer of 1970 by Dr. P. Petru.

33. *JbZentK* 2 (1904): 208 f., pl. 3; L. Nagy, *RM* 41 (1926): 82, 119.

34. Gnirs, Beibl. 99-164.

35. Ibid., p. 110.

36. St. Mlakar, "Novi anticki malaz u Puli," *Arheoloski radovi i rasprave* 2 (1962): 429-450.

37. H. Schwalb, "Römische Villa bei Pola," *Schriften Balkankommission Ant. Abt.* 2 (1902): 34 ff., pls. 10-13.

38. W. Radimsky, "Die römische Ansiedlung von Majdan bei Varcar Vakuf," *WMBH* 3 (1895): 248-256; Wilkes p. 405, where the text speaks only of "plastered walls decorated with geometric patterns"; the author omits the reference to these *painted* walls in his Index p. 572, s.v. wall paintings; for Varvar read Varcar in the Index, p. 562.

39. A. Colnago-J. Keil, "Archäologische Untersuchungen in Norddalmatien," *OeJh* 8 (1905: Beibl. 31-60; Wilkes p. 374.

40. M. Suić, "Peintures romaines récemment trouvées à Zadar," in *Le rayonnement des civilisations Grecque et Romaine sur les cultures periphériques* (1965). 8ème Congrès International d'Archéologie classique (Paris, 1963), pp. 353-355, pls. 74-75.

41. *Sirmium. Archaeological investigations in Syrmian Pannonia* II (1971), p. 40, figs. 6-7.

42. W. Radimsky, "Generalbericht über die bisherigen Ausgrabungen der römischen Stadt Domavia in Gradina bei Srebrenice," *WMBH* 1 (1893): 218-253.

43. J. Kellner, "Römische Baureste in Ilidze bei Sarajevo," *WMBH* 5 (1897): 131-162; Wilkes p. 382.

44. C. Patsch, "Archaeologisch-epigraphische Untersuchungen zur Geschichte der römischen Provinz Dalmatien," *WMBH* 9 (1904): 171-202; Wilkes p. 370, fig. 18.

45. Dyggve, *HSC,* p. 86, pl. IV, 49 (for the martyrs from the amphitheater); Ceci, *MC* pp. 244-247, pl. 31, figs. 2-3; p. 122, pl. 6,1 (tomb P); p. 199, pl. 22,5 (tomb in Marusinač); see also Dyggve, *Recherches* II, pp. 91, 108-111; Ceci, *MC* p. 224, pl. 22,7 (apse in basilica discoperta). D. Rendić-Miočević, "Neue Funde in der altchristlichen Nekropole Manastirine in Salona," *AI* 1 (1954): 53-70. M. Rostovtzeff noted the "flower-style" in Salona in his pioneering article on "Ancient decorative wall-painting," *JHS* 39 (1919): 144-163; for Salona see p. 162. Rostovtzeff refers no doubt to decoration such as that preserved in tomb P mentioned above and those discussed and figured in FS II, pp. 37 f.

46. Wilkes p. 379 with reference to FS I, pp. 109 ff. See also Ceci, *MP,* pp. 130-134, pls. 21-23, who does not mention any of the individual frescoes in his text.

47. Information sheet published by the excavation teams, 1968, p. 13, fig. 24. See also Urbanistički zavod Dalmacije, Split & University of Minnesota, *Diocleatian's Palace. Report on joint excavations in southeast quarter,* (Split, 1972), p. 44, with reference to "marbleizing design."

48. C. Truhelka-C. Patsch, "Römische Funde im Lasvathale," *WMBH* 3 (1895): 227-247; see especially p. 230, figs. 7-8.

49. F. Fiala-C. Patsch, "Untersuchungen römischer Fundorte in der Hercegovina," *WMBH* 3 (1895): 257-283; Wilkes, p. 397 (fig.) and 399 with n. 1. The Narenta valley is the site of numerous *villae rusticae,* many of which were decorated with wall-paintings for which archaeological investigations are lacking or the available evidence was never published. See Wilkes pp. 396-402. For Stobi which is, of course, within Yugoslav confines but strictly speaking outside our sphere of interest, see the comprehensive bibliography on wall-paintings in James Wiseman, ed., *Studies in the Antiquities of Stobi* (Beograd, 1973), pp. 247 f.

51. H. Kenner, *Carinthia* 153 (1963): 61-71, figs. 40 ff.

52. For human figures in panels, see also Zadar and note 40.

53. *Virunum,* pp. 173 ff.

54. M. Abramić, "Reste von Wandmalereien aus Vindobona," *JAK* 3 (1909): 88 ff.

55. E. Swoboda, *Carnuntum* (1958), pp. 147 ff.

56. Thomas, pp. 79 ff., 97 ff., 184 ff., 204 ff., 247 ff., 273, 374 ff., pls. 29-57, 77-79, 126-130, 171. See also A. Hekler, "Kunst und Kultur Pannoniens in ihren Hauptströmungen," *Strene Buliciana* (1924), pp. 107-118; J. Szilágyi, "Der Legatenpalast in Aquincum," *Budapest Regisegei* 14 (1945): 31-142 and summary 143-153); idem, "Die Bedeutung von Aquincum im Spiegel der neuesten Ausgrabungen," *Carnuntina* 3 (1956): 187-194; B. Horning Karoly, *Balacza* (1912), passim and especially pls. 1.2.5.

57. The only other country fully treated is Switzerland (in modern geographic terms). See Drack. Frescoes from other western provinces could only emphasize what has been noted earlier about their general dependence on the creative Italian centers and the simplification or even total abandonment of those essential features which characterized the four distinct phases of Pompeiian wall-painting. What we have is a mere skeletal survival with very often high technical quality and, depending upon the province or the site, a greater or lesser affinity with the spiritual and cultural background of Pompeiian painting. Comprehensive studies of wall-paintings found in France, Germany, Austria, Britain, and Spain are still lacking. Excavation reports in *BJb, Gallia* and many other local and hard-to-find bulletins usually give some information, as do general works about the Romans in these areas. For wall-paintings in Gaul see the out-of-date monograph by Blanchet, *Etude;* more recently the article by A. Barbet (see note 15) which raises interesting problems. For Britain see J.M.C. Toynbee, *Art in Roman Britain* (1962), pp. 213-217; Liversidge, pp. 39, 84 ff., pls. 14, 16-18. For Austria see also A. Schober, *Die Römerzeit in Österreich* (1953), passim and pp. 160 f. For Augsburg and Trier see Parlasca, *Augsburg* and note 2.

58. *Villen,* passim and L. Nagy, "Pannonisch-Römische decorative Stuccofriese," *Arch. Ertesitö* 41 (1927): 114-132, summary 306-310.

59. This is especially true for sites which are on major Roman roads, such as for instance Emona, Virunum, etc.

60. The overwhelming majority of the frescoes were found in the curia but excavation on the Forum also yielded fragments of wall-paintings. This is true especially for the Forum north site and trench 4. None of the patterned fresco fragments were found outside the curia with two notable exceptions, nos. 40-41, fragments of which were discovered in the curia and trench 4. This needs to be emphasized because the Forum at large yielded only fragments painted with plain colors and stripes (see nos. 1-37); moreover, the varieties of decoration attested in finds from the Forum at large stand much behind those made in the curia.

61. Only one stucco fragment was found on the Forum north site.

62. We are not concerned here with the apogee of Roman stucco decoration which in its finest specimens is only

available in Rome itself. All stucco decoration in the provinces is a faint echo of masterpieces, such as the stuccoes from the villa Farnesina, etc.

63. See pp. 53-54, for some revetment plaques found in situ and p. 212 for general references to colored revetment plaques.

64. Gnirs, p. 110.

65. Ibid., p. 142.

66. Schmid, p. 100.

67. W. Radimsky, "Ausgrabungen von Domavia in den Jahren 1892 und 1893," *WMBH* 4, 1896, 202-242, especially p. 210, figs. 15-18, p. 221, fig. 34.

68. Kellner (op. cit. note 43), p. 142, figs. 15 ff.

69. Thomas, pp. 79 ff., pls. 77-79; p. 219, pls. 126-130; p. 240, 267, pls. 162-163; p. 273, pl. 172 and p. 376. For Aquincum see J. Szilagyi, *Aquincum* (1956), p. 99. He refers to "Stukkaturpilaster" die "bis zur Decke hinaufliefen"; "die Stukkaturen wurden erst angefertigt und dann an der Wand befestigt."

70. R. Egger, Magdalensberg, p. 118. For stuccoes from Carnuntum see Swoboda (op. cit. note 55), pp. 122 f., fig. 64.

VII

Inscriptions

Hardly any inscriptions were found. As could be expected, some turned up in the huge surface *gomila* to the south of the Forum north porch. Included here are inscriptions on tiles.[1]

A. Inscriptions on Stone

1. (**Plate 26.**) From *gomila.* H. 17 cm; L. 16.5 cm; Th. 5.3 cm. White marble, weathered to gray. Broken on sides. Back is flat and roughly worked. Letters preserved in two lines. H. of letters, 4.5 and 3.7 cm.

   - - -] A MAT [- - -

   A] E SE͡VER [AE

   From a gravestone. A.D. 200-250.

2. (**Plate 26.**) From *gomila.* H. 13 cm; L. 15 cm; Th. 13.5 cm. Grayish-white marble. Broken on side and bottom. Two letters, A and D, are lightly incised on the underside of the stone which, in its primary use, may have served as a small pedestal or anta moulding.
3. From *gomila.* L. 20 cm; H. 16 cm; Th. 12.5 cm. Grayish-white marble. Broken on all sides except some distance at the top. The preserved edge suggests the left and central akroteria of a small gravestone with the letter D incised very coarsely to the left of the central akroterion. If the restoration of D M (Diis Manibus) is acceptable, the M was slightly to the right, below the central akroterion, in a position corresponding to that of the D.
4. From *gomila.* H. 24 cm; L. 17.5 cm; Th. 7 cm. White marble, probably limestone. Broken on top and at right edge; only part of lower edge intact. Torus-shaped moulding runs along left edge and bottom (as far as preserved) and probably formed a frame around the inscription. Letters roughly incised in two lines:

   < A
   H I

   Probably from a small tombstone.

B. Inscriptions on Tiles

5. (**Plate 26.**) From *gomila.* Max. Dim. 14 by 8 cm; Th. 3.8 cm. Light brick-red clay.

Broken at all edges. Some mortar adhering to tile suggests reuse. Inscription with stamped letters reads from right to left:

T C L O D [I U S

T(itus) Clod(ius)

6. (**Plate 27.**) Stray find. Max. Dim. 20.4 by 3 cm. Th. 3.2 cm. Tile fragment, gray-yellowish clay. Inscription is stamped:

L · P E · T R AV

L. Pe(tronius) Trau(sus)

7. (**Plate 27.**) From B6. L. 20 cm; H. 18 cm; Th. 2.6 cm. Fragment; brick-red clay. Stamped inscription is placed in oblong rectangle:

P A S I A N A

8. (**Plate 27.**) Stray find. Max. Dim. 7.5 by 4.3 cm; Th. 2.5 cm. Dark red clay. Stamped inscription:

P] A N S [I A N A

For tiles from the same factory see *CIL* III, 3213 and Suppl. III, p. 1654; also *CIL* V, 8110, no. 10 for the variant PASI·A·NA. See also Wilkes, Appendix XV, p. 499.

9. (**Plate 27.**) From A6-7. Max. Dim. 25 by 26 cm; Th. 3.25 cm. L.H. 1 cm. Fragment. Light red clay. Raised moulding, roughly square in section, runs along edge followed by a groove. On flat surface circular stamped inscription. To the left a second stamped circle somewhat lopsided and with irregular wide outline. This circle may have been abandoned and an improved circle eventually enclosed the inscription:

A T T I A E M V L S V L A E T F

Attiae Mulsulae T(iti) f(iliae)

For Mulsula cf. I. Kajanto, *The Latin Cognomina* (1965) p. 284; and for Attia, G. Alföldy, *Die Personennamen in der römischen Provinz Dalmatia* (1969), p. 63. For tiles with the same name see *CIL* III, 3214 and Suppl. III, p. 2275 (with references). Instead of T(iti) f(iliae), Ceci, *MP* p. 156 reads T(ertia) F(iglina).

Note to Chapter 7

1. Individual letters, some of them highly hypothetical, occur also on amphora lids to be published in the second fascicle. For uninscribed architectural tiles see the chapter on Clay Objects. The inscription which refers to the restoration of the curia is discussed on p. 50.

I wish to thank Professor Geza Alföldy for contributing to this chapter the readings of inscriptions nos. 1, 6, and 9.

VIII

Coins

[Since the author no longer had access to the original coins and was thus unable to give them a final check, the preparation of the catalogue of coins was a difficult task. The immediate cleaning of some of the coins in the Museum laboratory reduced their legibility. Many of the coins had been mixed up and shifted about in coarse building debris, and were poorly preserved. Indeed, the bronze coins were, on the whole, very worn and corroded. The catalogue does not, therefore, give the description of the actual coin, but its identification according to the standard reference works.[1] For actual identification of most of the legible coins of the fourth to the sixth century A.D., we are grateful to Dr. Herbert A. Cahn and Dr. W. Kellner, both in Basle, and to Professor A. Alföldi in Princeton. M.J.-B. Giard, Paris, was kind enough to make some valuable suggestions.[2]]

Among the coins there are no individual pieces of significant numismatic interest.

Considering the circulation of coins, no. 12 from Nemausus is noteworthy for having turned up on the Adriatic coast. There is only one Greek issue among the coins of the first century A.D. (no. 22, Claudius, Patras). The predominance of the issues of Pannonian and eastern mints among the coins of the fourth century A.D. is to be expected in Salona.

The composition of nominals does not yield, in our opinion, any striking pecularities. The reason for the scarcity of gold (which is completely absent, in fact, from among our finds) and silver coins on major sites during the early and middle Imperial period has recently been discussed again by H. Chantraine.[3]

Somewhat striking is the small role played by dupondii and sestertii. This could perhaps be explained by the scarcity of coins of the second century A.D. in our excavations.

It is remarkable that the silver coins of the Republican period find no counterpart in even a single denarius among the sixteen coins of the Augustan period and the first century A.D. (nos. 10-25). However, this fits well with facts already known for some time but recently substantiated again by C.M. Kraay and H. Chantraine.[4] Republican denarii share a considerable part of the silver coinage circulating in the first century A.D. The finds from Salona tend to confirm this rule. In other words, the six silver coins of the Republic are complementary to the bronze issues of the first century A.D. The high probability of this interpretation is supported, moreover, by the provenience of the coins themselves, especially in the Forum north site. Four out of the five silver coins of the Republic were found together with three bronze coins of the first century A.D. in the fill of period I/II to the north of the main east-west wall on the Forum north site (see chart 3).

The validity of the interpretation here proposed is enhanced also by the distribution of the minting dates of the Republican silver coins excavated. These correspond fairly precisely to those which C.M. Kraay has tabulated for coins from the treasuries discovered in Pompeii.[5] Thus, the series of Republican silver coins from Salona (excavations of 1969-70) parallels the Republican denarii circulating most commonly in Pompeii during the first century B.C. The Salona series seems to follow the Pompeiian pattern also with regard to the coins in group a which in Pompeii are, generally speaking, the most common as compared with groups b-d.

	Pompeii:	Salona:
a.	before or around 100 B.C.	nos. 2, 3, and 9 (Semis)
b.	80/70 B.C.	no. 6
c.	50/40 B.C.	no. 7 (Quinar)
d.	32/31 B.C. (Antony, Legionary)	no. 8

At military sites to the north of the Alps it was noted that the climax of circulation of Republican denarii is to be dated to the time of Claudius. The total number of coins from Salona (1969-70) is much too small, however, to determine whether or not they fit this pattern.

The distribution of the coins of the first century A.D. and their respective moneyers suggests with a high degree of probability that the Republican coins reached Salona together with the currency of the time of Tiberius.

The coins of both years of excavation provide an adequate, absolute chronology for the building periods I-IV which is supported in its turn by the finds of pottery. However, the discovery of less than a hundred coins does not provide a sufficient basis for elucidating the history of the city as a whole. Our excavations concentrated only on a very limited territory of the ancient town. Moreover, as stated earlier, the terrain was thoroughly disturbed. Since pillaging covered also objects of metal, the possibility is not to be excluded that coins, too, were removed. Finally, since our excavations were concerned largely with public quarters of the city, this enables us to assume a different percentage in the possible loss of coins as compared with the possible loss of coins in commercial and private quarters of cities.

It would seem to us that, from a methodical point of view, the use of coins as evidence can be justified at most only for the beginning and the end of the settlement of Salona in the territory which we examined. For the beginning of the settlement we must consider the period I finds from beneath the pavement of period II, to the east of the curia. The very small number of coins from this site—four all together (nos. 1, 4, 5, 12), all of pre-Christian date and found in relatively close proximity—does not in our opinion provide sufficient evidence for a *terminus post quem* of the settlement. However, we must point out the evidence from the pottery which would support such a conclusion. Since the earliest two coins are issues of Rome, we could surmise confidently that, in the second century B.C., Salona was included in the circulation of the currency of Rome. This interpretation finds confirmation not only in the economic sector, in the contemporary import of amphorae, but also in the literary sources which deal with Salona's political development. One would like to link the latest of the coins from beneath the pavement, an as of Nemausus (no. 12), with the commercial connections with the Po valley which can be observed in the latest pottery found in the same area of excavation.

The almost complete lack of coins on the Forum north and curia sites from the second century A.D. has a parallel in the paucity of pottery finds from that period. In search for an explanation of this cirumstance one cannot go further, in our opinion, than suggesting that this is due to the purpose which these localities fulfilled. In public quarters and usually paved areas (squares, streets, Forum, Capitolium, and curia), lost objects would be more easily noticed and retrieved than in commercial or private sectors of the city.

The great number of coins of the fourth century A.D. (nos. 40 ff.) might be surprising in view of the scarcity of contemporary structural remains; however, finds of fourth century pottery, which is plentifully attested, correspond to those of coins. Interpretation of this situation must be postponed until additional excavations and publication of further finds are made. In general it is clear that fourth century A.D. coins will have to be discussed in connection with the history of the currency of that period as well as in comparison with other sites which belong to the same area of coin circulation.

We are not at present in a position to give an interpretation for the gap in our Roman coins series in the fifth century A.D. This gap may very well be accidental.

The group of Justinian coins (nos. 72 to 76) together with the presence of sixth century A.D. pottery seems to indicate that the areas of the town excavated in 1969-70 were still inhabited in this period, rather than that the coins were lost by passers-by who lived in other sections of the town.

Notes on Chapter 8

1. Abbreviations and Specialized Bibliography

Chantraine	H. Chantraine, *Die antiken Fundmünzen der Ausgrabungen in Neuss.* Novaesium III, Limesforschungen Band 8, (Berlin, 1968).
CHK	R.H.G. Carson, P.V. Hill, and J.P.C. Kent, *Late Roman bronze coinage,* A.D. 324-448. (London, 1960).
DOAKS	A.R. Bellinger, *Byzantine coins in the Dumbarton Oaks Collection,* I. Dumbarton Oaks Center for Byzantine Studies, Washington, D.C., 1966.
Kraay	C.M. Kraay, *Die Münzfunde von Vindonissa (bis Trajan)*, (Basel, 1962).
Mor	C. Morrisson, *Catalogue des monnaies Byzantines de la Bibliothèque Nationale* I, (1970).
RIC	H. Mattingly and E.A. Sydenham, *The Roman Imperial coinage,* (London, 1923 ff.).
Syd	F.A. Sydenham, *The coinage of the Roman Republic,* (London, 1952).

Other abbreviations:

ANT	antoninianus	Quadr	quadrans
D	denarius	Qui	quinarius
DP	dupondius	S	sestertius

2. Cahn-Kellner identified the following coins: 1, 4, 5, 9, 12, 32, 39, 45-55, 58, 63-67, 70, 72, 77, 81, 83, 90-92; Alföldi identified coins nos. 59, 60, 87; Giard identified coins nos. 22, 34, 61a.
3. Chantraine, pp. 35.
4. Chantraine, p. 33; Kraay, pp. 15-16.
5. Kraay, p. 15.

CATALOGUE OF COINS

Coin numbers followed by 69 were found in 1969. All others were found in 1970.

No.	Denomination		Date of Issue	Bibliography	Mint	Inv. Nos. Forum Site	Inv. Nos. Curia Site	Period	Reference (ch.-charts)
	Unknown Hellenistic								
1	small bronze						C 105	I	ch.2;9;10
	Roman Republic								
2	D	C.Serveilius	c.110/108	Syd 525		C 69.26			ch.2;3.1
3	D	Mn.Aemilius Lepidus	c.109	Syd 554			C 69.25	III	ch.8;10
4	AS		2nd c.				C 102	I	ch.2;9;10
5	AS		2nd c.				C 103	I	ch.2;9;10
6	D	Q.C.Metellus pius	c.77	Syd 750		C 14			ch.2;3.2
7	Qui	M.[Porcius] Cato	47/46	Syd 1054		C 6		I/II	ch.2;3.1
8	D	Antony (Legionary)	c.32/31	Syd 1212		C 2		I/II	ch.2;3.1
9	Semis		90/80	Syd 681		C 35			ch.3.1
	Roman Empire								
	AUGUSTUS 27 B.C.–A.D. 14								
10	Quadr		c.5 B.C.	RIC 206	Rome		C 69.20	II	ch.8;9;10
11	AS		10/12	RIC 219	Rome	C 3			ch.3.1
12	AS		28/15 or 15/2 B.C.		Nemausus		C 104	I	ch.2;9;10
	TIBERIUS 14-37								
13	AS	for Divus Augustus	22/37?	RIC p. 95,6	Rome & elsewhere	C 29			ch.3.2
14	AS		"	probably RIC p.95,6	"	C 19			
15	AS		"	"	"		C 69.22	II	ch.9;10
16	AS		"	"	"		C 116	II	ch.8;10
17	AS		"	"	"		C 117	II	ch.8;10
	CALIGULA 37-41								
18	AS		39/40	RIC 31	Vesta	C 44			ch.3.3
	CLAUDIUS 41-54								
19	AS		41/50	RIC 69	Rome		C 69.15		ch.13;14
20	AS		41/52	RIC 66	Rome?		C 69.30	II	ch.9;10
21	AS		41/52	RIC 66	Rome?	C 10		I/II	ch.3.1
22	AS		post A.D.41	Legionary standards, eagle	Patras	C 9		I/II	ch.3.1
	VESPASIAN 69-79								
23	AS		71	RIC 494			C 69.6a		ch.13;14
24	DP		74	RIC 798a	Commagene?		C 69.7	II	ch.8;10
	For Titus								
25	AS		73	RIC 660a	Rome		C 69.6b	II	ch.8;10
	Probably lst cent. A.D.								
26	AS						C 109	IV	ch.9
27	AS					C 7			
	TRAJAN 98-117								
28	AS		98/102	RIC type 395			C 69.13	III	ch.8;10

1. B6-7, 0.60 m under pavement, completely corroded, June 27.
2. E1A, -1.20 m, well preserved, June 25.
3. A5, in fresco layer above drain, worn, June 20.
4. B6-7, under the pavement near foundation of east wall (0.125 m from east wall, 0.73 m from south wall), worn and corroded, June 27.
5. Same provenience as no. 4, B6-7, worn and corroded, June 27.
6. E2B/3C, -0.80 m, 0.50 m to the south of drain, well preserved, June 11.
7. E4A, -1.35 m, 0.85 m south and 0.50 m west of NE corner, well preserved, July 1.
8. E1A, between 0.60 m and -1.20 m, well preserved, May 27.
9. W5A, in topsoil, badly preserved, June 2.
10. A/A'5, just below burnt and fresco layers, nicely preserved, June 18.
11. E2A, -1.34 m, badly preserved, July 13.
12. B6-7, immediately below pavement, to the east of wall, completely worn and corroded.
13. W2B/2C, between -0.80 and -0.90 m, between walls in middle of trench, well preserved, June 9.
14. E2E, perforated, much worn, June 1.
15. A3, on levelled wall of period I, moderately well preserved, June 21.
16. Found together with no. 17, B5, just above corner slab of west cross wall of curia, worn and heavily burnt, June 1972.
17. Same provenience as no. 16, B5, worn and heavily burnt, June, 1972.
18. W2C, -0.75 m, on flat stone between walls, fairly well preserved, June 15.
19. Glass workshop, to north of wall B, in carbonized layer, worn and corroded, June 16.
20. A3, +6.13 m, in clay layer, worn, June 12.
21. E5AA, -0.60 m below top of east wall of portico, worn but nicely preserved, July 1970.
22. E5A, badly preserved, June 7.
23. Glass workshop, 1 m to the east of charcoal pit, well preserved, June 12.
24. A6, found together with no. 25, immediately below fresco layer, somewhat worn but nicely preserved, June 12.
25. Same provenience as no. 25, A6, well preserved, June 12.
26. B6-7, -0.30 m in topsoil, corroded, June 26.
27. E4A, corroded, June 28.
28. B6, in fresco level, very well preserved, June 13.

No.	Denomination	Date of Issue	Bibliography	Mint	Inv. Nos. Forum Site	Inv. Nos. Curia Site	Period	Reference (ch.=charts)
28a	1st or 2nd cent. A.D.					669.19	II	ch.8;10
	ELAGABAL 218-222							
29	S	218/222	RIC 359	Eastern	C 11			ch.3;4
	GALLIENUS 253-268							
30	ANT	260/268	RIC 251	Rome	C 36			ch.3;4
31	ANT	260/268	RIC 636?	Eastern		C 69.3		ch.13;14
	For Salonina							
32	ANT	250/260	RIC 192.2?			C 114		ch.14
	DIVUS CLAUDIUS II GOTHICUS							
33	ANT	270	RIC 265	Rome	C 69.27 (trench 4)			ch.14
	AURELIAN 270-275							
34	ANT	270/275	RIC type 244/245 S / XXIS	Siscia	C 33			ch.3;4
	TACITUS 275-276							
35	ANT	275/276	RIC 188 XXIT	Siscia	C 34			ch.3.4
	PROBUS 276-282							
36	ANT	276/282	RIC 714 V XXI	Siscia		C 69.18	III	ch.8;10
	DIOCLETIAN 284-305							
37	AE	c.296/297	RIC 46a ALE	Alexandria		C 69.2		ch.13;14
38	ANT			Alexandria	C 46			
39	Number not used.							
	GALERIUS MAXIMINIAN I emperor 305-311							
40			RIC		C 25			
	CONSTANTINE I emperor 306-337							
41	AE	330/333 or 335/336	SMTSA	Thessalonica		C 69.11		
42		326?	SMHA	Heraclea		C 69.14	III	ch.9;10
43	For Delmatius Caesar PROVIDENTIAE CAESSS	335/337	Type CHK I CONSA	Constantinople		C 69.14	IV	ch.8;10
44	For Constantius Caesar GLORIA EXERCITUS	324/335	Type CHK I 742	Siscia		C 69.16	IV	ch.9;10
	CONSTANTIUS II emperor 337-361							
45	AE FEL TEMP REPAPATIO	340/350	? BSIS	Siscia	C 43			
46	AE FEL TEMP REPARATIO	346/350	CHK II 881/882 N / AQP	Aquileia	C 5			

28a. A/A'6, from burnt level below fresco layer, June 18.

29. E4A/B, 0.50 m under drain of portico, partly corroded, July 9.

30. W5A, between -0.65 and 0.95 m, in charcoal layer, badly preserved, June 3.

31. Glass workshop (C7), from area of charcoal pit, heavily corroded, June 9.

32. D7, from furnace area, well preserved, July 8.

33. Trench 4, to the south of wall A, -40 m below surface, quite worn, June 25.

34. W7B, between -1.20 and -1.60 m, very well preserved, May 27.

35. W5A, in charcoal layer, well preserved, June 3.

36. A5-6, from fresco layer, worn but nicely preserved, June 18.

37. C6-7 (glass workshop), well preserved, June 9.

38. W2-4C/D, -0.12 m in topsoil, worn, June 17.

39. Number not used.

40. E2F, -0.52 m in topsoil, worn, June 1.

41. C7, +4.71 m, between walls A and B, well preserved, slightly worn, June 11.

42. A7, east of apse in a layer comparable to fresco layer, well preserved, June 16.

43. A/B6, 0.80 m below topsoil, slightly worn but well preserved, June 9.

44. A7, outside of apse, near east wall of curia, well preserved, slightly worn, June 17.

45. W5C, moderately well preserved, June 22.

46. E4A, moderately well preserved, June 26.

No.	Denomination		Date of Issue	Bibliography	Mint	Inv. Nos. Forum Site	Inv. Nos. Curia Site	Period	Reference (ch.=charts)
47	AE	FEL TEMP REPARATIO	346/350	?			C 113	IV	ch.9;10
47a	AE	FEL TEMP REPARATIO	c.350	?	Heraclea		C 69.17	III	ch.8;10
48	AE	FEL TEMP REPARATIO	351/354	CHK II 1681 A / SMTS	Thessalonica	C 37			
49	AE	FEL TEMP REPARATIO	351/354	CHK II 1681 — / SMTS		C 38			
50	AE	FEL TEMP REPARATIO	c.350	?	?	C 26			
51	AE		after 350	?	?	C 23			
52	AE	GLORIA ROMANORUM		CHK II 1179 ? / A SISC	Siscia	C 17		III	
	CONSTANTIUS ?								
53	AE		?	?	Constantinople	C 8			
	CONSTANS I emperor 337-350								
54	AE	GLORIA EXERCITUS	337/341	CHK I 1144 — / SMNA	Nicomedia	C 40			
55	AE	VICTORIA EDDAVGGQNN	341/346	CHK I 801 — / ASIS	Siscia	C 47			
56	AE	GLORIA EXERCITUS	after 340	?	?		C 69.12	III	ch.8;10
57	AE	GLORIA EXERCITUS	?	?	?		C 69.23	III	ch.8;10
	SONS OF CONSTANTINE								
58	AE	Type Victoriae		?	Siscia		C 112	IV	ch.9;10
59	AE	Type ?	?	?	?		C 69.9		
60	AE	Type ?	?	?	?		C 69.21	III	ch.8;10
60a	AE	Type ?	?	?	?	C 39			
60b	AE	Type ?	?	?	?	C 20a			
	JULIANUS CAESAR 355-361								
60c	AE			?	?	C 4			
61	AE	Type ?	?	?	?	C 16a			
	VALENS I 314								
61a				RIC 15b PIM / A SISC	Siscia	C 101 (trench 3)			ch.1;14
	VALENTINIAN I and VALENS 364-367								
62		Type ?					C 69.31		ch.14
63		Type: GLORIA ROMANORUM ?		?	?		C 115		ch.14

47. A7, in topsoil in middle of square, badly preserved, June 24.
47a. A/A'5-6, in fresco layer, nicely preserved, June 17.
48. W5A, on top of charcoal layer, very well preserved, June 2.
49. W2A, -0.60 m in topsoil, June 1.
50. E2F, between -0.40 m and -0.50 m, moderately well preserved, June 2.
51. E2F, between -0.40 m and -0.50 m, badly preserved, June 2.
52. Found together with no. 81, E2D, to the east of the column, nicely preserved, June 3.
53. E5A, badly corroded, June 12.
54. W5B/C, -0.96 m in topsoil, found together with no. 91, moderately well preserved, June 17.
55. W2C, 0.85 m in topsoil, well preserved, June 18.
56. B6, in fresco layer, moderately well preserved, somewhat worn, June 13.
57. B3-4, moderately well preserved and somewhat worn, June 25.
58. A7, 0.10 m in topsoil at south end of square, June 24.
59. C6-7, at +5.46 m, between walls A & B, badly corroded, June 11.
60. B3-4, in fresco layer, badly corroded, June 20.
60a. W5B/C, -0.64 m in topsoil, worn and corroded, June 17.
60b. E2E, found together with no. 72, badly preserved, June 3.
60c. E4A, in *gomile*, in northern part of square, corroded, July 2.
61. E2D, fairly well preserved, June 4.
61a. E2W/X (trench 3), -0.53 m, in middle of trench, badly preserved, June 26.
62. A1, +6.23 m, broken and worn, June 2.
63. D7, 0.60 m in topsoil, in middle of square, badly preserved, July 10.

No.	Denomination		Date of Issue	Bibliography	Mint	Inv. Nos. Forum Site	Inv. Nos. Curia Site	Period	Reference (ch.=charts)
64		SECURITAS REI PUBLICAE	?	?	Milan	C 13			
65		GLORIA EXERCITUS	?	? / PCONST	Arles	C 16			
	GRATIAN, VALENTINIAN II, and THEODOSIUS I 379-383								
66	AE	REPARATIO REI PUB		CHK II 751 / SMRP	Rome	C 15			
67	AE	REPARATIO REI PUB		CHK II 1821/28 ? / SMTES	Thessalonica	C 18			
	VALENTINIAN II, THEODOSIUS I, and ARCADIUS 383-392								
68	AE	VOT X MULT XX		?	Constantinople?	C 12			
69	AE	Type ?		?	?		C 106	III	ch.9
	THEODOSIUS I, ARCADIUS, and HONORIUS 394-395								
70	AE	SALUS REI PUBLICAE		CHK II 804/806 / R.P.	Rome		C 110		
	FIFTH CENTURY								
71	AE	Type ?		?	?		C 69.5	IV	ch.9;10
	JUSTINIAN I 527-565								
72	AE	DECANUMMIUM		DOAKS p.190,362; light wreath	?	C 20			
73	AE	DECANUMMIUM		DOAKS p.190,363; heavy wreath	?	C 24			
74	AE	DECANUMMIUM		DOAKS p.190,363; heavy wreath	?	C 22			
74a	AE	DECANUMMIUM		DOAKS p.190,363; heavy wreath	?	C 41			
75	AE	DECANUMMIUM		DOAKS p. 160 Masson,45			C 111		
76	AE	DECANUMMIUM		DOAKS p.190,362		C 27			
	JUSTINIAN ?								
77	AE	DECANUMMIUM				C 28			
	Undetermined Late Roman to Early Byzantine Coins (* = most probably 4th century A.D.)								
78						C 100 (E3J/K = trench 5)	C 100		ch.1;14

64. E2-3B, badly preserved, June 17.
65. E2D, only half of coin, well preserved, June 4.
66. E3B, moderately well preserved, June 25.
67. A1, -0.60 m, near center of square, worn but nicely preserved, June 3.
68. E5B/4C, small bronze, well preserved, June 11.
69. B6-7, -1.40 m, directly on pavement near west wall, corroded, July 9.
70. A'7, in *gomile* at south end of trench, somewhat worn, July 7.
71. A'6, outside southeast corner of curia, in rubble, completely corroded, June 11.
72. Found together with no. 60b, E2E, somewhat worn, June 3.
73. E2F, somewhat worn, June 1.
74. E2F, moderately well preserved, June 1.
74a. W5B/4C, 0.32 m in topsoil near east wall, averse completely worn, June 17.
75. A'7, 0.75 m in topsoil, much corroded, July 7.
76. E2B/3C, much corroded, June 11.
77. E2B/3C, 0.12 m in topsoil, completely corroded, June 11.
78. E3J/K, (trench 5), 0.70 m in topsoil, small bronze, completely corroded, July 2.

No.	Denomination		Date of Issue	Bibliography	Mint	Inv. Nos. Forum Site	Curia Site	Period	Reference (ch.=charts)
79							C 108	III	ch.9;10
80							C 107	III	ch.9
81*						C 17a			
82						C 30			
83						C 31			ch.7
84						C 32			ch.7
85							C 69.28		ch.14
86							C 69.8		ch.14
87							C 69.24	II	ch.8
88							C 69.1		ch.14
89						C 7			
90*						C 21			
91						C 40a			
92*						C 42			
93*						C 45			
94*						C 48			
95						C 1			

79. B6-7, completely corroded, above pavement, June 27.
80. B6-7, completely corroded, June 27.
81. E2D, found together with no. 52, small bronze, completely corroded, June 3.
82. W5B/4C, small bronze, completely corroded, June 8.
83. W6B, against Forum enclosure west wall, quinar ?, completely worn, July 7.
84. W6B, same provenience as no. 83, completely corroded, July 7.
85. A1, +6.60 m, completely corroded, May 30.
86. C6-7, (glass workshop), +4.71 m, between walls A and B, badly corroded, June 11.
87. B3-4, worn and corroded, June 25.
88. A1, in disturbed fill, completely corroded, June 2.
89. E4A, –1.90 m in *gomile*, in northern part of square, completely corroded, July 3.
90. E2E, completely worn, June 3.
91. W5B/C, found together with no. 54, 0.95 m in topsoil, small bronze, completely corroded, June 17.
92. W5B/C, 0.69 m in topsoil, at west wall, completely corroded, June 17.
93. W2C, 2 m west, on center wall, completely corroded, June 17.
94. W2-4C/D, small bronze, completely corroded, June 18.
95. E1A, completely corroded, June 17.
96. W2-4C/D, all of small bronzes wrapped in cloth, completely corroded, June 17.

IX

Roman Glass

INTRODUCTION

The glass from the Forum area excavations at Salona consists wholly of fragments, most of them very small; some 1000 were inventoried. 118 examples, of which 112 belonged to vessels, are catalogued individually. 650 sufficiently identifiable inventoried fragments in addition have been classified by type and listed in chart form. Glass manufacturing wasters found in connection with the glass furnace are also discussed.

A typological arrangement of the material was necessitated by the lack of sufficient stratified contexts. Each catalogue section is preceded by brief commentary and a chart which tabulates all similar fragments, including those catalogued as well as those not discussed individually. The arrangement of the catalogue is as follows:

- I. Fine Wares
  - A. Millefiori glass
  - B. Colored molded glass
  - C. Ribbed bowls: millefiori, colored and blue-green
  - D. Colored blown glass.
  - E. Colorless molded and engraved vessels
- II. Blue-Green Vessels
  - A. Shallow straight-sided dishes
  - B. Bowls and beakers
  - C. Bottles, jars, flasks
  - D. Unguentaria
  - E. Pointed unguentaria and amphoriskoi
  - F. Lids
  - G. Funnels
  - H. Stemmed goblets
  - I. Lamps with handles
- III. Non-Vessel Glass
  - A. Window glass
  - B. Mosaic tesserae
  - C. Game counters
  - D. Bead
  - E. Manufacturing wasters

Proportions of Different Glass Types

The preserved quantity of each type of glass, and its relation to the total amounts found at the Forum site, cannot be taken as accurate indications of the usage of glass at Salona as a whole. Since the Forum site was not a habitation area between the start of the early first century settlement and the fourth century abandonment of the public buildings of the Forum, most of the Roman glass must have come in as fill rather than as usage debris. Thus it is difficult from our finds to determine the types and quantities of glass in use at Salona at any given time.

For example, the Forum area yielded only three molded and engraved vessel fragments, whereas half a dozen other variants of this technique came from the houses near the Porta Caesarea. However, in general it is clear that as might be expected plain blue-green blown fabrics predominated. Among these the high proportion of drinking vessels should be noted, some 70% of the blue-green examples inventoried. Although there is a representative selection of both recognizably early and late glasswares, it is impossible to establish proportionate quantities of glass used in each century at Salona. The earliest fine wares may have undue prominence since they are identifiable even in the smallest fragments, whereas many blue-green glass sherds could not be assigned to any particular shape.

Salona Glass in General: Types and Origin

As might be expected from its location, Salona's early Roman fine glass seems to be of Italian origin. None of the Syro-Palestinian mold-blown small vessels have been found. A good proportion of plain glass comparable to Salona's can be found in Western European sites; however, a significant number of the plain glasses from the site could have come from or been modelled on Eastern or Egyptian types. These include large diameter thread-decorated rims (Egypt), sack-shaped beakers (Cyprus), and blown facet-cut beakers (Egypt or the Near East). Since remains of a glass furnace were found on the site, it is fair to assume that some of the glass found was made at Salona itself.

Trade

After the establishment of the Roman colony at Salona (47 B.C. or shortly after) and the annexation of the Dalmatian coast to the Empire, a great number of items were imported to the Dalmatian cities from Italy, such as pottery, bricks and building tiles, and metal goods and luxury objects, including glass.[1] Although there were several cities from which these things could have come, the probable port of shipment was Aquileia on the northwest shore of the Adriatic.[2] To Aquileia came pottery, bronzes and marbles from the rest of Italy, metals from Noricum and Pannonia, and amber from the Baltic.[3] There is also evidence in the form of a glassworker's signature for the manufacture of glass at Aquileia itself.[4] Thus some of the Italian glass found at Salona and other Dalmatian cities such as Zadar may very well be Aquileian. Although there are no distinctive types which can be precisely localized, the colored blown glass found at Salona is very similar to that seen at Aquileia and elsewhere in North Italy. Other types of early Imperial glass at Salona are so similar to examples from Pompeii and Herculaneum that they must have a common origin.[5]

Evidence for trade after the first century is scanty. In his book on the province of Dalmatia Wilkes mentions without any documentation that Italian trade was losing its dominance along the Dalmatian coast in the later second and third centuries.[6] Aquileia provides indirect evidence for the movement of people to that city from Cos, Cyprus, Byzantium, Asia Minor, Palestine and Syria.[7] Of course these individuals do not necessarily demonstrate commercial contacts. However, a ship's captain from Corinth is known,[8] as is also a certain merchant who brought grain and oil from Cyrenaica to Aquileia.[9] Since trading ships took advantage of the many sheltering islands and good harbors along the East coast of the Adriatic, some of the foreign goods at Salona could have arrived via this route. Direct mention of trade to Dalmatia and to Salona in particular comes in the late Roman empire. In Diocletian's Edict on Maximum Prices highest allowable charges are given for freight between Alexandria and Dalmatia, Asia and Dalmatia, and Africa and Salona.[10] This attests to the presence of trade between these areas and Salona. It is thus not improbable to suppose that some glass was imported along with other products from these more easterly and southerly regions in the later Roman empire.

Local Manufacture of Glass

The discovery of a fragmentary glass furnace and workshop area north of the curia at Salona makes it certain that glass was locally manufactured (see pp. 56 ff.). What is not so certain is the starting date and duration of use of the furnace. According to the excavated remains, this could range from the first to the fourth century. Speaking for a later rather than earlier usage span is the fact that glassmaking was probably a secondary reuse of an area originally devoted to metal smelting. Further, it seems unlikely that an industrial establishment which would generally be relegated to the less populated areas of a Roman city because of the danger of fire[11] should have been located so close to a major public building while it was in use.

As noted in more detail in the section concerning the scientific analysis of vessel glass and cullet following the catalogue, the fragments of glass cullet adhering to the melting crucibles differ in their composition from the vessel fragments analyzed. Briefly, while the composition of the vessel glasses corresponds in general to that of North Italian glass, the composition of the cullet corresponds either to certain early Roman glasses or to those of Eastern Roman origin. The latter possibility seems more probable here. We know that craftsmen from the eastern parts of the Roman empire worked at Salona, especially from the late second century onwards.[12] Travelling Eastern glassmakers are known both from the early Roman empire and from later centuries as well.[13] Such Eastern glassworkers might well have brought with them their traditional formulas for glass composition. Alternately, Eastern glassware melted down for reuse by the Salona workshop could account for the different compositions of cullet and vessel glass.

Unfortunately there is insufficient evidence not only for the date and duration of glass manufacture at Salona, but also for the types of vessels made. The glass found adhering to the crucible represents only one batch; the same furnace may have made glass with compositions similar to the vessel glass analyzed. Alternately, the small selection of analyzed vessel glass may not have picked up samples made at the Salona workshop. Further careful study of glass compositions from other parts of the Salona site, as well as from neighboring Dalmatian coast cities would be needed to clarify the problems of the glass produced at the Salona glasshouse.

Comparison of Salona Glass with Other Yugoslav Finds

It is difficult to compare the Salona glasses with those from other Yugoslav sites due to the scarcity of publications dealing with the many glass finds. To my knowledge, no other non-cemetery site apart from Salona has received a systematic publication. Among Dalmatian coast cities, Zadar and Aenona have yielded the richest finds from their necropolises. This material is, however, mentioned and illustrated only briefly in summary publications issued over many years.[14] A recent careful publication has been devoted to the glass from the cemetery of Doclea,[15] near modern Titograd. For other parts of the country we are dependent on reports of individual or chance finds. The following listing makes use of published sources available in the U.S.A.

Salona and vicinity: Although excavations have been going on at Salona since the nineteenth century, the glass finds have received scant attention in writing. F. Bulić, the editor of the local archaeological publication for many years, gave careful attention to inscriptional finds, while dismissing pottery, glass, etc. with the briefest mention. Only one piece is treated in any detail: a bottle from Promona, north and inland from Split, which had a base inscribed VICTOR AUGUSTOR FEL (IX) with a central victory figure.[16] Von Saldern recently published the fine glass from the Archaeological Museum at Split, which came from Salona and its vicinity.[17] Certainly from Salona itself are: a gold-band bottle, millefiori bowl, blown "basket," latish head flask, geometric cut bowls, and a diatretum fragment. Some of the unpublished finds from the recent excavation at the Porta Caesarea area of Salona are mentioned later.[18]

Zadar: The glass from the cemeteries of Zadar, nearby Asseria, and Aenona (modern Nin) form the richest complex discovered along the Dalmatian coast. The bulk of the material is now in the Museo Vetrario in Murano, while the remainder is on display in the museum of the University of Zadar. These burial gifts form an interesting comparison with the material used by the living at nearby Salona. From the cemeteries come some specifically funerary types, for example, the large glass urns also found in North Italian burials,[19] and numerous unguentaria and dolphin bottles for oil.[20] The early luxury glasses correspond in general to those from Salona, with the addition of imported Eastern Mediterranean pieces: mold-blown Greek inscribed beakers, lotus beakers, and small mold-blown flasks with various designs.[21] Many of the plain glasses are similar to those of Salona; however later luxury pieces include a molded jug, oval dish, and round plate with allover facet cutting.[22] A few graves have been recently found at Zadar, but they do not add significantly to the repertoire of glass already known from the area.[23]

Dalmatian coast; Sarajevo region: Further up the coast, at Bakra near Rijecka was found many years ago a cemetery of inhumation burials with generally early glass, including a funnel, a drinking horn, and a tall square bottle with Latin inscription on the base. There is also a later narrow-necked flask and jar within a jar.[24]

Details of the Roman glass from the region of Pola were not available to me. Older publications list what seem to be numerous glass finds from the cemeteries around the Roman city.[25]

Going south from Salona, one finds mention of unguentaria found at Narona, probably an indication of another cemetery.[26] Further inland in the region of Sarajevo, a number of individual finds have been reported. In Roman building remains from Ilidže near Sarajevo were found an olive-green trulla or ladle handle, a flat bowl with incised decorated horizontal rim, and a millefiori fragment.[27] From Stolac towards the coast south of Sarajevo a late nineteenth century report describes a mausoleum containing three burials with second-third century glass, including a beaker shallowly engraved with a band of diamond pattern, and a footed bowl with horizontal rim.[28] More recent is a report of glass from a Roman villa of this region. The finds are said to date from the second-fourth centuries and include colorless engraved examples, fragments with colored blobs, and window glass.[29]

Doclea: The Roman city of Doclea, near modern Titograd, has yielded numerous glass finds from its southeast necropolis, which was excavated as a salvage operation.[30] Only the late Roman glass has been published, although the presence and relative scarcity of earlier glass is mentioned.[31] Coins ranging in date from Marcus Aurelius through Constantine are noted in association with individual finds.[32] The glass corresponds to well-known plain-ware types of the third-fourth centuries: footed bowls with outsplayed rim, bowls with round and rice-shaped facet cuts, tall conical beakers, narrow necked and funnel mouthed flasks, and fusiform unguentaria. Although the author of the Doclea publication draws many parallels with Western European and Pannonian material, and concludes that a great number of the examples were imports from the west,[33] it seems to me that many of the glasses illustrated could rather have an Eastern origin. Direct comparison with the Salona glass is difficult since, apart from the plain bowls, the Doclea glass contains a preponderance of types such as unguentaria and flasks which are poorly represented at Salona.

Emona: Some finds have been recorded from the region of Emona (modern Ljubljana). Tomb finds from the city have been reported, one with inhumation burials of the first-second century, along with a fourth century grave. One glass urn is noted, some plain bowls including one straight-sided example, and a bell-shaped unguentarium.[34] First century glass associated with a funerary monument is also recorded, as are portrait cameos.[35]

From Celeia graves are reported with late Roman narrow-necked flasks.[36] Near Maribor on the road to ancient Poetovio a grave mound with more extensive finds was discovered. These included, along with a coin of Vespasian, a handleless glass urn, bottles (one cylindrical and one square with base design), a one-handled modius, high-handled ladle, two trullas, and four bowls.[37] The finds are dated to ca. A.D. 100. North Italian parallels are evident. The relatively early glass from this area is not surprising, given its proximity to Aquileia. Two late finds of gold glass from Poetovio have also been published.[38]

Finds from other parts of Yugoslavia will not be cited, since they do not seem relevant to the patterns of manufacture or trade which brought glass to Salona. It is obvious even from this necessarily sketchy survey that glass was widely distributed in the areas of Roman settlement along the Yugoslav coast and the areas adjacent to it. Perhaps the firmest conclusion which can be drawn is that much excavation and publication of both old and new glass finds are needed before a survey of the Roman glass of this region can be written.

I. FINE WARES

A. Millefiori Glass

The millefiori glass from Salona may seem to have an undue prominence in the picture of the glass from the site, since even the smallest fragments are recognizable. Nevertheless, their number is small, even in proportion to the other fine wares. Early types such as the striped fragments are seen, along with later examples such as the speckled ware and the millefiori ribbed bowls. For the latter see the section on ribbed bowls. All of the Salona types are paralleled by examples known from Italian and provincial sites, and they are undoubtedly imports from Italy.

1. (**Plate 32.**) Bowl rim. Amber ground with white and green canes. D. 12 cm. From W2B. Mosaic bowl of hemispherical shape. The rim ground smooth on interior and exterior. No top thread at rim. This example does not resemble the Hellenistic millefiori bowls recently discussed by Andrew Oliver in matrix color or rim treatment,[39] but belongs rather in the early Imperial period.
2. Wall fragment of bowl. Purple matrix with white canes. From W2A. Slight bulge in the fabric suggests that this may have belonged to a ribbed bowl, but too little is preserved to be certain.
3. Fragments of streaked millefiori bowl. Blue with white canes. From E2B. Ten non-joining fragments, apparently from a shallow bowl. Pattern formed of long, thin cane sections laid slantwise to produce a firework-shower effect. Vindonissa no. 8 is a similar pattern, differing in the addition of multicolored canes.[40]
4. (**Plate 32.**) Rim of streaked millefiori bowl. Originally purple matrix with white sprinkled canes. Now weathered and iridescent. From E5A. Part of shallow bowl, pattern similar to no. 3 above. Exact parallel in a complete shallow bowl of the same color and pattern in the Archaeological Museum in Split, said to have come also from Salona.[41] Another fragmentary bowl of this type with amber and white patterning was found by us.[42]
5. Striped mosaic fragment. Flat section with stripes of rose, blue, and colorless wound with opaque yellow. Max. Dim. 2.4 cm. From E4A. This is probably part of the flat base of a bowl in ribbon mosaic technique. It may have included mosaic cubes or chunks of colored glass such as those in a similar complete example in the Archaeological Museum of Split.[43] Hellenistic examples of the technique seem to have been made with bases, and with a more

rounded, deeper bowl than our piece. The earliest well-dated specimen of the type known to me is that from the Antikythera shipwreck (80-50 B.C.).[44] Early first century A.D. examples of the more shallow type, generally without base rings, are cited by Berger.[45] It is to this group that our fragment must have belonged. A further Dalmatian coast parallel to the Salona fragments should be noted: a hemispherical bowl from Zadar.[46]

6. Fragment of color-band vessel (?). Pale yellow stripe edged with colorless lines adjoining green stripes on either side. Weathered. From E1B.
7. Three layered fragments. From E1B; E5B/4C; E1B respectively.
   A. Side A–translucent deep blue and opaque white. Side B–opaque medium blue.
   B. Side A–opaque white. Side B–medium translucent deep blue.
   C. Side A–deep translucent blue with thin opaque white stripe and translucent purple stripe. Side B–purple, colorless, and pale blue opaque.

   These fragments seem to belong to the same vessel, but since their size is very small, none larger than 2-3 cm., it is impossible to tell which side of each is the interior or exterior. Thus the designations of sides "A" and "B" are arbitrary. The pieces must have come from a complex layered vessel of variegated stripes or blocks of colored glass, fused in such a way as to be different inside and out. The closest parallel in technique is to be found in gold-band alabastra, which use a color scheme different from that preserved in the Salona pieces.[47]

B. Colored Molded Glass

The molded glass vessels of Salona, apart from the colorless examples, which will be discussed separately, are characteristic of this tableware found elsewhere in the first century A.D. The conical molded bowls, however, of which several examples were found, are a Hellenistic shape.

Table 1 lists all of the Salona molded Roman glass fragments, both catalogued and uncatalogued, by shape and color. Most are of small size, although a few are of larger serving-dish dimensions. Pale blue is the only opaque color represented at Salona, while emerald green has a slight preponderance over the other translucent colors. Many of the shapes are derived from contemporary terra sigillata pottery,[48] for example the Salona bowl no. 8 of Dragendorf shape 27, for which numerous parallels in glass also exist.[49] Parallels for Salona examples can be found on many pre-Flavian sites: at Pompeii and Herculaneum, from North Italy, in trans-Alpine sites such as Vindonissa, and westward into Britain.[50] The source for this glass in Salona must have been Italy.

Conical molded bowls have been widely found in Hellenistic contexts, most recently at Tel Anafa in Israel, where they were in use from at least 150 B.C. down to 75 B.C.[51] Mrs. Weinberg, in her preliminary publication of this glass, cites additional dated finds of it, most from the early second to early first century B.C.[52] Another recent find of this type of bowl, from one of a group of graves near Pylos, is well dated to the early second century B.C.[53] Hemispherical versions of the same bowl seem to have continued later than the strictly conical variety,[54] for which the dated examples do not continue far into the first century B.C.

TABLE 1: MOLDED GLASS BY COLOR AND SHAPE

	Amber	Blue	Emerald	Black	Opaque Blue	Opaque Turquoise	Totals
Straight-sided dish			6		1		7
Dragendorf form 27		1	1				2
Ceramic-like shape		2					2
Conical bowl	2	2					4
Rims	4	1	3				8
Ring feet		1	1		1		3
Handles		1		1			2
Wall fragments					2	2	4
Totals	6	8	11	1	4	2	32

8. (**Plate 28.**) Slightly outflared rim from conical bowl. Deep blue. Now weathered bluish-gray. D. 10.2 cm. From E3-4A. Rim has strongly profiled ridges on interior. Probably from conical shape, although lower part not preserved. For Hellenistic parallels, see n. 51.
9. (**Plate 28.**) Bowl rim with interior grooves. Deep amber. D. 14 cm. Grooves 1 and 1.8 cm below rim. From E2D. Rim ground, with 2 grooves on interior just below rim. Conical shape, similar to no. 8 above.
10. (**Plate 28.**) Bowl of Dragendorf shape 27. Deep blue. Now weathered gray-blue. Rim D. 8.4 cm. From E1A. Almost complete profile of small molded bowl: characteristic ceramic form. One of the common shapes of early Roman molded bowls, generally made in small sizes such as this one, and in a variety of colors, both translucent and opaque.
11. (**Plate 28.**) Bowl imitating ceramic form. Deep blue. Now weathered violet-green and iridescent. D. 16.8 cm. From E1A. Six non-joining fragments of same bowl. Compare Dragendorf form 16, and Vindonissa no. 31[55] from a Claudian-Neronian grove.
12. (**Plates 28 and 32.**) Bowl with small horizontal rim. Deep blue. Now iridescent and pitted on surface. D. 30.4 cm. From E1A. Upper portion preserved. This could be reconstructed as a shallow shape[56] or with another convex curve below this one as in a comparable example from Fishbourne.[57]
13. Bowl wall fragment. Bright translucent aquamarine. From E5A. Strongly grooved upper portion above carinated shoulder. Jar of opaque turquoise with similar carinated shoulder is in the British Museum.[58]
14. (**Plate 28.**) Bowl. Emerald green. Rim D. 16 cm. From E5A. Original height about 3 cm. Profile of narrow outcurving rim, gradually sloping rounded body and probable base ring. Very similar example in same fabric from Vindonissa.[59]
15. (**Plate 28.**) Straight-sided dish. Emerald green. Rim and base D. 14 cm. H. 2 cm. From W5B/C. Complete profile of typical shape for this emerald molded fabric. Isings cites the Pompeiian parallels.[60] From Salona comes another example of the same shape and fabric with a diameter of 20 cm[61] while a second example from Vindonissa with a diameter of 14 cm suggests a range of standard sizes for the shape.[62]
16. Rim and handle attachment. Deep blue. Almost opaque. D. 10.8 cm. From W5A. Rim exterior shows fine grinding lines. Although the Salona example is very fragmentary, it seems by fabric and shape to be a handled cup, perhaps related to the two-handled variety of Isings form 25.
17. Two fragments of opaque vessel. Opaque pale blue. White incrustation. From E2-3B/C and E5A[63]. Two non-joining fragments, one with part of a circular groove, apparently from the interior of the base. Second fragment has a small molded circle, possibly part of an inscription.

C. Ribbed Bowls: Millefiori, Colored, and Blue-Green

Ribbed bowls in millefiori, deep solid-colored fabrics, or in plain blue-green, form one of the most characteristic glass types of the first century A.D. The millefiori examples follow the chronological patterns of other millefiori in general,[64] possibly starting slightly later than other shapes, while blue-green ribbed bowls are typical of the fifties of the first century and later.[65]

At Salona as elsewhere the blue-green bowls are much more common than the colored variety, all of which are catalogued here. In both colored and blue-green ribbed bowls, some mold-blown examples were found along with the more common molded variety. Only 6 fragments of ribbed bowls in millefiori or plain deep colors were found at the site, in contrast with 36 blue-green fragments (see Table 2). It is impossible to determine how many bowls these 36 blue-green fragments represent; 11 bowls with different rim diameters and rib shapes were found. The smaller fragments could belong to these or to additional bowls beyond this number.

TABLE 2: BLUE-GREEN RIBBED BOWLS BY TYPE AND DIAMETER

Type	Diameter 10	12	14	16	18	No Diam.	Total, All Types
Straight-sided, heavy ribs			1	1	1		
Straight-sided, close ribs			1			1	
Shallow, small ribs	1					1	
Thick ribs, rim	2	1	1				
Shallow, heavy ribs			1		1		
Mold-blown						4	
Bases of ribs						9	
Single ribs						10	
Total no.	3	1	4	1	2	25	36

18. (**Plate 32.**) Millefiori bowl wall. Opaque purple ground with white flecks. From A3. Two non-joining fragments with 3 ribs from what seems to be a large bowl.
19. Wall with marbled pattern. Amber ground with white canes. From curia burnt layer. Two further small fragments found in different parts of the site may come from this same bowl. Not enough to reconstruct shape or size.
20. Deep colored fragment. Thick, translucent dark amber. From E5A. One rib with very small rim portion.
21. Deep colored fragment. Translucent deep blue. From E5A/E4C. Top portion of shallow, closely-spaced ribs.
22. Deep colored wall fragment. Opaque blue-black. From E5A. Portion from base curve of ribs.
23. (**Plate 32.**) Mold-blown wall fragment. Thin translucent amber; remains of white thread decoration. From E3A. Portion from top of ribs showing characteristic arcaded appearance, incurving rim, and horizontally wound threads of the *zarte Rippenschalen* type.[66]
24. (**Plate 28.**) Shallow bowl fragment. Blue-green. D. 10.8 cm. Rim H. 1.1 cm. From W5A. Shallow shape with slightly incurved rim.
25. (**Plates 28 and 32.**) Deep bowl with wide-spaced square-topped ribs. Blue-green. D. 14 cm. Rim H. 1.6 cm. From E5A.
26. (**Plates 28 and 32.**) Medium deep bowl with square-topped ribs. Blue-green. D. ca. 18 cm. From E3A. Remains of interior groove at base.
27. Four fragments of mold-blown bowl. Colorless-blue green. Thin. D. not known. From E5A; E3A; E1A. All fragments apparently from the same vessel. All wall portions. Two pieces from two different find-spots join; the remaining two fragments do not.[67] Differing from the more common molded variety, this type of bowl is generally smaller, and has a sharply incurved rim and base portion.[68]

D. Colored Blown Glass

Fine blown tableware in deep-colored translucent glass is found in a variety of shapes at Salona. There are deep bowls of the "Hofheim" type,[69] footed dishes, plates, and handle fragments, one possibly from a trulla. The distribution of colors and forms in the group is interesting (see Table 3). As in the molded glass, emerald predominates over the other colors, with about half of the total in that fabric, 40% blue, and 10% amber.[70]

In emerald, there are multiple examples of folded rims and ring feet in graduated sizes. The folded rims range upward in size in almost perfect two centimeter gradations from 10 to 18 centimeters, with a cluster of examples at 14 centimeters. The ring feet come in an even broader size range, from about 4 to 16 centimeters. Some of these rims and bases may have belonged together in footed plates or shallow bowls of increasing diameters. The very large diameter ring feet could have belonged either to straight-sided dishes similar to the blown blue-green examples,[71] or to plates of very large size. The blue examples have a similar but less precisely graduated series of folded rims and bases. It is curious that all of the handles found were deep blue; they could have belonged to any type of small vessel, even to mold-blown novelty vases with blown necks and handles.

At other sites, colored blown glass was used for tableware from the Claudian to early Flavian periods. The peak of popularity for the ware came at about mid-century, and blue-green and colorless glass was more extensively used thereafter.[72] There is evidence for the use of deep-colored blown glass after the first century, for example in a late group of deep blue one-handled jugs with mold-blown bodies,[73] but the Salona fragments seem to fit rather with the early fabrics and forms.

TABLE 3: COLORED BLOWN GLASS BY SHAPE AND DIAMETER

Shape	No. of Exs. in Emerald	Diam., cm.	No. of Exs. in Amber	Diam., cm.	No. of Exs. in Blue	Diam., cm.
Folded rim	3	10			1	6
	1	11			1	8
	6	14			1	9
	3	16			5	12
	2	18			1	12.8
					1	15.2
					1	20
Fire polished rim	1	9.2	1	7.2	1	12.8
	1	12	1	10	1	18
			1	16	1	24
Ground rim	1	6.4	2	8	1	- - -
			1	- - -		
Horizontal rim	3	10			1	7.3
	1	14				
Ring foot	3	3-5	1	18	2	4
	1	6			1	8
	1	8			1	10
	1	10			1	12
	1	12				
	1	14				
	1	16				
Other bases	2					
Handles					4	
Total	33		7		25	

28. (**Plate 28.**) Globular bowl. Emerald. D. at rim 10 cm. Rim W. 0.7 cm. From W5B. Horizontal grinding marks on exterior and top of rim.
29. (**Plate 28.**) Two fragments from bowl with flaring rim. Deep blue. Blowing striations on exterior. Rim D. 12.8 cm. From W5B; W2C.[74] Gradually outflaring bowl folded outwards at rim. Both fragments are from the same vessel, but they do not join. Compare Isings form 41B.[75]

30. (**Plate 28.**) Rim of small bowl. Emerald. Thin. D. 6.4 cm. From E4A. Outflaring rim of small, probably deep, shape, tentatively reconstructed with ring foot.
31. Two fragments of outfolded rim. Emerald. D. 18 cm. From W5B. Narrow folded rim from a bowl, possibly of the straight-sided type seen more often in blue-green fabric. For further examples, see Table 3.
32. Beaker or bowl. Portion of wall near base. Emerald. From E1A. Horizontal wheel-cut groove and polishing marks visible on exterior. This fragment appears to come from a straight-sided bowl or beaker with rounded base. It may belong to one of the deep bowls with wheel-cut horizontal lines popular in the first half of the first century A.D. (Isings form 12.[76])
33. Beaker rim. Amber. D. 8 cm. From E5A. Rim fire polished and ground, with exterior horizontal grinding marks visible.
34. Rim with opaque white edge. Deep blue with added white marvered thread. D. 10 cm. From E4A. Slightly incurving rim from bowl or beaker. A footed beaker from Vindonissa has a similar rim with additional white threads wound horizontally around the lower part of the body of the base,[77] while a comparably decorated vase from Zadar has an opaque white thread around a heavy upward-folded rim.[78]
35. (**Plate 32.**) Rim with white-splashed design. Deep amber. Opaque white splashes. Max. dim. 4.3 cm. From E5A. This type of decoration is found on glasses from North Italian sites, and is generally on jug shapes.[79]
36. Fragment possibly from the end of a trulla handle. Deep blue. W. 1.9 cm. From W5A. Fragment with straight edge, folded over and fire polished. Original width preserved, and part of length. This could come from the handle of a vessel of trulla type (Isings form 75) or possibly from a long-handled ladle.[80]
37. (**Plate 28.**) Ring base of flat dish. Deep blue. Pitted. Base D. 8 cm. From W5A. Pad base extending into the flat bottom of a plate or bowl. For further examples in a range of sizes, see Table 3. Not enough to reconstruct complete shape.

E. Colorless Molded and Engraved Vessels

The three colorless molded glasses and single blown engraved piece listed below represent the total number of finds of this type of glass from the Forum area of Salona, a good indication that we are dealing here with a luxury imported ware. This kind of glass was made in the second and third centuries,[81] and its presence at Salona indicates that in contrast to the first century evidence a very small amount of luxury glass was being used in proportion to the blue-green blown wares.

It should be noted that the Porta Caesarea habitation site at Salona yielded half a dozen cut fragments of more varied cutting patterns than those from the Forum site.[82] There are, for instance, two examples comparable to the geometric patterned flat plate in the Split Museum,[83] and some plainer facet-cut wares.[84] As noted below in the discussion of individual pieces, the place or places of manufacture of this ware is not certain, so that the pattern of trade which led to their arrival at Salona must remain at present a matter of conjecture.

38. (**Plates 29 and 32.**) Bowl with engraved figure. Originally thick, colorless fabric. Now cloudy with weathering. D. 22 cm. From E2B. Shallow molded bowl of thick fabric with wheel-cut ridged rim above a band of facet-cut ovals. Below, fragmentary figure of a gladiator or warrior, of which the front portion of the head, part of the arm and shield are preserved. The figure seems to be wearing a hat or helmet designated by a horizontal groove above the forehead, and a horizontal line at chin level (a strap ?). The arm is cut diagonally with a pattern of short scratched lines. The upper curve of a round shield is visible. The figure is depicted with a combination of wheel-made facet cuts and hand-cut shallowly scratched lines. The fragmentary state of the piece makes identification of the figure difficult. The round shield and apparently bare arm (on which, as often in figure engraved glass, shallow cuts are used to indicate skin)[85] suggest a gladiator of the lightly armed "Thracian" type.

The form of the helmet is not clear, although it seems to have a flat visor over the forehead, and another portion covering the side of the head, which may have gone down into the neck-protecting form of some gladiators' helmets,[86] or may have finished as a round hat. A warrior figure, for example the hoplite engraved on a beaker from Begram,[87] could also look like the Salona fragment, with helmet, bare torso, and round shield. However, the greater frequency of gladiator representations on Roman glass makes the first identification more probable.

Given the shallowness of the bowl, it is likely that only two figures could have been engraved on it, hence the probability that a gladiatorial contest was depicted. Such contests between pairs of combatants are represented on mold-blown, painted, and engraved glasses. Earliest is the group of mold-blown gladiator beakers of the first century A.D., possibly to be traced to a South Gaulish workshop.[88]

Not well dated, but undoubtedly also early, is a series of four tall goblets with painted gladiatorial combats from Begram.[89] Closest to the Salona figure in costume and weapons is the Thracian gladiator on the left-hand panel of the best-preserved goblet. His bare left arm carries a small round shield, his legs and right arm are protected by bands. On his head is a helmet with a flat brim (as in the Salona example) and a fantastic tassel of plumes fastened above.

Unusual in having only one gladiator depicted is a blown glass cup from Aquincum.[90] Although the combination of facet cutting and scratched line engraving is the same, the style of cutting is quite different from the Salona example, the Aquincum example being bolder, and making use of many ornamental swirls and background fillers.

The example of the Aquincum bowl makes clear the difficulty of using engraving technique as a reliable criterion for comparison. Facet-cut figures with added scratched lines are seen on numerous engraved pieces, which range in date from the second to the fourth centuries.[91] The colorless fabric, molding technique, and fine wheel-cut ornament of the Salona fragment provide better indicators for placing it with other fine glass of the second century.

39. (**Plate 29.**) Engraved rim. Originally thick colorless fabric. Now whitish and almost opaque. Rim W. 2.2 cm. Overhand H. 0.7 cm. From B6. Wide horizontal rim with overhang. Molded and cut, with a pattern of ridges and grooves on the overhang, and on the underside of the flat rim a band of stylized flowers: double tulip-like leaves and stems made with oval and elongated facet cuts, the flowers each with a single round facet. One complete flower and parts of two others preserved. Diameter cannot be determined.

This rim belongs to a group of colorless molded and engraved pieces, generally large shallow bowls. Datable examples are from the second century A.D. An especially fine bowl was found in the Cave of Letters in Israel, deposited there in Hadrian's reign along with other valuables in the course of the Bar Kochba revolt.[92] The Cave of Letters plate, almost 34 cm in diameter, uses a bead and reel pattern of more complex form than the Salona example on its rim overhang, but a design of alternating round facets and lines on its rim which is similar in the repetitive use of a simple pattern of cutting shapes. The remainder of the plate is plain, save for a small circular band of facets around the center of the base.

Closer in provenance to the Salona example is a honeycomb pattern plate with bead and reel border from Zadar now in the Museo Vetrario, Venice. There is also an oval dish from Zadar with cut-out handles in the same technique in Venice,[93] and a smaller one still at Zadar, on display in the museum of the University.[94] The Zadar plates differ from the Cave of Letters example in their overall honeycomb ornamentation. It is hard to say whether this indicates any difference in date or workshop. Also similar in its rim design is a deep dish found in Cambridge, England,[95] with horizontal rim ornamented with a row of facets. Although clearly akin to these examples, the Salona rim differs in its use of a natural if stylized floral element in its design. Plain unornamented molded plates and bowls of similar fabric and shapes, such as the following example, were also made, perhaps from the same molds as the more ornate pieces which were finished with facet cutting.

Although these molded engraved glasses show marked affinities in fabric, shapes and cutting techniques, it is not possible to determine as yet the place or places of manufacture. Clairmont, in connection with the rich Dura finds of cut glass, makes a case for the Near Eastern but not Durene origin of the cutting technique,[96] while Harden would favor Alexandria.[97] Both authors suggest a subsequent spread of the technique to Western European glassmaking centers. In general opposition to this view is Fremersdorf, who had long argued for the primacy of Cologne.[98] The long distances travelled by glass products[99] and glass workers[100] makes it difficult to reconstruct the pattern of manufacture and distribution of this type of glass.

40. Plain rim with overhang. Originally colorless, thick fabric. Now cloudy and pitted. Int. D. ca. 12.5 cm. Rim W. 1.6 cm. From E2F. Wide horizontal rim with narrow overhang. Grinding lines and very small bubbles visible on both top and underside of rim. This type of rim is similar to the molded and engraved Salona rim discussed above. Its closest parallel is to a deep footed bowl from Karanis.[101]

41. (**Plates 29 and 32.**) Rim and wall of blown facet-cut bowl. Originally colorless, pale green. Now whitish and opaque. D. 12.4 cm. Grooves 0.5 cm and 2 cm below rim. From D7. This blown bowl is included here because of its facet-cut decoration. Slightly concave rim grooved below, and continuing in plain band to a second horizontal groove; below, two rows of quite widely spaced oval facet cuts are preserved. The characteristic concave rim, grooves, and deep bulging walls of this bowl correspond closely to deep facet-cut bowls found at Karanis and at Dura.[102] The Dura bowls follow a regular pattern of rows of roundish facets at the base of the bowl separated from the oval facets by a line of "rice grain" shape. Bowls of this general type are known also from Cologne, Scandinavia, and other areas.[103]

II. BLUE-GREEN VESSELS

A. Shallow Straight-Sided Dishes

Straight-sided shallow dishes are generally found in contexts of the middle and second half of the first century A.D.,[104] and imitate in their shape the more luxurious versions in deep-colored molded glass. At Salona, the greatest number of surviving examples are very shallow, no more than 2 cm deep, with an apparently concave base and folded rim.[105]

Finds at Pompeii and in Vervoz Tumulus 1 in Belgium[106] suggest that these flat dishes were used in sets for dinnerware. The remaining Salona examples range upward in approximately 2 cm steps from 11 to 24 cm in diameter, with 16 and 18 cm sizes represented by several examples each (see Table 4 below). Only 20% of the surviving Salona examples are from the smallest sizes, and it is possible that deep bowls were more commonly used for the smaller dishes.[107]

The large number of these dishes found in Italy indicates the probability of their importation to the cities of the Yugoslav coast. Local manufacture in other parts of the Roman empire at a slightly later date seems likely, however, in view of the finds from Belgium and Germany.

TABLE 4: STRAIGHT-SIDED SHALLOW DISHES BY TYPE AND DIAMETER

D., cm	Folded Rim	Fire-Polished Rim	Ring Foot	Rim with Collar	Totals
11		1	1		2
12	1		1	1	3
14	1				1
16	4	1	1		6
17	2		1		3
18	5		1		6
19			1		1
20	1				1
22	1				1
24	1				1
Total	16	2	6	1	25

42. (**Plates 29 and 32.**) Shallow straight-sided dish with outfolded rim. Blue-green. D. 16.8 cm. H. 2 cm. From W3-5C/D. This dish probably had a concave base without an added base ring, although the type is also known with the bottom cantilevered out from a small central base ring, and with pulled out foot almost the full diameter of the bottom of the dish.[108]
43. (**Plate 29.**) Shallow straight-sided dish with fire polished rim. Pale olive. Bubbly. D. 16 cm. From W2A.
44. (**Plate 29.**) Ring foot of shallow dish. Colorless-blue green. D. 15.6 cm. From E5A.

B. Bowls and Beakers

Since it is difficult to distinguish in form or function between some types of bowls and vessels for drinking, the whole group is treated together here. Hardly any complete vessels were found, hence they are divided by rim and base types as follows:

Ground or unworked rims	Integral bases
Folded rims	Footed bases
Horizontal and outflared rims	Handles
Rims from large dishes	
Fire polished rims	
Fluted rims	

Tabulation of both catalogued and uncatalogued examples (see Table 5) has yielded the following results: of a total of 207 rim fragments and 112 base fragments only 10 bases and 23 rims were sufficiently informative to be catalogued. The largest number of rims, but also the most fragmentary, are of the simple fire-polished type, with 82 examples of great size range, from 4.8 to 30 cm in diameter. The greatest concentration of examples is at the 8, 10, and 12 cm sizes. The same concentration of sizes occurs with the straight ground rims, which are also the second most numerous rim type with 44 examples; this suggests manufacture of bowls and beakers in convenient sizes as sets for table use. The only other rim which shows a concentration at one size range is the outflared rim with 7 and 5 examples of 8 and 10 cm respectively.

The bases are not as numerous as the rims and are both less informative and less well preserved. The largest category of 59 examples is that of the integral bases generally found on beakers. Next come the ring bases with 44 examples and a concentration of examples at 4 cm and again at 8 and 10 cm for the larger shapes. However, there is no indication of the shapes to which they belonged. These ring bases have been included with the table of bowl bases; for integral and other bases which may have belonged either to bowls or to flasks, see the section on Bottles, Jars and Flasks. A few handles which seem to have belonged to bowls or beakers are listed here also.

Both catalogued and uncatalogued examples show that the Salona bowls and beakers were glasses for table use, with only a few heavier and larger examples of storage type. Some of the vessels with sharp outflared rims may have been used not for tableware, but as in the Cypriote glass, for small covered jars.

It is hard to place many of these examples closely by time and place of manufacture. Fragmentation of the pieces is one difficulty, persistence of some of the shapes another. For example, the beaker with indented sides (no. 71) is in use from the mid-first century through the Antonine period.[109] It is, however, interesting to note that of the 33 catalogued bowl and beaker fragments, 11 can be dated early (to the first century), only 4 can be dated definitely late (fourth century), while an equally small number definitely belong in the second and third centuries. The uncatalogued fragments, were they more complete, might change this picture.

Some of the early examples such as the "Hofheim bowl" type are paralleled primarily on Italian and W. European sites, and it is probable that like the finer glasswares of this period they were imported to Salona from Italy. For the later types, on the other hand, parallels are more with the Eastern part of the Roman Empire. For example, the large diameter rims with thread decoration on the underside (no. 61) are known elsewhere only from Egypt, and should thus be Egyptian imports. The colorless, well-shaped bowl (no. 49) of second century type may also be an imported item.

However, it should not be thought that the greater part of the later Salona bowl and beaker fragments were imported, for the simplicity of forms and their considerable number speak for local production.

TABLE 5A: BOWL AND BEAKER RIMS BY TYPE AND DIAMETER

Ground Rims

D., cm	6	7	8	9	10	11	12	14	16	Total
No. of Ex.	3	3	8	1	7	5	11	3	3	44

Folded Rims

D., cm	8	10	12	13	14	16	18	20	22	24	26	28	Total
No. of Ex.	5	4	7	1	3	6	4	4	3	1	2	1	41

Horizontal or Outflared Rims

D., cm	6	8	10	12	15	16	18	28	30	Total
No. of Ex.	1	7	5	3	1	1	1	2	1	22

Rims with Folded Collar

D., cm	8	10	12	13	14	16	18	Total
No. of Ex.	1	2	1	1	3	3	4	15

Fire Polished Rims

D., cm	4.8	6	6.8	8	9	10	12	14	16	18	20	22	24	26	28	30	Total
No. of Ex.	2	1	2	17	2	21	13	6	8	2	2	1	2	1	1	1	82

TABLE 5B: BOWL AND BEAKER BASES BY TYPE AND DIAMETER

Integral Bases

D., cm	3	3.5	4	4.5	5	5.5	6	6.5	8	No D.	Total
No. of Ex.	1	1	2	3	10	1	12	2	5	22	59

Ring Bases

D., cm	2.5	3.5	4	4.5	5	5.5	6.5	7	7.5	8	10	12	15	Total
No. of Ex.	1	1	10	3	5	1	2	3	1	7	7	2	1	44

	Disk Bases				*High Pad Bases*			
D., cm	4	4.5	Total		6.5	8	10	Total
No. of Ex.	1	2	3		1	2	3	6

Ground Rims

45. (**Plate 29.**) Inward-slanting bowl rim and wall. Blue-green. Brown weathering. D. 8.4 cm. Groove 0.4 cm below rim. From E5A. Smooth ground rim with deep groove below. Wall curves slightly out, then in towards base. Isings form 12, so-called "Hofheim type,"[110] examples of which are generally found in mid-first century levels.[111]

46. (**Plate 29.**) Bowl with rim groove and engraved horizontal lines. Colorless. Green in breaks.

D. 11.2 cm. From W2A. Slight rim groove, with two horizontal lines 1.5 cm apart on bowl wall. Sides go down almost vertically before tapering in towards base. Similar to above, with wider proportions.

47. (Plate 29.) Beaker top portion with wheel-cut exterior groove at rim. Colorless-pale green. D. 9.5 cm. W. of rim groove 0.5 cm. Sides taper downwards slightly. Narrow horizontal engraved lines 1.5 cm below rim groove, and at its base.
48. (Plate 29.) Rim and wall of sharply tapering bowl. Thick blue-green. D. 8 cm. From E1A. Ground rim with pronounced groove just below. Wall thickens towards base.
49. (Plate 29.) Outflaring rim and convex wall of shallow bowl. Originally colorless. Hard whitish coating. D. 18 cm. From W2B. Ground rim, with thin horizontal grooves just at rim and at start of convex curve of body 1.4 cm below. This is a second century type in its colorless fabric and wheel-cut decoration, although similar shapes are seen earlier in the first century in fancier fabrics. The closest comparable example was found in Israel at Nahal Hever, and must date from the first third of the second century.[112] Similar but deeper shapes have also been found at Dura.[113]
50. (Plate 29.) Beaker wall tapering sharply upward to outflared rim. Colorless-blue green. D. 6.8 cm. From E1A. Group of faint horizontal wheel-cut lines at junction of rim and body and 1.4 cm below. Very like the Cypriote "sack-shaped" beakers,[114] which were sometimes lidded.
51. (Plate 29.) Bowl with convex wall and bulging rim. Colorless. D. 12 cm. From W5AA. Horizontal wheel-cut lines form grooved band at rim and 3 cm below. This is a third-fourth century bowl type.[115]
52. (Plate 29.) Vertical beaker rim canted out from sides. Colorless-blue green. D. 6.8 cm. From E5A. Rim ground, with fine exterior polishing lines. Very slight upward taper of wall below rim. Parallels date from the late first-second century.[116]

Folded Rims

53. (Plate 30.) Outfolded rim. Pale olive. D. 9.4 cm. From E1A. This rim and the following example may belong to the common type of deep bowl with base ring and folded rim. The parallels are so widely spread geographically and chronologically that without a more extensive fragment it is impossible to place this piece very closely.[117]
54. (Plate 30.) Deep outfolded rim. Blue-green. D. 19.8 cm. Rim H. 1.4 cm. From W3-5C/D. A thicker and deeper rim fold than the above example. The Karanis bowls on high pad bases have this kind of rim,[118] as does a third century example of comparable diameter found in Kent, England.[119]
55. (Plate 30.) Inward folded rim, hollow in section below edge. Pale blue-green. D. 20 cm. From E1A. This profile was probably achieved by pinching in a folded rim around the edge. The angle suggests an open bowl shape, but I know of no parallels for this type of rim.

Outflared or Horizontal Rims

56. (Plate 30.) Fire polished horizontal rim. Colorless-pale green.Ext. D. 16.4 cm. Rim W. 1.7 cm. From W3-5C/D. This rim is similar to those of the deep bowls from Cyprus published by Vessberg with tubular base rings or high pad feet.[120] Dura bowls similar in shape and fabric seem molded rather than blown.[121] These parallels are of the late first to early second century.
57. (Plate 30.) Outflared fire polished rim. Colorless-blue green. D. 12 cm. From C7. Parallels as for above example. Compare also Isings form 41B, a deep bowl with outsplayed rim and downward tapering sides.[122]
58. (Plate 30.) Outcurved rim from bulbous bowl. Pale olive; bubbly. D. 9 cm. From W3-5C/D. Compare Isings form 94, a second to early third century form.

Decorated Rims

59. (Plate 30.) Complete profile, shallow bowl with horizontal rim. Colorless-green. Ext. D.

11 cm. H. 3.5 cm. From C7. Fire polished horizontal rim with exterior coil just below rim. Irregular scratched lines on exterior. Base probably concave without foot. I have found no exact parallels, but the type seems to be related to Isings form 42, late first to second century.[123]

60. **(Plate 30.)** Flaring rim with coil decoration. Colorless; green in breaks. Ext D. 10 cm. Rim W. 1.9 cm. From W2A. Rim fire polished. This rim could belong to a bowl with a high foot;[124] it is of too large a diameter to have formed the mouth of a funnel-mouthed flask. There is a similar rim, also fragmentary, from Corinth.[125]

Rims from Large Dishes

61. **(Plates 30 and 32.)** Rim with thread decoration on underside. Colorless-green tint. Thick fabric. D. 30 cm. From W3-5C/D. Rim has thickened edge folded under, three raised coils applied to underside in same glass color. There is another Salona fragment of this type in olive glass with a diameter of 16 centimeters.[126] Both rims come from an Egyptian bowl type of the late third to fourth century.[127] These are shaped like shallow truncated cones with straight flaring sides and small base rings. Harden lists many Karanis examples with both self-colored and contrasting applied coils at the rim.[128] Unlike the Karanis examples, the Salona rim fragments are round rather than oval in section. However, since this type of bowl does not seem to be paralleled elsewhere, I think it fair to assume that these are Egyptian imports.

62. **(Plate 30.)** Rim with overhanging lip. Pale olive. D. 24 cm. From W5A. The curve of the wall suggests that this came from a very shallow bowl.

Fire Polished Rims

63. Slightly incurved bowl rim. Colorless, green tint. D. 12 cm. From A'7. Rim slightly thickened. This rim could belong to a straight-sided bowl with small base ring, similar to Cypriote types.[129] With smaller diameters, such rims are found on second century cups.[130] There is a concentration of fire polished bowl rims among the Salona glass at the 12 cm dimension, suggesting here as in other shapes, a standardization of sizes for table use (see table 5A above). However, a greater number of these rims are of the smaller cup sizes, as in the following example.

64. **(Plate 30.)** Fire polished rim. Pale olive. Bubbly. D. 8 cm. From E4C.

65. Rim of conical vessel. Thick deep olive. Blowing striations. D. 10 cm. From E3D. This is a characteristic late and post-Roman shape, used for lamps or drinking vessels.[131]

Fluted Rims

66. Rim fragment with scalloped edge. Deep olive. From A'7. This probably formed part of a footed bowl with scalloped edge comparable to examples from Egypt and other areas.[132] The rims of such bowls are worked into 13-18 irregular scallops.

67. **(Plate 32.)** Portion of octagonal rim. Colorless, thin. L. of side 4.5 cm. From C7. Added self-colored thread on rim edge shows mark of instrument used to push rim into points. The closest parallel to this rim comes from a footed bowl with a five-sided rim in the Niessen collection.[133]

Integral Bases

68. **(Plate 30.)** Base and partial side of straight-sided beaker. Pale green. Base D. 4.5 cm. From E1A. Base flat. Two horizontal grooves on sides 2 cm apart. The pattern of grooves probably continued up the sides of the beaker;[134] other finds indicate that this is a common type of the second half of the first century A.D.[135]

69. **(Plate 30.)** Flat base with conical center kick. Blue-green. Blowing spirals. D. 4.5 cm. From B6-7. From a straight-sided beaker shape.

70. **(Plates 30 and 32.)** Slightly concave beaker base with sharply outflared sides. Colorless-blue green. Thin. Base D. 2.5 cm. D. 1.5 cm above base: 5 cm. From W3-5C/D. This

fragment may belong to a type of beaker whose sides rise almost vertically to the rim from a sharply outflared base. There are many Cypriote examples,[136] and one from an Augustan-Tiberian context from Samothrace.[137]

71. Slightly concave base of beaker with indented sides. Colorless-pale green. From C6. The only preserved Salona example of this well-known type, Isings form 32.[138] It is known from first and second century contexts in Yugoslavia and other areas.[139]

Vessels with Footed Bases

72. (**Plate 30.**) Beaker with applied coil base. Pale green. D. 4.2 cm. From W6B. One of a group of small Salona beakers with bases made by this method. Another fragmentary example (72A) is also illustrated because it shows the technique very clearly.[140]
73. (**Plate 30.**) Ring foot from bowl. Originally colorless. Now white opaque weathered surface. D. 5.6 cm. From E4A.
74. (**Plate 30.**) Thick disk-shaped foot. Pale blue-green. D. 4 cm. Thickness of base disk 1.5 cm. From E5A. This unusually thick applied disk foot with flaring walls is paralleled in a series of 9 conical beakers of Flavian date from Vindonissa.[141]
75. (**Plate 30.**) Disk-shaped foot. Blue-green. D. 4.5 cm. From B6. A lower version of the above example. This seems more closely related to Dura examples;[142] comparisons range from late first to early third century.
76. (**Plate 30.**) Pad base. Bright pale green. D. 5.6 cm. From W5A. Clumsy and thick. There are many comparable examples from Cyprus and Egypt,[143] mainly used for bowl bases.
77. (**Plate 30.**) Base ring with crimped edge. Colorless-pale green. D. 3.5 cm. From D7. This type of base is sometimes described as having "toes." This example, like the very similar Cypriote piece,[144] was probably used for a beaker with sides flaring at the base, then going up almost vertically towards the rim. From Dura and Karanis come comparable bases which are thought to come primarily from flasks;[145] the Dura examples are dated to the second to early third century.

Handles

78. Ear-shaped handle. Pale blue-green. H. 3.2 cm. From E4A. This handle was attached to the underside of the rim and rose above it. 2 ribs. The small size of this handle would make it suitable for a high-handled drinking cup.
79. "Teacup" handle. Blue-green. W. 1.7-1.9 cm. H. 4 cm. From A5. Flat strap handle with attachment points at both ends preserved. This handle seems to have been attached below the rim of the vessel.

C. Bottles, Jars, Flasks

Although not enough survives to reconstruct any one of the Salona bottles in its entirety, sufficient fragments remain to deduce that most come not from large packing or storage shapes, but from table-size vessels, especially narrow-necked bottles and jugs with handles. The better preserved jug fragments belong to the predominantly first century conical or bulbous-bodied types. It is curious that all of the surviving jug rims are of the heavy folded type, while no pouring spouts remain. Only one rim could go with a storage jar of kitchen size. Pottery must have been used here in place of glass at Salona.

Remains of bases show that some of the bottles were of the square type; both mold-blown bases and those flattened after blowing are represented. Free-blown bottles with the sides flattened to a square shape are more commonly found on Eastern than on Western sites.[146] Their appearance at Salona might well suggest importation from the East, since it cannot be determined whether such bottles were locally made. Square bottles of all types were in use from the mid-first century A.D., and find their widest distribution in the second century.[147]

The most interesting of these bases is mold-blown with a two-letter fragment of a Greek inscription: OΥ. Bottle bases with Greek inscriptions are rare and are not well recorded.[148] Many more of the bottle-base inscriptions are in Latin and they thus presumably come from the Latin-speaking provinces of the Empire.[149] Since free-blown uninscribed bottles are more common on Eastern sites than the mold-blown ones, is it not possible that the mold-blown bottles with Greek inscriptions were made in the West by Eastern workmen?

There is a notable lack of bases which can be definitely associated with the round-bottomed bottles, jars and flasks. Some of the integral and ring bases listed under bowls and beakers may have belonged to bottles or flasks. The majority of the bottle and jug fragments fit with early types of the first and second centuries. Many were found in the "A" numbered trenches of the Forum north site, in which concentrations of early material were found. Less common, but still in evidence, are the funnel-mouthed flasks of olive fabric, typical of the third and fourth centuries.

TABLE 6: BOTTLE, JAR AND FLASK PARTS BY TYPE AND SIZE

Bottle Rims

D., cm	3	3.5	4	4.5	5	5.5	6	7	Total
No. of Ex.	1	5	7	3	1	3	1	1	22

Flask Rims / *Jar Rims*

	Flask Rims				*Jar Rims*						
D., cm	5	8	9	Total	8	9	10	12	14	15	Total
No. of Ex.	2	1	2	5	2	3	1	1	1	1	9

Handles

	2 Rib	3 Rib	Strap	Round	Total
No. of Ex.	6	6	8	1	21

Bases, Bottles and Flasks

	Square Bottles	Pushed-In Center	With Inscription	With Knob Feet	Total
No. of Ex.	8	2	1	4	15

Bottle and Jug Rims and Necks

80. (**Plate 30.**) Jug rim and neck with part of handle attached. Pale olive. Ext. rim D 3.5 cm. H. 5.4 cm. No provenience. Rim folded down, up and out to form a lip. Complete neck pinched in at base. Handle attachment with thumb rest. Curve below neck suggests either conical or bulbous body. The general shape is that of Isings form 55A of which the examples date from mid-first to early second century A.D.[150]

81. (**Plates 30 and 32.**) Jug rim and neck, with handle attachment. Blue-green. Ext. rim D. 3.8 cm. Int. D. 1.8 cm. Neck H. 4.2 cm. From W2A. Rim folded out, up and in. Neck, pinched in at base, probably continued into conical body shape. Handle attachment point low on neck preserved. The handle probably had a long horizontal top section like other examples of this type.[151]

82. (**Plate 30.**) Jug rim, neck and handle attachment. Blue-green. Blowing spirals. Rim D. 5 cm. From E2A. Rim is formed from an added, unevenly flattened coil, with join visible on upper surface of rim. Remnants of attachment point of handle 1 cm below rim.

83. (**Plate 30.**) Portion of bottle neck and rim. Pale green. Ext. rim D. 4 cm. From W2A. Rim turned out, up and in. Neck bulges slightly below rim. Sturdy rim of the type used on mid-first to second century molded bottles.[152]

84. (**Plate 30.**) Bottle rim of large diameter. Thick pale green. Ext. D. 6.8 cm. Rim W. 1.3 cm. From E5A.

Flask Rim

85. (**Plate 31.**) Widely flaring funnel-shaped rim. Pale yellow-olive. Rim D. 8.8 cm. From W3-5C/D. Thin scratched diagonal lines on exterior down to 2 cm below rim. The funnel-mouthed flask, to which this rim belonged, is a characteristic shape of the third and fourth centuries.

Jar Rims

86. (**Plate 31.**) Wide-mouthed jar rim. Blue-green. Rim D. 11.6 cm. Max. rim W. 1.7 cm. From E1A. Thick horizontal rim folded out and under. Uneven in width. This belongs to the type of wide-mouthed storage jar found among the household goods of Pompeii, and widely used also in the second century.[154]
87. (**Plate 31.**) Rim of small wide-mouthed jar. Colorless. Very thin. D. 8.6 cm. From W6B. A very similar complete example from Aquileia with rounded body and no base is 11 cm in height. It is a second and third century type.[155]
88. (**Plate 31.**) Rim of large jar or urn. Blue-green. Rim D. 15 cm. From A'7. The inner fold of this rim seems designed for holding a lid.

Handles, Bottles and Jugs

89. (**Plates 31 and 32.**) Jug handle with spur attachment at base. Pale green. H. 6.5 cm. W. 1.9 cm. From E5A. One central rib joins attachment plate at base. Attachment plate long, with horizontal nicks on surface. This type of handle is seen on small jugs.[156]
90. (**Plates 31 and 33.**) Jug or amphora handle with three ribs. Blue-green. Bubbly. H. 8.5 cm. W. at base 4 cm. W. at top 1.8 cm. From E3-4A. Handle complete except for top attachment portion. From a table-size jug or amphora on base ring, Isings form 15.[157]
91. Strap handle fragment. Pale green. Bubbly. W. 4 cm. From E4A. Shallow vertical combed design on exterior of handle. This probably came from a heavy shape such as a square molded bottle.[158]

Bases, Bottles and Jugs

92. Base fragment of square molded bottle. Pale green. Very thick fabric. From E1C/D. Corner portion preserved. Not enough to determine original dimensions.
93. (**Plates 31 and 33.**) Fragmentary bottle base with molded letters. Colorless-blue green. Max. Dim. 3.8 cm. From curia south. Raised letters appear to be OΥ.[159]
94. (**Plate 31.**) Three-toed flask base. Colorless-pale green. From C1. Glass pinched out to make three toes for a base. This kind of base belongs to a type which generally has more toes than the Salona example, often arranged to form a ring; additional "warts" are sometimes pinched out on the body of the vessel as well. The flasks, deep bowls and beakers to which these bases go, were found at Dura, at Karanis in Egypt, on Cyprus, and at other Near Eastern sites.[160] However, the distribution of finds makes it fair to assume with earlier writers that this is a type made in Egypt or Syria,[161] in use in the second and early third centuries.

D. Unguentaria

The Salona unguentaria are quite uniform in shape, and scarce in comparison with other types of glass from the site. 34 fragments were found, of which only 3 showed a complete profile, 19 were base and body fragment, 3 were bodies to the neck, and 9 were rims and necks. Even the fragments indicate that all of the unguentaria were of the type with a narrow conical body and flattened base which was made primarily in the first and second centuries.[162] There were none of the later "candlestick" unguentaria.[163] Vessberg makes the reasonable suggestion that narrow unguentaria of the type found by us were used for packing and sending small quantities of liquids such as perfume,[164] and this may be the explanation of their appearance at Salona apart from their usual funerary context.

95. (**Plates 31 and 33.**) Unguentarium with slightly flaring conical body. Thick blue-green.

H. 5.5 cm. Base D. 1.7 cm. Body H. 3.3 cm. From W3-5C/D. Body slightly more than one-half the complete height. Flaring unworked rim.

96. **(Plates 31 and 33.)** Long-necked unguentarium. Blue-green. H. 6.8 cm. Base D. 1.7 cm. Body H. 1.8 cm. From W3-5C/D. Flaring, inward-folded rim. Long neck with constriction at base. Body only about one-third of total height. This type is in use for a longer period into the second century than the preceding one.[165]

E. Pointed Unguentaria and Amphoriskoi

There are five fragmentary bases from Salona which could belong either to amphoriskoi or to tubular unguentaria with drop-shaped bases. All are of a similar colorless-green glass. Of the two best-preserved examples, the narrower, no. 97, fits well with the dimensions of complete long-necked unguentaria with drop-shaped bases. Examples of this type are known from Cyprus, Aquileia (four examples), and Zadar;[166] three others, two probably of Augustan date, come from the necropolis of Samothrace.[167] Two further dated examples of the Tiberian-Claudian period come from the Tessin necropolis near Locarno.[168] The Salona fragments seem closely related to these first century examples.

The second well-preserved base fragment is of too widely flaring a form to have belonged to one of these unguentaria, which are generally quite tubular in shape, but may have been the base of an amphoriskos. Many early examples of this form are known from Pompeii,[169] and a few undated pieces from Cologne, Bonn, and Warsaw.[170]

97. **(Plates 31 and 33.)** Drop-shaped base, probably from tubular unguentarium. Colorless-pale green. H. 3.7 cm. D. at top 3 cm. From C6.

98. **(Plates 31 and 33.)** Flaring base with drop-shaped point. Colorless-pale green. Thin. H. 3.2 cm. D. at top 3.5 cm. From C1.

F. Lids

Two lids of Isings "bottle neck" type survive.[171] However, these Salona lids are very small, and would have belonged not with urns but with cosmetic jars or similar shapes.

99. **(Plates 31 and 33.)** Almost complete lid. Thin colorless-olive. D. 3.5 cm. Preserved H. 1.8 cm. From E2D. Flat-topped lid having a vertical flange with unworked edge and the start of a hollow central knob.

100. Lid knob. Blue-green. H. 1.3 cm. From A'7.

G. Funnels

Of the four fragmentary funnels found, one is short and the other three are of a very long, thin type which has sometimes been identified as a wine decanting device.[172] It is of interest that an example of this apparently rare long type comes from Aquileia,[173] a probable source for Salona's first century glass. However, the small diameter of these tubes would make them impractical for funnelling a liquid with sediment. An alternate suggestion is that they may have been used in bloodletting devices. Ancient authors cite the use of glass in bleeding cups when it was desired to know the quantity of blood taken.[174] However, no complete glass bleeding cup has survived to verify this identification.

101. Complete tube. Pale green. Tube H. 6 cm. D. 0.7 cm. From E1A. Tubular portion preserved, with start of flaring section.

102. **(Plate 33.)** Top portion of tube. Pale olive. Present L. 12 cm. D. at rim 0.4 cm. From A5.

H. Stemmed Goblets

Sixty-seven recognizable fragments from glasses of the stemmed goblet type were found at Salona. The majority consist of bases and stems, while a few thin-walled upper portions have survived as well. The goblets are variable in form, care of manufacture, and fabric (see Table 7).

TABLE 7: NUMBER OF EXAMPLES OF GOBLETS BY COLOR

	Olive	Blue-Green	Pale Green	Colorless	Bright Green	Total
No. of Fragments	27	14	13	11	2	67
No. Catalogued	9	4	3	1	--	9

Within each color group there is variation, with some examples thin and free of flaws, others thick and bubbly. No reasonably complete base and cup portions were found together in the Forum area, but better preserved specimens from the Porta Caesarea area give some aid in reconstructing the original appearance of the goblets.[175] The bases are quite uniform in manufacture, folded up or under to form a definite rim. The goblet stems are of three types: straight and long, curving outwards at both ends, or of knob shape. The preserved goblet bowls are of at least two types: gradually spreading like a modern wine glass, and with straighter sides sharply angled in to a narrow stem (nos. 109 and 109a below). The Salona goblets are of the type in which bowl and base portions were blown in one.[176]

In the small available sampling of Salona goblets, narrow stemmed examples are more frequent than the knobbed variety. The solid knob-stemmed example (no. 103), the only truly colorless piece, may be of earlier date than the other types.[177] There is no evidence of any ornamentation on these vessels, which seem to have been made for everyday use.

The goblet form with knob stem is found in third century contexts, but the type in all its variations is a much more usual drinking vessel of the fourth century, and continues with only slight modifications for several hundred years.[178] The range of colors, qualities, and shapes in the Salona goblets suggests origin from a number of different places, and also manufacture over a period of time. The earlier theory that the stemmed goblet was probably a purely Eastern Mediterranean type[179] can no longer be maintained after recent finds in Italy, and as far west as England.[180] We do not as yet have sufficient evidence to suggest which of the Salona pieces might have been made locally, and which imported. Except for the knob-stemmed examples, the Salona goblets fit well with dated pieces from the fourth century, although the fragmentary state of the material precludes attempts at closer dating.

Stems and Bases

103. **(Plate 31.)** Solid knob stem. Colorless. White weathering. Knob H. 1.1 cm. From W5A. Curves up into rounded bowl. Preserved angle of foot suggests a high-domed shape for it.[181]

104. **(Plate 31.)** Hollow knob stem and folded foot. Medium olive. Foot D. 5.2 cm. From A6-7. Profile less bulbous than no. 103. The hollow stem knob is unusual.[182]

105. **(Plate 31.)** Tempered stem with complete foot. Deep olive. Dulled pitted surface. Foot D. 4 cm. Stem H. 2 cm. From A1. Rim of foot folded under. Top of stem curves out gradually, probably to rounded bowl.

105a. **(Plate 31.)** Tapered stem, complete foot, and portion of bowl. Blue-green, bubbly. Blowing spirals on base. Foot D. 4.7 cm. Stem H. 1.8 cm. From Porta Caesarea, I-7. Rim of foot folded under. Tool mark inside goblet bowl.

106. **(Plates 31 and 33.)** Short tapered stem and base. Pale olive. Good fabric without bubbles. Foot D. 4 cm. Stem H. 1.6 cm. From B7 between walls S. of workshop. Rim of foot folded upwards. Shape similar to no. 105, with shorter stem.

107. **(Plate 31.)** Short stem curved outwards at top and bottom. Blue-green. Stem H. 1.2 cm. From W5A. Whole stem preserved, with small portion of foot.

107a. **(Plate 31.)** Short outward-curved stem with foot. Colorless-pale green. Foot D. 4.2 cm. Stem H. 1.1 cm. From Porta Caesarea, I-4. Rim of foot folded under. Only lower part of goblet bowl preserved. May rise from sharply angled bottom portion to fairly straight sides.

108. **(Plate 31.)** Base with small stem portion. Blue-green. D. 4.8 cm. Ext. stem D. 0.5 cm. From E1C/D. Rim fire-polished, not folded. Shallow conical foot rises to narrow hollow stem.

Goblet Bowls

109. (**Plate 31.**) Portion of goblet bowl and stem. Thin blue-green. From E1C/D. Bowl curves smoothly from narrow stem, very like bowl of no. 105a. Stem probably narrow and tapered.

109a. (**Plate 31.**) Portion of goblet bowl and stem. Colorless-blue green. D. 3.6 cm above stem junction: 4 cm. From Porta Caesarea, G4. Straight sides with slight outward slant, angling sharply into narrow stem. This goblet bowl would have had an unusually small rim diameter.[183]

Stemmed Bases for Larger Vessels

The two examples listed here have been included because of their similarity to the goblets. They are, however, noticeably thicker, with wider stems, and may have belonged with large bowls, or possibly stemmed flasks.[184]

110. (**Plate 31.**) Foot and lower portion of wide stem. Olive. Brown weathering. Foot D. 6 cm. Ext. stem D. 1.5 cm. From A6-7. Large rim folded upwards; high domed foot rising to hollow stem.

111. (**Plate 31.**) Base of footed bowl. Thick pale green. Foot D. 6 cm. Present H. 4 cm. From W5-6C/D.

I. Lamps with Handles

Some fragments of late Roman three-handled lamps have been found scattered throughout the Salona Forum site, presumably part of the domestic equipment of the people who inhabited the site after the Forum area fell into disuse. Lamps of this type are known from the East, notably from the site of Jerash,[185] and from Italy, where they are found in the catacombs.[186] Datable examples come from the fourth and fifth centuries.[187]

There were 7 of these fragments of lamps with rims of from 8 to 10 centimeters, with a handle attached; 9 separate handles and 8 handle base plates. All are made of colorless glass with a slight olive or green tint.

112. (**Plates 31 and 33.**) Rim and handle fragment from lamp. Colorless-olive. D. 8.4 cm. From E3J/K. Narrow downward-folded rim. Wall tapers towards the base. Comparable examples have an integral base with a fairly high kick; 2 further handles were spaced around the rim.

III. NON-VESSEL GLASS

A. Window Glass

Twelve fragments which are certainly window glass are listed here; flat pieces without finished edges are not included, since they may have belonged rather to square-sided bottles. Both thick so-called matte-glossy glass and thin double-glossy panes were found. Of the double-glossy type four certain fragments can be noted. Most of the rest, however, although heavily iridescent, were probably of the matte-glossy type and very thick, varying from 0.35 to 0.7 cm.

Stratified sites in Roman Britain indicate that between the first and fourth centuries A.D. there was an evolution from thick window glass matte-surfaced on one side to thin double-glossy panes.[188] The thin glossy glass does not appear before the late third century.[189] There is, however, no indication that the chronology of the Salona window glass followed the same pattern. The small number of fragments found and their even scatter over the site are insufficient to indicate whether any of the Salona buildings, such as the curia, were originally windowed with glass.

113. (**Plate 33.**) Large fragment of thick matte-glossy glass. Blue-green. Slight weathering. Small bubbles throughout. L. 10.4 cm. W. 5.8 cm. From C6. One side flat and rough textured, the other of varying thickness, from 0.4 to 0.6 cm at the rounded edge.

114. Three fragments of double-glossy glass. Colorless-yellow. Thin. Some elongated bubbles. Largest piece: 4.5 x 6.4 cm, ca. 0.2 cm thick. From W3-5C/D. Non-joining fragments, each with smooth finished edge.

B. Mosaic Tesserae and Inlays

Ninety-two single glass mosaic tesserae were found on the site, the majority of them in the upper layers of the Forum area, and a few outside the apse of the curia building. Almost half were deep translucent blue, with translucent dark green the second most fequently found color (see Table 8). A section of mosaic tesserae in a cement backing was also found, as were six flat thin fragments larger than mosaic tesserae, which were probably used as inlays. These latter fragments came in the same color range as the mosaic tesserae.

TABLE 8: MOSAIC TESSERAE BY COLOR

Color	Number of Tesserae
Blue-green	7
Pale blue opaque	3
Deep blue	46
Light blue	7
Medium green	19
Turquoise	10

115. (**Plate 33.**) Section of glass mosaic with backing. Light blue opaque tesserae. Individual sections 0.7 to 1.2 cm. From B6. 7 tesserae of uneven size, both square and oblong, laid in whitish cement.

C. Game Counters

Of four round disks with flattened bases found at Salona, two are catalogued here.[190] These objects are found at many sites; they could have been used either as counters for games,[191] or possibly as imitation gem stones.[192] The former use seems more probable here.

116. Complete counter. Pale green. Slight weathering. D. 1.3 cm. From E1A. Sphere, flattened on bottom.

117. Chipped counter. Originally opaque black, now burnt. D. 1.3 cm. From E1B.

D. Bead Fragment

Parallels for beads of this type vary widely in date. At the single site of Corinth, similar cylindrical specimens with blue ground and white thread patterns have been found, dating to the fourth or fifth century B.C., and to the late Roman-Byzantine period.[193] The Salona fragment is more likely to be late or post-Roman.

118. (**Plate 33.**) Fragment of cylindrical bead. D. ca. 1 cm. From A3. Opaque medium blue ground color. Festooned thread pattern. Glass of threads worn away. Rough grayish interior surface.

E. Manufacturing Wasters

A large quantity of glass-working wasters was found in the Glass Workshop area, and a scatter elsewhere on the site. These wasters consisted of sharp-edged chunks of slag, and small drop-shaped and twisted pieces from the blow-pipe. Over 100 fragments of this type were found (**Plate 33**). These pieces will not be catalogued separately. Also discovered were layers of glass material adhering to curved plaster fragments, which were probably the remains of glass melting crucibles. The relation of these latter crucible fragments to the glass furnace has already been discussed. It is interesting to note the presence of two hollow iron tubes in the glass furnace area; these may have come from blow-pipes.[194] (See pp. 59 ff. for a discussion of the glass furnace.)

The working wasters from Salona are comparable to those from other glassmaking operations both Roman[195] and post-Roman,[196] and there is no doubt that along with the glass furnace and crucible remains, scanty as they are, they give evidence for the working of glass at Roman Salona.

Notes on Chapter 9

The following abbreviated titles will be used in the notes:

Arh. Vest.	*Arheološki Vestnik,* Ljubljana.
Berger	L. Berger, *Römische Gläser aus Vindonissa* (Veröffentlichungen der Gesellschaft pro Vindonissa, 4, Basel, 1960).
BD	*Bullettino di Archaeologia e Storia Dalmata.*
Calvi	M.C. Calvi, *I Vetri Romani del Museo di Aquileia* (Associazione Nazionale per Aquileia 1968).
Clairmont	Ch. W. Clairmont, *The excavations at Dura-Europos, Final Report 4, part 5, the Glass Vessels* (New Haven: Dura-Europos Publications, 1963).
Corinth 12	Gladys R. Davidson (Weinberg) *Corinth, Results of Excavations Conducted by the American School of Classical Studies at Athens, 12, The Minor Objects* (Princeton, 1952).
Doclea	Aleksandrina Cermanović-Kuzmanović, "Late Roman glass from Doclea," *Archaeologia Iugoslavica* 9 (1968): 31-43.
Dusenbery E.	"Ancient glass from the cemeteries of Samothrace," *JGS* 9 (1967): 34-49.
Fremersdorf, *FGG*	Fr. Fremersdorf, *Figürlich Geschliffene Gläser* (Römisch-germanische Forschungen, 19, Berlin, 1951).
Fremersdorf 4	Fr. Fremersdorf, *Das naturfarbene sogenannte blaugrüne Glas in Köln* (Die Denkmäler des römischen Köln 4, 1958).
Fremersdorf 6	Fr. Fremersdorf, *Römisches geformtes Glas in Köln* (Die Denkmäler des römischen Köln 6, 1961).
Fremersdorf 8	Fr. Fremersdorf, *Die Römischen Gläser mit Schliff, Bemalung und Goldauflagen aus Köln* (Die Denkmäler des römischen Köln 8, 1967).
Harden, *Karanis*	D.B. Harden, *Roman Glass from Karanis* (University of Michigan Studies, Humanistic Series, 41, Ann Arbor, 1936).
Harden, *Camulodunum*	D.B. Harden, "The Glass," in C.F.C. Hawkes and M.R. Hull, *Camulodunum. First Report on the Excavations at Colchester, 1930-1939* (Oxford, 1947), pp. 287-307.
Harden, *Fishbourne*	D.B. Harden and Jennifer Price, "The glass," in *Excavations at Fishbourne 1961-1969* (Reports of the Research Committee of the Society of Antiquaries of London no. 27, 1971), pp. 317-370.
Isings	Clasina Isings, *Roman Glass from Dated Finds* (Archaeologica Traiectina II, Groningen, 1957).
Isings II	C. Isings, "The glass," in Vermaseren and Van Essen, *The Excavations in the Mithraeum of Santa Prisca in Rome* (Leiden, 1965).
JGS	*Journal of Glass Studies,* the Corning Museum of Glass.
Kisa	A. Kisa, *Das Glas im Altertume,* 3 vols. (Leipzig, 1908).
Marconi	P. Marconi, "Vetri romani del Museo di Zara," *Boll. d'Arte* 26 (1932): 33-42.
Mariacher 1963	G. Mariacher, "Vetri antichi del Museo di Zara. I Vetri del Museo di Zara depositati al Correr," *Bollettino dei Musei Civici Veneziani* 8 (1963): 3-15.
Mariacher 1966	G. Mariacher, "Vetri di Zara restaurati," *Boll. dei Musei Civ. Venez.* 11 (1966): 1-15.
Mariacher, *Vetrario*	G. Mariacher, *Il Museo Vetrario di Murano,* n.d.
Masterpieces	*Masterpieces of Glass.* A selection compiled by D.B. Harden, K.S. Painter, R.H. Pinder-Wilson, Hugh Tait (Trustees of the British Museum, London, 1968).
Panciera	S. Panciera, *Vita Economica di Aquileia in età Romana* (1957).
Ray Smith Coll.	R.W. Smith, *Glass from the Ancient World. The Ray Winfield Smith Collection* (Corning, N.Y., 1957).
Vanderhoeven	M. Vanderhoeven, *Verres Romains (1er-111me siècle) des Musées Curtius et du Verre à Liège* (Liège, Journées Internationales du Verre, 1961).
Vessberg	O. Vessberg, "Roman glass in Cyprus," *Opuscula Archaeologica* 7 (1952): 109-165.
von Saldern	Axel von Saldern, "Ancient glass in Split," *JGS* 6 (1964): 42-46.

Weinberg	G. Weinberg, "Hellenistic glass from Tel Anafa in Upper Galilee," *JGS* 12 (1970).
Wilkes	J.J. Wilkes, *Dalmatia* (Harvard University Press, 1969).
WMBH	*Wissenschaftliche Mitteilungen aus Bosnien und der Hercegovina.*

1. Wilkes, p. 237.
2. Panciera, p. 87.
3. Ibid., pp. 85-7. For the pottery evidence from our Salona excavation, see chapter 11.
4. Two bottles found at Linz (Lentia) in Austria with the signature "Sentia Secunda Facit Aquileiae" and "Sentia Secunda Facit Aq. Vit." Panciera, p. 41. A C. Salvius Gratus whose bottles have been found at Aquileia and other North Italian sites, may also have worked at Aquileia. (G. Brusin, *Aquileia Storica e Artistica,* Udine, 1929, p. 232).
5. For example, the emerald molded and blown bowls, and the straight-sided blue-green bowls.
6. Wilkes, p. 409. For information on this question from the pottery of our Salona excavation, see chapter 11.
7. Panciera, p. 88.
8. Ibid., p. 87.
9. Ibid., p. 91.
10. Tenney Frank, ed. *An Economic Survey of Ancient Rome* vol. 5 (1940), pp. 305 ff.; N. Lewis and M. Reinhold ed. *Roman Civilization, sourcebook II:* the Empire, pp. 471-472. For further information on this question from the pottery of our Salona excavation see chapter 11.
11. M.L. Trowbridge, *Philological Studies in Ancient Glass* (University of Illinois Studies in Language and Literature 13, 1930), p. 119, an edict of Julian of Ascalon concerning location of glass workshops.
12. G. Alföldy, *Bevölkerung und Gesellschaft der römischen Provinz Dalmatien* (Budapest, 1965), p. 188.
13. See note 100 below.
14. A. Hölder, *Führer durch das K.K. Staatsmuseum in S. Donato in Zara* (Vienna 1913); R. Valenti, *Il Museo Nazionale di Zara* (Rome 1932); Marconi; M. Suić, *Muzeji i Zbirke a Zadra* (Zagreb 1954); Mariacher 1963; Mariacher 1966; a few illustrations of choice pieces in G. Mariacher *Vetrario,* n.d., figs. 1-5, pl. 1; G. Mariacher, *Il Vetro Soffiato, da Roma antica a Venezia,* pls. 5, 9, 13, 19. See also Batović, Beloševic, and Suić, *Nin, Problems of Archaeological Excavation* (Zadar 1968), pp. 50-51, pl. 31,1.
15. Doclea.
16. F. Bulić, "Ritrovamenti antichi a Oklaj di Promina (Promona)," *BD* 32 (1909): 45-48.
17. von Saldern.
18. I am grateful to Mssrs. Cambi and Rapanic, directors of the Porta Caesarea excavation, for permission to mention these examples.
19. Mariacher 1963, fig. 18.
20. Unpublished material seen in the Museo Vetrario at Murano.
21. Mariacher 1966, fig. 11; Mariacher 1963, figs. 14, 15; Mariacher 1966, fig. 2. A rare Argonaut flask is shown in Mariacher *Vetrario,* fig. 4.
22. Mariacher 1963, fig. 20; Mariacher 1966, fig. 10.
23. These are reported in *Diadora* 2 (1960-61): 199-213; *Diadora* 3 (1965): 211-212; *Diadora* 4 (1968): 211-214. The early publication by Abramić and Colnago, "Untersuchungen in Norddalmatien," *JÖAI* 12 (1909): 51 ff., illustrates only 2 grave groups from the extensive cemetery found by them (pl. 20-21).
24. S. Ljubić, "Arkeologičko izkapanje u Bakra," *Vjesnik Hrvatskog Arheološkog Društva,* Zagreb 4 (1882): 1-9, pls. 1-4.
25. U. Dusati, *Catalogo del Museo Civico di Pola,* (Pola, 1907). Finds of glass by grave groups mentioned throughout, but with no illustrations or inventory numbers.
26. A.J. Evans, "Antiquarian researches in Illyricum," *Archeologia* 48 (1884): 75-6.
27. J. Kellner, "Römische Baureste in Ilidže bei Sarajevo," *WMBH* 5 (1897): 119-123.
28. C. Truhelka, "Zenica und Stolac, Beiträge zur Röm. Archaeologie Bosniens und der Hercegovina," *WMBH* 1 (1892): 285-286.
29. Irma Cremosnik, "Rimska villa u Višičimo," *Glasnik Zemaljskog Muzeja u Sarajeva* N.S. 20 (1965): 196-198; 219.
30. Doclea, n. 2, p. 42.

31. Doclea, p. 31. Wilkes, p. 259-60 notes that Doclea was founded under the Flavians, possibly by Titus; presumably nothing pre-Flavian has come from the necropolis.
32. Doclea, pp. 44-47 passim.
33. Doclea, p. 41.
34. Plesničar-Gec Ljudmila, "Caractère et chronologie des tombes antiques sur la Prešernova et la Celovka ceste à Ljubljana," *Arh. Vest.* 18 (1967): 137-146.
35. Sonja Petru, "Sul monumento del cittadino di Emona," *Arh. Vest.* 13-14 (1962-3): 497-524. Comparison is made with the similar monument from Aquileia (G. Brusin, *Gli Scavi di Aquileia,* 1934: pp. 197-203). Cameos: R. Noll, "Zwei unscheinbare Kleinfunde aus Emona," *Arh Vest.* 19 (1968): 79-83. Further early glass finds of a marbled millefiori bowl, conical flask and mold-blown beaker with gods under garlands are noted in P. Petru, "Einige Probleme der provinziell römischen Archäologie in Slowenien," *Arh. Vest.* 15-16 (1963-65): figs. 8 and 12.
    The following publications: Sonja Petru, *Emonske Nekropole* (odkrite med leti 1935-1960), Catalogi et Monographiae editi cura Musei Nationalis Labacensis 7 (1972), and Ljudmila Plesničar-Gec, *The Northern Necropolis of Emona.* Catalogi et Monographiae editi cura Musei Nationalis Labacensis 8 (1972) were not available to me.
36. Bolta Alojzy, "Römisches Gräberfeld 'na Bregu' in Celje," *Arh. Vest.* 8 (1957): 317-327.
37. Stanko Pahic, "Antike Grabhügel mit Grabkammer in Miklavz bei Maribor," *Arh. Vest.* 20 (1969): 104-109.
38. Mikl Iva, "Two fragments of glass vessels adorned with gold from Poetovio," *Arh. Vest.* 13-14 (1962-3): 491-5.
39. A. Oliver Jr., "Millefiori glass in Classical antiquity," *JGS* 10 (1968): 58-65.
40. Berger, p. 14, pl. 1, no. 8.
41. von Saldern, p. 43-44, no. 4, inv. no. G36 with parallels listed.
42. Inv. no. 7.32, from E3A.
43. von Saldern, p. 44, fig. 5. From Dalmatia.
44. G. Weinberg, "The glass vessels," in "The Antikythera shipwreck reconsidered," *TAPS* 55 pt. 3 (1965); pp. 37-8, fig. 19.
45. Berger nos. 1-3, pp. 13, 16; pl. 1.
46. Marconi, color pl. opp. p. 36.
47. A. Oliver Jr., "Late Hellenistic glass in the Metropolitan Museum," *JGS* 9 (1967): 21-22.
48. Illustrative tables of contemporary pottery and glass shapes from the Tessin necropolis in Lamboglia, review of Simonett, *Tessiner Gräberfelder, in Rivista di Studi Liguri* 10 (1944): 176-77; 192-3.
49. Berger, p. 24-30, pl. 3, 38.
50. Pompeii and Herculaneum examples are displayed in the Naples Museum and the Pompeii and Herculaneum Antiquaria. Most unpublished. Many examples from local excavations in the Museo di Antichità, Torino; at Este, Aquileia and Locarno. Vindonissa: Berger, see preceding note. Britain: Harden, *Camulodunum,* pp. 298-299; 300-301; nos. 42-47; 53-60.
51. Weinberg 1970, p. 18. See also Weinberg, "Notes on glass from upper Galilee," *JGS* 15 (1973): 35-45.
52. Ibid., p. 19, n. 6.
53. G.A. Papathanasopoulou, "Hellenistic glass vessels from the Pylos Museum," (in Greek) *Deltion* 21 (1966), part a, *Meletai,* p. 188 ff.
54. Dusenbery, nos. 9 and 12, p. 39, probably Augustan in date. An uncatalogued fragment which could be either a conical or hemispherical bowl was found in the closed deposit on the curia site beneath the pavement.
55. Berger, p. 25-26, pls. 3, 31 and 17, 1.
56. Berger, p. 27, pl. 3, 32; 17, 3; Isings form 5, p. 21.
57. Harden, *Fishbourne* no. 15, p. 328, fig. 137.
58. British Museum 59-3-1-10, "From Hertz sale."
59. Berger no. 32. (See note 56 above.)
60. Isings form 22, p. 38.
61. Inv. no. 7.339. Prov. W2C. See chapter 10 for analysis of fabric of no. 15.
62. Berger no. 37, p. 28.
63. 7.4 E2B/E3C; 7.70 E5A.
64. Berger nos. 16-21, p. 10, pls. 1 and 2.

65. Isings p. 17-21, form 3a-c; Harden, *Fishbourne* p. 328-330; Berger p. 21-22, parallels from many W. and N. European sites.
66. W. von Pfeffer and T.E. Haevernick, "Zarte Rippenschalen," *Saalburg Jahrbuch* 17 (1958): 76-88.
67. Inv. no. 7.4 E5A; inv. no. 7.61 E3A; inv. no. 7.65 and 7.66, E1A. Nos. 7.61 and 7.65 join.
68. Cf. Berger no. 139 p. 55, pl. 9. Comparable bowls of this design measure between 9-11 cm at the rim and ca. 5.5 cm in depth. The type, known in the pre-Flavian period, continues later in the first century. Calvi, color pl. 16, 2, shows a deeper beaker-like shape with similarly ribbed body, while there is in the Naples Museum a pair of two-handled jugs with ribbed mold-blown bodies.
69. Ritterling, "Das frührömische Lager bei Hofheim in Taunus," *Annalen des Vereins für Nassauische Altertumskunde* 40 (1912), types 3 and 4, p. 366 ff.
70. I have not included here the far less homogeneous group of fragments in various shades of purple, many of which seem not to be deliberate, but the result of accidents in mixing the glass batch.
71. See section II A below.
72. Harden, *Fishbourne,* pp. 321-322; Berger, pp. 87-88.
73. Ray Smith Coll. no. 279, p. 141; Clairmont no. 565, table p. 4 (late examples in blue opaque, amber and purple).
74. Inv. no. 7.357 W5B; inv. no. 7.335 W2C.
75. Isings p. 57.
76. Isings pp. 27-30; Berger, pp. 43-45 with additional refs.
77. Berger no. 82, p. 39, pl. 5.
78. Marconi, fig. 4, p. 36.
79. F. Fremersdorf, "Römische Gläser mit buntgefleckter Oberfläche," *Festschrift für August Oxé* (1938): 116-121.
80. A "cup handle" of similar form with molded signature comes from Corinth (*Corinth 12* no. 650 fig. 10, p. 163). An undecorated example forming the top of a skyphos handle was also found there (no. 649). These are both of smaller dimensions than the Salona example, and are more flattened. An example in plain colored glass of a trulla is in the National Museum in Prague (J. Čadík, *Graeco-Roman and Egyptian Glass.* A guide to the Exhibition at the National Museum in Prague (Prague 1970), pl. 11, p. 31).
81. Clairmont, pp. 56-57; Harden, *Fishbourne,* p. 334.
82. See note 18.
83. von Saldern, fig. 11, p. 46.
84. Comparable to: Harden *Karanis* no. 189, 211, pl. 13; no. 316, pl. 14. 2nd-early 3rd cent. A.D. Clairmont, geometric cut glass group B (2nd cent.) p. 63; group C (2nd-early 3rd cent.) p. 65.
85. F. Fremersdorf, *FGG* pl. 7. George C. Boon, "A Roman figure-cut vessel from Caerleon," *JGS* 10 (1968): p. 81, figs. 1, 3, 5.
86. As on Begram painted glass frag. B37 no. 199; P. Hamelin, "Materiaux pour servir à l'étude des verreries de Begram," *Cahiers de Byrsa* 4 (1954), pl. 18 no. 3.
87. Hamelin, *Cahiers de Byrsa* 2 (1953), pl. V.
88. Berger, p. 58-60; Origin: D.B. Harden, "A Roman sports cup," *Archaeology* 11 (1958): 2-5. On Neronian date of certain gladiator beakers from names inscribed on them, see Henry T. Rowell, "The gladiator Petraites and the date of the Satyricon," *TAPA* 89 (1958) 14-24. See also J. Price, op. cit. note 194 below.
89. Hamelin, *Cahiers de Byrsa* 4 (1954), pl. 18, 2, 3; pl. 19, 5.
90. Fremersdorf *FGG,* pl. 8, 1 and 3.
91. *Masterpieces,* no. 94, p. 70-71; Leuna Merseburg Artemis bowl (2nd cent. with companion Actaeon piece from Dura; Clairmont 57-59; the Hohensülzen bottle (Fremersdorf, *FGG,* pl. 7), and the Caerleon fragment (Boon, op. cit. note 85, p. 84) are dated to the late 3rd-early 4th cent. by associated finds. On the question of the place of origin of figure-cut pieces cf. notes 96 and 97 below.
92. Y. Yadin, *The Finds from the Bar Kochba Period in the Cave of Letters* (Jerusalem, 1963), no. 12, p. 107.
93. Plate: Mariacher *Vetrario,* fig. 3, p. 15. Oval dish, Mariacher 1966, fig. 9.
94. Inv. no. 6297.
95. Harden, *Karanis* fig. 1c.
96. Clairmont, p. 57.

97. Harden, *Karanis* p. 66; Harden, "The Wint Hill hunting bowl and related glasses," *JGS* 2 (1960): 46 on Alexandrian origin of figure-engraved glasses.
98. Fremersdorf, *FGG*, pp. 22-24. Against the unity of Fremersdorf's "Cologne workshop" see Harden in *JRS* 43 (1953): 201-2.
99. G. Eckholm, "Orientalische Gläser in Skandinavien während der Kaiser-und frühen Merowingerzeit," *Acta Arch.* 27 (1956): 35-59; Harden, *Karanis* 102 (export from Egypt to Rhine area).
100. For example, Ennion from Syria to N. Italy: Harden, "Romano-Syrian glasses with mould-blown inscriptions," *JRS* 25 (1935): 164-5. See also R.J. Forbes, *Studies in Ancient Technology* 5 (Leiden 1966): 154-155, n. 124-133.
101. Harden, *Karanis* no. 166, p. 66, pl. 12. Plain molded rim of similar profile from Harden, *Fishbourne* no. 26, p. 332 fig. 138; additional refs. p. 331.
102. Harden *Karanis* no. 317, p. 99, pl. 14. Dated 2nd-early 3rd cent. Clairmont, cut glass geometric patterns group C, p. 65 fig. 2.
103. Fremersdorf 8, pl. 32, 3; 48; 75. Eckholm (op. cit. note 99), fig. 2J; Clairmont, p. 65 n. 160 (Zagreb, Athens, Virunum, Saalburg).
104. Isings form 46, form 48, pp. 61-63. The majority of the finds listed come from North Italy (Calvi no. 238 p. 94). Examples are also known from Germany (Fremersdorf 3, p. 35, pl. 46; Fremersdorf 4, p. 36, pl. 67), Belgium (Vervoz Tumulus 1. J. Phillipe, "Les verres des tumuli de Vervoz," *Hommages à Albert Grenier* vol. 3, p. 1243-1253. Also in Vanderhoeven I, nos. 47-50, pl. 10 and 11) and Zadar (now in Museo Vetrario, Murano. Mariacher 1966, p. 11, fig. 15). Compare also two 2nd cent. examples from Corinth, 17 and 22 cm in diameter resp. (*Corinth 12* nos. 628, 629, p. 99, fig. 8).
105. Only folded rim examples which are certainly from shallow dishes are included here. Other folded rims are listed under Bowls and Beakers nos. 53-55 in the catalogue.
106. Phillipe and Vanderhoeven (op cit. note 104), 4 plates of identical manufacture, varying in diameter from 14.6 to 14.9 cm, 2 cm in height, were found at Vervoz.
107. In the Antiquarium at Herculaneum for example can be seen a stack of 4 identical blown bowls (no. 2365) while at Vervoz, along with the shallow dishes were found 8 deeper bowls of the same straight-sided type. (Vanderhoeven I nos. 33-40, pl. 7-9).
108. Isings form 47, p. 62; form 48 p. 63.
109. Yugoslav example from Doclea. *Doclea,* grave 208, pl. 12, p. 84 (2nd cent. A.D.); grave 85, pl. 7 (Flavian). Cypriote dated example is Antonine (Vessberg, p. 154-5), Samothracian one mid-first cent. (Dusenbery, no. 45, p. 47). There are two N. African examples, one found with a Domitianic, the other with a Hadrianic coin (S. Lancel, *Verrerie Antique de Tipasa,* 1967, nos. 147, 157, p. 78.
110. Isings p. 27-29.
111. See note 69. Cf. Berger, no. 100 (p. 44, pls. 7 and 17) "Claudian-Neronian" in date; Dusenbery, no. 36, p. 45; Harden, *Fishbourne* no. 46-48 (pp. 344-345, fig. 139) 43-75 A.D.
112. D. Barag, "Glass vessels from the cave of horror," *Israel Exploration Journal* 12 (1962): 208; fig. 9 p. 209.
113. Clairmont, no. 426, p. 96, pl. 10, also of the 2nd or early 3rd century.
114. Vessberg, beaker type A IIa, p. 121 pl. 3, 9-18. Examples with lids pl. 14, 2-4. Two similar examples from Zadar are now on display in the Museo Vetrario at Murano (unpublished; nos. not available). A piece from Samothrace is dated to the first half of the lst cent. A.D. (Dusenbery, no. 37, pp. 45-46).
115. Cf. Isings form 96a, pp. 113-114; Clairmont no. 427 pl. 10.
116. Cf. Harden, *Fishbourne* no. 57, fig. 140, p. 347. 100-270 A.D. Also an example from the Cologne area with 3 horizontal grooves and base ring. Late 1st cent. A.D. Fremersdorf 4, p. 38, pl. 72.
117. First cent. A.D.: Fremersdorf 4, pl. 71; 2nd cent.: *Corinth 12* no. 634, p. 99, 2nd-3rd cent.: Harden, *Karanis* nos. 242 and 260; Isings form 44 (1st cent.) and form 115 (4th cent.).
118. Harden, *Karanis* nos. 83-116, pp. 72-76, pl. 12.
119. *Masterpieces,* no. 110, p. 84.
120. Vessberg, pl. 2; 10, 15 and 18, pp. 114-117.
121. Clairmont, nos. 76 and 77, pl. 2; pp. 2 and 22.
122. Isings p. 57.
123. Isings p. 58,
124. Cf. Vessberg pl. 2, 16; p. 117.

125. *Corinth 12* no. 653 p. 103, fig. 9.
126. Inv. no. 7.195. Prov. W3-5C/D. Olive green fabric.
127. Harden, *Karanis* p. 47.
128. Harden, *Karanis* nos. 30-66, pl. 11. No. 60 shows complete shape.
129. Vessberg, pl. 1, 27.
130. Isings form 85, p. 101; Harden, *Fishbourne* no. 74 p. 352; L. Barkoćzi, "Die datierten Glasfunde aus dem II Jahrhundert von Brigetio," *Folia Archaeologica* 18 (1966-67): no. 9, pl. 26, 3.
131. Harden, *Karanis* nos. 464-465, with rounded rim and base knob, pl. 16, pp. 155-158; 164. More commonly this type has an unworked rim. Post-Roman examples in G.M. Crowfoot and D.B. Harden, "Early Byzantine and later glass lamps," *JEA* 17 (1931): 196-208.
132. Cf. Harden, *Karanis* no. 257, p. 111, pl. 14; n. 2, p. 111, fig. 2g (Toledo Museum 354.9871). The examples cited by Harden were thought by him to have been made in Egypt. Cf. also N. Kunisch, "Neuerworbene antike Gläser der Antikenabteilung der Staatlichen Museen Berlin," *AA* 1967, p. 188, fig. 19. Found in W. Anatolia.
133. S. Loeschke, *Beschreibung Römischer Altertümer gesammelt von Carl Anton Niessen* (Cologne 1911), no. 1096, pl. 45.
134. Still-life fragment in National Museum, Naples. B. Maiuri, *Museo Nazionale di Napoli.* Musei e Monumenti (1957), color pl. opp. p. 134.
135. Isings pp. 28-9; Vanderhoeven I, nos. 14 and 15, pl. III, pp. 18-21. From Vervoz tumulus I, with refs. Vessberg pl. 1, 25; p. 115, deep bowl type A III.
136. Vessberg beaker type A1A, pl. III, 1-3, pp. 119-120.
137. Dusenbery, fig. 40, p. 46.
138. Isings pp. 46-7.
139. See note 109.
140. Inv. no. 7.598, from W6B.
141. Berger no. 105, pl. 19, 51; p. 46.
142. Clairmont, nos. 432-435, pl. 10, pp. 97-98, with refs.
143. Vessberg pl. II, 8-14, type B IIa and b, pp. 116-117; Harden *Karanis* nos. 122-130, pl. 12, pp. 77-78. The Egyptian bases differ from other examples in having slanting marks on the outer edge. Clairmont nos. 76-85, pls. II and III, pp. 22-23, are comparable in form but not in fabric.
144. Vessberg, pl. 4, 12, Beaker type B III. Other bowl and beaker cf. Clairmont, p. 51, n. 101.
145. Clairmont, nos. 200-213, pl. 5, pp. 50-52. Dated 2nd-early 3rd cent., and thought to be of W. Syrian-Egyptian make. Harden, *Karanis* nos. 682-685, p. 220.
146. Harden, *Karanis,* pp. 237-238; Vessberg pp. 126-129, pl. 6, 1-5; *Corinth 12,* nos. 656-658; Clairmont, p. 121 identifies numerous molded bottle bases found at Dura as imports on the basis of affinities with Western material.
147. Dorothy Charlesworth, "Roman square bottles," *JGS* 8 (1966): pp. 30-32. Clarlesworth also details the limited evidence for a continuation of the square bottle form in the East in the 3rd-4th cent.
148. Clairmont, p. 127 and n. 330, mentions a hexagonal bottle with the Greek inscription ΓΕΡΜΑΝΟΣ. Reference here to G131, an unpublished piece from the Athenian agora, inscribed with the Greek name *Tryphonos*. (Information on the inscription kindly provided in a personal letter by Mrs. Weinberg.) There is a dubious reference, possibly a misreading, of a supposed Greek bottle base inscription in Kisa vol. 3, p. 939, 2. Also Calvi, no. 214, inscribed Αλεξανδ[ρου], and the unpublished base from an octagonal bottle from the Eugene Schaefer Collection, The Newark Museum (50.1620) inscribed ΠΡΙΟΚΟΣ. The same signature appears on a bottle in the Rockefeller Museum, Jerusalem, inv. no. G 340-1262.
149. Charlesworth (op. cit. note 147) p. 33. Examples from England and Germany, pp. 34-36; Fremersdorf 4, pp. 50-55; Kisa vol. 3, pp. 947-954.
150. Isings pp. 72-73. Both body forms shown in Calvi, pl. B, 8 and 9.
151. For a very long-necked example see Fremersdorf 6, pl. 74, p. 43.
152. Vanderhoeven 1, nos. 51-66 illustrates many comparable examples.
153. Isings form 104, pp. 122-125.
154. Isings form 62, p. 81.

155. Calvi, no. 301, pl. 22, 7, p. 146, n. 42 with additional refs.
156. For example: Vessberg, pl. 5, 15; Fremersdorf 4, pl. 47, 57.
157. Isings pp. 32-34.
158. Cf. note 147.
159. See note 148.
160. Clairmont, nos. 200-222, pls. 5 and 6; Harden, *Karanis* nos. 678-685, pl. 19; Vessberg, p. 123, pl. 4, 12, a beaker.
161. Clairmont, p. 51, n. 101 and Harden, *Karanis* n. 3, p. 220 for German examples thought to be Eastern imports or copies from them. Also Barkoczi, *Folia Archaeologica* 19 (1968), p. 63, pl. 39, 4 for a flask with base toes and body warts found at Brigetio in Hungary.
162. Isings form 28, pp. 41-43; Vessberg, p. 140.
163. Vessberg, p. 137, pl. 22.
164. Vessberg, p. 140.
165. Isings, pp. 42-43.
166. Cyprus: Vessberg, p. 141, pl. 9, 30; 20, 2. Aquileia: Calvi nos. 188-189, pl. C, 13. Zadar: Mariacher 1966, no. 5, p. 4.
167. Dusenbery, fig. 32, no. 32, p. 44.
168. Chr. Simonett, *Tessiner Gräberfelder,* (Basel 1941), p. 79, fig. 62. Further examples cited under Isings, form 9, p. 25.
169. V. Spinazzola, *Le Arti Decorative di Pompeii* (Milan, 1928), pl. 223.
170. Cologne: Fremersdorf 6, pl. 40, p. 33. Bonn: Morin-Jean, *La Verrerie en Gaule sous L'Empire Romain* (Paris 1922-3) form 29, p. 80. Warsaw: B. Filarska, *Muzeum Harodowe Warszawie, Szkla Starozytne Katalog Naczyn* (Warsaw 1962) no. 165 inv. 42249.
171. Isings form 66B, p. 85.
172. Berger nos. 224-26, p. 85, with references to similar Pompeiian finds.
173. Calvi, nos. 242-43, pl. 18, 1.
174. John Stewart Milne, *Surgical Instruments in Greek and Roman Times* (Oxford, 1907), pp. 102-3.
175. I would like to thank our Yugoslav colleagues, particularly Mr. Cambi and Mr. Rapanic, for their kind permission to publish these glasses from their excavation area. The pieces have been given "a" numbers in the catalogue to distinguish them from the Forum examples.
176. Isings, pp. 139-40 for distinction between one and two part techniques (partly hollow stem vs. solid stem respectively). The one piece technique is seen in Cypriote examples (Vessberg, p. 124, pls. 4, 17, and 18) while examples of both techniques were found in the glass of the Santa Prisca Mithraeum in Rome (Isings II, figs. 437-39). Goblets from Karanis in Egypt are distinguished by their almost exclusive adherence to the two part technique and their distinctive tooled feet (Harden, *Karanis,* nos. 479-92, pp. 167-71). Further local variation is suggested by the almost stemless, pushed-in bases of tall goblets found in the late 4th century glass factory at Jalame near Haifa (information kindly provided by Sidney Goldstein; see Sidney M. Goldstein, *A Preliminary Study of the Glass Manufactured at Jalame in Israel,* unpublished Ph. D. dissertation, Harvard University, 1970, pp. 108-9; 126-28, pl. 10).
177. Cf. Clairmont, nos. 460-67, p. 101. These examples, dated 2nd to 3rd century A.D., are likely to have been of the ornate snake-thread type.
178. Dated examples from earlier literature cited by Isings, pp. 139-40. See also: *Corinth 12,* p. 81 no. 654, a 4th cent. example; Isings II, p. 508, pre-A.D. 400, and the Jalame examples of the late 4th cent. (note 176). For later continuation of the goblet form: A. von Saldern, "Glass from Sardis," *AJA* 66 (1962): 9-10, nos. 10a-10g.
179. Harden, *Karanis* p. 168; Vessberg, p. 124; Isings, p. 139.
180. Among these, the Santa Prisca Mithraeum glasses (Isings II, figs. 437-39) and goblets from a Suffolk grave group of the 4th to 5th cent. A.D. ["Recent important acquisitions," no. 16 in *JGS* 5 (1963): 144-45].
181. Cf. *Corinth 12,* no. 654. All goblet stems found at Dura are also of this type (Clairmont pp. 101-2, nos. 460-67). A complete example of this type from the Porta Caesarea section of Salona (P.C. 14, 1.20 M) has an unusually wide foot, 7 cm in diameter.
182. I know of one parallel for this type from Kish, dated 5th-6th cent. A.D. D.B. Harden, "Glass from Kish," *Iraq I* (1934), fig. 5, 16.

183. This contrasts in size with other goblet bowls. The complete Karanis examples are ca. 7 cm in upper diameter, while this narrow example could hardly have been more than 5 cm.

184. Example of flask with bulbous body, narrow straight neck and base of this type in Split Museum, inv. 7338.

185. G.M. Crowfoot and D.B. Harden, "Early Byzantine and later glass lamps," *JEA* 17 (1931), p. 199, type C1.

186. Isings II, p. 508, fig. 432. Additional refs. in Isings p. 162.

187. Isings form 134.

188. D.B. Harden, "Domestic window glass: Roman, Saxon and Mediaeval," in E.M. Jope ed. *Studies in Building History. Essays in Recognition of the Work of B.H. St. J. O'Neil.* (London, 1961) pp. 47-48. This article (pp. 39-63) gives a very complete treatment of the subject, with full refs. Diverging from Harden's view that most Roman window glass was cylinder-blown, opened and flattened in a furnace, is George C. Boon ["Roman window glass from Wales," *JGS* 8 (1966): 41-45], who believes that the Welsh glass published by him was made by pouring into molds.

189. Harden (op. cit. note 188), p. 47.

190. The other two are olive green and pale green, and have the same shape and dimensions as the catalogued examples.

191. *Corinth 12,* p. 217, p. 223 note 1b; nos. 1787-1789. Also similar counters in bone (p. 169 no. 1693). Harden, *Karanis,* p. 291, n. 2 and 3, nos. 895-927.

192. *Corinth 12,* p. 223.

193. *Corinth 12,* p. 288, no. 2456; p. 289, no. 2481.

194. From a Roman industrial area outside the ancient city walls of Merida in Spain come comparable hollow tubes of bronze, which may also have been used for glass-blowing. Jennifer Price, "Some Roman glass from Spain," *Annales du 6e Congrès de L'Association Internationale pour L'Histoire du Verre.* Cologne, 1-7, July 1973 (Liège 1974), pp. 66, 69-72.

195. *MUSE. Annual of The Museum of Art and Archaeology, University of Missouri* 2, p. 13.

196. Corinth: Gladys R. Davidson, "A Mediaeval glass factory at Corinth," *AJA* 44 (1940), pp. 304-5, fig. 2. Bulgaria: Georgi Chr. Djingov, "Le Verre dans l'antiquité et au moyen âge en Bulgarie," *Annales du 3e Congrès des Journées Internationales du Verre,* Damas 14-23 Nov. 1964, pp. 104-115, figs. 35-36.

ACKNOWLEDGEMENTS

I would like to thank the Smithsonian Institution for the Research Travel Grant which enabled me to return to Yugoslavia in the summer of 1971 to study the glass material from Split and other areas; Mssrs. Mladen Nikolanci, Nenad Cambi and Jelko Rapanic for their aid during my work in the Split Museum; the photographer of the Split Museum for photographing the glass; Profs. Wiseman and Ochsenschlager, directors of the Stobi and Sirmium excavations respectively, for letting me look at their glass finds; the Rutgers University students Robert Scheetz, Ann Zeloof and Richard Mowery for assistance during the 1970 excavation; Robert Brill, Corning Museum of Glass, for his generous assistance in analyzing the Salona glass fragments; and last, but by no means least, the co-authors of this report for their advice and encouragement throughout this project.

CHEMICAL ANALYSES OF SOME GLASSES FROM SALONA

by Robert H. Brill

Eighteen fragments of glass excavated at Salona were submitted by Dr. Susan Auth to The Corning Museum of Glass for laboratory examination and chemical analysis. The fragments include parts of vessels, pieces of cullet, and materials which might have been waste from a glass-working operation. The fragments are from known locations in the excavations, and it is suspected that occupations of different dates are represented, but there are no particular dates associated with particular specimens. The glasses are believed by Dr. Auth to date from the first to fourth century A.D.

The main objective of our analyses was to determine if the glasses could have been manufactured locally. While it is not generally possible to make precise identifications of places of manufacture from analytical data, it does sometimes happen that peculiarities occur in chemical composition as a result of the use of some unusual local raw material. But even if a group of glasses does not show some such peculiarity in composition, it is nonetheless useful to be able to assign glasses to one or the other of two compositional categories which predominate among ancient glasses.[1,2] These categories are the high potassium-high magnesium type (high K_2O-high MgO) and the low potassium-low magnesium type. It is the author's opinion that the former includes glasses made with plant ash as a source of soda, while the low K_2O-low MgO glasses were probably made with natron. Ancient glasses from certain periods and places can also often be classified according to those which contain intentional additions of manganese (MnO) and those with antimony (Sb_2O_5). (Occasionally both are found in a glass.) These ingredients were probably added as decolorizers to offset the greenish tints caused by iron impurities, but the Sb_2O_5 could also have functioned as a fining agent, to remove small bubbles.

The results of our chemical analyses are presented in Table 1. Quantitative analyses, by atomic absorption, were carried out for Na_2O, CaO, K_2O, MgO, and Al_2O_3. Atomic absorption was also used for Fe_2O_3 and MnO where prior spectrographic analysis indicated that the contents of these elements are more than a few tenths of a percent. All the other values are by emission spectrography, except for silica (SiO_2) which was estimated by difference from 100%.

There are three conclusions which can be drawn from the data. The first is that if the glasses were made locally, they do not seem to be characterized by any chemical peculiarity resulting from the use of some unusual local raw material. The compositions are normal in the sense that they do not differ (at least not markedly so) from analyzed glasses from other sites. They appear to have been made from the conventional materials. This, however, does not necessarily argue against either local manufacture of the glass itself or the local fabrication of vessels from imported cullet.

Secondly, the basic compositions of the fragments of vessel glass (with one exception) are all very similar. The similarity is close enough, in fact, that they could well have come from the same factory. These are all of the low K_2O-low MgO group, and most contain intentional additives of manganese. The compositions are of the type believed to result from the use of natron as an alkali. Although the analyses place the glasses within a broad compositional category, they do not answer the question of whether or not the glass was manufactured locally. They do, however, relate the Salona finds to a tradition of manufacture. In the way of comparison we have as yet unpublished analyses of a large suite of glass samples from the site of Cosa, on the west coast of Italy above Rome. These glasses, provided by Dr. David Grose, date to the second quarter of the first century A.D. The Cosa glasses are a homogeneous group, chemically, and although the compositions can be distinguished from the Salona data, the two groups of glasses do resemble one another quite closely.

The sample 3014, from a dish of emerald-green glass, differs significantly from the other vessel fragments in its composition. It is colored with copper (CuO) and contains traces of tin (SnO_2), lead (PbO), and silver (Ag_2O). The presence of tin suggests that the copper was introduced in the form of an ingredient derived from bronze, a common characteristic of early blue and green glasses. The lead also probably came in with this ingredient and, in turn, probably brought along the silver as an impurity. Even the minor elements in this glass differ somewhat from the rest of the vessel fragments, substantiating that it had a different origin. (The K_2O and MgO values bring it close to the limits of the high K_2O-high MgO group.)

Thirdly, it is noteworthy that three of the five specimens of cullet differ somewhat from the vessel glasses (nos. 3000, 3002, and 3003). They contain antimony at an additive level, whereas none of the vessel fragments contain any antimony. (The light blue opaque glass, no. 3012, has a high antimony content, but this is due to the presence of the white pigment, $Ca_2Sb_2O_7$, which makes the glass opaque. Antimony also often found its way into strongly colored mosaic tesserae, like nos. 3016 and 3017.) This confuses the picture somewhat, for it brings in examples of cullet which represent a rather different glassmaking tradition than that used for making the vessels—at least those vessels which were analyzed. On the other hand, the other two samples of cullet (nos. 3001 and 3004) and the rounded droppings of waste glass (no. 3005) are quite close to the vessel glasses and could, indeed, well be waste from the same factory where the vessel glasses were made. The confusion might be the result of variation in levels or date among the samples, but without more definitive excavation information, it is difficult to make a judgment on this point.

It might be added that both antimony and manganese are occasionally found among wares from archaeologically homogeneous groups, and sometimes both occur in the same glass, as is the case with our no. 3002. This could be attributed to an overlapping of technological traditions or to the salvaging and remelting of scrap glass. The salvaging process, still in practice today in small factories throughout the world, leads to the mixing of glasses of varying compositions. Glasses containing both antimony and manganese most often date from between about 150 and 350 A.D.

The cullet sample no. 3003 is unusual in that its CaO content is so low. The analysis was repeated, and the low CaO content was verified. This glass is totally colorless to the eye, giving it an appearance which raises the question of whether it could be a modern intrusion.

The compositions of the mosaic tesserae (nos. 3016 and 3017) are quite close to the vessel fragments, after allowances are made for the presence of the colorants. The blue tessera owes its color to cobalt (CoO) and possibly contains some $Ca_2Sb_2O_7$ opacifier. The green tessera is colored with copper (CuO) as modified by the lead (PbO) which could be "in solution" or, possibly, in the form of the yellow colorant-opacifier $Pb_2Sb_2O_7$. In both cases, the copper contents show associated tin (SnO_2) which again suggests that the copper was introduced in the form of an ingredient derived from bronze.

Dr. Auth also submitted samples of conglomerates which contain highly fractured remains of glass adhering to what appears to be a refractory substance. The refractory substance could be the remains of an actual furnace structure or tank, or a floor adjacent to a furnace. This material was obviously heated to high temperatures, and the adhering glass, while softened, was in contact with it. This is clear from the observation that there are interaction zones between the glass and other substance. The conglomerate resembles debris found in abundance at known early glass-manufacturing sites, for example, Jelemie, in Galilee. When found in substantial quantities, such materials can be taken as evidence that glass manufacturing did take place nearby. This conglomerate, along with the rounded droppings of softened glass (no. 3005), are the most convincing evidence the author has seen that glass was manufactured in the vicinity of the Salona excavations.

Notes on Chapter 10

1. E.V. Sayre and R.W. Smith, *Advances in Glass Technology,* part 2, pp. 263-282 and 283-291, Plenum Press. These are the proceedings of the Sixth International Congress on Glass. (Held in Washington, D.C., 1962.)

2. For a general discussion of the examination and analysis of early glasses, see: R.H. Brill, "The Scientific Investigation of Ancient Glasses," *Proceedings of the Eighth International Congress on Glass.* (Held in London, 1968.)

Sample Descriptions*

Cullet and Glass Waste

3000 Pale aqua
3001 Greenish aqua
3002 Bluish aqua
3003 Colorless
3004 Lump of dark green cullet (7.866 B6-7)
3005 Small rounded droppings of dark green glass (7.720 W7B)

Vessel Fragments

3006 Goblet base, green glass (7.374 E2F)
3007 Vessel fragment, colorless with purple streaks (7.9 W3-5C/D)
3008 Vessel bowl (?) fragment, with pincered tip, colorless glass (7.719 W3-5C/D)
3009 Goblet base, colorless glass with brown weathering scum (7.119 E5A)
3010 Vessel wall fragments, pale purple glass (7.850 W5AA)
3011 Vessel fragment, rounded shape, amber glass, weathering pits (7.73 W2A)
3012 Mold-blown vessel fragment, squared-off corner, light blue opaque glass (7.72 W2A)
3013 Rim fragment of flask, aqua glass (7.149 W2A)
3014 Fragment of straight-sided dish, emerald-green glass (7.152 W5B/C; see above p. 151, no. 15)
3015 Wall fragment, pale yellowish glass with horizontal cut decoration
3016 Mosaic tessera, dark blue glass
3017 Mosaic tessera, green opaque glass

*Nos. in parentheses were provided by Dr. Auth.

ANALYSES OF GLASSES FROM SALONA

Cullet and Waste Glass

		3000	3001	3002	3003	3004	3005
SiO_2	(d)	~ 71	~70	~69	~78	~70	~68
Na_2O	(a)	19.2	18.1	18.4	14.1	17.2	17.2
CaO	(a)	5.24	7.14	7.14	4.39	6.03	5.70
K_2O	(a)	0.44	0.43	0.53	0.43	0.61	0.85
MgO	(a)	0.41	0.33	0.38	0.30	0.54	0.82
Al_2O_3	(a)	2.13	2.20	2.04	1.87	2.26	2.51
Fe_2O_3	(a)	0.66	0.59	0.73	0.48	1.19	2.34
TiO_2		0.15	0.18	0.35	0.25	0.80	0.90
Sb_2O_5		0.40	n.f.	0.32	0.45	n.f.	n.f.
MnO		0.18	1.12	0.69	0.04	1.54	1.08
CuO		0.00X	0.00X	0.00X	0.00X	0.00X	0.00X
CoO		n.f.	n.f.	n.f.	n.f.	n.f.	n.f.
SnO_2		0.15	n.f.	n.f.	n.f.	n.f.	n.f.
Ag_2O		n.f.	n.f.	n.f.	n.f.	n.f.	n.f.
PbO		0.07	0.00X	0.00X	0.00X	0.10	n.f.
BaO		0.01	0.02	0.01	$<$0.01	0.04	0.07
SrO		0.07	0.05	0.07	0.05	0.10	0.07
B_2O_3		0.03	0.02	0.02	0.05	0.05	0.05
ZrO_2		n.f.	n.f.	n.f.	n.f.	0.025	0.035

Notes: (a) Analysis by atomic absorption
(d) SiO_2 estimated by difference.

All other analyses by emission spectography.

Also sought but not found: Li_2O, Rb_2O, V_2O_5, Cr_2O_3, NiO, ZnO, Bi_2O_3. P_2O_5 = less than 1%, not found.

No. 3000 contains 0.00X Bi_2O_3; No. 3005 contains some V_2O_5.

ANALYSES OF GLASSES FROM SALONA

Vessel Fragments

		3006	3007	3008	3009	3010	3011	3012	3013	3014	3015	tess. 3016	tess. 3017
SiO_2	(d)	~70	~75	~72	~71	~74	~73	~68	~76	~69	~72	~72	~72
Na_2O	(a)	16.4	14.9	19.1	16.8	15.0	17.3	14.5	14.8	15.5	18.8	16.4	16.0
CaO	(a)	5.02	5.75	4.75	5.51	6.06	5.75	5.54	5.63	5.08	6.35	4.95	4.66
K_2O	(a)	0.63	0.63	0.39	0.85	0.66	0.49	0.51	0.52	2.13	0.48	0.64	0.65
MgO	(a)	0.69	0.27	0.23	0.69	0.30	0.26	0.30	0.25	1.18	0.43	0.33	0.33
Al_2O_3	(a)	2.62	2.13	1.55	2.13	2.05	2.25	1.80	2.15	1.64	1.73	2.13	2.00
Fe_2O_3	(a)	1.93	0.63	0.63	1.07	0.46	0.32	1.39	0.43	1.41	0.37	0.89	1.21
TiO_2		0.90	0.15	0.17	0.25	0.10	0.10	0.12	0.12	0.35	0.10	0.12	0.11
Sb_2O_5		n.f.	n.f.	n.f.	n.f.	n.f.	n.f.	~7	n.f.	n.f.	n.f.	1.75	0.3
MnO		1.87	0.82	0.59	1.42	1.19	0.1	0.39	0.06	0.73	0.00X	00.30	0.25
CuO		0.00X	0.00X	0.00X	0.00X	0.00X	0.00X	0.50	0.00X	1.71	0.00X	0.15	(a) 1.35
CoO		n.f.	n.f.	n.f.	n.f.	n.f.	n.f.	0.05	n.f.	n.f.	n.f.	0.08	n.f.
SnO_2		n.f.	n.f.	n.f.	n.f.	n.f.	n.f.	n.f.	n.f.	0.50	n.f.	0.00X	0.03
Ag_2O		n.f.	n.f.	n.f.	n.f.	n.f.	n.f.	n.f.	n.f.	0.000X	n.f.	0.000X	0.000X
PbO		0.00X	n.f.	n.f.	0.00X	n.f.	n.f.	0.00X	n.f.	0.20	n.f.	0.15	0.55
BaO		0.18	0.07	0.02	0.03	0.02	0.01	0.02	0.02	0.03	0.01	0.01	0.01
SrO		0.07	0.05	0.15	0.05	0.05	0.05	0.06	0.05	0.07	0.04	0.02	0.02
B_2O_3		0.05	0.05	0.02	0.03	0.03	0.02	0.03	0.03	0.03	0.03	0.05	0.02
ZrO_2		0.04	n.f.	n.f.	0.01	n.f.	n.f.	n.f.	n.f.	0.01	0.01	n.f.	n.f.

Notes: (a) Analysis by atomic absorption.
(d) SiO_2 estimated by difference.

All other analyses by emission spectography.

Also sought but not found: Li_2O, Rb_2O, V_2O_5, Cr_2O_3, NiO, ZnO, Bi_2O_3.
P_2O_5 = less than 1%, not found.

No. 3006 contains some V_2O_5.

X

Pottery from Closed Deposits

The writer is heavily indebted to the kindness of many colleagues who are much more at home in the field of Greco-Roman pottery in the Mediterranean area than she is, and whose knowledge and experience were helpful on frequent occasions. Her gratitude is due to A. Carandini and G. Carettoni of Rome, H. Comfort of Haverford, who in addition read and identified all the sigillata stamps, E. Ettlinger of Zürich, J. Hayes of Toronto, F. Jones of Princeton, S. Marović of Split, F. Morel, formerly of Rome, H.S. Robinson of Cleveland, J.W. Salomonson of Leyden, and Homer A. Thompson of Princeton. It goes without saying that the author bears full responsibility for the opinions stated hereafter, as well as the remaining shortcomings.

In the study of the pottery excavated in Salona in 1969-70, two main difficulties had to be coped with. One is inherent in the material itself. Practically all pottery finds are part of destruction debris, often used as fill. The pottery is consequently broken up throughout into small fragments with no complete and few nearly complete profiles preserved. If, as is usual, the types of the finer table wares can often be determined on the basis of fabric and rim profile alone, this is only rarely the case with the coarse household wares and even less so with amphorae.

The second difficulty arose from the fact that all the time spent on the excavation and during later sojourns in Split had to be devoted exclusively to the classifying, recording, and drawing of the vast amount of pottery found during the excavation on the Forum north, Forum central, and curia sites (in 1970) by the writer alone. All research connected with the preparation of the publication had to be done later, when the originals were no longer at hand. This is especially unfortunate with regard to the various Hellenistic groups of black glazed wares. It is to be hoped, however, that the intended publication of the much larger group of pottery from the Forum north and Forum central sites and from the 1969 excavation will clarify some of these and other problems left open here.

The pottery presented in this volume has been selected exclusively for the purpose of providing chronological evidence for the various building periods. The following catalogue therefore presents finds from closed deposits from the 1970 excavation only (see also the chapter on the chronological evidence, and the charts 1-15). The overwhelming majority of such finds comes from the destruction debris of period I, which is sealed off to the east of the curia by an extended street or piazza pavement laid in the immediately following period II (Figs. A-G). A second, very small complex comes from Trench 1, dug into the foundations of the *Capitolium* (see Figs. F2 and G2). The third complex, without having been truly sealed off, can nevertheless be treated confidently as a "closed deposit." It is a pit on the Forum north site in which several amphorae were dumped together, probably at the end of period I or at the very beginning of period II, to judge by the association of types (see Fig. G3).

Two more complexes are presented in this volume. One is from a drain of period III on the Forum north site; its contents belong mainly to the second to sixth century A.D. (see chart 12). The other is a homogeneous group of pottery of the second to fourth century A.D. dumped most probably as destruction debris against the western face of the Forum enclosure wall west on the Forum north site (see chart 7). Both these groups of finds are rather small and the latter is not from a closed deposit in the strict sense. They are presented in the charts together with some profile drawings without further discussion. Otherwise, pottery from the 1970 excavations dating from the second century B.C. to the sixth century A.D. is mentioned together with the coins from the years 1969 and 1970 only in the charts (1-15), the function of which is to provide chronological evidence for the dating of building periods I-IV.

However few, then, the closed deposits from the 1970 excavations may be, it is fortunate that the pottery complex of period I found to the north and east of the curia (squares A'7, B7 and B6 East) is sizeable enough to provide a *terminus post quem* for the beginning of the settlement on the eminence. The following catalogue therefore presents in Figs. A-G all the rims and bases which were found, with only insignificant exceptions, among the coarse ware. Even so it is self-evident that these remains represent a more or less random selection of the pottery in use during building period I. However, the wide range of wares included in this complex suggests that the 150 odd fragments constitute a representative cross section.

Only two main aspects of these finds will be discussed in the following pages: their implication for the duration of period I and, where possible, their provenience. Purely typological problems are usually neglected.

The undeniable existence of what might be called a late-Hellenistic and Republication pottery *koinē*, including the coarse wares, reaching from Greece to Spain comes to the fore in the material found at Salona, too. In view of the more specific geographical location of Salona, however, it is indeed not surprising that, generally speaking, the closest parallels for our pottery of period I, seen as a whole, are to be found in Italy and the Mediterranean region to the west of that peninsula. It is also mainly these regions that provide the necessary framework of reference for dated finds.

The basic chronology of Roman pottery from the time of Caesar onwards has been established, of course, on the military sites to the north of the Alps. Among those, we shall have to refer more often to the Petrisberg and to Haltern. Our knowledge of pottery of all categories current in the West during the first two centuries B.C., however, has been greatly advanced in more recent times by the publication of finds from various sites, especially in Italy and along the northern coast of the Tyrrhenian sea. Each of these sites has provided a broad range of different wares. Some can be dated within wider limits only, while others, above all the finds from some shipwrecks, can be assigned to a more limited time range. Those sites which provide dated finds and to which we refer more frequently in the following pages are listed hereafter together with their presumable duration in terms of absolute chronology. In dealing with the problem of dating of individual types of pottery, however, one has to keep in mind that the pace of development of ceramics generally speaking is not as fast in the last centuries B.C. as it is from roughly the time of Augustus onwards, witness the rapid evolution of the typology of terra sigillata.

The following abbreviations are used in this chapter:

Akrai	G. Curzio, "Akrai(Siracusa), Richerche nel territorio," *NSc* 24 (1970): 438 ff.
Albenga	N. Lamboglia, "La nave di Albenga," *RivStudiLiguri* 18 (1952): 131 ff.
Albintimilium	N. Lamboglia, *Gli scavi di Albintimilium e la cronologia della ceramica Romana* (1950).
Ampurias	M. Almagro, *Las necrópolis de Ampurias,* vols. I-II (1953, 1955).
Athens *Agora*	H.S. Robinson, *Pottery of the Roman Period,* vol. V, *The Athenian Agora* (1959).
Athens HellPott	H.A. Thompson, "Two Centuries of Hellenistic Pottery," *Hesperia* 3 (1934): 311-480.

Baldacci, commercio anfore	P. Baldacci, "Le principali correnti del commercio di anfore romane nella Cisalpina. Importazioni ad esportazioni alimentari della pianura padana centrale del III sec. a.C. al II d.C.," in *I problemi della ceramica romana di Ravenna, della Valle padana e dell'alto Adriatico* (1972).
Gabii	M. Vegas, "Römische Keramik von Gabii(Latium)," *BJb* 168 (1968): 13-53.
Goudineau	Ch. Goudineau, *La céramique arétine lisse. Fouilles de l'Ecole Française de Rome à Bolsena* (Poggio Moscini) 1962-1967, vol. 4, Ecole Française de Rome, *MélArchHist,* suppl. 6, Paris 1968.
Grand Conglué	F. Benoît, *L'épave du Grand Conglué à Marseille. Gallia* Suppl. vol. 14 (1961).
Haltern	S. Loeschcke, *Keramische Funde in Haltern, MittAltertürkommWestfalen* 5, 1909.
Hs	J.S. Hayes, *Late Roman Pottery* (1972).
La	N. Lamboglia, "Terra Sigillata Chiara," *RivIngauna e Intemilia = RivStudiLiguri* 7 (1941): 7 ff. idem, "Nuove osservazioni sulla Terra Sigillata Chiara," *RivStudiLiguri* 24 (1958): 257 ff.; 29 (1963): 145 ff.
Labraunda	P. Hellström, *Labraunda. Swedish excavations and researches* vol. II:1. *Pottery of classical and later date.*
Lamboglia, Classificazione	N. Lamboglia, "Per una classificazione preliminare della ceramica Campana." *Atti del I° Congresso Internazionale di Studi Liguri.* Bordighera, 1950 (Bordighera 1952); pp. 139 ff.
Lindenhof	E. Vogt, *Der Lindenhof in Zürich* (1948).
Loeschcke, *Vindonissa*	S. Loeschcke, *Lampen aus Vindonissa* (1919).
Moevs	M.T. Marabini Moevs, *The Roman thin walled pottery from Cosa* (1948-1954), *Memoirs AmAcaRome,* vol. 32 (1973).
Numantia	K. Koenen, *Die Keramik aus den Lagern des Scipio und den Lagern bei Renieblas* in A. Schulten, *Numantia. Die Ergebinisse der Ausgrabungen 1905-1912,* vol. IV, *Die Lager bei Renieblas* (1929).
Oxé-Comfort	A.Oxé-H. Comfort, *Corpus Vasorum Arretinorum. A Catalogue of Signatures, Shapes and Chronology of Italian Sigillata* (1968).
Petrisberg	L. Loeschcke, "Alteste römische Keramik vom Petrisberg über Trier," *Trier Ztschr* 14 (1939): 93 ff.
Pollentia I	M. Vegas, "Vorläufiger Bericht über römische Gebrauchskeramik aus Pollentia (Mallorca)," *BJb* 163 (1963): 275 ff.
Pompeii CdF	A. Bruckner, "Küchengeschirr aus der Casa del Fauno," *Rei Cretariae Fautorum Acta* 7 (1965): 7 ff.
Sutri	G.C. Duncan, "Roman Republican Pottery from the Vicinity of Sutri," *Papers BritSchoolRome* 33 (1965): 134 ff.
Vindonissa	E. Ettlinger, *Römische Keramik aus dem Schutthügel von Vindonissa* (1952).
Zevi, Appunti anfore	F. Zevi, "Appunti sulle anfore romane," *ArchClass* 1966: 208 ff.

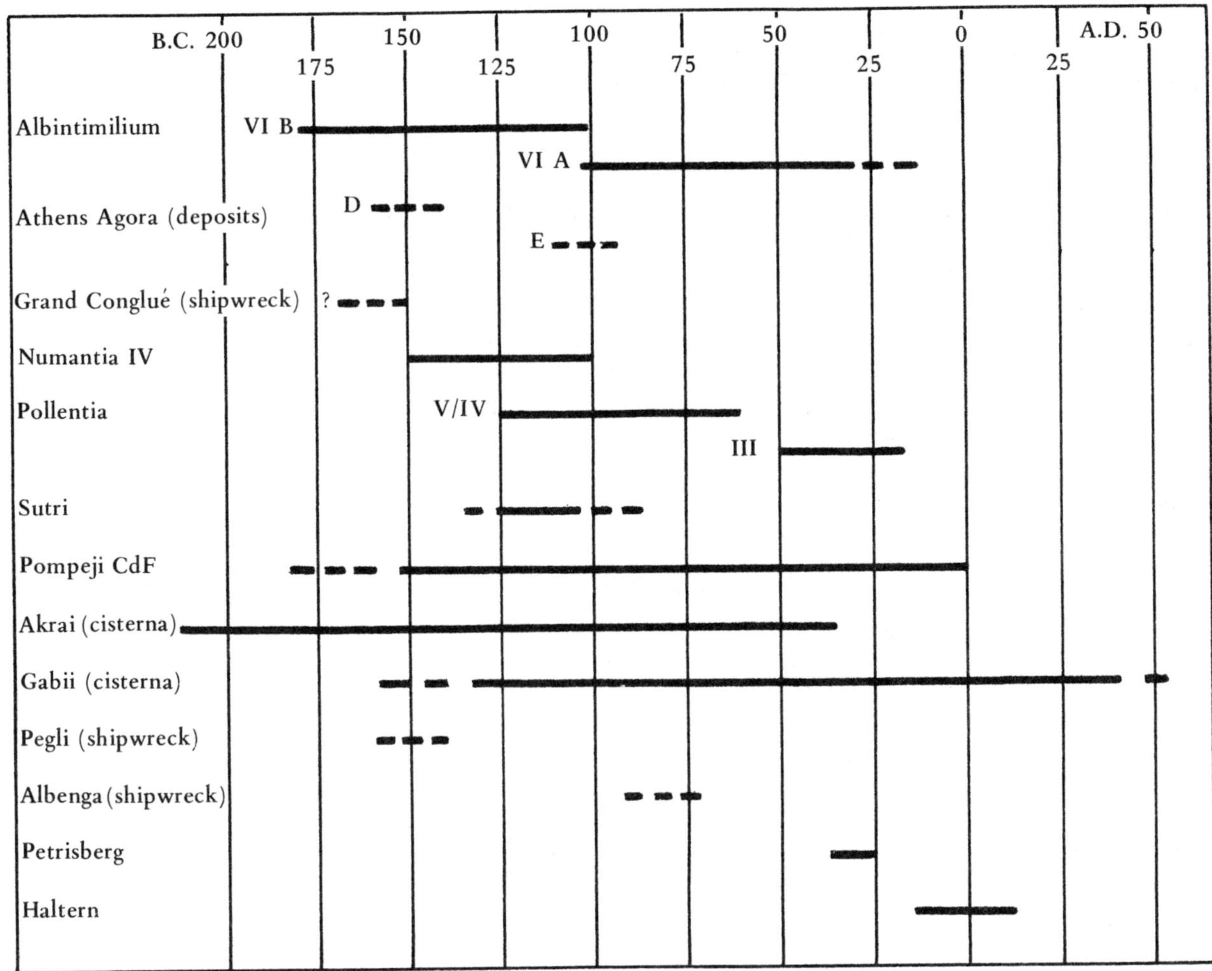

Chronology of the Sites of Reference

I. LATE HELLENISTIC TABLE WARES

A. Black Glaze on Light Clay (P 1-21, Fig. A, Plate 34)

This extremely fragmentary group is characterized by a homogeneous, at times very heavy fabric: the coarse, salmon-colored clay is fired medium hard, leaving the unglazed surfaces very smooth. The glaze at its best is black to blueish with a metallic luster, more often diluted to brownish and mat, and applied to the outside somewhat carelessly (P 6, 12). Some types seem to reflect affinity with Italian Campana ware; this impression is enhanced by sherds among the finds from the Forum north and central site (see charts 1, 2, 6). Nevertheless, the ware is definitely not genuine Campana A ware. In view of the decorated fragments (P 15a, 17, 18a), which belong to the orbit of late Gnathia and related wares, an Apulian origin for at least some of the fragments might perhaps be considered. This problem cannot, of course, be dealt with appropriately before the large amount of Late Hellenistic black-glazed pottery from the cemeteries on the islands along the coast of Dalmatia, now in the Split museum, is adequately published.

The more characteristic profiles such as Krateriskoi (P 14, 15), together with the decorated fragments, would suggest a date for the whole group somewhere in the late third or perhaps rather in the second century B.C.

B. Black Glaze on Light Buff, Light Brown Clay (Campana B Imitations?, P 19-21, Fig. A, Plate 34)

The identification of this group on the basis of a few fragments alone is, of course, arbitrary enough. Nevertheless, the fabric, if not always the glaze, is different enough from the previous group so as to recommend separating them. The more so, as the finds of this variety of black-glazed pottery from the Forum north and Forum central sites are more numerous (see charts 1, 2, 6). The leather-colored clay is fired medium hard, the glaze is rather thin and dull, the fabric is thin and the breaks are smooth. A very few fragments of genuine Campana B ware, not from the complex published here, have been kindly identified by Jean Morel. But our group is definitely of an inferior quality than that ware. The few profiles are too fragmentary to warrant any attempt to further identify the small group. It might be tentatively called a regional imitation of Italian Campana B, which itself does not appear before the middle of the second century B.C. Our group then could be dated tentatively to the latter half of that century.

For Campana wares see Lamboglia, Classificazione. See also the authors cited under *Plain Gray Ware,* section IE.

C. **Megarian Bowls (P 22-38, Fig. B, Plate 35)**

These bowls were the most popular relief-decorated pottery drinking bowls of the Hellenistic world. They were in all probability first produced in Athens in the third century B.C. and then imitated in several different centers and distributed widely until the first century B.C. The ware has, however, so far never been found associated with late Republican or later pottery.

In this rather large group only P 22 represents what we might call the "standard" type of Megarian bowl with regard to its fabric as well as scant remains of its decoration. Otherwise, the fragment is too insignificant to permit closer attribution. The fact that this piece presents the only example from the 1969 as well as the 1970 excavations might suggest perhaps a rather early date within our complex in the first half of the second century B.C.

Almost all the other fragments of Megarian bowls (P 23-35) form a surprisingly homogeneous group by themselves. Although with regard to their general shape as well as their decoration they belong clearly to this multifarious family of relief-bowls, they show distinct characteristics of their own. The clay, besides being an unusual medium gray, is not of the normal gritty quality but is finely textured without any impurities. The fabric is not as thin-walled as usual (except P 26) and fired hard, but only moderately fired and rather heavy. The glaze is not thin and hard but soft and soapy. The semi-oval shape with out-turned moulded rim, apparently higher than it is wide, is in contrast to most of the more standard versions too. It is a beaker rather than a deep bowl. A reasonably good parallel is a piece at Yale, attributed by Baur to Athenian workmanship of the second century B.C.[1] For the lip profile, the general shape, as well as the plastic feet, beakers from Città di Castello of a possibly later date can be compared (see sectional bibliography below). The relief itself is of medium to poor quality due, in part at least, to what seems to have been the use of worn moulds. The principle of decoration for the lower half of the vessel is an overall pattern of imbricated leaves or other motives. All features mentioned can, of course, be found singly or combined to a degree in the vast corpus of Megarian bowls published so far, but we are unable to find parallels for them in the same combination. This is true also of the plastic feet of P 31. P 37 and 38 represent a different group on account of the fabric which has much more mica in the clay, a more adherent black slip and, besides, possibly a different style of decoration and a shallower shape (P 37).

The homogeneity of P 23-35 points undoubtedly to a single place of manufacture. The large number of bowls in this group, emphasized by further identical pieces from the Forum north and Forum central sites, might suggest a provenience perhaps not too distant from Salona. On the other hand the presence of at least three other varieties of Megarian bowls (P 22, 36-38) cautions us from lending too much importance to the greater number of one group. The astonishing diversity of Megarian bowls from various centers of production which can be found on a single site such as, for instance, Labraunda, certainly reflects a definite pattern of trade relations. The presence of products of different workshops in Salona is probably to be explained on similar lines.

The presence of mica in the clay distinguishes these relief-bowls from the otherwise almost identical fabric of the plain undecorated gray ware (P 40 ff., Fig. C). Besides the general habitus of the whole group, the highly micaceous clay of P 37 and 38, identical in slip and degree of firing with the black variety of Eastern sigillata B (certainly imported to Salona), prompts one to consider a place of manufacture of P 23-38 possibly somewhere on the coast of Asia Minor or in the Aegean. As to the date of the whole group, the second half of the second century B.C. seems to be the most likely. To this period can be assigned with all probability P 36 from the 1969 excavation on the curia site, which belongs to a more "standard" type in terms of its thin fabric as well as its decoration. Such "long-petal-bowls" are thought not to appear before the middle of the second century B.C. [cf. Athens, HellPott, pp. 475 f., figs. 70-73; *Labraunda* p. 22; del Chiaro (see bibliography below), fig. 32, 3.].

The latest brief and cautious account of the present state of knowledge of this ware, most valuable for a complete bibliography up to 1961, is given by M.A. del Chiaro in the *EncArteAnt* s.v. "Megaresi Vasi." To this should now be added the excellent discussion of Megarian bowls by P. Hellström in his publication of the large group found in Labraunda (*Labraunda* pp. 19 ff.). To the comprehensive list of plastic feet under Megarian Bowls and other Hellenistic fine wares given by P.V.C. Baur [*AJA* 45(1941): 240] can be added examples from Athens, Kerameikos [Schwabacher, *AJA* 45 (1941): 223, pl. IX B, no. 15]; from Labraunda (*Labraunda* p. 45, nos 338, 371-373); from Rome (catalogo della Mostra, "Roma Medio Repubblicana," Rome, 1973, p. 133, no. 160, pl. 13); from Città di Castello [B. Adamsheck, "Hellenistic Relief Wares from Italy," *Rei Cretariae Romanae Fautores, Acta* 14/15 (1973-73): 5 f., group 3, pl. 1, p. 2, figs. 1-2]; from Pompeii [J. Morel, "Céramique à vernis noir de Pompeji," *Rei Cretariae Romanae Fautores, Acta* 7 (1965): 84, no. 8, figs. 2, 2; 5, 1].

D. Gray Clayed Bowl with Relief-Medallion Inside on the Bottom (P 39, Fig. B, Plate 35)

Too little is preserved of this unique piece, unparalleled among the finds from the Forum north and Forum central sites to allow any more specific interpretation. The fabric as well as the profile of the base preclude any direct comparison with Calenian wares which otherwise might be possible. Fabric and glaze are the same as in P 23 ff., which might speak in favor of related provenience as well as date.

E. Plain Gray Ware (P 44-58, Fig. C, Plate 36)

With the exception of P 44 and P 59 this group shows rather consistently the same fabric. The clay is medium gray and fine-textured, without impurities and mica; it is fired medium hard. The glaze is of poor quality, the sheen rather dull, resembling at times mere burnishing. Its color is more often than not uneven, varying from gray to greenish to brownish, with sometimes a mottled effect on the same vessel. Despite their apparent homogeniety, one might hesitate to attribute all fragments to one group on the basis of the fabric alone in view of the small number of fragments. The same is even more true in regard to the types represented. Without the inclusion of the much larger amount of similar pottery from the Forum north and Forum central sites a discussion of this ware cannot be attempted.

It is evident, nevertheless, that this group is to be set in the larger framework of variants and imitations of the Italian Campana B and C wares of the later second and first centuries B.C. The fabric of P 44-58 is, however, definitely not Campana C, of which fabric only exceedingly few fragments were found in 1969-70 and not in the complex published here. P 59 is of much the same fabric as P37-38; the quality of the glaze is also the same as in the reduced variant of Eastern sigillata B (black ESB), which suggests here too a related provenience.

For Campana wares see besides Lamboglia, Classificazione; D.M. Taylor, "Cosa. Black-glaze pottery," *MemAmAcaRome* 25 (1957): 65 ff.; F. Morel, "Notes sur la céramique etrusco-campanienne," *MélEcFr Rome* 75 (1963): 7 ff.; idem, *La céramique à vernis noir du Forum romain et du Palatin* (1965); G. Fiorentini, "Sulla ceramica campana nella valle del Po," *RivStudiLiguri* 29 (1963): 7 ff.

F. Thinwalled, Unglazed Beaker (P 60-61, Fig. C, Plate 35)

This group of beakers (Form Moevs I) with delicately moulded lip and extremely fine fabric fired very hard is well known from dated contexts of the second and early first centuries B.C. (Ampurias I, p. 395, fig. 6; Athens, Agora F 24; Grand Conglué, p. 108, fig. 69; Entremont, *Gallia* 14, 1956, fig. 221).

The first comprehensive study of this group is published by Moevs, pp. 49 ff.

II. EARLY ROMAN TABLE WARES

A. Vitreous Glazed Ware (P 63, Fig. D, Plate 37)

Of the skyphos P 63 only the lower half was found. It was broken in antiquity just below the two ring handles attached to the rim. The shape as well as the style of the relief-decoration assign this handsome vessel to the end of period I, probably the last quarter of the first century B.C. The fabric as well as the color or colors of the glaze point to an origin somewhere in the Po valley. Among the few examples of vitreous glazed pottery found in Cisalpina and published so far, two fairly close parallels can be cited for the numbers of berries in the cluster: one from Sarsina, now in the Museo Sarsinate, the other from Palazzolo Vercellese in the Museo archeologico in Torino.

The only comprehensive general account of Roman vitreous glazed ware in the Po valley published is the short section in the chapter on pottery by A. Stenico in the volume published on the occasion of the Bologna exhibit of 1965, *Arte e civilità romana nell' Italia settentrionale* I, (Bologna 1965), pp. 329-330. Cup from Sarsina: G.V. Gentili, "Le ceramiche invetriate romane di Sarsina," in: *I problemi della ceramica ... Atti del convegno internazionale di Ravenna,* 10-12 maggio, 1969 (Bologna, 1972), pp. 180 ff., fig. 2a. Cup from Palazzolo Vercellese: *Arte e civilità romana nell' Italia settentrionale* II (1965) no. 293, pl. 140, no. 507.

B. Italian Terra Sigillata (P 64-73, Fig. D, Plate 38)

The eight fragments, though a small group, permit some observations to be made, the validity of which is confirmed by the study of the vast amount of Italian terra sigillata from the Forum north site. There is no trace of the "pre-sigillata" as recently defined by Goudineau (pp. 57-63) which is otherwise well represented in such export areas as, for instance, on the Magdalensberg in Noricum or on early sites to the north of the Alps. Also missing are the immediate predecessors of Haltern Service I as well as its earliest types. The large plates P 64-65 may well not be earlier than about 10 B.C. and may possibly be later. The corresponding cups of Service I, Ha 7, are not represented. Instead, the plates are apparently accompanied by cups of Service II, Ha 8 (P 69-71), a phenomenon observed elsewhere too. As the features mentioned are also characteristic of the finds from the Forum north and the Forum central sites, they thus permit tentative chronological interpretation: Italian terra sigillata seems to have reached Salona about 10 B.C. at the earliest.

All three stamps found (P 67, 68, 71) are rectangular. The legible ones show that the ware was imported from the Po valley; the fabric of all fragments points to the same conclusion. The fabric with orange to salmon clay of rather coarse texture, is markedly different from the "Arretine" ware of Arezzo. The two stamps found during the 1969 campaign on the curia site in contexts comparable to levels of period I are rectangular, too (*P 72, fig. D) and one is illegible (PE 69.418).

Stamps in *planta pedis* are absent. Together with the absence of the cups and bowls Ha 11.12 and 15, which appear only in later Augustan times and which are well represented among the Forum north finds, this fact points to an end of period I before the reign of Tiberius.

For a discussion of the predecessors of Haltern Service I & II see Goudineau pp. 13 ff. with the review by E. Ettlinger, *Germania* 49 (1971): 264. For the chronology and distribution of the earliest types see E. Ettlinger, "Keramik Datierungen der frühen Kaiserzeit," *JbSchweizGesellsch.Ur-undFrühgesch.* 54 (1968-69); 69 ff.

C. **Eastern Sigillata (P 74-77, Fig. D)**

Of the three major Late Hellenistic and Early Roman red-glazed wares, two are represented by a few fragments in our complex. Both A and B ware as well as the third C ware (Çandarli ware) are well represented on the Forum north site. For reasons which seem to us very cogent and well stated by Hellström, we prefer his nomenclature, an expansion of that established by Kenyon, to the older one, and will use it hereafter (Labraunda pp. 28 ff.):

Eastern Sigillata A I	(Hellenistic Pergamene)	ESA I
Eastern Sigillata A II	(Early Roman Pergamene)	ESA II
Eastern Sigillata B I	(Samian B)	ESB I
Eastern Sigillata B II	(Samian A)	ESB II
Eastern Sigillata C	(Çandarli ware)	ESC

1. ESA I and II (P 74-75)

In the larger series from the Forum north site, ESA I ware can be fairly easily distinguished from ESA II ware on the basis of the fabric as well as of some of the types. In our complex there is, however, one fragment of ESA I (PE 143); it belongs most probably to a large, shallow plate. The clay is cream-colored, with very fine texture and includes no impurities; the glaze is dark red with dipping patches. The ware was widely distributed from the coasts of Cilicia to Egypt and beyond during the first century B.C., appearing first perhaps as early as the end of the second century B.C. Of our two fragments of ESA II ware (P 74-75), P 75 displays in its foot the characteristics of this group, the shapes of which show the general influence of Italian sigillata. The two fragments can be assigned to the last two decades of the first century B.C. or first century A.D.

2. ESB I (P 76-77)

The relationship with Italian sigillata is unmistakable also in the two fragments of plates in ESB ware which were found. In our opinion P 77 displays affinities with plate Ha 1, Service I, which has been noticed already for this type in earlier ESA I ware (see the discussion by Goudineau pp. 345 f.). P 76 echoes very closely the plate Ha 2, Service II and can therefore not be earlier than about 10 B.C. and possibly not much later than about A.D. 20. The fabric of both fragments shows the characteristics of the ESB I ware. The cinnamon-colored clay is highly micaceous; the strongly orange glaze is glossy and silky and very well adhering. The large series of different shapes and the few stamps with Greek letters found leave no doubt that the ware was imported from somewhere in the Aegean or in Asia Minor, where it is most widely represented.

The latest account of the present state of our knowledge of the Eastern sigillata that has come to our attention is given by P. Hellström, together with a succinct and illuminating resume of the previous discussion and an up-to-date bibliography (Labraunda pp. 28 ff.). See also Goudineau pp. 338 ff., who is dealing, however, primarily with the hypothesis of Eastern inspiration for the creation of Arretine ware.

III. COARSE HOUSEHOLD WARES

A. Plain Household Wares (P 78-124, Figs. E, F and Plate 39)

The most striking feature of the repertory of shapes in all groups of utility vessels is their common Greco-Roman and Mediterranean character, as opposed to an indigenous late-Iron-Age "Illyrian" one. The only exceptions, as could be expected, are a few handmade kitchen and larger storage vessels (P 112-114, 118). (P 114a, not from our complex, is shown here because it is the only complete vessel of that kind; see pl. 39.) Naturally enough, specimens of the latter part of period I, that is the first century B.C., might be expected to be in the majority. Taking the debris character of the entire complex, however, together with the indestructibility especially of remains of heavy household wares, specimens of an earlier time can be expected to be quite numerous too.

Unguentarium Ha 30: The late slender variant (P 78) is attested from Greece (Athens HellPott E 138) to Spain (Ampurias I p. 397) from the second century B.C. through Augustan times.

Ewers (P 81-82): This wide-mouthed type with handle departing from the lip is as a strictly functioning form a long-lived and ubiquitous type (cf. the dated series from Athens, HellPott pp. 464 ff. and *Ampurias* I p. 394).

Flagons and Jugs (P 83-87): The salient feature of this group is its uniformity, the delicate fabric, fired astonishingly medium-hard only. As the complete shape is unknown the type is difficult to assess. But Sutri form 27, A 36-39, seems a reasonably close parallel. The angular shoulder of P 88 of a different fabric echoes the lagynos type (see Athens HellPott E 70-73). With the delicate ring on the base of the neck it might still be pre-Augustan (without parallel at Haltern).

Small Storage Jar (P 92, 93): These "Honeyjars" of the earlier military sites on the Rhine frontier (Ha 62, Vindonissa p. 23) are of very light clay as usual. They have a flaring rim intended to receive a flat lid of the same fabric (as P 91, 92, 120-124). An example very close to this jar with the usual ear-shaped double handles was found in a first century B.C. tomb in Syracuse with its lid still on.[2] To the larger variant P 95 may well belong a bulbous body such as our P 117, Fig. F (cf. Sutri form 25, Gabii 131).

Baking Plates (P 96, 97) and Cooking Casseroles (P 98-101): These are a very characteristic group. The two basic shapes, the flat plate and the deep casserole with angled wall and round bottom, are very often associated in the Mediterranean region as well as to the north of the Alps. Their related functions of baking and cooking are also clearly indicated by a typical fabric which is more or less unchanged from at least the second century B.C. This has led to the hypothetical assumption of a limited number of centers of manufacture and exportation (Pompeii CdF pp. 7f.). Convincing as this seems to anyone familiar with the material found both north and south of the Alps, this assumption can be verified only on the basis of a petrographic analysis of the clays used. P 96 with the characteristic thick red paint on the inside of these "Pompeianisch rote Platten" has a thickened rim typical of the earlier part of the first century B.C. (Albintimilium VI A, fig. 31, 63-64; Pollentia IV, fig. 3, 1-2 and p. 282; Pompeii CdF fig. 1, 1). The belief that the thickened rim is not carried on into the first century A.D. is strengthened by the numerous finds from the Forum north site, where the majority of "Pompeianisch rote Platten" show the simple, slightly in-turned rim (as Pompeii CdF fig. 1, 2-3). P 97 with slightly rolled lip is paralleled in Sutri form 22 (Pompeii CdF fig. 1, 6 with further references p. 8).

The shape of the deep casserole with flaring lip intended for a lid with angular wall and rounded bottom (P 98-101) has a long pre-Hellenistic history (Athens HellPott pp. 466 ff., fig. 121). Our series with its clearly slanting lip profiles seems to reach well back into the second century B.C. (Cf. Athens HellPott D 72, E 141, fig. 121; Sutri forms 23-24, A 21-24; Pompeii CdF fig. 2:1, 2, 6; Pollentia IV, fig. 3, 10-11.) P 102 with flat, horizontally out-turned rim is attested from the early first century B.C. onwards (Albenga fig. 30, 11-12; Gabii 151-152) and associated usually with a deeper, rounded bottom (Haltern Ha 56).

Cooking Jars (P 103, 104): The presence of only two wheel-made examples as compared to the number of deep casseroles seems at first astonishing, particularly in view of the respective proportion at Sutri. We would like to assume that there was in Salona during period I still a substantial number of handmade cooking jars in use. This is also suggested by the presence in our complex of at least two specimens (P 112, 118, fig. F). P 103 with its almond-shaped thickened rim, the "orlo a mandorla" of Lamboglia, is the most popular cooking jar in the second and first centuries B.C. (see Pompeii CdF fig. 1, 1 with a list of dated finds on p. 10, to which can be added Sutri form 38b, A 89-92). The type does not last into the first century A.D. P 104 with out-turned rim is a long-lived type, as would be expected for this simplest of rim profile. In a second century B.C. context it is attested in Sutri form 34a, A 52-54; but our specimen cannot be dated more closely and may as well be Augustan.

Mortaria: The fabric of the only two rim fragments (P 105, 119) shows the close affinity with that of clay A of the amphorae as often noted in Republican context (see, for instance, Gabii p. 44). For P 119 only one dated fragment of similar type has come to our attention (Numantia pl. 72). Most mortaria datable within the last century B.C. show the vertical collar with deep furrow of P 105 (Albintimilium VI A, fig. 29, 50-51; Petrisberg fig. 7, 18-19).

Small Lids for Storage Vessels (P 91, 92, 106-108, 120-124): The more than thirty specimens found belong to two rather easily distinguishable, homogeneous groups, plus, of course, some intermediary examples. Type A lid is of somewhat conical shape with the center pushed up from the underside and a small hand-shaped, irregular knob. The only decoration is an occasional concentric grooving near the rim (P 107). The fabric is always light and the clay most often related to the type used for the "Honeyjars" and clay A of the amphorae. Type B lid is rather thick with a flat underside and a center knob, usually rounded. The fabric is heavy, the clay and firing often related to clay B of the amphorae. On this type markings occur (P 108). In our period I complexes these two basic types are present in a proportion of roughly four to one. Type A is frequently found in second and first centuries B.C. context (Albintimilium VI B fig. 45, 39; Pollentia IV fig. 3, 3; Petrisberg figs. 3-4, no. 43). From their size, averaging from 7 to 10 cm, it becomes quite clear that these lids could not be used on more wide-mouthed types of amphorae. The evidence of amphorae found in shipping condition shows that in Republican times amphorae were quite often sealed by means other than clay lids (Grand Conglué pp. 52 ff.; F. Benoît, *Gallia* 14, 1965, pp. 24f.). In Salona type A is the predominant type of lid during period I. The evidence from the Forum north site where the overwhelming majority of these lids is of type B (almost all with markings) leads to the assumption that this heavier type was introduced here as the standard lid for large jugs and amphorae perhaps only in the later first century B.C. This assumption is of course connected also with the question of provenience of such packaging material as the amphorae

Double-Handled Heavy Jug (P 109): We are not able to give a parallel for this peculiar type of stepped collar which, however, appears to be not earlier than Augustan.

Handmade Vessels (P 112-114, 118): It would be only reasonable to assume that in the scant remains of handmade pottery, elements of the indigenous late-Iron-Age tradition might be detected, especially in details like the moon-shaped hand-hold on P 114. Yet, on the one hand, most of the handmade fragments were found outside our period I complex (see *P 114a, pl. 39) in 1969; on the other hand, up to this date not enough dated late-Iron-Age pottery has been found on the Dalmatian coast to permit any well-founded idea of its character, as Mr. Marović has kindly informed me.

B. Amphorae (P 127-154, Fig. G)

The interpretation of the group of about twenty amphorae from under the pavement to the east of the curia and from Trench 1 which could be identified is somewhat hampered by the lack of complete profiles. Nevertheless, taking into account also the few fragments of handles and bases found besides the rim fragments, it becomes sufficiently clear that the great majority of amphorae belonged to the three main types current in the second and first centuries B.C. in the western Mediterranean region. In addition, two more types could be identified which, while both developing in Late Hellenistic times, are also well attested to through the first century A.D. The lack of stamps, with the exception of the illegible fragment P 151, is perhaps best explained by the fragmentary state of the finds on the whole. This sole stamp occurs on an amphora type Dressel I A and is presumably not earlier than the second half of the second century B.C. It was discovered with the complex of amphorae found dumped in the Forum north site, W2C pit, (Fig. G.3).

1. *Greco-Italian type* of the second century B.C., lasting into the first century B.C. For dated finds see: *Albintimilium,* VI B-(VI A); *Grand Conglué; Numantia;* Sutri; Pollentia V, III: Akrai.
2. *Amphorae type Dressel I A* ("Sestius-amphora," "Marseille-amphora,") of the second century B.C. to about 20 B.C. (Oberaden 77). For dated finds see: *Albintimilium* VI B-(VI A), figs. 32, 39, 50; *Grand Conglué; Numantia* IV; Pollentia V and III; Akrai; Albenga.
3. *Amphorae type Dressel I B* of the first century B.C. For dated finds see: *Numantia;* Polentia; Gabii; Akrai; Albenga; Altenburg; *Lindenhof.*
4. *Amphorae type Dressel 3* of the later second century B.C. to Flavian times (Oberaden 78). For dated finds see: Pegli (see bibliography below); Pallentia IV-I; Gabii 180-182.
5. *Amphora P 154* of the later second century B.C. through the first century A.D. For dated finds see: *Numantia* IV; Gabii 184; Albenga; *Vindonissa* 588.

1. Greco-Italian type (P 129-139, Fig. G): Our fragments show the characteristic triangular or at times slightly undercut profile, the yellow to dirty white clay with specific inclusions and a medium hard firing (see Grand Conglué 37 f.). The origin and history of this type of amphorae has been more recently discussed on the basis of earlier observations by F. Benoît, and by Baldacci, commercio anfore, pp. 109 ff. These amphorae were in their earlier form, from about 300 B.C., a product of the Hellenistic koinē of the Aegean world. At the later stage, in the second century B.C., they were manufactured in various centers of Sicily and Southern Italy.

In Salona the products of this later type are represented. They were imported here, as elsewhere in the Adriatic, most probably from Apulia (Brundisium). Due to the lack of complete profiles it is impossible for us to identify the more specific "Apulian" variants of the Greco-Italian type. Our P 129-139 might, however, possibly be compared with Baldacci's Apulian Type I (Baldacci, commercio anfore, figs. 7, 11, 16). One may wonder whether the striking affinity of the rim profile of our white-clayed P 145-147 to that of the straight-collared amphora Dressel I A, which is usually red-clayed, however, is an indication of a parallel development of the Greco-Italian type in its latest stage. (For this problem see Zevi, Appunti anfore, p. 214, and Baldacci, commercio anfore, pp. 110 f.)

2. and 3. Amphorae Dressel I A and I B (P 145-151, Fig. G): This spindle-shaped amphora with long neck and sharp shoulder angle is characterized by the rather long collar-rim and a more or less straight, slightly undercut lip; by a salmon to brick-red clay, fired rather hard. The centers of production are thought to be in Campania and in southern Latium. In these amphorae the wine of those regions was exported. The type is represented in all three complexes (Fig. G 1-3). The majority of the fragments show the salmon colored clay (clay B) containing much mica.

Some show a somewhat lighter surface, possibly the remains of a whitish coating. All pieces are fired hard. Of the 9 amphorae found in the pit on the Forum north site (W2C; Fig. G 2), four were of type Dressel I A (P 144-147), two of type Dressel I B (P 150-151), while the only three pieces of Greco Italian type (P 135-137) no longer show the classical triangular lip of that type. This spectrum of types assembled in the pit speaks in favor of our assumption (see chapter 4) that the amphorae were dumped together sometimes toward the end of period I or the very beginning of period II. A very good parallel to a similarly dated small assemblage of amphorae types are the finds from the early military site of Altenburg-Rheinau, where still earlier types are found (about 50 to 15 B.C.) together with a majority of specimens of type Dressel I B.

4. *Amphorae Dressel 3 (Oberaden 78):* The two rim fragments (P 152-153) belong most probably to this type as is also suggested by fragments of sharply bent handles with 8-section. The short neck is cylindrical on a conical shoulder. This type most likely developed in Italy during the second century B.C. from Greek types, probably Rhodian or Coan. These amphorae were used for the transportation of wine. They are found in dated context until Flavian times.

5. *Amphora with bell-shaped mouth and overhanging lip (P 154):* The general type is long-lived, but the profile of the mouth varies and the body associated with it is varied too. The widely out-turned lip of our P 154 may well belong to the first century B.C. (For reasonably close parallels see Numantia, pl. 74, 10).

We mention only the most important of more recent discussions of Late Hellenistic and Republican amphorae, in which a complete bibliography can be found. N. Lamboglia, "Sulla cronologia delle anfore romane del' età repubblicana (II-I secolo a.C)," *RivStudi-Liguri,* 21 (1955): 241 ff.; F. Benoît, "Epaves de la côte de Provence, Typologie des amphores," *Gallia* 14, 1956, pp. 23 ff.; Otto Uenze, *Frührömische Amphoren als Zeitmarken im Spätlatène* (1958); with the review by E. Ettlinger, *Germania* 38, 1960, pp. 440 ff. Uenze's book is most valuable for his collection of dated amphorae both north and south of the Alps, presented in profile drawings and accompanied by an evaluation of the chronology of each site. While Lamboglia and Uenze stressed the typological evolution perhaps too much in establishing their chronology, F. Zevi, in his very important "Appunti anfore," introduces other, equally relevant criteria which will necessitate a partial modification of these chronological systems. For a full bibliography of aspects of trade and distribution of amphorae between southern Italy, the Adriatic, Istria, and the Cisalpina see: Baldacci, commercio anfore.

For Altenburg-Rheinau see: F. Fischer, "Das oppidum von Altenburg-Rheinau," *Germania* 44 (1966): 286 f. For Pegli see: *RivStudiLiguri* 21 (1955): 263 f., fig. 19.

SUMMARY

The duration of building period I in terms of absolute chronology as it results from the study of the coins and the pottery has been discussed above in the chapter dealing with the chronological evidence. The evidence from the pottery can therefore be summarized here briefly as follows. The settlement (emporion) of Salona is in all probability well established around the middle of the second century B.C., with the possibility of a slightly earlier beginning some time during the first half of that century. Period I lasted through the time of Augustus, very likely until ±A.D. 10. In terms of the known history, this would indicate that the end and the beginning of period I and period II respectively coincide roughly with the successful campaigns of Tiberius in Illyria (A.D. 6-9).

Despite the extremely fragmented state of the pottery finds of period I, a few observations can be made with regard to their general character as well as their provenience. There can be, in our opinion, no doubt that the earliest settlers on the eminence of Salona were not Dalmatians nor did they come from the hinterland. Witness the complete lack of sufficient number of specimens of pottery of a clearly native-Illyrian late-Iron-Age character. The few handmade kitchen and storage vessels found could be expected under all circumstances to have been manufactured on the spot or to have been purchased in the neighborhood. We had, on the contrary, to stress the thoroughly Hellenistic Greco-Roman character of the wares in use. Wherever the settlers came from, they were used to pottery current in the Hellenistic world. Trade relations between the Aegean and the Adriatic are attested, of course, since the establishment of Greek colonies in the Adriatic. Moreover, we certainly have to assume the existence of regional centers of manufacture, be it on the islands or on the Dalmatian coast, to provide for the needs of the Greek colonists in this very area.

Some groups of finer wares, however, seem to speak in favor of more specific connections of Salona with the Aegean world during period I (in the earlier part of period I see the "Megarian" bowls, in the latter part see the Eastern sigillata). Such relations were to continue throughout later centuries as shown by the finds from the Forum north and Forum central sites. But in the presence of various black-glazed pottery the connection with Italy and, most probably, specifically with Apulia is evident too. These groups could perhaps be partly imports (witness the rare fragments of Campana B and C ware) but it is much more likely that limited Italian imports were influencing older, already established local or regional workshops. Direct imports from the Cisalpina, such as preeminently terra sigillata, reached Salona at a surprisingly late stage of period I, not before about ±A.D. 10.

This phenomenon is complemented by the not less astonishing fact that apparently not one, or, in any case not many, amphorae of the characteristic "Istrian" type Dressel 6, have been found. It then seems that no amphora—or, in other words—no oil shipments from the Istrian peninsula reached Salona in any considerable amount before the time of Tiberius. This in spite of the fact that at least since about 50 B.C. Istrian as well as Venetian oil was distributed widely in the Cisalpina and beyond. The reason for this might well be the circumstance that Salona continued to import its oil as well as its wine mainly from Apulia and Campania. However, this situation changed during the first century A.D. as the study of the amphorae from the Forum north site can show. From the beginning of period II onwards, the importation of pottery from northern Italy is large and varied.

Notes on Chapter 11

1. P.V.C. Baur, *AJA* 45 (1941): 238 f., no. 195, fig. 9; also M.A. del Chiaro, "Megaresi Vasi," in *EncArteAnt*, fig. 33, 2.
2. G.V. Gentili, *NSc* 10 (1956): 154, fig. 5.

CATALOGUE OF POTTERY

Note: In inventory numbers, PE refers to pottery from curia and Forum central sites; PN refers to pottery from Forum north site. Pottery illustrated is designated by pl.

Fig. A (P 1-21) Late Hellenistic Table Wares; Black Glaze on Light Clay (1:2), Plate 34.

The glaze or slip is indicated on the drawings only if the contrast to the reserved surface is relevant. An asterisk indicates that there is no drawing.

P 1-18 Clay orange to salmon

P 1	Patera.
P 2	Patera.
P 3	Deep bowl, rim reserved.
P 4	Deep bowl, brownish glaze.
P 5, pl.	Lid.
P 6, pl.	Cup. Grooved, out-turned lip incomplete.
P 7-9	Bases of open forms. Outside and underside of feet reserved.
P 10	Neck of closed vessel, unglazed.
P 11	Jug or beaker. Glaze outside dark olive green, inside brown to dark orange.
P 12	Bell-shaped form with grooved rim. Outside reserved but for irregular zone under the rim.
P 13	Base of small cup (?). Outside and underside reserved.
P 14, pl.	Lower part of stemmed vessel.
P 15, pl.	Lower part of stemmed vessel. Lowest part and underside reserved.
*P 15a, pl.	Wall fragment of closed vessel. Inside reserved.
P 16	Basis of krateriskos (?) or skyphos (?). Outside and underside reserved.
P 17, pl.	Neck-shoulder fragment of jug; handle broken. Glaze brownish-black. Decoration incised and painted with white paint mostly rubbed off (two horizontal parallel wreaths).
P 18, pl.	Wall fragment of ribbed open vessel. Glaze outside brownish, inside lustrous black. From the curia site, 1969.
*P 18a, pl.	Small wall fragment of open ribbed vessel. Black glaze inside and out.

P 19-21 Clay buff to light brown

P 19	Patera, lustrous black glaze.
P 20	Lid (?). Outside reserved but for lip zone. Glaze inside brownish.
P 21	Base of cup or beaker. Mat black glaze.

	Inv. Nos.	Provenience	Further Ref.
P 1	PE 667	B 7	Charts 2 & 6
P 2	PE 666	B 7	↓
P 3	PE 668	B 7	
P 4	PE 846	A'7	
P 5	PE 830	A'7	
P 6	PE 831	A'7	
P 7	PE 671	B 7	
P 8	PE 663	B 7	
P 9	PE 686	B 7	
P 10	PE 837	A'7	
P 11	PE 836	A'7	
P 12	PE 847	A'7	
P 13	PE 838	A'7	
P 14	PE 664	B 7	
P 15	PE 817	B 7	
P 15a	PE 818	B 7	
P 16	PE 832	A'7	
P 17	PE 819	B 6 East	
P 18	PE 69.619	curia	
P 18a	PE 684	B 7	
P 19	PE 815	B 7	
P 20	PE 816	B 7	
P 21	PE 860	A'7	

Figure A

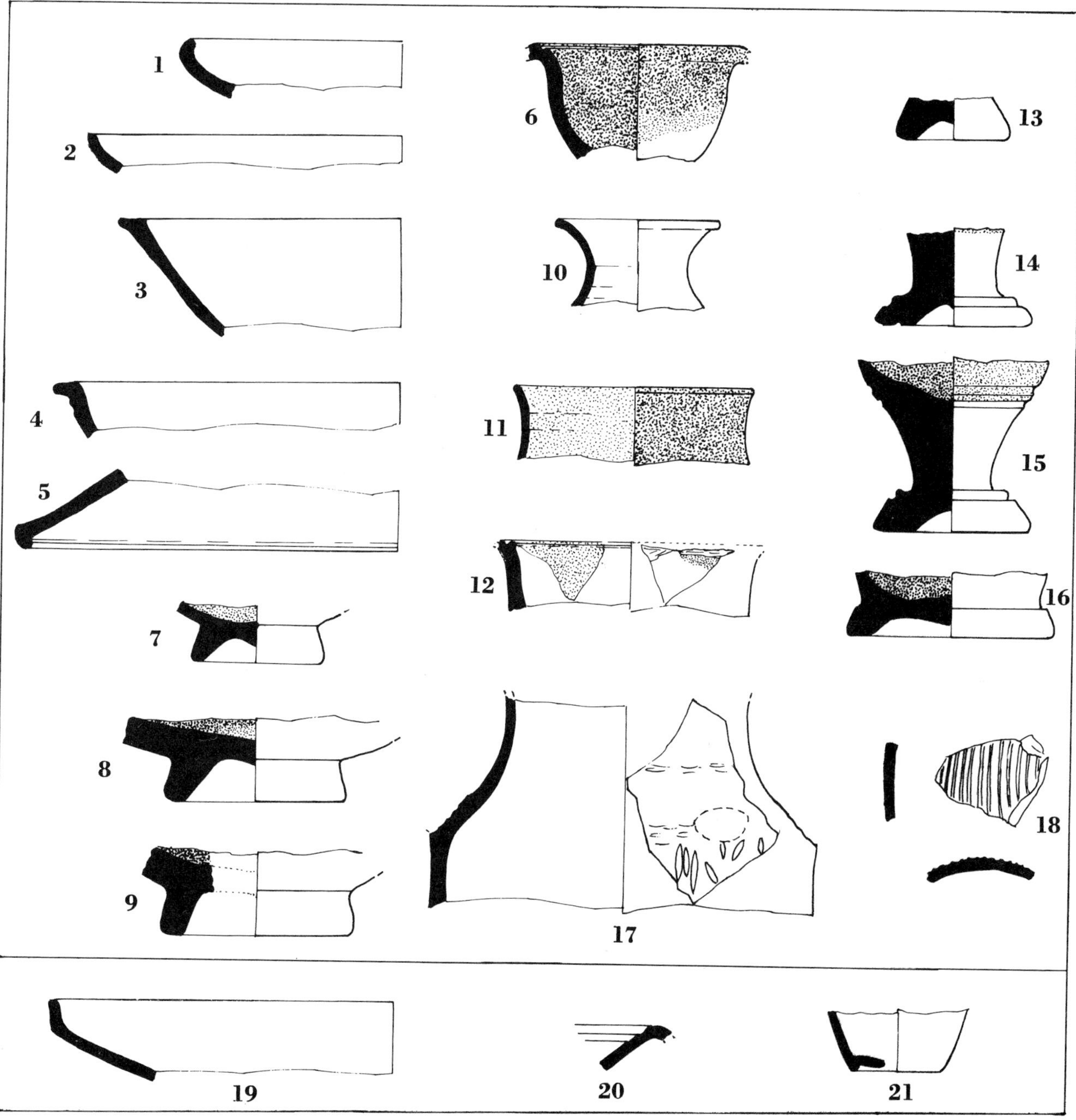

Fig. B (P 22-42) Late Hellenistic Table Wares with Relief Decoration (1:2), Plate 35

Megarian bowl of "normal type"

P 22, pl. Rim fragment of shallow bowl. Clay dark orange-brown, gritty, some mica; remains of mat brown-reddish glaze. First register egg and dart.

Megarian bowls (P 23-38)

Clay gray with some mica, fine textured; fired medium hard; black glaze soft, soapy, dark gray to olive green.

P 23, pl. Rim fragment. Relief almost rubbed off; first register: alternating larger and smaller rosettes (or masks ?).

P 24, pl. Rim fragment. Relief blurred. First register: whirl rosettes and smaller vertically paired rosettes (or masks ?).

P 25-30 Rim fragments, broken above first register.

P 31, pl. Base fragment resting upon three plastic feet. Overall pattern imbricated veined leaves. The feet are most likely not shell or mask-shaped. They rather resemble the crab-shaped feet on a fragment from the Forum north site (PN 58).

P 32, pl. Wall fragment. First register: six petalled rosette; second register: reclining figure.

P 33, pl. Wall fragment, Second (?) register: imbricated, veined leaves.

P 34, pl. Wall fragment. First register: imbricated stylized shells (?).

P 35, pl. Wall fragment (?). Relief almost abraded. ? register: wide-spaced palmettes.

P 36, pl. Wall fragment. Straight long petals, wreathed (?) at intervals (?). From 1969 excavations.

P 37, pl. Wall fragment. Clay more micaceous, slip thicker, relief higher than in previous series. Upper register: ? and palmette; row of lying double spirals; lower register: reclining figure and eight-petalled rosette.

P 38, pl. Wall fragment. Clay, slip, and relief as in P 37. First register: large pointed dots.

P 39, pl. Base fragment of bowl with false base ring. Relief medallion on inside of bottom: pine cone (?) or tip of thyrsos (?).

P 40-42, pl. 36. Bases of (undecorated ?) bowls with false base rings.

	Inv. Nos.	Provenience	Further Ref.
P 22	PE 686a	B 7	Charts 2 & 6
P 23	PE 826	A'7	
P 24	PE 696	A 7	
P 25	PE 678	B 7	
P 26	PE 677	B 7	
P 27	PE 679	B 7	
P 28	PE 822	B 7	
P 29	PE 821	B 6 East	
P 30	PE 849	A'7	
P 31	PE 820	B 6 East	
P 32	PE 833	A'7	
P 33	PE 854	A'7	
P 34	PE 697	B 7	
P 35	PE 874	A'7	
P 36	PE 69.626	curia	
P 37	PE 812	B 7	
P 38	PE 698	B 7	
P 39	PE 861	A'7	
P 40	PE 699	B 6 East	
P 41	PE 835	A'7	
P 42	PE 813	B 7	

Figure B

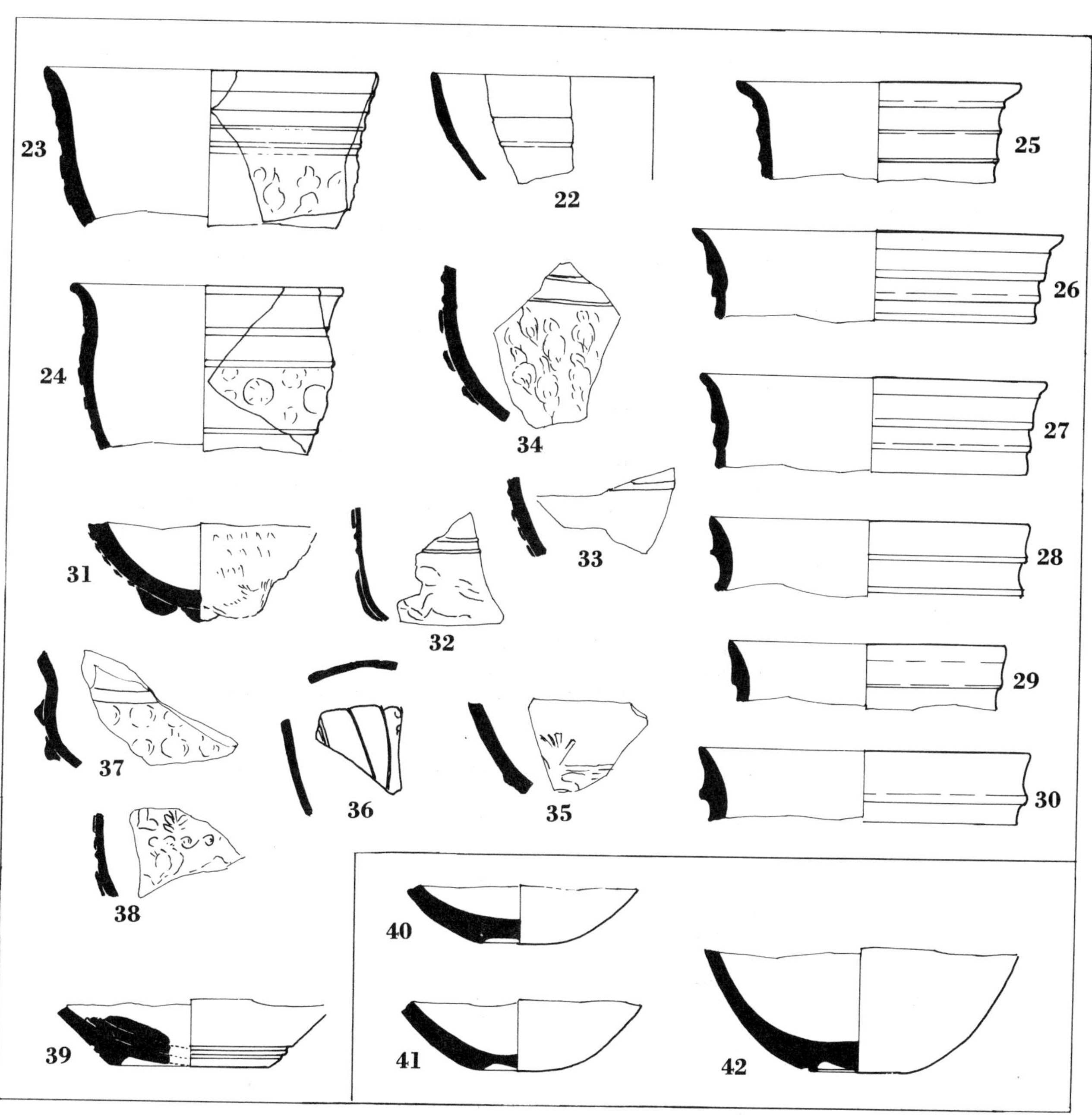

Fig. C (P 44-62) Late Hellenistic Table Wares (1:2), Plate 36

An asterisk indicates that there is no drawing. P 43 has been deleted.

P 44-58	Clay gray fine textured, fired medium hard; glaze soft, soapy, black to dark green to olive green.
P 44, pl.	Bowl with grooved upper wall, full form uncertain. This vessel stands out from the others in this group for the quality of the clay which is between beige, buff and gray, with mica, and fired hard.
P 45	Beaker or small jug (?).
P 46-47	Handles.
P 48	Shallow bowl.
P 49-50a	Paterae.
P 51-52	Bases of open forms.
*P 53, pl.	Base fragment of plate with two bands of fine rouletting between concentric rings.
P 53a	Base fragment of similar plate with one rouletted band, found together with P 59 (see below).
P 54-55	Deep, large bowls.
P 56	Plate with out-turned rim.
P 57, pl.	Neck of flagon with built-in five-holed sieve; schematic drawing.
*P 57a	Neck of similar flagon with four-holed sieve.
P 58	Base of flagon or jug.

P 59	Clay as above but very micaceous, like the clay of black Eastern sigillata B (not represented in our period I, 1970 complex). Soft semi-lustrous soapy black glaze, mostly rubbed off.
a,b	Large plate with "eastern" shape of base and wide rouletted band between concentric rings. It was found broken into many fragments used as a cover for the graphite-covered hand-made *Dolium* P 114 (Fig. F). Fragments of rim and foot are shown here. Found together with P 53a and P 113.

P 60-62 Light clayed ware

P 60	Rim fragment of beaker (form Moevs I) with "décor clouté."
P 61	Base of beaker (form Moevs I) with remains of pine scale decoration.
P 62, pl. 39	Large plate with out-turned rim; tip of rim broken. Surface polished very smooth.

	Inv. Nos.	Provenience	Further Ref.
P 44	PE 827	B 7	
P 45	PE 871	A'7	
P 46	PE 680	B 7	
P 47	PE 828	A'7	
P 48	PE 834	A'7	
P 49	PE 869	A'7	
P 50	PE 872	A'7	
P 50a	PE 866	A'7	
P 51	PE 682	B 7	
P 52	PE 829	A'7	
P 53	PE 875	A'7	
P 53a	PE 681	B 7	
P 54	PE 870	A'7	
P 55	PE 857	A'7	
P 56	PE 865	A'7	
P 57	PE 851	A'7	
P 57a	PE 850	A'7	
P 58	PE 867	A'7	
P 59	PE 672	B 7	
P 60	PE 1200	B 7	
P 61	PE 868	A'7	
P 62	PE 1204	B 7	

Figure C

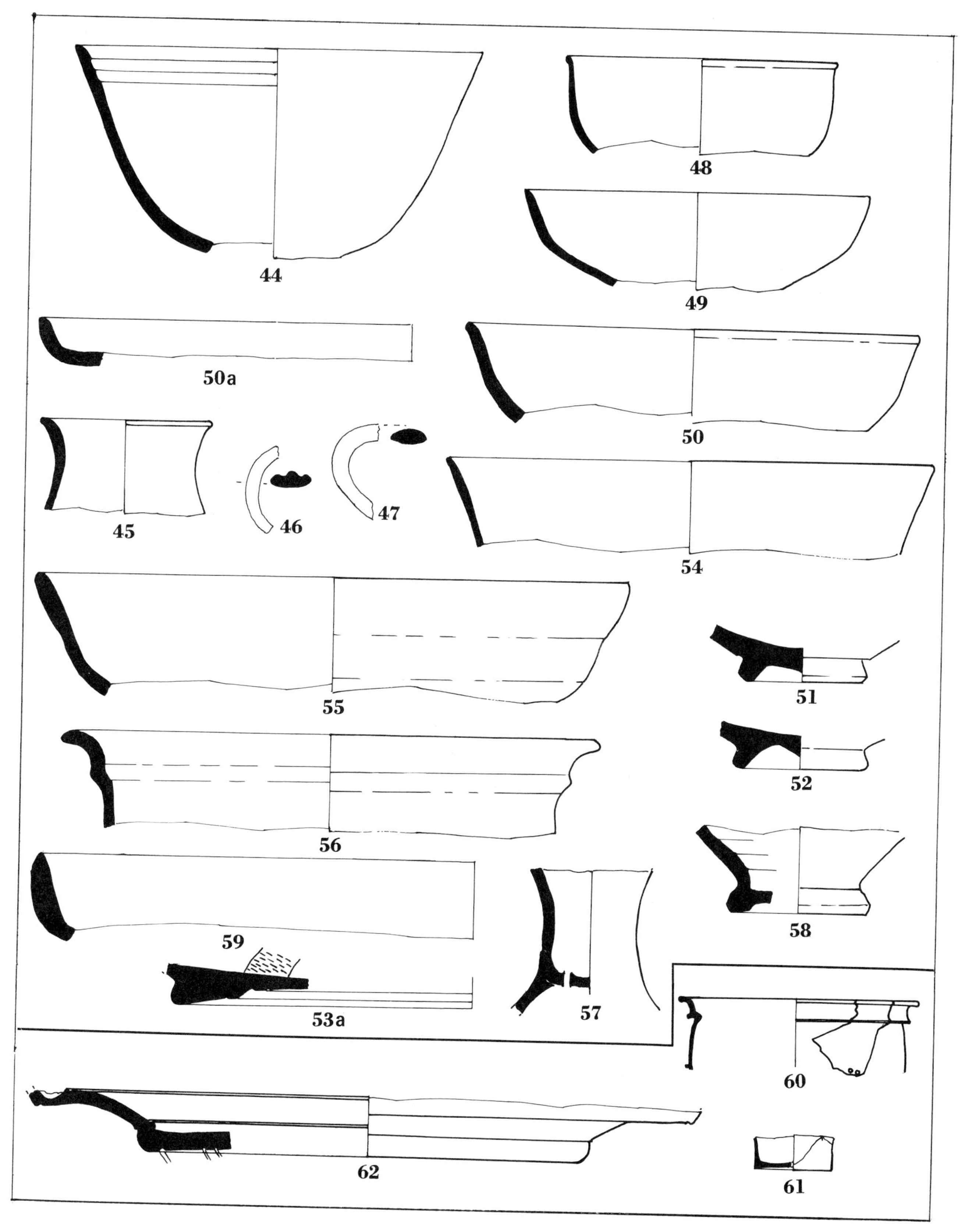

Fig. D (P 63-77) Early Roman Table Wares (1:2 Sigillata Stamps 1:1), Plates 37-38

An asterisk indicates that there is no drawing. These are comparative pieces, not from curia site 1970.

Vitreous glazed ware

P 63, pl. 37 Skyphos with base ring and mould-formed; relief decoration: garland of ivy leaves and berries. Clay coarse grained, white to ivory, some black inclusions; glaze outside: green with olive green, brown, and turquoise patches; inside: olive green to light green.

P 64-73 Italian Terra Sigillata

P 64 Plate *(catinus)* Ha 1b, Service I. Clay salmon, "Glanzton" with silky shine; very fine quality.

P 65 Plate *(catinus)* Ha 1b, Service I. Clay salmon, "Glanzton" with silky shine; mat; fine quality.

P 66 Plate *(catinus)* Ha 1c, Service I. Clay salmon; "Glanzton" silky, mat; fine quality.

P 67, pl. 38 Plate *(catinus)* with rectangular stamp LIBANI (not in O.-C.). Clay reddish, some mica or quartz; "Glanzton" mat, with glossy patches.

P 68, pl. 38 Plate *(catinus)* with rectangular stamp R]O[MANI (O.-C. 1581). Clay orange; "Glanzton" mat, somewhat diluted; fair quality.

P 69 Cup *(paropsis)* Ha 8, Service II. Clay salmon; "Glanzton" silky, somewhat diluted on the outside; very fine quality.

P 70 Cup *(paropsis)* Ha 8 with flat bottom, Service II. Clay beige to salmon; "Glanzton" silky, somewhat diluted on the outside; very fine quality.

P 71 Cup *(paropsis)* Ha 8 with lightly curving bottom, Service II, with rectangular stamp NICO (O.-C. 1121). Clay salmon to orange; "Glanzton" silky, somewhat mat, diluted underneath the base; fine quality.

*P 72, pl. 38 Cup *(paropsis)* Ha 8 with flat bottom, Service II, with stamp NICO. Curia site, 1969.

*P 73, pl. 38 Cup *(paropsis)* Ha 8 with flat bottom, Service II, with rectangular stamp DASI (O.-C. 587). From Forum central site, Trench 2.

P 74-75 Eastern Sigillata A II (ESA II)

P 74 Wall fragment of cup. Clay pale buff, fine texture, very light fabric; scant remains of yellow-orange glaze.

P 75 Foot of small cup. Clay and fabric like P 74; very thin-walled; remains of mat, thin glaze orange to yellow, marbled (?), partly rubbed off.

P 76-77 Eastern Sigillata B I (ESB I)

Clay cinnamon-red, very micaceous; glaze dark orange, somewhat soapy, very glossy, and very well adhering.

P 76 Plate corresponding to Ha 2a, Service II.

P 77 Rim fragment of footless plate. Clay and glaze as P 76.

	Inv. Nos.	Provenience	Further Ref.
P 63	PE 700	A'7	
P 64	PE 843	A'7	
P 65	PE 841	A'7	
P 66	PE 842	A'7	
P 67	PE 420	A'7	
P 68	PE 417	A'7	
P 69	PE 852	A'7	
P 70	PE 853	A'7	
P 71	PE 416	A'7	
*P 72	PE 69.419	curia	
*P 73	PE 82	Trench 2	Chart 1
P 74	PE 824	B 6	
P 75	PE 845	A'7	
P 76	PE 687	B 7	
P 77	PE 688	B 7	

Figure D

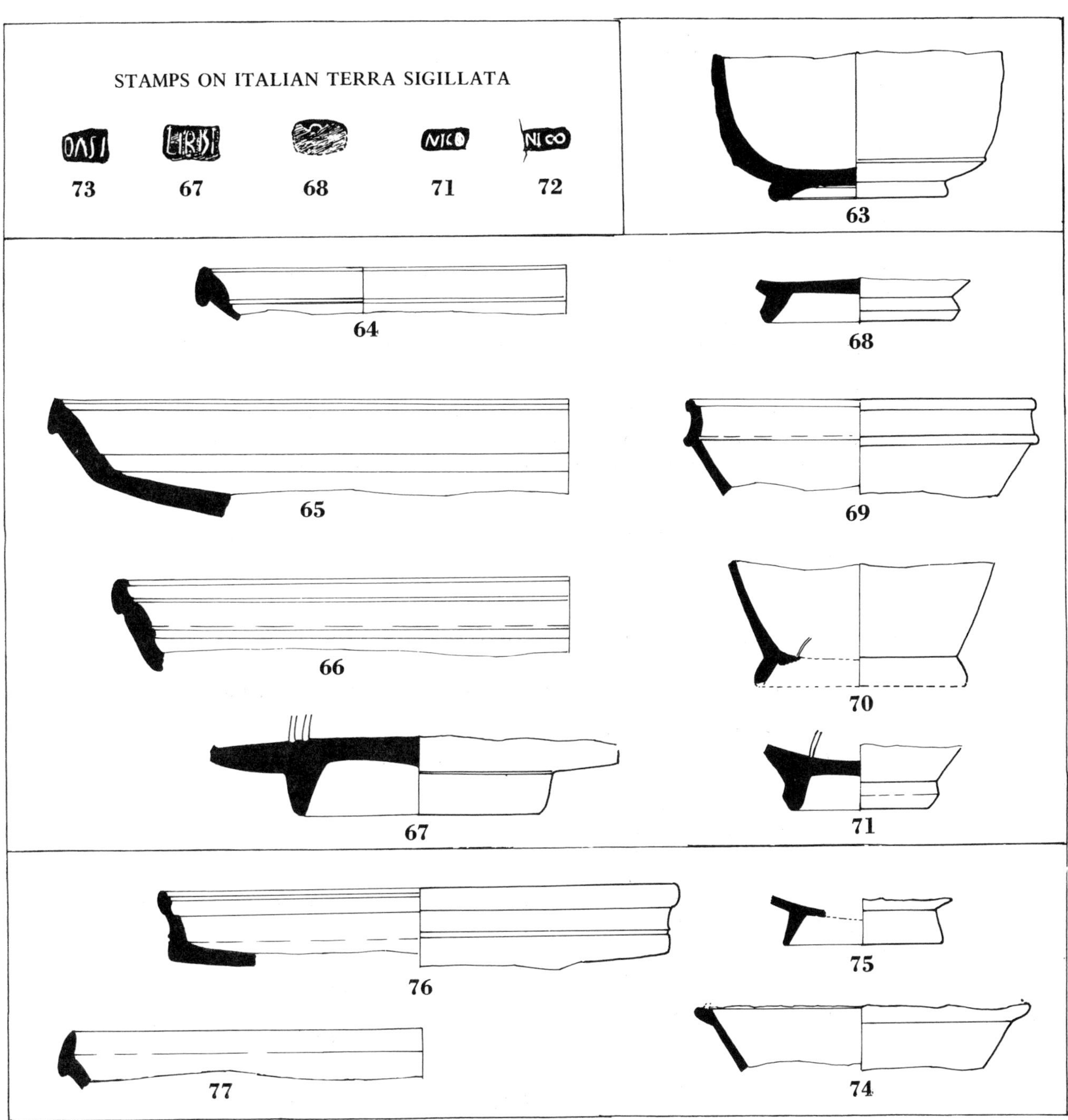
STAMPS ON ITALIAN TERRA SIGILLATA
73
67
68
71
72
63
64
68
65
69
66
70
67
71
76
75
77
74

Fig. E (P 78-104) Plain Household and Cooking Wares (1:3)

An asterisk indicates that there is no drawing.

P 78-95 Light clayed household wares

P 78	*Unguentarium,* fusiform (Ha 30). Clay light brown, remains of brown slip.
P 79	Deep bowl, thin walled with grooved rim. Clay salmon, much mica; white slip on outside.

P 80-82 Ewers

P 80, pl. 39	Fragment of handle joining rim. Coarse grained, cinnamon colored clay with white and quartz inclusions.
P 81-82	Clay as P 80.
*P 82a	Base as P 82.

P 83-89	Flagons or jugs with horizontal moulded lip. Very delicate fabric, fired medium hard.
P 83-85	Clay off white to yellow with greenish tinge.
P 86-87	Clay salmon colored with mica.
P 88	Clay buff to salmon, surface very smoothly polished. Found crushed but almost complete.
P 89	With cylindrical neck and rolled lip.
P 90-91	Small lids (see also P 120 ff., Fig. F).
P 90	Type A, conical with large knob. Clay off white with white and black inclusions. About 23 more lids (not catalogued) of type A were found.
P 91	Type B, flat with small knob. Clay salmon with red inclusions. About 10 more lids (not catalogued) of type B were found.

P 92-95	Storage jars ("honeyjars") with probably two handles on shoulder. Clay beige, very fine, fired medium hard.

P 96-104 Cooking and baking vessels.

	The clay is coarse-grained, cinnamon brown to salmon with quartz and other large inclusions as in P 80-82 and with much mica.
P 96	Baking plate ("Pompejanisch rote Platten") with thickened rim, light groove under the rim on the outside.
P 97	Baking plate. Inside painted red, outside blackened by use.
P 98-101	Casseroles with angular wall; flaring lip for accommodation of lid.
P 102	Later variant of P 98-101.
P 103	Deep cooking jar with "orlo a mandorla."
P 104	Deep cooking jar with out-turned rim.

	Inv. Nos.	Provenience		Inv. Nos.	Provenience
P 78	PE 662	A'7	P 92	PE 1198	B 6 East
P 79	PE 1201	B 7	P 93	PE 1199	B 6 East
P 80	PE 1195	B 7	P 94	PE 1196	B 6 East
P 81	PE 1192	B 6 East	P 95	PE 1195	A'7
P 82	PE 1194	B 7	P 96	PE 1155	A'7
P 83	PE 1186	B 7	P 97	PE 1153	B 7
P 84	PE 1187	B 7	P 98	PE 1143	A'7
P 85	PE 1190	B 7	P 99	PE 1145	A'7
P 86	PE 1189	B 7	P 100	PE 1144	A'7
P 87	PE 1188	A'7	P 101	PE 1146	A'7
P 88	PE 652	A'7	P 102	PE 1152	B 7
P 89	PE 825	B 6 East	P 103	PE 1147	A'7
P 90	PE 638	A'7	P 104	PE 1154	B 6 East
P 91	PE 639	A'7			

Figure E

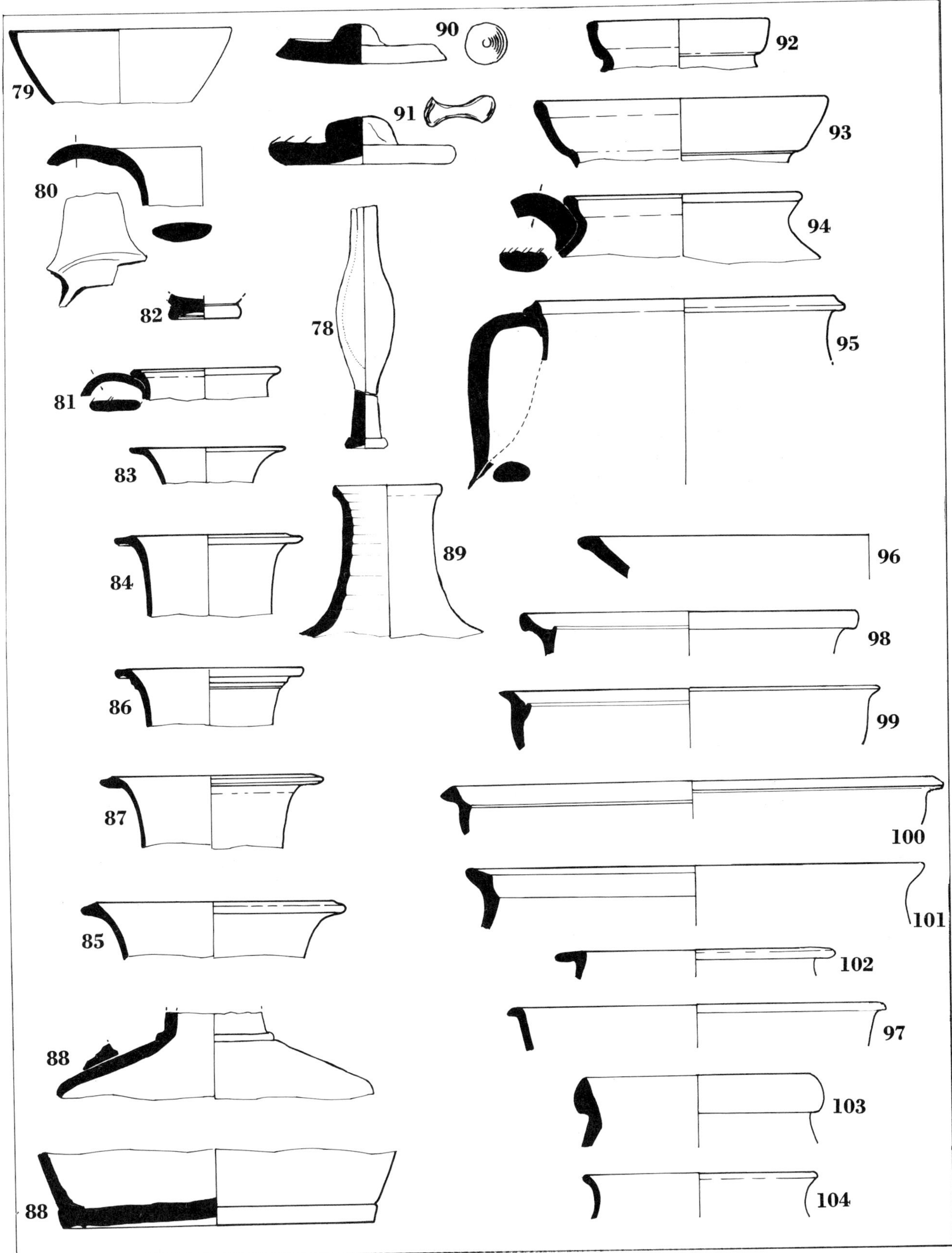
79
90
91
92
93
94
80
82
78
95
81
83
89
96
84
98
86
99
87
100
85
101
102
88
97
103
88
104

Fig. F (P 105-124) Plain Household Wares (1:3), Plate 39

An asterisk indicates that there is no drawing.

P 105-111 Light clayed vessels

P 105 — *Mortarium.* Clay off-white, fired medium hard.

P 106-108 — Lids. P 106 has beige clay with brown inclusions. P 107-108 have beige clay with mica.

P 109-111 — Large double-handled jugs ("table amphorae"). P 109 beige clay with red and white inclusions. P 110 brownish-red clay, surface is lighter with mica. P 111 salmon clay with white and black inclusions, surface lighter.

P 112-114 Handmade cooking and storage vessels

Clay is more gray, surface reddish-brown, many white inclusions; coarse-grained and fired hard.

P 114 — With soapy, thick black graphite (?) coating easily washed off. P 113-114 were found crushed but complete together with P 55a and P 59 (see Fig. C).

*P 114a, pl. — Cup from the glass workshop (1969).

P 115-124 From Capitolium trench (trench 1, closed deposit)

For amphorae belonging to this complex see P 130-134, fig. G 2.

P 115 — Wall fragment, clay gray as in P 44-59, with polished or slipped surface.

*P 115a — Wall fragment of straight sided beaker (?). Clay as in P 115.

P 116 — Base fragment of jug. Clay salmon, fired medium hard.

P 117 — Wall fragment probably of storage vessel ("honeyjar" see P 95). Clay with gray core, surface reddish, fired very hard. Secondary burning (?).

P 118 — Cooking jar. Clay as in P 96-104. Outside blackened by use.

P 119 — *Mortarium.* Clay and firing as in *Mortarium* P 105.

P 120-124, pl. Small lids for small jugs or storage vessels (for designation of clay see Fig. G).

P 120, 123, 124 — Clay A.

P 121 — Clay off-white without inclusions.

P 122 — Clay B

9 more lids, mostly clay A, were found (inv. nos. PE 145, 149, 152-158).

	Inv. Nos.	Provenience		Inv. Nos.	Provenience
P 105	PE 1204a	A'7	P 115	PE 23	Trench 1
P 106	PE 660	A'7	P 115a	PE 22	Trench 1
P 107	PE 658	A'7	P 116	PE 28	Trench 1
P 108	PE 659	A'7	P 117	PE 26	Trench 1
P 109	PE 1205	A'7	P 118	PE 25	Trench 1
P 110	PE 636	A'7	P 119	PE 27	Trench 1
P 111	PE 637	A'7	P 120	PE 148	Trench 1
P 112	PE 661	B 6 East	P 121	PE 151	Trench 1
P 113	PE 690	B 7	P 122	PE 147	Trench 1
P 114	PE 695	B 7	P 123	PE 146	Trench 1
P 114a	PE 69.694	Glass workshop (1969)	P 124	PE 150	Trench 1

Figures F1, 2

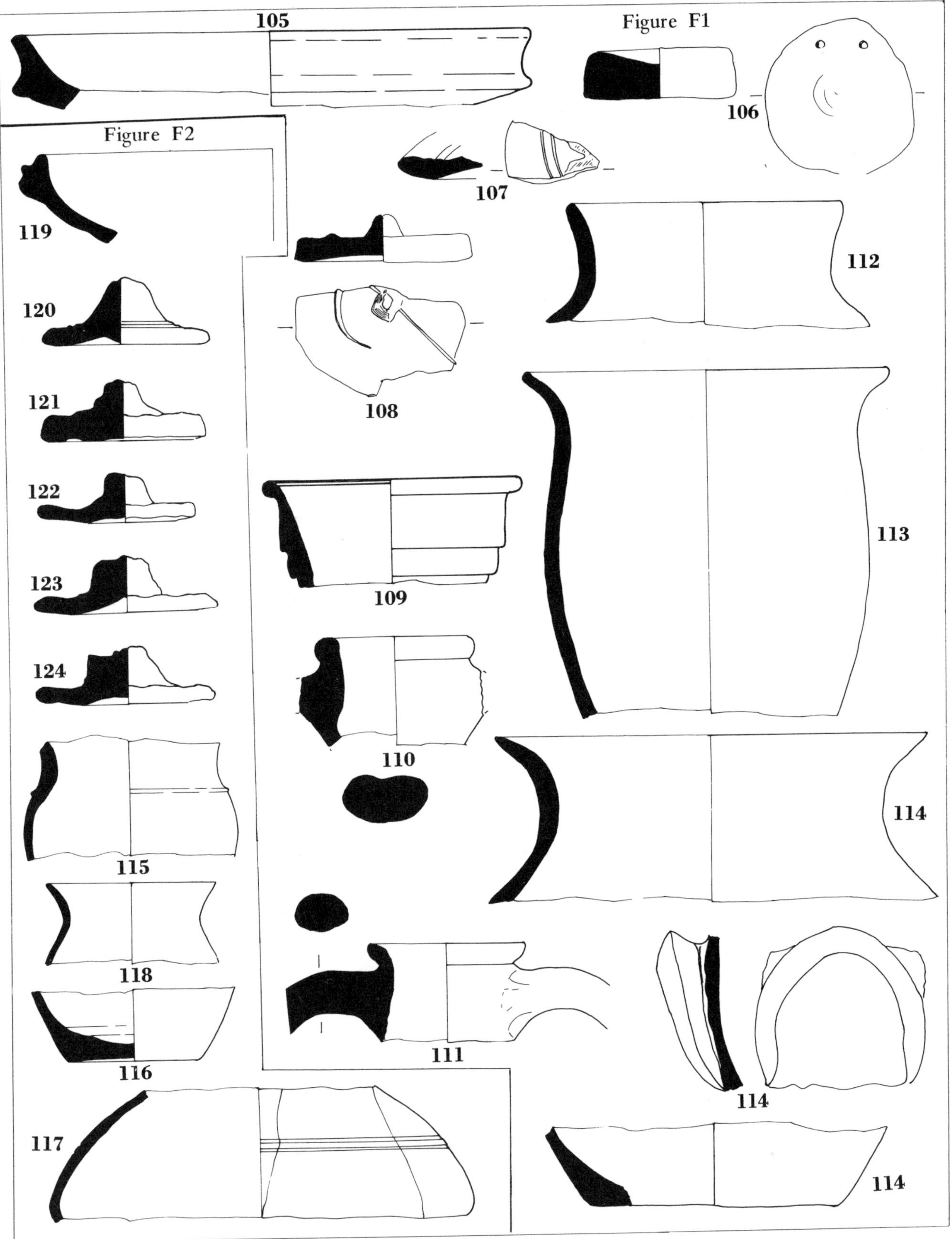

105
Figure F1
106
107
108
109
110
111
112
113
114
114
114
Figure F2
119
120
121
122
123
124
115
118
116
117

Fig. G (P 125-154) Amphorae (1:3), Plate 38

G 1 From curia site, under the pavement of period II.

G 2 From *Capitolium* trench (trench 1, closed deposit).

G 3 From Forum north site, W2C (Amphora pit).

P 125-139 (P 134 not drawn). Amphorae of Greco-Italian type and variants thereof. P 138-139 Apulian type I (?). Clay A.

P 140-144 Amphorae Dressel I A.

P 145-148 Amphorae Dressel I A (?) in fabric of Greco-Italian type amphorae. Clay A.

P 149-151, pl. Amphorae Dressel I B. P 151 with stamp on collar. Clay B.

P 152-153 Amphorae Dressel 3. Clay brownish with much mica, remains of white coating (?).

P 154 Amphora with out-turned rim and overhanging lip. Clay brick-colored, surface lighter with many white inclusions. White coating on inside of fragment; on outside rubbed off (?).

Clay A Sandy, ivory to dirty white often with black and tile-colored inclusions and at times fairly much mica; rather fine texture, fired medium hard.

Clay B Salmon to reddish with mica; heavy fabric with coating at times; fired very hard.

	Inv. Nos.	Provenience
P 125	PE 649	A'7
P 126	PE 643	A'7
P 127	PE 644	A'7
P 128	PE 650	A'7
P 129	PE 655	A'7
P 130	PE 111	Trench 1
P 131	PE 142	Trench 1
P 132	PE 140	Trench 1
P 133	PE 141	Trench 1
P 134		Trench 1
P 135	PN 1156	W2C Forum N
P 136	PN 1160	W2C Forum N
P 137	PN 1157	W2C Forum N
P 138	PE 640	A'7
P 139	PE 651	A'7
P 140	PE 644a	A 7
P 141	PE 642	A'7
P 142	PE 143	Trench 1
P 143	PE 144	Trench 1
P 144	PN 1162	W2C Forum N
P 145	PN 1161	W2C Forum N
P 146	PN 1159	W2C Forum N
P 147	PN 1158	W2C Forum N
P 148	PE 648	A'7
P 149	P 1182	A'7
P 150	P 1163	W2C Forum N
P 151	P 423	W2C Forum N
P 152	P 634	A'7
P 153	PE 635	A'7
P 154	PE 647	A'7

Figure G1

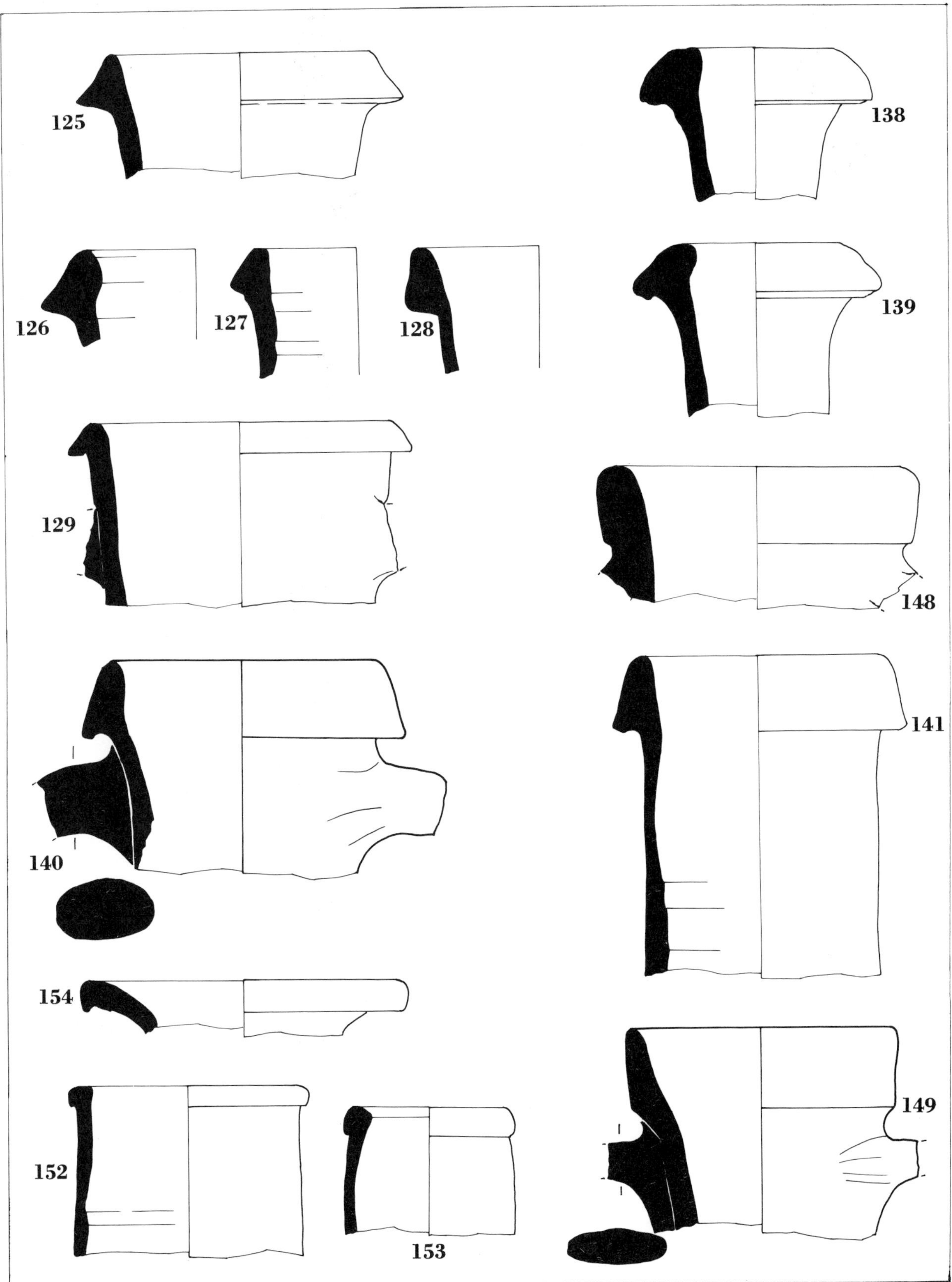

Figures G2, 3

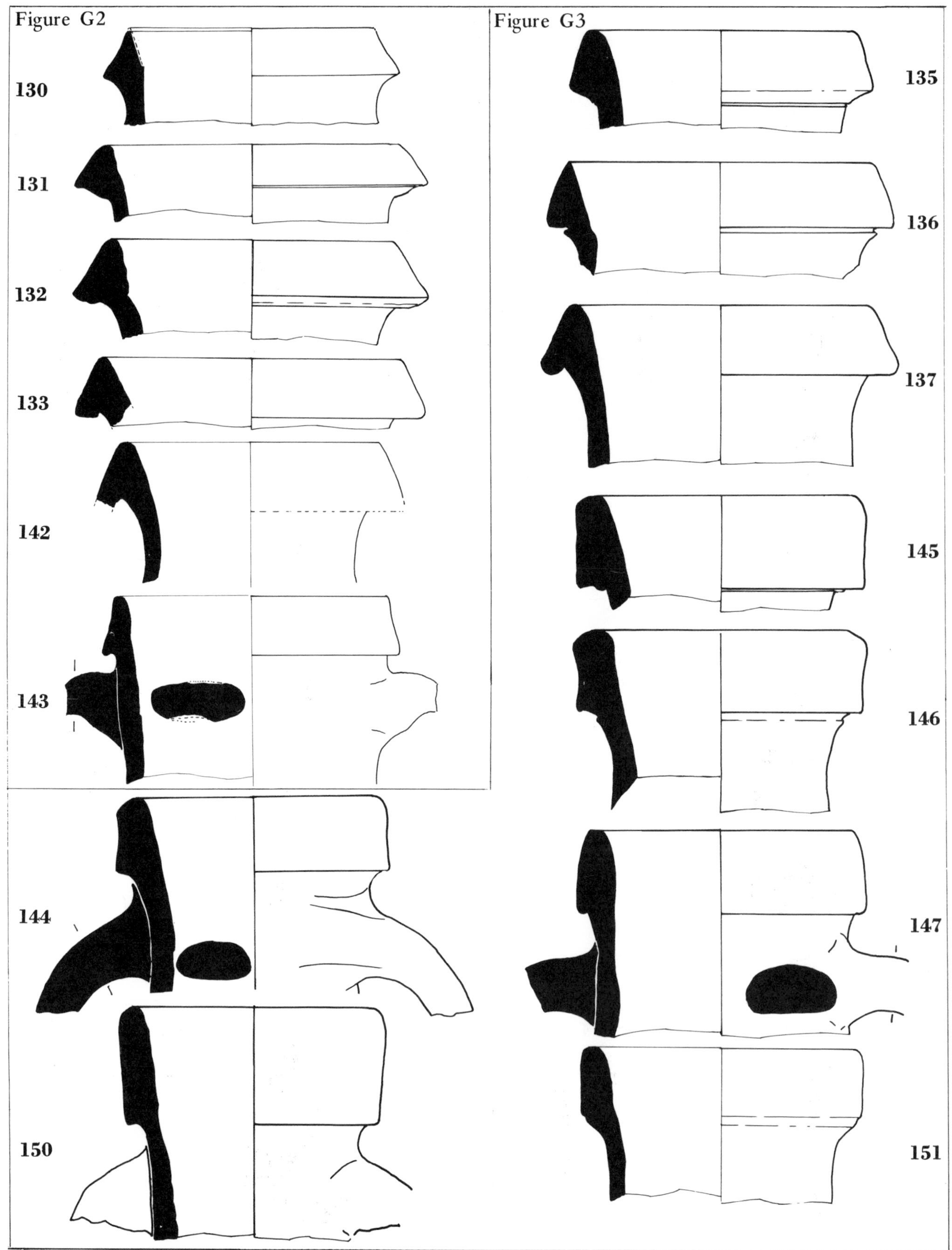
Figure G2
130
131
132
133
142
143
144
150
Figure G3
135
136
137
145
146
147
151

XI

Stone Monuments

Among the monuments in stone (**Plates 40-47**) the majority were retrieved from the surface *gomile* in the Forum north site when it was decided to tunnel through it in order to extend excavation further to the south. Considering the size of the *gomile* and its location amidst former Roman buildings, the harvest from it was quite poor; especially surprising was the almost total absence of fragments with inscriptions which one might hope to find among the many thousand broken and discarded stones. Other *gomile* in the excavation trenches proper yielded some of the finds catalogued below. Very few stone objects were found in other than *gomile* contexts. This shows how much the site was systematically searched for stones either for reuse in buildings in Christian times, for use in lime kilns, or simply in clearing the earth for cultivation.

From among 149 fragments inventoried, 38 are published here. In this selection are included all fragments of sculpture (nos. 1-3). As for sculpted architectural pieces (nos. 4-26), a choice of the better preserved fragments from among many similar pieces was made. Finally, fragments of stone objects are gathered in a miscellaneous group (nos. 27-38). A listing of revetment marbles follows.

I. SCULPTURE

1. (**Plate 40.**) From W4B. L. 24.5 cm; H. (including strut) 12 cm. White marble, heavily weathered on underside. Lower arm of male figure with a strut attached at the point where the arm passes into the wrist. This point of attachment suggests that the arm of the figure was lowered and was secured to the body by means of a strut at the upper thigh.

   For an illustration of the pose described see Lippold, *Griechische Skulptur* (Handbuch) pl. 59.1 (Doryphoros in Naples); pl. 60.1 (Westmacott boy); pl. 68.1 (Ares Borghese).
2. (**Plate 40.**) From B5. Gray-green basalt with light speckles, probably of Egyptian provenience; broken on all sides. Surface of fragment is very sensitively modelled and smoothed. Could be from the limb of a figure, imported from Egypt. It is worth noting that some Egyptian sculptures came to light in the palace of Diocletian in Split. See P. Selem, "L'état de recherche concernant les sphinx du palais de Dioclétien à Split." *Adriatica Praehistorica et Antiqua. Miscellanea G. Novak* (1970), pp. 639-656.
3. (**Plate 40.**) From W5B. Grayish marble. H. 16 cm, D. at top 18 cm, at bottom 24 cm. Irregularly broken on top leaving a circular concavity; convex sides are smooth with traces of granular weathering; some smaller and a large chip off the side. Concave underside is only roughly smoothed. In general shape, the fragment is reminiscent of a hoof. The oval, concave underside suggests the above interpretation.

II. ARCHITECTURAL FRAGMENTS

A. Plain Mouldings

The mouldings are on the whole too fragmentary to be assigned to specific elements of architectural decoration. Some fragments may belong to pedestals, podia, and the like; others could have belonged to simae, geisa, jambs, orthostates, and antae. Thus, while attempting some identification, final attributions must remain vague. Some attributions have been suggested by comparison with monuments in W. Altmann, *Die römischen Grabaltäre der Kaiserzeit* (1905) and with mouldings in L. Shoe, *Profiles of western Greek mouldings* (1952). The date of the plain and ornamented mouldings, sculpture and stone objects is the middle Imperial period (second to third century A.D.). The use of the drill is very prominent in some objects.

4. (**Plates 40, 45.**) From B3-4. White marble; brown incrusted weathering. H. 11.8 cm; 23.7 cm by 15.8 cm at sides. Two sides of moulding, one long and one short; break goes from one corner of long side to back which is cut vertically. Underside flat. Fragment as preserved may not be of original size; if original, the vertically cut side was placed against a wall, pilaster, etc. The moulding is that of a pedestal or a base.
5. (**Plate 45.**) From E3D. Grayish-white marble. H. 7.5 cm; L. 17.5 cm. Broken on all sides. Thick layer of mortar adheres to back side of fragment and has spilled over profile, probably indicating reuse of architectural fragment. Moulding from geison sofit (?).
6. (**Plate 45.**) From *gomile,* E2E/F. Grayish-white marble. H. 14 cm; L. 15.5 cm. Broken on all sides. Surface of moulding carefully smoothed. Cornice moulding (?).
7. (**Plate 45.**) From *gomile,* E2E/F. Grayish-white marble. H. 11 cm; L. 7.5 cm; D. 6.5 cm. Broken on all sides. Surface smoothed. Could have belonged to lowermost portion of pedestal, altar, or revetment.
8. (**Plate 45.**) From *gomile,* E2E/F. Grayish-white marble. H. 18 cm; L. 12 cm. Broken on all sides. Surface of moulding only roughly smoothed. Possibly from anta capital (?).
9. (**Plate 47.**) From *gomile,* E2E/F. Gray marble. H. 9.5 cm; L. 12.5 cm; max. D. 7.5 cm. Broken on all sides. Torus moulding (broken at lower edge) continues above in stepped moulding. Perhaps from an anta base.
10. (**Plate 45.**) From *gomile,* E2E/F. Grayish-white marble. H. 15 cm; L. 18 cm. Broken on all sides. Slanting underside is roughly picked. Base has torus moulding above, followed by short vertical, then concave profile. Perhaps from an anta base or column-shaped support (?).
11. (**Plate 41.**) From *gomile,* E2E/F. Grayish-white marble. H. 14 cm; L. 23 cm; D. 28 cm. Broken on all sides. Dentil pattern and stepped moulding suggests that this fragment is part of a frieze.
12. (**Plate 41.**) From A3. Gray-blue, local marble. Heavy traces of weathering. H. 18 cm; W. 2.2 cm; D. 6 cm. Reused fragment, broken at left edge and lower side. Upper edge deliberately cut when reused, leaving only lower half of cyma decoration. Below, a tongue pattern and fragmented volute design. From a small Ionian capital (?); the tongue pattern is in a reversed position.
13. (**Plate 41.**) From W4B. White marble. H. 14 cm; L. 9 cm; Th. 5.5 cm. Long edges broken. One short end complete. Surface decorated with band ending in volute; in center of band rows of knobs framed by raised edges. Fragment comes from console.
14. (**Plate 41.**) From *gomile,* E2E/F. Grayish-white marble. H. 12 cm; L. 19.5 cm; max. Th. 5.5 cm. Broken on all sides. Fragment of cable pattern framed by triangular moulding with concave moulding below.

B. With Plant Decoration

15. a-c (**Plate 41.**) From *gomile,* E2E/F. Grayish-white marble. Three fragments, L. of biggest 17.5 cm. Acanthus leaf with broken ends. Deep rectangular groove possibly added later (?).
16. (**Plate 42.**) From *gomile,* E2E/F. Grayish-white marble. H. 9.5 cm, L. 19.5 cm, Th. 4 cm.

Broken on all sides, except at right edge. Corner fragment with acanthus leaf. Oblong rectangular slot in lower right leaf added when reused (?).

17. (**Plate 42.**) From W7B. Grayish-white marble. H. 5 cm. Surface somewhat weathered. Rosette-like flower, possibly from coffer or related decoration.
18. (**Plate 42.**) From *gomile,* E2E/F. Grayish-white marble. H. 11 cm; W. 11 cm; average Th. 5 cm. Broken on all sides. Surface much weathered. Fragment with leaf design, probably an oak leaf.
19. (**Plate 42.**) From *gomile,* E2E/F. Grayish-white marble. H. 12.5 cm; max. L. 18 cm. Right edge horizontally cut, broken at other edges. Underside flat and roughly picked. Possibly corner fragment with three symmetrically placed oak leaves (?).
20. (**Plate 42.**) From E3D. Grayish-white marble. H. 6.5 cm; L. 10 cm; average Th. 5.75 cm. Broken on all sides. Slightly curved fragment with egg-and-dart pattern between mouldings.
21. (**Plate 42.**) From *gomile,* E2E/F. Gray marble. H. 10 cm; L. 13.5 cm; Th. 3 cm. Edges broken, underside flat and roughly picked. Two elements of *cyma reversa.*
22. (**Plate 43.**) From B3-4. Grayish-white marble. H. 25 cm; max. W. 19 cm; max. Th. 11 cm. Left edge complete, otherwise broken on all sides. Surface damaged and weathered. Decoration consists of acanthus, horizontal moulding, *cyma reversa,* and egg-and-dart pattern. Probably from a pilaster capital.
23. (**Plate 43.**) From *gomile,* E2E/F. Grayish-white marble. H. 17 cm; L. 13 cm; Th. 12 cm. Surface weathered and many small chips off the leaves. Edges broken. Console decorated with acanthus leaf. On a recessed plane scanty remains of an egg-and-dart pattern. Four small rectangular slots in surface are due either to a secondary use of stone or to a metal (?) revetment fastened to leaf (?).
24. (**Plate 43.**) From *gomile,* E2E/F. Grayish-white marble. Max. Dim. 14.5 cm. Broken on all sides. Two planes forming edge at right angle, the edge being only partly preserved. On right plane scanty remains of a volute (?), on left plane very scanty remains of acanthus decoration.
25. (**Plate 46.**) From *gomile.* Grayish-white marble. Max. L. 18 cm; H. 15 cm; max. D. 11 cm. Fragment partly covered with mortar attesting secondary use. Broken on all sides. Relief (shell motif ?) decorates vertical surface above concave-convex moulding; to the right of shell a raised edge, part of some additional decoration.
26. (**Plate 43.**) From *gomile,* E2E/F. Grayish-white marble. H. 23 cm; L. 23 cm; Th. 12 cm. Surface much weathered. Remnants of three rows of oval-shaped leaves, probably forming a wreath.

III. MISCELLANEOUS STONE OBJECTS

27. (**Plate 47.**) From B5. Gray granite. H. 17 cm; Th. 3.5 cm. No weathering. The fragment belongs to a large open and deep basin whose diameter exceeds 25 cm. There is relief decoration on the outside: two ears and a tiny bit of the neck above the upper ear. The left ear is seen frontally, the right (upper) ear more in profile. The position of the ears would suggest that the animal walked to the right, with head bent and turned into frontal view. The heart-shaped form of the frontally represented ear points to a feline creature. The relief decoration is from near the upper edge of the sidewall of the basin. The mouth of the vessel has a raised edge, no doubt for the fitting of a lid. The inside of the vessel is smoothed but not as much as the relief decorated side.
28. (**Plate 44.**) From C6-7. White marble. Streaks of brownish weathering. L. at rim 13.9 cm; H. 6.3 cm; D. ca. 34 cm. Fragment of shallow marble basin (*labrum*). Horizontal rim set off from sidewall by very shallow groove. Outer edge of rim slightly raised.
29. (**Plate 44.**) From C6-7. Gray marble with white veins. L. 8 cm; W. 5.7 cm; Th. 4 cm. Heart-shaped flat handle broken off rim of vessel.

30. **(Plate 46.)** From C6-7. White marble. H. 12 cm; W. 5.5 cm; D. 9 cm. Akroterion-like projection with palmette design. Below, a rectangle framed by mouldings; further down a vertical surface with raised frame moulding. The palmette akroterion suggests that this fragment belonged to a small altar (Tomb altar).
31. **(Plate 44.)** From A1. White limestone. L. 5.3 cm; H. 4 cm. Broken on all sides. Lower end of triglyphs, horizontal moulding, and guttae. Vertical surface of metope panel to the right. Fragment belongs to metope-triglyph frieze of small altar or related object.
32. **(Plate 44.)** From *gomile,* E2E/F. Grayish-white marble. L. 11 cm; Th. 7.5 cm. Broken at upper and lower edge, diagonal break at back. Surface weathered. Torus-shaped moulding with diagonal grooves. Narrow, oblong pointed leaves forming a calyx are topped by volute. Fragment represents less than half of symmetrical design often encountered as crowning element on top of altars; instead of the volute there is usually a rosette.
33. **(Plate 44.)** From *gomile,* E2E/F. White marble. H. 30 cm; D. at top 14 cm, at bottom 20 cm. Cone-shaped object; towards bottom an irregularly wide raised moulding, much damaged. Below, rounded surface, some chips.
34. **(Plate 44.)** From *gomile,* E2E/F. Grayish-white marble. H. 13 cm, D. 7 cm at top and 9 cm at bottom. Broken on top, lower end almost flat. Surface smooth except for some weathering. Object is cone-shaped and may have served as pestle (?).
35. **(Plate 44.)** From *gomile,* E2E/F. Limestone with traces of red paint. H. 14.7 cm, W. 14 cm; Th. 4.5 cm. Surface fairly well smoothed; chipped (just below center of cross). Center of cross with two of its arms very scantily preserved. Grooves on surface of cross; in vertical upper arm grooves separates into two forming Y-shaped letter. Later than A.D. 300.
36. **(Plate 44.)** From A6. White marble. D. 7.2 cm; H. 3.5 cm; D. of hole 1.4 cm, depth of hole 2.6 cm. Some chips off the edge. Disk with hole bored in center, not going through the entire thickness.
37. **(Plate 44.)** From C1. Grayish stone. L. 4.8 cm; W. 3.8 cm; Th. 7 mm. Axe head with cutting edge preserved and finely polished. Slightly chipped along cutting edge.
38. **(Plate 47.)** From E2F. Light brown with gray speckles. L. 2.5 cm, average H. 1.3 cm. Flint stone, many edged, some of the edges sharp, others more blunt.

IV. REVETMENT PLAQUES

Revetment plaques come from many locations in the curia and the Forum north sites. Individual pieces are quite small, measuring at most 15 cm by 10 cm although the majority are smaller. A clear indication of the use of the plaques is the mortar which adheres to the backside of many fragments. A short portion of wall with plaques still in situ was also found. There is a wide range of colors in the marbles of the plaques: gray-blue, gray-green, pink, pale green, and slate gray are among the favorite colors. White marble is fairly rare. Some of the marbles are veined, white with salmon, white with green, white with purple, green with dark green, and white with gray-blue. Some marbles are speckled, bright or light green in dark green or pink in purple. In one heavily weathered fragment there are traces of red paint in grooves, some of which are very narrow, others more wide and deep. The former are very scanty; perhaps they are the remains of a letter T (?). The use of painting to enhance letters is very common. The thickness of this exceptional fragment also suggests that it may have formed part of a small tombstone (tomb plaque ?) rather than being a revetment plaque.

XII

Lamps

As is to be expected, the lamps found at Salona do not substantially add to what is already known about the typology and chronology of this group of artifacts. As all periods in the history of the settlement are well represented by these finds, the group in its entirety is a welcome addition because of its provenience from a region on the eastern Adriatic coast, an area where few lamps from supervised excavations have so far been published.

For reasons already discussed, only one lot of lamps can be securely dated (*terminus ad quem*) on the basis of stratification. This is the small but significant group of late Hellenistic to Augustan specimens from east of the curia (period I).

Lamps of the Roman Imperial period from Salona reflect the situation stated more emphatically by the pottery from the first to the sixth century A.D., namely that the predominant trade orientation of Salona after the Hellenistic period is towards Italy. This gives way to a wider geographic spectrum in the second century A.D., even more so in late Roman times when imports come from the eastern and western Mediterranean and the North African coast.

The few complete or better preserved lamps come from areas which have also yielded the less fragmentary specimens of pottery. These are: (1) the area inside and to the east of the curia (period I); (2) Trench 5 in the Forum central site—here was found the great majority of the earliest, Hellenistic to late Republican, lamps; and (3) squares W6-7B in which lamps were found among the second and third century A.D. debris which was dumped here (see chart 7).

Of the lamps found, the sturdier Firma and African lamps fared better in the long process of destruction, levelling, rebuilding, dumping, and looting than the extremely brittle and delicate picture lamps which, however, accounted for the majority of fragments found. Due to the consistently fragmentary state of the material it is very difficult to assess correctly the number of post-Hellenistic lamps found. Judging from the evidence of the fill of period I-II north of the main east-west wall in the Forum north site where the greatest number of fragments were found, it is perhaps safe to assume that three or more fragments stand for one lamp only. The finds from other areas, always extremely fragmented, would then have to be interpreted in the same way in terms of "quantity-analysis."

It seems therefore perhaps more realistic to reduce the number of 170 to 180 picture- and Firma lamp fragments which represent, of course, the entire lamp material of the early and middle Imperial period found, to about 60 to 70 lamps. More meaningful than this necessarily rather vague figure is the numeric proportion between picture- and Firma lamps in any limited complex of finds, as for instance in fill of period I-II.

In the latter, the proportion between picture- and Firma lamps is about 3:1. Since finds of period II included in that fill cover the time span from about A.D. 10 to A.D. 110/20 (see chart 6), this proportion seems adequate, because Firma lamps are unlikely to have made their appearance before the last third of the first century A.D.

The catalogue will present the lamps in the order listed below. Each group will be preceded, where necessary, by a brief discussion of its typological and chronological implications.

I. Hellenistic to late Republican.
   Campana lamps
   "Warzen" lamps
   "Vogelkopf" lamps
II. Picture lamps, first to third century A.D. (Loeschcke types I-VIII).
III. Firma lamps, first to third century A.D. (Loeschcke types IX-X).
IV. African lamps, fourth century A.D. and later.
V. E. Asia Minor lamps, sixth century.

The following abbreviations are used in the catalogue:

Broneer	O. Broneer, *Terracotta Lamps.* Corinth vol. IV. ii (1934).
C. Curzio, Akrai	G. Curzio, "Akrai (Siracusa), Richerche nel territorio." *NSc* 24 (1970), 438 ff.
Deneauve	J. Deneauve, *Lampes de Carthage* (1969).
R. Hanoune, Graviscae	R. Hanoune, "Lampes de Graviescae," *MélEcFr Rome* 82 (1970) 237-262.
Hayes	J.W. Hayes, *Late Roman Pottery* (1972).
Lamboglia	N. Lamboglia, *Gli scavi di Albintimilium e la cronologia della ceramica romana. I. Campagne di scavi 1938-1940* (1950).
Loeschcke, *Vindonissa*	S. Loeschcke, *Lampen aus Vindonissa* (1919).
Menzel	H. Menzel, *Antike Lampen im römisch-germanischen Zentralmuseum zu Mainz* (1954).
Perlzweig	J. Perlzweig, *The Athenian Agora.* vol. VII. *Lamps of the Roman period* (1961).
Pohl	G. Pohl, "Die frühchristliche Lampe vom Lorenzberg bei Epfach, Landkreis Schongau," *Aus Bayerns Frühzeit.* Friedrich Wagner zum 75. Geburtstag (1962), pp. 219-228.
Salomonson	J.W. Salomonson, *Spätrömische rote Tonware mit Reliefverzierungen aus nordafrikanischen Werkstätten. Scripta Minora. BABesch.* 44, 1969.
M. Vegas, *Gabii*	M. Vegas, "Römische Keramik von Gabii," *BJb* 168 (1968), 13 ff.
M. Vegas, *Novassium*	M. Vegas, *Die römischen Lampen von Neuss* (1966).
Walters	H.B. Walters, *Catalogue of the Greek and Roman Lamps in the British Museum* (1914).

I. HELLENISTIC TO LATE REPUBLICAN LAMPS

All of the types represented in Salona have in common a biconical body. The nozzle is elongated, widening towards the end, which has a straight termination. Hence, the differing general terminology: "à bec d'enclume," or, "a testa d'incudine." There may or may not be a handle. The filling hole is placed in the center of the usually slightly convex disc.

A. Campana Lamps (Menzel 22f.).

The Hellenistic tradition of these lamps is evident in their brownish to black slip, typical also for Campana ware. They show no relief decoration. Such lamps are well attested in dated contexts all over Italy from the Narbonnensis to Sicily in the second and first centuries B.C.

From dated contexts: *Grand Conglué*: F. Benoît, *L'épave du grand conglué à Marseille. XIVe supplément à Gallia* 14 (1961), 108, pl. 16, 4-5. *Gabii:* M. Vegas, *Gabii* 48 f., nos. 195 ff., figs. 86a-b.

1. **(Plate 48.)** From curia, B3-4, destruction level of period I. L. 7.7 cm; 2. 5.6 cm. Buff clay; black glaze partly worn. Filling hole (d. 2 cm) with horizontal edge followed by raised ring. About one third of nozzle missing; tip of (ring?) handle preserved.

B. "Warzen" Lamps (Dressel-Lamboglia 2; Menzel 23 f., nos. 70-71).

The form of this group, thought to be derived from Dressel type 3, is characterized by a stand-ring, a handle composed of several contiguous bands or ribs, and the presence of one or two symmetrically arranged protrusions at the side. The upper part of the body is usually decorated with wart-like globules in a variety of arrangements, hence the name "Warzen" lamps. The typology and chronology of this type has recently been thoroughly discussed by M. Vegas in her publication of the lamps of Novaesium (Neuss) together with an up-to-date list of parallels. Thus it will be sufficient to refer here to these parallels with an (*) and to add a few other references. The type appears in about 50 B.C. and dies out around the turn of the millenium. According to its distribution it is typical for the western part of the Mediterranean and Italy.

Dated parallels: France: Mt. Beauvray,* Provence. *Noricum:* Magdalensberg.* *Africa:* Bulla Regia,* Tipasa.* *Italy:* Albintimilium,* Rome, House of Livia,* Alba Fucens.*

Undated parallels: Graviscae, R. Hanoune, Graviscae 240, nos. 406, pl. 3. *Akrai,* G. Curzio, Akrai 495 f., figs. 86c-d.

2. **(Plate 48.)** From trench 5. L. 9.5 cm; W. 7.1 cm. Handle and point of fin-like projection broken off. Light yellow-brown clay; scanty remains of black wash inside and out. Heavily incrusted.

   Concave central disc with small filling hole. Two rings, the outer much broader than the inner. Rows of "warts" on the rounded shoulder. Fin-like projection. Broad, slightly convex-ended nozzle with large opening. Between disc and nozzle a raised surface the outlines of which are worn off, but it is not unlikely that a frog is depicted with his head facing the nozzle. Disc-shaped foot. In the concave center two raised letters: RO. Cf. Deneauve, type I, p. 103, no. 265, pl. 34 and type IVF, pp. 122 ff., nos. 374-402, pls. 43-44. For the shape see Walters, nos. 50-51, pl. 40; and for the "warts" no. 320, pl. 45, fig. 46. Deneauve no. 265 is important because of the letter R at the underside of the lamp; see his pl. 15, p. 238.
3. **(Plate 48.)** From curia A'7, under pavement. Max. Dim. 6 cm. Grey clay, black glaze worn off. Rim and some of disc of lamp; curvature towards nozzle. Three rows of "warts" around rim.

C. "Vogelkopf" Lamps (Dressel-Lamboglia 4; Menzel 24 f., nos. 22 ff.)

This type, similar in general to the preceding, is also derived from Dressel type 3. It is characterized by the following decoration and pecularities: The bottom may be flat or have a raised ring foot; side projections are usually lacking; the band handle is furrowed. The upper part of the rather steep body is usually ribbed; the nozzle is often decorated with two symmetrically arranged bird-heads, hence the term "Vogelkopf." These heads can take a variety of shapes and sometimes degenerate into unrecognizable patterns.

This type of lamp seems to have been in use from about 5 B.C. to about A.D. 10. According to its distribution pattern the type is characteristic for the western part of the Mediterranean and for Italy. Some examples are attested for Delos.

The "Vogelkopf" lamps have been discussed by M. Vegas in the publication already mentioned with a list of dated parallels. To these we will refer again with an asterisk, adding a few other examples.

Dated parallels: France: Fréjus.* *Germany:* Veters,* Haltern.* *Africa:* Carthage.* *Italy:* Albintimilium,* Alba Fucens,* Gabii (M. Vegas, Gabii 50, no. 200, fig. 20. Akrai (from context dated 250-50 B.C., see G. Curzio, Akrai 496, figs. 85c-d), Graviscae, undated, R. Hanoune, Graviscae 240 f., nos. 9-11, pl. 3.

4. **(Plate 48.)** From east of the curia, sealed level of period I. Max. Dim. 9.6 cm; D. of

lamp 6 cm. Part of nozzle broken, one side of body broken off. Flat bottom. Handle in two parts of eight-shaped section. Ring around central concave disc; a section of a ring divides nozzle from center of lamp. Tongues decorate shoulder.

5. (**Plate 48.**) From fill of period II to the north of main east-west wall, E5A. Fragment of nozzle with scant remains of "Vogelkopf" decoration.

The following fragments may belong to either group II or III.

6. From sealed level of period I to the east of the curia, square B7. Buff-ivory colored clay; thin brownish, matte slip. Fragment of nozzle.
7. Same provenience as no. 6. Gray clay; remains of black slip. Fragment of nozzle.
8. From fill of period I/II to the north of the main east-west wall of period II, W2A.
   We include this disc fragment tentatively in this group. If the interpretation is correct, the fragment might be part of a lamp of Dressel type 3, from the latter part of the first century B.C. For a dated parallel see shipwreck "Titan," about 50 B.C., F. Benoît, *Gallia* 16 (1958), 5 ff., fig. 4.

II. PICTURE LAMPS FROM THE FIRST TO THE THIRD CENTURY A.D.
(Loeschcke types I-VIII)

The bulk of the material in this group consists of tiny fragments from the fill of period I/II to the north of the main east-west wall of period II. This fill has been dated securely to the first century A.D. overlapping into the first quarter of the second century. For obvious reasons, mentioned already in the introduction above, it is almost impossible to distinguish with any degree of accuracy the different types of Loeschcke I-VIII because the foremost criterion for such a differentiation is the type of nozzle and/or its connection with the disc.

This is especially true for the distinction of the different variants of type I. The only attempt at some possible differentiation would be the one between the lamps with angular nozzle (I-III) and those with rounded nozzle (IV, V, VIII). This is meaningful to the extent that the latter types do not come into existence before the middle of the first century A.D., while the former appear from Augustan times onwards. Nevertheless, the numeric proportion of angular and round nozzles from the fill turned out to be so utterly unconvincing so as to prove only the impossibility of using the nozzles for statistical purposes. There are, of course, some other means to identify the different types, characteristics such as shoulder form and disc decoration. But here, too, the poor state of preservation defeated attempts at identification. Thus, the catalogue gives a selection of the material, namely those fragments in which some part of the disc decoration is preserved.

Mercury

9. (**Plate 49.**) From W5A. Max. Dim. 5.1 cm. About a third of the disc is preserved. Yellow clay; red-brown glaze.
   Mercury moving to left, probably as on a lamp from Novaesium, M. Vegas, *Novaesium* no. 217, pl. 6. Cf. also no. 218.

Human Figures

10. (**Plate 49.**) From curia. Max. Dim. 7.4 cm. Little more than top half of lamps is preserved. Pink clay, red-brown glaze.
    Rider with floating hair mounted on horseback to left, looking back. Around the waist there are traces of a garment. His right hand brandishes a sword, in his left hand he holds an oblong, rectangular Gaulish shield. Harnessing and saddle cloth are shown.
    Three rings.
    Identical lamps come from Scardona, *WMBH* 7, 1900, p. 108, fig. 89; Loeschcke, *Vindonissa* nos. 96-98, pl. IX, with reference on p. 368 to Italy and Yugoslavia; Deneauve, no. 326,

pl. 38 and, a less good example, no. 327, pl. 38.

11. & 12. (**Plate 49.**) From E4A and W4B. Max. Dim. 6.3 cm and 7.2 cm. In (11), less than top half of lamp is preserved, in (12) close to top half of lamp. Gray-pink clay, red-brown glaze (11), yellow clay, brown glaze (12). Essentially the same representation of a seated gladiator with loin cloth around the waist, arm guard, short sword in right hand (11); in (12) the left foot and the shield in front can be seen. Three rings. In (11) one volute on shoulder preserved. For the subject matter cf. Deneauve, nos. 459-460, pl. 49; Loeschcke, *Vindonissa* nos. 444-447, pl. 10.

13. (**Plate 49.**) From W4B. Max. Dim. 7 cm. Close to half of top of lamp is preserved. Yellow clay, brown glaze.

Gladiator is seen with left leg to the right, his body probably in frontal view (see comparisons below); the left hand has a short sword and a shield is probably fastened to the arm; an arm-guard is also visible. Three rings.

Loeschcke, *Vindonissa* nos. 435-436, pl. 10; Deneauve nos. 317-320, pl. 38.

14. (**Plate 49.**) From W5A. Max. Dim. 4.2 cm. Small fragment of disc and attachment of nozzle. Yellow clay; red-brown glaze.

Left foot of male figure in running position to right. Three rings.

15. (**Plate 49.**) From E4A. Max. Dim. 4.3 cm. About a fifth of top half of lamp. Yellow clay; brown glaze.

Male figure with upper body (as far as preserved) in frontal view, the head turned slightly to the left. The left upper arm is lowered, but the lower arm is raised, judging from the hand, the fingers of which are barely indicated. Three rings. Erotic scene, Symplegma?

Horse

16. (**Plate 49.**) From E3A. Max. Dim. 3.7 cm. About a fourth of disc is preserved with the design intact. Grayish clay, brown glaze almost completely worn off. The lamp is a direct parallel to a lamp found in Corinth (Broneer, no. 428, fig. 100 on p. 173). The description of the Corinth lamp fits our's exactly (what is missing on our lamp is given in brackets): "Discus of a [large] lamp with the figure of Pegasus to right; on his breast is a small cross incised; in front is a tree growing out from a cantharus and above [one circular and one oblong shield]; behind Pegasus the feet of a small horse appear, but the rest of the figure is broken away."

Loeschcke, *Vindonissa* no. 199, pl. 16, Pegasus alone, also with a cross on his breast (the lamp is cited by Broneer).

Eagle

17. (**Plate 49.**) From E4A/B. Max. Dim. cm. Yellow clay; orange glaze.

Wing; probably of eagle with outspread wings. Cf. Loeschcke, *Vindonissa* nos. 280-281, pl. 14.

Vegetal Decoration

18. (**Plate 49.**) From E3A. Max. Dim. 3 cm. Fragment of disc. Yellow clay; brown glaze.

Left part of Kantharos with vine branch growing from it.

Loeschcke, *Vindonissa* nos. 463-465, pl. 11; Menzel no. 176, fig. 31 (with reference to other parallels); Deneauve, no. 736, pl. 70.

19. (**Plate 49.**) From E3B. Max. Dim. 3.6 cm. Tiny fragment of disc. Yellow clay; orange glaze.

Right-hand section of double cornucopia. This is the more stylized variant of this motive.

Loeschcke, *Vindonissa* no. 343, pl. 4; Deneauve no. 454, pl. 48.

Rosettes

20. (**Plate 49.**) From E1A. L. 6 cm. Yellowish clay; red-brown glaze. Fragment comprises some of rim with grooves and three petals of rosette. When intact there were probably ten petals.
21. (**Plate 49.**) From E1C/D. L. 4.5 cm. Yellowish clay; red-brown glaze. Fragment comprises the ends of two petals and shoulder with one groove. The fragment belongs to a rosette with eight petals. Between the petals a groove projecting for a short distance. The petals are in sharp relief from an excellent mould.

    Several other fragments identical to those described were found. Two fragments (both from E3A) with originally eight petals; four fragments with more than eight petals from E2F, E5A, W2C/D, and W5B/C.

Shells

22. (**Plate 50.**) From E4A. L. 6 cm. Less than half of lamp with tiny piece of nozzle. Yellowish clay; red glaze.

    Shell on opposite side of nozzle; near nozzle perhaps 5-7 petals rather than a second shell design (?). Two rings. Grooves leading to volute on rim of lamp but volute itself is apparently broken off.
23. (**Plate 50.**) From E5A. Max. Dim. 6.9 cm. Yellowish clay; red-brown glaze. Some of disc and shoulder with double groove preserved; groove indicating volute, and vertical tip of volute remain. Only two lowermost ends of a shell design survive.

    Cf. Loeschcke, *Vindonissa* nos. 559-567; Menzel no. 226, fig. 34, 10 (from Miletos). Numerous parallels come from Cyprus in the East to Pannonia and Germania.

Egg and Dart

24. (**Plate 50.**) From curia, square A4. Max. Dim. 5.7 cm. Gray-pink clay; brown glaze. One of four identical fragments (all from curia site). Horizontal rim is set off from disc by groove. Sharply moulded egg and dart pattern on rim. Two more grooves and perhaps a short raised line on disc.
25. (**Plate 50.**) From W2A. Max. Dim. 4.7 cm. Yellow clay; glaze worn. Small fragment of disc and shoulder.

    Concave disc. Two rings, second one much wider and forming transition to sloping shoulder. Egg and dart pattern is fairly well done but flurred as compared with no. 24. No. 25 is one of two identical fragments. Possibly a local (?) imitation of an imported prototype.

    For a parallel from Scardona see *WMBH* 7, 1900, p. 113, no. 44, fig. 104; Loeschcke, *Vindonissa* nos. 693-694; Menzel no. 250, fig. 33, 19. Cf. also Perlzweig nos. 133-134, pl. 5, late first-early second century A.D.

With Plain Disc

26. (**Plate 50.**) From W2A. Max. Dim. 4.5 cm. Beige clay; traces of red glaze; lamp is much weathered. About one-third of disc, grooves, and some of volute. Cf. Perlzweig nos. 80 ff., pl. 4, about A.D. 50-100.

The following three lamps were found together with the Firma lamp of type X (no. 39) from the debris dumped against the Forum enclosure west wall in W6-7B (nos. 27-28 from W6-7B, no. 29 from W7B); see chart 7.

27. (**Plate 50.**) From W6-7B. D. of disc 5.5 cm. Gray-pink clay. Disc is preserved, rim fragmentary. Venator staving off bear. The venator wears chlamys and holds a lance in both hands; he is turned in three-quarter view to the right, the bear in profile to the left. There are two concentric grooves around disc. Venator and bear stand on base indicated by two grooves. On rim, groups of three knobs regularly distanced.

For subject matter see Perlzweig no. 844, pl. 19, dating from A.D. 250-300; for decoration of rim see Perlzweig, no. 707, pl. 16, nos. 779 and 805, pl. 18, ranging from mid- to late third century.

28. (**Plate 50.**) From W6-7B. Max. Dim. 4 cm. Small fragment comprising some of disc and shoulder. Lamp was possibly of oval shape. Tendril and feather design. Late third to early fourth century A.D. (?).

29. From W7B. Max. Dim. 8.3 cm. Preserved almost half of rim and small portion of disc. Yellowish clay; brown glaze.

    Many petalled rosette with pairs of leaves and narrow interspaces.

    Three rings around disc. On the slightly convex shoulder a moulded pattern, consisting of small heart-shaped leaves. The rosette is probably like Loeschcke, *Vindonissa* no. 670, pl. 3. See also F. Miltner, *OeJh* 26 (1930), Bb. p. 84, no. 44, fig. 34.5, for a combination of rosette and ivy leaves on shoulder.

The following lamp is of second to third century A.D. date.

30. (**Plate 50.**) From E2W/X: trench 3, Forum central site. Max. Dim. 2.2 cm. Some of disc and broad rim is preserved. Light salmon-colored clay; glaze has peeled off.

    Disc has rays in sharp relief and is divided from rim by ring. Tendril and rosette design on the rim. For an exact parallel from Corinth see Broneer no. 566, pl. 11, type XVII, group 2; Perlzweig, no. 1581, pl. 29 (first half of third century A.D.).

III. FIRMA LAMPS, FIRST TO THIRD CENTURY A.D.
(Loeschcke types IX-X)

With the presence of a large group of Firma lamps it becomes clear again that this part of the Dalmatian coast is more associated with Italy and the northern provinces than with the southern Mediterranean in the early and middle Imperial period (see Menzel p. 61). As the distinction of the main types in this class of lamps rests on rather minute typological differences, the fragmentary state of preservation made it impossible, here too, to establish a valid numeric proportion between examples of the earlier type IX (Flavian to about A.D. 110) and those of the later type X, which make their appearance in about A.D. 100.

As is to be expected, both groups of lamps are well represented. The specimens of type IX show predominantly the well-known hard fired brownish to brick colored clay and usually have a fairly sharply articulated profile. These are in all probability imported from northern Italy. Among the group of type X, in which there is a greater variety in size (cf. nos. 38, 39 and 40-42) there may well be local products, too. In the latter the contours are generally softer.

In the fill of period I/II from to the north of the main east-west wall of period II about 15 Firma lamps were found. This fill was sealed off some time between A.D. 100-120 (see pp. 86 ff.). Type IX only is securely attested in this fill. The presence of two stamps of *Communis* who was active into the early years of the emperor Trajan (see Loeschcke, *Vindonissa* pp. 275 f., Menzel no. 360) generally associated with type IX support the *terminus ad quem* which was established for the fill.

The only other stamp usually associated with type IX is one of Modestus (no. 31): cf. Loeschcke, *Vindonissa* p. 256; Menzel p. 60). Among the signatures associated with type X, one example each of *Fortis* (no. 37), commonly thought to be the "inventor" of the type in about A.D. 100 (cf. Loeschcke, *Vindonissa* pp. 92 f.; Menzel p. 60) and of *Cresces* (no. 38), active from the time of Hadrian onwards (cf. Loeschcke, *Vindonissa* p. 108; Menzel no. 387), is attested. The presence of a lamp of *Cresces* wherever actually made, shows that Salona is within the sphere of Noricum and Pannonia rather than that of Germania and Gaul as far as the distribution of Firma lamps is concerned; this is really not surprising (cf. Schnurbein, *Regensburg, Bayerische Vorgeschichtsblätter* 36, 1971, pp. 285 ff., especially p. 261).

Loeschcke type IX

31. (**Plate 52.**) From W4B. L. 9.2 cm. Brick red clay; without handle. This is the best preserved Firma lamp. Two perforated lug handles. MODES(TI) framed by a narrow and a larger raised ring. Separating the base from the sidewall is a groove.
32. (**Plate 51.**) From E5A. Max. Dim. 5 cm. Lamp of COMMUNIS (with ligature in the M's).
33. (**Plate 51.**) From W4B. Max. Dim. 6.4 cm. Lamp of [COM]MUNIS.
34. (**Plate 51.**) From curia, square A4. Max. Dim. 8 cm. Pink clay; two-thirds of disc preserved. Comic mask in center of disc; filling hole is to the left. Cf. Loeschcke, *Vindonissa* no. 937.
35. (**Plate 51.**) From E5A. Max. Dim. 7.5 cm. Light gray clay; red-brown glaze. Disc is concave; lug handle is not perforated. The ring handle has three grooves.
36. (**Plate 51.**) From E5A. Max. Dim. 9.8 cm. About half of lamp preserved. Handle is plain.

Loeschcke type X

37. From curia, square B4. Small fragment comprising almost complete bottom: F]ORTIS. Fortis is commonly thought to be the "inventor" of type X.
38. (**Plate 51.**) From curia site, square A'7. Max. Dim. 6 cm. Body of lamp only partly preserved and small portion of bottom with the letters CR]ESCE[S, the final S most likely on the second line.

    For Cresces see Loeschcke, *Vindonissa* p. 296; Schnurbein, *Regensburg*, pp. 00).
39. (**Plate 51.**) From W6-7B. Max. Dim. 5.4 cm. Beige clay. Nozzle partly missing. Lamp is coarse, assymetrical; two concentric grooves on bottom.

    From second-third century A.D. dump in W6-7B; see chart 7.
40. (**Plate 52.**) From E2E. Max. Dim. 10.9 cm. Light red-brown clay. Complete except for section of upper side of nozzle. Heavy traces of burning around nozzle. Shoulder ring opens into broad canal and curves around nozzle. Three very low, knob-like handles with a very shallow groove in the middle seen especially in the handle opposite the nozzle. Two very faint rings on underside. The shape is heavy and plump.
41. (**Plate 51.**) From W4B. Max. Dim. 5.8 cm. Small fragment of shoulder. A cross is incised on the perforated lug handle.
42. (**Plate 51.**) From curia, square C6. Max. Dim. 9.2 cm. Portion of upper half of lamp with some of nozzle is preserved.
43. (**Plate 51.**) From curia, square A6. Max. Dim. 5.5 cm. Nozzle broken off; traces of burning. Pink clay.

    Shoulder ring is very irregularly moulded. Filling hole is slightly off center; lug handles are very roughly formed.

IV. AFRICAN LAMPS, FOURTH TO SIXTH CENTURY A.D.

The study of the African lamps of the fourth to the sixth century has been given a solid chronological and typological framework in recent years by the studies of Pohl and Salomonoson, the result of which is now incorporated in a brief section of J.W. Hayes' work on Late Roman pottery (see Bibliography).

The two main groups of these lamps are represented among the finds at Salona where they are certainly imports from centers of production thought to be in Tunisia. These lamps, especially type II, are intimately connected with sigillata chiara C and D, also products of Africa, and well attested in Salona from the third to the sixth century. The connection between pottery and lamps is not only visible in the basic identity of the quality of the clay, its firing, and slip, but especially for type II also in the decoration. As Salomonson has shown, the relief decoration of the lamps is taken mainly from the decoration repertory of the sigillata chiara C and D.

We adopt the more logical typology of Hayes which takes into account that type 2 of Pohl is somewhat earlier than type 1, as this author has realized. Hayes I (Pohl 2) belongs to the fourth century, while Hayes II (Pohl 1) is probably not fully developed before the end of the fourth or early fifth century A.D.

Type I is represented by only two specimens (nos. 44-45) which show all the characteristics observed by Pohl. They are of poorer workmanship, more plump and of slightly different material than specimens of type II. Type II, the "classical" type of African lamp, is represented by six examples (nos. 46-51), which include one almost complete lamp (no. 46). In the decoration of no. 46 and the fragmentary motive in no. 47, the relationship to the sigillata chiara is especially obvious (on this relationship see Salomonson pp. 80 ff.). That the small geometric and stylized vegetal motives of the shoulder zone of these lamps are patterns created for the sigillata chiara C and D is also evident. In the following catalogue only a few parallels are given for the shoulder zones of type II. There is now available for comparison in Hayes (pp. 211 ff., especially pp. 229 ff., including 336 items) the catalogue and repertory of stamps which occur on the sigillata chiara.

Hayes, type I

44. (**Plate 53.**) From W2-4C/D. Max. Dim. 6.9 cm. Orange clay; light brown glaze. Less than half of lamp is preserved. The general form is rhomboid. In center of disc the vertical bar and right-hand side of horizontal bar of a cross; relief design on the surface of the cross to suggest decoration with gems. On the shoulder a hanging palm-leaf. For the cross cf. Pohl 222, pl. 23.5; cf. also Broneer no. 1456, pl. 22.

45. (**Plate 53.**) From curia, A'7. Max. Dim. 8 cm. Brick-colored clay. Almost half of lamp (without bottom); handle intact.

    Relief decoration in the shoulder zone has almost completely faded. Only some geometric decoration can be recognized. From the same location comes a tiny fragment (Max. Dim. 2.6 cm) with triangles and circles on the rim.

Hayes, type II

46. (**Plate 54.**) From outside of curia, B6-7. Max. Dim. 12.5 cm. Brick red clay. Body of lamp is complete except for part of nozzle, some of handle and piece missing from disc. The decoration on the disc consists of a tree of life. On the shoulder a very stylized frieze of trefoils alternating with concentric circles.

    For the tree cf. Salomonson p. 80, fig. 104 (Carthage); Salomonson p. 82, fig. 112 (for the roundels). See also Pohl 222, pl. 23.6; R. Hanoune, Graviscae 249, no. 44, pl. 7; Miltner, *OeJh* 24, 1929, pp. 151 f., fig. 63, no. 13.

47. (**Plate 53.**) From curia. Max. Dim. 5.5 cm. Probably brick-colored clay, but fragment is gray-black from burning. Fragment comprising some of disc and shoulder. On the latter geese and palm trees seem to alternate. On the disc remains of the left arm of a figure holding a bow, perhaps one of the mythological figures which appear frequently on lamps of this type.

    For geese see Pohl 222, pl. 23,4 (Carthage).

48. (**Plate 53.**) From D7. Max. Dim. 6.3 cm. Red-brown clay. Heavy traces of burning. Less than half of lamp is preserved. A bird (peacock ?) stands on disc to the left, its feet not preserved although the body, head, and wings are rendered in detail. The disc is surrounded by a ring; concentric circles alternate with vine leaves on shoulder zone.

    For peacocks on these African lamps see Menzel no. 601, fig. 77.6; for the vine leaf Menzel no. 598, fig. 77, 3.

49. (**Plate 53.**) From W3-5C/D. Max. Dim. 6.6 cm. Brick-red clay. Half of shoulder zone

and some of nozzle. S-shaped and heart-shaped motifs filled with dots on shoulder zone. For the S-shaped motifs cf. Salomonson fig. 105 (Carthage).

50. **(Plate 53.)** From curia, square D7. Max. Dim. 5.8 cm. Brick-colored clay. Small section of shoulder zone and departure of nozzle.
Concentric circles and vine leaves in shoulder. Cf. no. 48.

51. **(Plate 53.)** From E2B/3C. Max. Dim. 4 cm. Brick-colored clay. Small fragment of shoulder zone decorated with antithetical triangles; some hatching in triangles.
Cf. Salomonson fig. 104 (Carthage); fig. 115 (Rome); Pohl, p. 222, pl. 23.3 (with monogram in center). Cf. also R. Hanoune, Graviscae, 249, no. 44, pl. 7 (with Constantinian monogram in center).

V. LAMP FROM ASIA MINOR

52. **(Plate 53.)** From E2D. Max. Dim. 3.8 cm. Orange clay; brownish glaze. Very small fragment of shoulder with some of handle. This lamp may come from Asia Minor (?); the date is probably the sixth century A.D. Cf. Perlzweig no. 2807, pls. 44, 50.

XIII
Metal Objects

Many of the bronze and iron objects have suffered badly from corrosion and are thus difficult to recognize and to interpret. All of the objects published here are small in themselves; some, however, formed part of larger objects (see military equipment) which have totally disappeared. It is not unlikely, therefore, that in the post-Roman period there was a systematic search for metal objects and that we are left with only a small fraction of the metal objects originally in use. Scraps of bronze, mostly from thin plaques, were plentifully found in all locations and in a more concentrated fashion in the West trenches of the Forum north site and to the east of the curia. Iron scrap was also found in many different locations. Most noteworthy are the bun-shaped pieces of iron slag which come almost exclusively from the workshop area to the north of the curia in C/D7. The relevance of the slag is discussed in connection with the workshop itself.

An attempt is made to classify the objects according to their use, but in some cases definition has proved to be difficult because of their poor state of preservation.

I. BRONZE OBJECTS

A. From Vessels

1. (**Plate 55.**) From A5-6. L. 10 cm; W. 4.5 cm. Handle. The wing-like projections were probably soldered to the rim of a shallow, pan-like vessel.
2. (**Plate 55.**) From A'7. L. 7 cm; W. 7 cm. Handle from jug(?)-shaped vessel. Fin-like projections may suggest that handle was made in stem shape with small leaves coming off it.
3. From E3B. L. 8 cm; W. 1.1 cm. Handle from jug, bent out of shape and heavily corroded. Central rib runs along handle.
4. (**Plate 58.**) From A4. H. 2.9 cm; D. 3 cm. Circular mouth of flask; thickened rim; below rim horizontal rib wound around mouth.
5. From C6. H. 2 cm; D. 4 cm. Circular mouth of flask (?) with rounded rim and inside a concave profile sloping towards narrow opening.
6. From C7. H. 1.5 cm; D. 3.2 cm. Circular mouth of vessel (flask ?); flat rim is thickened with horizontal fluting below.
7. (**Plate 58.**) From E5A. L. 7.5 cm; greatest W. 4.7 cm. Heart-shaped leaf terminating in short stem, the purpose of which must have been insertion into some other object, very likely a vessel so that the leaf would have served as handle.
8. From E4A. L. 20 cm. Loop-handle of a bucket(?)-shaped vessel. One end of handle missing, central portion considerably thickened.

B. Fibulae

9. (Plate 58.) From W5A. L. 5.5 cm. Aucissa-type fibula. Pin is missing.
10. (Plate 58.) From E3B/2C. L. 2 cm; H. 1.3 cm. Pin head of Aucissa-type fibula.
11. From E5A. L. 6.5 cm. Fragment belongs to the bow of an Aucissa-type fibula. Heavily corroded and bent out of shape with a deep crack near the pointed end.
12. From W5A. Fragment of fibula.
13. From E4A. L. 7 cm. Wire fibula (?); bent out of shape; disk-shaped pin head.

C. Jewelry

14. (Plate 58.) From W2C. L. 35 cm; W. 1.9 cm. Pendant somewhat corroded. Flat plaque-like member ending in ring which holds crescent-shaped pendant or possibly a pomegranate fruit with the characteristic calyx-shaped leaves.
15. (Plate 58.) From W2-4C/D. D. 1.8 cm. Earring (?). Pinched center may have held pendant or gem.

D. Military Equipment

16. (Plate 58.) From E2B. H. 5.5 cm. W. in center 2.8 cm. Hinge. Corroded. One of the two symmetrical parts slightly damaged. Surface is decorated with round knobs.
17. (Plate 58.) A4. L. 9 cm; H. 2.7 cm; Th. 5 mm. Slightly arched hinge plate, wider at one end, with another, now broken hinge attached by means of a nail. Somewhat corroded. Bronze is exceedingly thin.
18. (Plate 58.) From E3A. H. 2 cm. Core of knob, probably of iron, covered with bronze. Small hole on underside for fitting of rod or peg. Perhaps from a helmet, serving as crest-holder (?).

E. Utensils, Tools

19. (Plate 55.) From A'7. L. 6.2 cm; H. 3 cm. Sickle. Heavily corroded. Curving blade with a faint groove parallel to the cutting edge. Triangular tang with semicircular indentation is for attaching the handle.
20. (Plate 55.) From W5B. L. 8.5 cm; W. 3.5 cm. Flat, fairly thin blade with slightly dove-tailed ends. Heavily corroded. The left-hand end broken off.
21. (Plate 58.) From W4B. L. 7.8 cm. Edge of circular spoon slightly damaged, end of handle broken off. D. of spoon 2.6 cm.
22. (Plate 58.) From C7. L. 7 cm; W. 2.2 cm. Chisel. Edge slightly damaged, end of handle probably missing.
23. (Plate 55.) From A7. L. 4.3 cm. Needle with fairly large eyelet, now bent out of shape.
24. (Plate 55.) From E4A. L. 4 cm. Small key. Corroded.

F. Miscellaneous

25. (Plate 58.) From E5A and E3JK. D. 2.7 and 3 cm. Two identical bronze disks (the smaller of the two is illustrated), the disk incomplete, in center of disk a vertically projecting rod.
26. From various locations. Parts of chain and buckles with chapes fastened to buckle rings. Fragments of small bronze rings, probably from chains rather than worn on fingers.
27. From various locations. Fragments of wires of various thickness. More scarce are fragments of tubes with very small opening.

II. IRON OBJECTS

A. From Vessels

28. (Plate 55.) From E3B. L. 5.3 cm. Loop-handle, one end of handle bent back to form suspension hole; vessel may have been bucket-shaped. Heavily corroded.

29. (**Plate 55.**) From A'7. H. 5.2 cm; W. 2.3 cm. The definition of this object as a handle attached vertically to the wall of the vessel is tentative. Some corrosion.

B. Military Equipment

30. (**Plate 58.**) From C7. L. 7.2 cm; W. 3.5 cm. Spearhead. Tube for setting in of wooden shaft only fragmentarily preserved. Some corrosion.
31. From A7. L. 9.5 cm. Blade of knife (?). One edge sharply curved, other edge was probably straight. Heavily corroded.
32. (**Plate 55.**) From W6B. L. 12 cm (unfolded). Hinge with folded-back plaque. Longer plaque of hinge has small raised square bolt (?) and small rectangular perforation. Square-shaped folded plaque has also a raised square knob opposite the one on the obverse.
33. (**Plate 55.**) From A'7. 4.9 by 3.9 cm. Buckle with rounded corners. Some corrosion.
34. (**Plate 55.**) From W5AA. 6 by 3.5 cm. Buckle with rounded corners; chape, 5 by 1 cm, attached to buckle. Some corrosion.
35. (**Plate 56.**) From B6-7. L. 11.8 cm. Part of harness, mouthpiece (?). Corroded.
36. (**Plate 56.**) From E3J/K. L. of central ring 4.5 cm. Ring with two smaller rings inserted through its opening. All three rings are oval in shape. Perhaps part of harness (?). Corroded.
37. From W2C. L. 9.5 cm. Point of lance or dagger. Heavily corroded.
38. From W2C. L. 6.1 cm. Point of dagger (?). Heavily corroded.

C. Utensils, Tools

39. Stray find. L. 12.9 cm. L. of top bar 12.2 cm; W. 2.6 cm. Small pickaxe (?). Heavily corroded. Handle part of object widens towards rounded end. Crossbar, symmetrically soldered on its handle, has rounded ends.
40. (**Plate 56.**) Stray find. L. 17.3 cm; W. 1.5 cm; Th. 9 mm. Part of lock (?). Slightly corroded. Crossbar with three holes, tapering outwards at one end, with the other end curved up and serving as joint.
41. (**Plate 56.**) From A7. L. 14.5 cm; W. 1.5 cm. Lock comprising bar with rounded ends fitted with holes. Through one hole is attached a hook. Heavily corroded.
42. (**Plate 56.**) From W5AA. L. 5.7 cm; W. 3 cm. Possibly this is part of a key. Corroded and fragmentary. Rounded end formed complete ring.
43. (**Plate 57.**) From inside glass tank in C7. L. 9.2 and 5 cm. Tubes, one of somewhat wider diameter than the other which has a thicker and more tapering part. Thinking in terms of the manufacture of glass, it is possible that we have here the remains of blowing pipes. Considerably corroded.
44. (**Plate 57.**) From C7. Various utensils and scrap found together in glass workshop. From l. to r.: 3 nails, candleholder, chisel (?), bar, and scrap (above nails).

D. Miscellaneous

45. (**Plate 57.**) Stray find. 6.5 by 6 cm; Th. 2 cm. Solidly cast, almost square, socket-like object with shallow circular depression in center. Heavily corroded.
46. Stray find. L. 14.5 cm. Dove-tailed clamp. Heavily corroded.
47. From A'7. L. 16.5 cm. Clamp, circular in section, with ends bent in same direction and tapering towards a point now broken. Heavily corroded.

E. Nails

Nails were found plentifully distributed in most locations on the curia and the Forum north site. Their use in timber construction is obvious, and if we are correct in believing that reed mats served as background for the mortar and stucco layers of walls painted with frescoes, quantities of nails would have been needed.

Many nails are fragmentarily preserved and most of them are corroded. Attempting a classification according to their length, the following results emerge.

	Approx. L.	D. of Head	Number Found
A:	15 cm	ca. 2 cm	5
B:	10 cm	ca. 2.5 cm	26
C:	6 cm	ca. 2.5 cm	48
D:	5 cm	ca. 1.5 cm	43
E:	3.5 cm	ca. 2.5 cm	15

B, C, and D seem to have been standard nails. Noteworthy in E is the large diameter of the head. These nails are very thick and must have had a very specific use. In a variant to E, represented by only a few nails, the head has a diameter of ca. 1 cm. Fragmentary nails which could not be assigned to any of the above groups number about three dozen.

III. LEAD (Plate 57.)

From C6, below the charcoal pit: (a) L. 35 cm + 33 cm, opening 7.5 by 3 cm; (b) L. 33 cm. Squeezed but in good state of preservation. (b) more fragmentarily preserved. Fragments of pipe; ridges on surface may indicate soldering of originally flat piece of lead.

The significance of the pipes underneath the charcoal pit is not quite clear but it is likely that the pieces had already been discarded. These were the only specimens of lead pipe found in the excavation, other similar pieces having probably been removed as valuable material already in antiquity or in later times. Lead scraps as single specimens with no recognizable shape come from trenches on the Forum north site (E1A, E3A, E4A, E3JK, W4B) and one scrap from A'7.

XIV

Bone and Ivory

Besides the individual objects published here, pieces of unworked ivory and bone were found in the excavations. From the glass workshop come three oblong fragments of ivory. The green coloring on their surface suggests oxidation from metal objects. Other ivory scraps come from A7 (small tubular pieces, plaques) and E3A (Fragment of a shaft).

Some bone fragments, and in particular one from E4A, show initial carving but were never finished. Other bone fragments come from A7.

I. PINS, NEEDLES, AND OTHER UTENSILS (Plate 59, Nos. 1-16)

1. From E5A. L. 8.8 cm; max. W. 7 mm. Bone. Spindle. Oblong head separated from shaft by two ring-shaped mouldings. Shaft thickens, then tapers toward blunt end.
2. From glass workshop. L. 8.1 cm. Bone. Hairpin (?). Small berry-shaped end with some decoration on top now broken off. Two ring-shaped mouldings below berry; shaft of pin tapering.
3. From A7. L. 6.5 cm. Ivory. Hairpin (?). Thickened oval-shaped upper end. Shaft thickening, then tapering. Lower end broken off.

4,5. From E2B/3C. L. 8.8 and 4 cm. Bone. Spoons (?). Scoop-shaped upper end. Shaft tapering. Both lower ends broken off.

6. From W2-4C/D. L. 11.7 cm. Bone. Shaft. One side rounded, other flat. Small end intact, break at other end.
7. From B6-7. L. 5.8 cm. Bone. Awl (?). Sharply pointed end. Shaft tapers and is broken.
8. From glass workshop. L. 6.6 cm. Bone. Shaft, tapering, both ends broken.
9. From E3D. L. 5.8 cm. Bone. Awl (?). Sharp triangular point at one end. A rectangular small slot 1.1 cm below point. Tapering shaft is broken.
10. From E4A. L. 3.5 cm. Bone. Hairpin (?). Upper end carved into a knob. Shaft thickening, then tapering. Lower end broken off.
11. From E3J/K. L. 9 cm. Bone. Needle. Tapering shaft. Wider end is pierced by hole, other end broken off.
12. From E4A. L. 8.5 cm. Ivory. Shaft has levelled off end and just below it a deep diagonal intentional cut with some incised parallel strokes. Not a hook, but possibly used by fishermen in repairing nets (?).
13. From A7. L. 7.5 cm. Ivory. Awl (?). Pointed end, tapering shaft is broken.
14. From E2D. L. 5 cm. Bone. Saw. Very fine shaft, slightly arched and toothed. Point preserved, broken at other end.
15. From A7. L. 9 cm. Ivory. Hairpin (?). Upper end of shaft rounded off; shaft tapering, lower end broken.

16. From A4. L. 13 cm. Ivory. Hairpin (?). Broken at both ends. Hollow, tapering shaft.
17. From E4A. L. 9.5 cm. Bone. Hairpin (?). It may have been colored red in antiquity, the color having faded to pink. Spiraling band of white running up the length of the pin, the upper end of which is scooped.
18. From E4A. L. 5.5 cm. Bone. Fragment of shaft.
19. From E4A. L. 4 cm. Bone. Awl (?). Identical to no. 7.

II. DISKS, BUTTONS, AND MISCELLANEOUS PIECES (Plate 60, Nos. 20-30)

20. From E1A. D. 4.4 cm. Bone. Disk. Tangential break. Surface decorated with concentric ridges; underside flat. Central hole 1.2 cm in D.
21. From B5. D. 3.9 cm. Ivory. Spindle-whorl (?). Surface has two concentric ridges. Central hole is 5 mm in D.
22. From B3-4. D. 3.5 cm; Th. 4.5 mm. Ivory. Spindle-whorl (?). Surface slightly convex with two concentric ridges. Central hole 8 mm in D. Underside flat with concentric ridges.
23. From E2B/3C. D. 2.3 cm. Bone. Button (?). Very shallow surface; in center ridge around centrally raised perforated knob. Reverse correspondingly convex with raised triangle design.
24. From *gomila.* D. 2.8 cm. Bone. Button (?). Edge thickened and rounded. Surface has shallow groove, slight bulge, and again a depressed central area with a hole. Reverse is flat with two concentric ridges.
25. From A'7. D. 2.8 cm. Bone. Disk. Shallow surface with central hole. Reverse correspondingly convex with two grooves.
26. From B5. D. 2.2 cm; Th. 4 mm. Ivory (?). Button. Very shallow with slightly raised, ridged center. Tiny rectangular projection on underside which shows minute tool marks, while the upper side is highly polished.
27. From W2-4C/D. L. 3.4 cm; H. 2.1 cm. Bone. Hinge. Decoration is incised and consists of concentric circles and three parallel grooves. Also preserved is the small joint with perforation.
28. From W5A. L. 2.2 cm; D. 7.5 mm. Bone. Bead. Cylindrical with three grooves at each end and twisted (diagonal) incision between.
29. From E3A. L. 3.5 cm; H. 2.3 cm; Th. 5 mm. Bone. Inlay (?). Convex-concave moulding with raised edges enclosing groove.
30. From W2-4C/D. D. 3.7 cm. Bone. Child's bracelet (?). Ring with flat edges. Thickness of ring is divided up by ridges into three sections.
31. From E3J/K. D. 2.7 cm; W. 1 cm. Bone. Pendant (?). About half of ring-shaped pendant with flat surface. At one end the ring is pierced with a small hole.

In addition to these objects, several gaming stones of bone were also found (beside others of glass, already mentioned). These usually have a slightly convex upper side and a flat bottom. Their diameters vary between 1 and 1.5 cm.

Numerous animal bones were recovered in all locations in the curia and Forum north sites.

XV
Clay Objects

Some of the architectural tiles published here are representative types, found in each case in few numbers. We distinguish between tiles made of yellow, and those made of red clay. The former are distinctly earlier than the latter; this is especially clear from the finds of yellow clay tiles in the soundings within and without the temple to the south of the central Forum drain.

Many small and crushed fragments of tiles indicate that they were plentifully used in buildings. The few more-or-less intact tiles actually discovered suggest that similarly well-preserved tiles were carried away by looters as valuable building material.

Among tiles other than architectual are hypocaust tiles and tiles probably used for the paving of floors. The other clay objects include a unique piece which served a very specific purpose and some miscellaneous small finds.

I. ARCHITECTURAL TILES

A. Yellow Tiles

1. From C7. L. 25 cm; W. 11 cm; Th. 6 cm. Broken at two sides. One edge of tile has convex profile, the other edge is vertical.

2. & 3. From W3B. Max. Dim. 10 by 5.5 cm; Th. 5 cm; 18 by 17.5 cm; Th. 7 cm. Tiles have one flat and one slightly convex side. The latter passes with concave profile into projecting moulding which has a narrow flat edge.

4. From W3B. 12.5 by 6 cm; Th. 5.5 cm. Yellow clay is covered with brown glaze. Moulding, if any, not preserved.

5. (**Plate 61.**) From B6-7. Max. Dim. 33.5 by 22 cm. Brownish weathering on surface. Tile has convex profile. The preserved length suggests that it may be almost complete.

B. Red Tiles

6. From within glass tank. Max. Dim. 28.8 by 16 cm; H. of moulding 3.5 cm. Heavily weathered. An oblique plane connects the flat part of the tile with the moulding.

7. (**Plates 61 and 63.**) From within glass tank. Max. Dim. 21.5 by 12 cm; H. of moulding 3.9 + 6.7 cm. Heavily weathered. Moulding is irregularly high and indented, reducing its width from a total of 6.6 cm to 2.65 cm. Several other fragments of this type of indented tile were found.

8. From A1. Max. Dim. 12.7 by 15 cm; Th. 3 cm. Dark red clay, with some brownish weathering. Clay has large and small bubbles. Moulding has convex-concave profile forming deep recess at juncture with horizontal part of tile.

9. (**Plate 62.**) From within glass tank. Max. Dim. 17.5 by 15.4 cm; Th. 2.1 cm; H. of moulding 3.1 cm. Light red clay, completely covered with gray-brown weathering.

Exceptional tile with regard to the pronounced concave profile and the deep recess where moulding meets the horizontal part of the tile. On the latter's surface two concentric circles are embedded in the clay.

10. & 11. **(Plates 61 and 63.)** From glass workshop. Av. Th. 1.8 and 1 cm. Some weathering. Two of the few curved tiles found in the excavation. One shows a steeper curvature than the other. Some traces of mortar adhering to tiles may suggest later use.

12. **(Plate 63.)** From B6. Max. Dim. 41.5 by 27 cm; Th. 5 cm. Light red clay. One corner missing, chips off edges, otherwise the only complete tile which lacks moulding.

II. OTHER TILES

13. to 15. Stray finds. Brick red color. Three small complete tiles served for floor pavement. Their dimensions are as follows: 11 by 7.2 by 2.8 cm; 12 by 7.5 by 2.2 cm; 9.6 by 6.5 by 2.2 cm.

16. **(Plate 63.)** From Forum central site. D. 17 cm; Th. 4.5 cm. Dark brick-red color. Circular hypocaust tile with worn surface and edges. This is one of several identical.

17. to 19. **(Plate 64.)** From B3-4. D. 5.3 cm; Th. 4.6 cm. Brick-red color. Hexagonal hypocaust (?) tile, possibly also used for paving. Two identical tiles with some traces of mortar still adhering come from E4A and W2B.

20. **(Plate 63.)** From *gomile*. Max. Dim. 14 by 13 cm; Th. 3 cm. Gray-pink clay. Broken on all sides. On one of the surfaces stamped decoration consisting of three vertical grooves with, above them, horizontal grooves curving into a pseudo-volute, suggesting an Ionic capital upside down.

III. OTHER CLAY OBJECTS

21. **(Plate 64.)** From within glass furnace. H. 6 cm; W. of rim 2 cm; Est. D. 20 cm. Light brick-red clay covered with brown weathering. Circular opening is rather irregular; about one-third of mouth is preserved. Immediately below the mouth an incomplete flat "shoulder" excludes the possibility that the fragment belongs to a vessel. Its function is rather that of the crowning member of a chimney and/or ventilation structure. The provenience of the fragment corroborates this function.

22. **(Plate 63.)** From A3. H. 12 cm; Ave. L. 6.5 cm; Th. 3.3 cm. Yellowish-gray clay. Loom weight. Large triangular portion at wider end missing. Two holes at narrower end do not meet in center.

23. **(Plate 63.)** From A'6. H. 10 cm; W. of base 4.5 cm. Light pink clay. Top of pyramidal object (loom weight ?) is missing. Suspension hole could have been in missing end.

24. **(Plate 63.)** From A5. H. 3 cm; D. of hole 8 mm. Light yellowish-brown clay. Spindle whorl, roughly spherical.

25. **(Plate 64.)** From A/B6. H. 3.2 cm; D. of hole 1.2 cm. Greenish-gray clay. Spindle whorl.

26. **(Plate 63.)** From C6. Max. L. 8.5 cm. Yellowish-brown clay. Head and neck of a very coarsely modelled horse. Eyes are bored, the right one being higher up. The ears are added with lumps of clay, partly broken off. Some incision, indentation, and clay particles on head which are hardly intentional. Neck is thick-set, heavy.

27. From B6-7. Max. L. 17.5 cm. Yellow clay. Clay pipe; several cracks in wall and some of the wall of the pipe broken out. Tapering towards one end (now missing), while the other complete end has a D. at the opening of 8.5 cm. The total L. of the pipe may have reached ca. 30 cm.

XVI

Miscellaneous Finds

In reporting on the excavations proper, we have already mentioned a number of miscellaneous finds such as charcoal, glass slag, iron slag, etc. which seem to point to very specific tasks that were accomplished mainly within the workshop area to the north of the curia.

Beside these finds, cobalt was plentifully found. The glass workshop and both the East and West trenches on the Forum north site are the principle sources of provenience. Usually the cobalt is preserved in ball shape, with a diameter of 1.5 to 2 cm; flecks of white, gray and charcoal often cover the surface of the balls. The use of cobalt as a coloring substance in the glass workshop is very appropriate; the same holds true for the use of blue color in fresco painting. Lastly, it could also have served for cosmetic purposes.

STONE MOSAIC TESSERAE

In addition to the very fragmentary mosaic found in C1, stone tesserae were found in great numbers dispersed over the entire site. Individually collected, they come mostly from the late building period; as disturbed as the levels generally are, this would nevertheless indicate that these stone tesserae come from mosaics which were laid sometime in the third century A.D., which is also the date of the mosaic in C1. It is very possible that these mosaics replaced earlier ones; however, judging by the almost total absence of mosaic tesserae underneath the pavement in A'7, A7, and B6-7, it is clear that mosaics date only from the Augustan period onward. Occasionally a few mosaic tesserae were found clustered together in their original mortar bedding. The predominant white color of the stones, with black and gray in minor quantities, is in keeping with the color scheme of the mosaic discovered in C1. We should therefore conclude that mosaic floors elsewhere in the curia and Forum north sites resembled the one in C1, with black patterns on a white background. The few mosaic stones in other colors (blue, yellow, red, and green) could belong to sparse subsidiary decoration. The sizes of the mosaic tesserae are very consistent, there being two sizes: 2.5 by 1 by 1 cm and 1.5 by 1 by 1 cm.

TABLE OF DISTRIBUTION

Provenience		White	Gray	Black	Other colors
Curia site:	A'7	61	33	5	10
	B6-7	59	23	6	4
	C6	2	1		
	D7	15	3	6	
Forum north site:	E trenches	225	65	32	65
	W trenches	176	63	34	30

CONCORDANCES

[Catalogue and Inventory Numbers]

Glass		Glass		Glass		Stone Monuments	
Cat. Nos.	Inv. Nos.	Cat. Nos.	Inv. Nos.	Cat. Nos.	Inv. Nos.	Cat. Nos.	Inv. Nos.
1	7.31	38	7.1	81	7.126	1	7A24
2	7.75	39	G 56	82	7.891	2	69S1
3	7.28	40	7.357	83	7.146	3	7A27
4	7.12	41	7.881	84	7.495	4	69A19
5	7.567	42	7.224	85	7.666	5	7A7
6	7.329	43	7.406	86	7.273	6	7A17
7	7.330	44	7.488	87	7.603	7	7A8
	7.14	45	7.207	88	7.901	8	7A80
	7.19	46	7.455	89	7.117	9	7A39
8	7.324	47	7.462	90	G 94	10	7A32
9	7.24	48	7.471	91	7.544	11	7A99
10	7.340	49	7.479	92	7.108	12	69A17
11	7.568	50	7.458	93	G 67	13	7A23
12	7.177	51	7.847	94	G 22	14	7A29
13	7.18	52	7.234	95	7.77	15	7A34
14	7.150	53	7.201	96	7.76		7A28
15	7.152	54	7.225	97	7.728		7A49
16	7.316	55	7.203	98	G 15	16	7A49 bis
17	7.4	56	7.192	99	7.303	17	7A64
	7.70	57	G 27	100	7.614	18	7A31
18	G 86	58	7.360	101	7.99	19	7A33
19	G 70	59	G 25	102	G 93	20	7A38
20	7.21	60	7.408	103	7.385	21	7A46
21	7.15	61	7.424	104	7.800	22	69A18
22	7.174	62	7.217	105	G 71	23	7A71
23	7.34	63	7.605	106	G 44	24	7A70
24	7.36	64	7.476	107	7.262	25	7A72
25	7.37	65	7.402	108	7.365	26	7A93
26	7.49	66	7.618	109	7.442	27	69S2
27	7.41	67	G 32	110	7.867	28	69M7
	7.61	68	7.461	111	7.191	29	69M17
	7.65	69	7.868	112	7.635	30	69M20
	7.66	70	7.513	113	7.727	31	69S1
28	7.351	71	7.887	114	7.665	32	7A18
29	7.357	72	7.600	115	G 47	33	7A94
30	7.557	73	7.550	116	7.35	34	7A56
31	7.358	74	7.525	117	7.331	35	7A57
32	7.342	75	G 49	118	G 33	36	69M21
33	7.22	76	7.301			37	7St1
34	7.809	77	7.882			38	7St3
35	7.11	78	7.546				
36	7.311	79	G 68				
37	7.310	80	Stray find				

Metal Objects

Cat. Nos.	Inv. Nos.
1	69B9
2	7B65
3	7B29
4	69B11
5	7B64
6	69B1
7	7B34
8	7B43
9	7B66
10	7B6
11	7B33
12	7B35
13	7B44
14	7B39
15	7B37
16	69B12
17	69B10
18	7B5
19	7B54
20	7B36
21	7B1
22	69B13
23	69B14
24	7B50
25	6B31
26	69B15
27	7B38
28	7Ir4
29	7Ir40
30	69Ir10
31	7Ir41
32	7Ir29
33	7Ir30
34	7Ir34
35	7Ir36
36	7Ir18
37	7Ir9
38	7Ir10
39	7Ir11
40	7Ir12
41	7Ir23
42	7Ir37
43	69Ir13
44	69Ir7-9
	69Ir1
	69Ir5
	69Ir14

Metal Objects

Cat. Nos.	Inv. Nos.
45	69Ir15
46	69Ir16
47	7Ir31

Bone–Ivory

Cat. Nos.	Inv. Nos.
1	7Bo5
2	69V12
3	7V8
4	7Bo8
5	7Bo9
6	7Bo11
7	7Bo27
8	69V16
9	7Bo7
10	7Bo21
11	7Bo20
12	7Iv2
13	7Iv4
14	7Bo6
15	7Iv6
16	69V13
17	7Bo16
18	7Bo17
19	7Bo18
20	7Bo3
21	69V11
22	69V14
23	7Bo1
24	7Bo2
25	7Bo28
26	69V7
27	7Bo14
28	7Bo10
29	7Bo4
30	7Bo13
31	7Bo15

Lamps

Cat. Nos.	Inv. Nos.
1	69P153
2	7L169
3	7L224
4	7L225
5	7L226
6	7L227
7	7L228

Lamps

Cat. Nos.	Inv. Nos.
8	7L229
9	7L74
10	69P107
11	7L172
12	7L16
13	7L12
14	7L88
15	7L153
16	7L158
17	7L231
18	7L148
19	7L167
20	7L139
21	7L138
22	7L174
23	7L191
24	69P142
25	7L55
26	7L58
27	7L232
28	7L233
29	7L234
30	7L146
31	7L27
32	7L192
33	69P90
34	69P126
35	7L213
36	7L186
37	69P51
38	7L218
39	7L237
40	7L144
41	7L11
42	69P145
43	69P33
44	7L65
45	7L238
46	69P52
47	69P50
48	7L239
49	7L235
50	7L222
51	7L141
52	7L143

Clay Objects

Cat. Nos.	Inv. Nos.
1	69T2
2	7T1
3	7T2
4	7T3
5	7T19
6	69T3c
7	69T3a
8	69A9
9	69T3d
10	69T10
11	69T11
12	69P72
13	7T8
14	7T9
15	7T10
16	69T9
17	69T8
18	7T16
19	7T12
20	7A55
21	69T4
22	69T1
23	69T7
24	69T5
25	69T6
26	7T17
27	7T18

Inscriptions

Cat. Nos.	Inv. Nos.
1	7A53
2	7A50
3	7A58
4	7A33
5	7A54
6	69T12
7	69P87
8	7T7
9	69P89

GENERAL INDEX

(All numbers refer to pages)

Aequum, 49
Ancona, 26, 32 f.
Anemo, 87
Antony, 6, 18, 36 f.
Aquileia, 3, 27, 146
Aquincum, 115
Appian, 4 ff., 18, 36
Aspalathos, 1, 19 f., 107
Asseria, 21, 32 f., 148

Bato, 7
bone, 59, 227 ff.
Brattia, 2
bronze, 59, 62, 223 ff.
  jewelry, 224
  military equipment, 224
  utensils, 224
  vessels, 224
Brundisium, 26, 191
Burnum, 32 f.
Byzantium, 27

Caesar, 3, 6, 12, 18 f., 36 f., 106
Carnuntum, 115
Celeia, 149
charcoal, 59
Clambetae, 114
Claudius, 15, 21
clay, 229 f.
Clodius, Titus, 131
Cnidos, 2
cobalt, 59, 231
coins, general, 54, 65, 83 ff., 92 ff., 133-44, and charts
colonization
  Greek, 1 ff.
  Sicilian, 1
colony, double, 7
Communis, 219 f.
Corcyra nigra, 3
Corinth, 27
Cosconius, C., 6, 18
Cresces, 219 f.

Dacian(s), 26 f.
Danube, 33
Dasi, 86
Decree of 56 B.C., 3, 6, 37
Delmatae, 2 ff., 20, 36 f.
Delminium, 4 f., 36, 49, 79, 114
Dio Cassius, 10 n. 32
Diocletian, 7, 107, 114, 147
Dionysios I, 2
Doclea, 49, 147
Domavia, 114, 125
double colony, 7
Dyrrhachium, 27

eagle, 217
Emona, 113, 125
Epetion, 1 ff., 19 f., 106
Epetium, see Epetion
Epidaurum, 1
Eutropius, 9 n. 28

Fannius, Gaius, 4
Fasti Ostienses, 26
fibula, 224
Figulus, M., 4
floral design, 115 ff., 210, 217
Fortis, 219 f.
fresco, 49, 54, 65, 67, 107, 109-124
fruit design, 125 ff.
furnace
  bowl type, 62
  shaft type, 62
  see also glass

Gabinius, 6
Gellius, 87
gladiator, 217
glass, general, 58, 65, 92 ff., 145-175
  analyses, 176-180
  batch, 59
  furnace, 58, 61 ff.
  slag, 58 ff.
  tank, 59, 146 f.

Hadrian, 112
Hilarus, 87
horrea, 12
horse, 217, 230
Hortus Metrodori, 20 ff.

Iadastini, 3
Iader, river (Zadar), 3 f., 39
  town, 21, 32 f., 107, 114, 146 ff.
Illyrians, 2, 6, 106
Ilidze, 114
inscriptions, painted, 115
  on stone, 131 f.
iron, general, 224 f.
  slag, 62, 223
Issa, 2 ff., 36 f., 106
Issaeans, 36
Istria, 1, 114
ivory, 59, 227 ff.

Jelsa, 21
Jupiter, 15
Justinian, 90

Kairos, 2
Klis, 3, 19, 38

lamps, general, 90, 92 ff., 213-222, and charts
  African, 213 f., 220 ff.
  Campana, 214
  E. Asia Minor, 214, 222
  Firma, 88, 213 f., 219 ff.
  Hellenistic-Republican, 214
  picture, 213 f., 216 ff.
  "Vogelkopf," 214 f.
  "Warzen," 214 ff.
Lasva, valley of, 115
lead, 59, 226
Lesina, 21
loom weight, 230
Lumbarda, decree of, 2 ff.
Lysippos (sculptor), 2

Magdalensberg, 115, 125
Majdan, 114
Melite, 2
Mercury, 216
metal smelting, 147
Metellus, C., 5 f.
Metrodorus, see Hortus M.
Modestus, 219 f.
mosaic tesserae, 49, 53, 65, 231
Mulsula, Attia, 131
municipia, 1
Murrius, C., 87

nails, 65, 225
Naissus (Niš), 27
Narona, 148
Nin (Aenona), 147
Noricum, 115, 146, 219

Octavian, 6
Orosius, 6, 9 n. 28
Ostia, 21, 112

Pannonia(ns), 7, 115, 125, 146, 219
Pansiana, 132
Pasiana, 132
Petronius, L., 132
Pharos, 1
pipe, 230
Piraeus, 27
Poetovio, 114, 149
Pola, 114, 148
Polybius, 4, 9 nn. 20-21
Pompey, 37
pottery, general, 54, 62, 83 f., 91 ff., 181-208, and charts
  Campana B, 185 f., 193
  Campana C, 186, 193
  coarse ware, 5, 59, 85 f., 189
  earliest, 86
  Eastern Sigillata, 88, 186, 188, 193
  Gnathia, 184
  Greek connections, 5
  Greco-Roman, 181, 191, 193
  handmade, 84
  Hellenistic black glaze, 84
  household, 84
  lids, 65, 85
  Megarian, 84, 185, 193
  Nigra ware, 85
  plain gray, 186
  Roman, later, 84
  Sigillata chiara, 88, 90
  Sigillata, Italian, 85 ff., 182, 187
  Sigillata stamps, 87, 95, 105, 187
  vitreous glazed, 187

Ravenna, 27
reed(s), 49, 109 f.
refuse pit, 59
revetment plaques, 53, 65, 125, 212
rosette, 218
rostra, 79

Salona
  amphitheater, 11, 17
  arcades, 11, 32, 39
  basilica, Christian, 38, 56
  basilica iuxta portum, 18
  building period I, 41 ff., 70, 83, 106, 181, 192
  building period II, 45 ff., 63, 70 ff., 86 ff., 106, 192
  building period III, 47 ff., 63, 74 ff., 88 ff., 106
  building period IV, 54 ff., 77 f., 90, 107
  Capitolium, 15, 17, 32 f., 38 f., 50, 63, 65, 85 f., 106, 181
  cemetery, pagan, 21
  Christian, 2, 20, 38, 107
  chronological evidence, 82 ff., 181 ff.
  closed (sealed) deposits, 83 ff., 87, 181
  Colonia Martia Iulia, 6
  complexes of finds, 101, chart 11
  conventus, 3, 6, 13, 36 f.
  curia, 33, 45 ff., 106
  deposits, see closed (sealed) deposits
  drains, 39, 41, 44 ff., 63, 67, 69 ff., 90, 106 f.
  earliest settlement, see Hellenistic settlement
  eminence, Caesar's *collis,* 13, 15, 19, 39, 45, 63, 69, 77, 83, 85, 181
  emporion, 2 ff., 38
  Forum, 13, 17, 19, 32, 54, 63 ff., 181
    enclosure, 39, 77 f., 86, 107
  gate, Greek, 19 f.
  gomila, gomile, 39 ff. passim
  harbour, 32
  Hellenistic settlement, 20, 38 f., 41, 78, 83, 181, 192
  looters, in, 40, 59, 83, 90, 229
  mole, 17, 21, 32
  native settlement, 4
  pavement, 47, 50 f., 83 ff., 90, 107, 181
  platform, 11, 17, 45, 106
  port (see also harbour, mole), 17
  Porta Caesarea, 18 f., 38, 69
  portico(es), 17, 32, 74 ff., 79, 86, 90, 106 f.

stratification, 40, 83
tetrastyle temple, 13, 15, 17, 31
theater, 13, 15, 17, 29, 32 f., 106 f.
Thermae, 17, 53, 63
torcularium, 17, 38 f., 53
urbs nova, 17, 19, 39
urbs occidentalis, 11 ff.
urbs orientalis, 11 ff., 39
urbs vetus, 11 ff.
via munita, 18, 20 f.
view of, 26
walls, 39
Greek, 19
Republican, 21
workshop, 56 ff., 107, 147
Salonae (plural form), 36
Sarajevo, 148
Scardona, 1, 32 f.
sculpture, 209-212
architectural, 79, 210 f.
imported, 209
sedra, 49
Sergia (voting tribe), 6, 19
Severa, 131
shell, 218
Sirmium, 33, 114
small finds, 39, 41, 59, 65 ff., 84
see also Table of Contents
spindle whorl, 230
Split, see Aspalathos
Stolac, 115, 148
stone, see sculpture
Strabo, 4 f., 18, 36
stucco(es), 49, 107, 109, 124-126
Syracuse, 2 f., 6

Tarsatica, 1
Tergeste, 27 f., 32
tiles, 86, 229
chimney, 62, 230
hypocaust, 65, 230
roof, 65
Tiberius, 7, 87, 106, 192
Timavo, 27
Tivoli, 112
trade, 84, 146 f., 191 ff., 217
Tragurion (Tragurium), 1 ff., 19, 36, 38, 106
Trajan, 7, 27
column of, 7, 26 ff.
Trogir, see Tragurion
Tromentina (voting tribe), 6, 19

Vandals, 38
Varvaria, 21
Vindobona, 115
Virunum, 115, 125
Vitruvius, 15, 125
voting tribes, 6, 19

walls, see Salona s.v.
wall, plastered, 70
workshop, see Salona s.v.

Zadar, see Iader, town

Texts of Ancient Authors Quoted
(For other references, see page xv)

Appian, *Illyrike* II. 11, 4 f.
Caesar, *B.C.* III. 9, 9 n. 31
B. Alex. 43, 9 n. 32
CIL III. 2072, 24 n. 42
III. 2207, 24 n. 42
CIL III. 8817, 50
Eutropius VI. 4, 9 n. 28
Orosius, *Hist.* V. 23. 23, 9 n. 28
Vitruvius, VII. 3. 11, 110

Plate 1

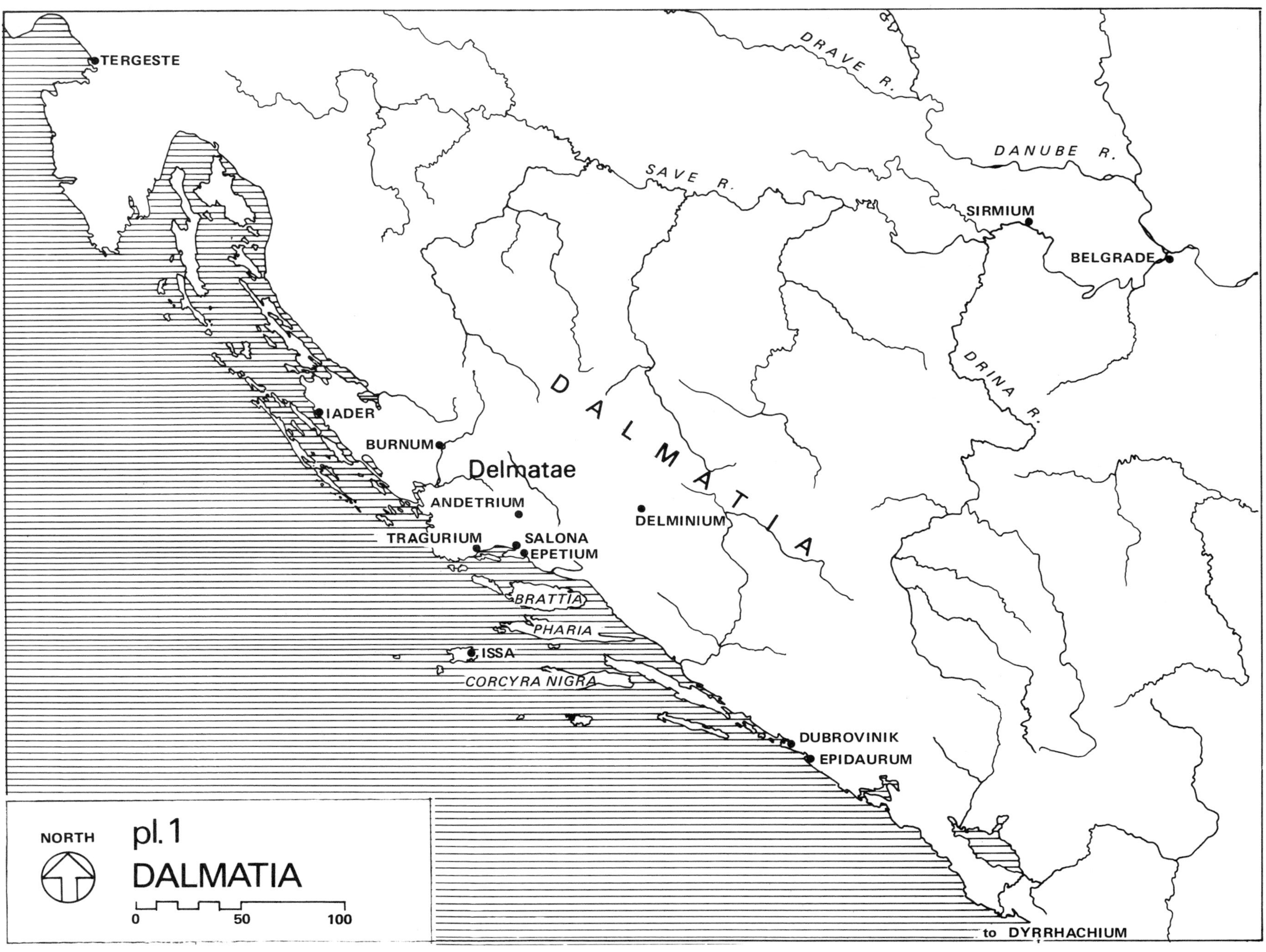

TERGESTE
DRAVE R.
DANUBE R.
SAVE R.
SIRMIUM
BELGRADE
DRINA R.
DALMATIA
IADER
BURNUM
Delmatae
ANDETRIUM
DELMINIUM
TRAGURIUM
SALONA
EPETIUM
BRATTIA
PHARIA
ISSA
CORCYRA NIGRA
DUBROVINIK
EPIDAURUM
to DYRRHACHIUM
NORTH
pl.1
DALMATIA
0
50
100

Plate 2

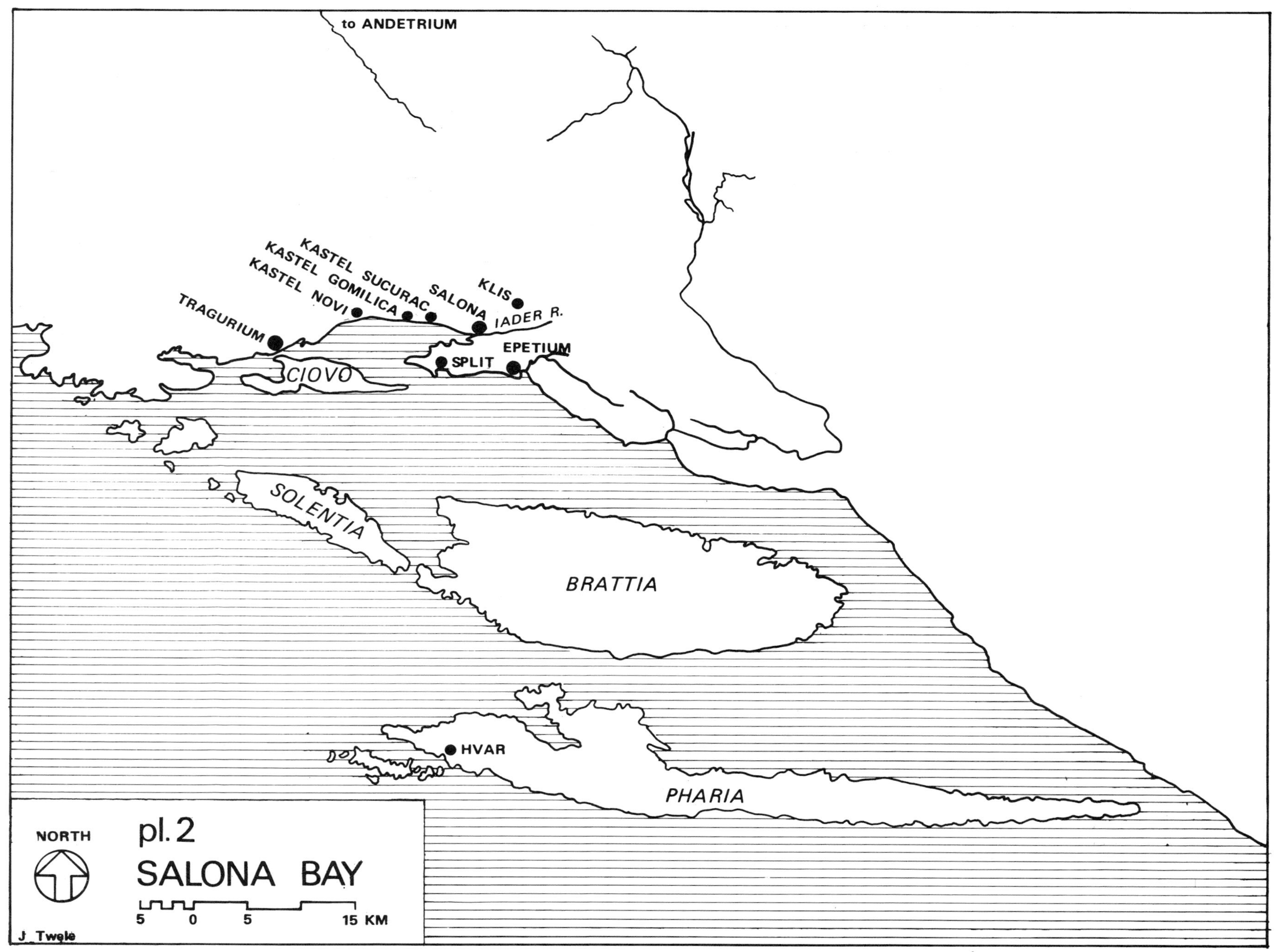

to ANDETRIUM
KASTEL SUCURAC
KASTEL GOMILICA
KASTEL NOVI
TRAGURIUM
SALONA
KLIS
IADER R.
EPETIUM
SPLIT
CIOVO
SOLENTIA
BRATTIA
HVAR
PHARIA
NORTH
pl. 2
SALONA BAY
5 0 5 15 KM
J. Twele

Plate 3

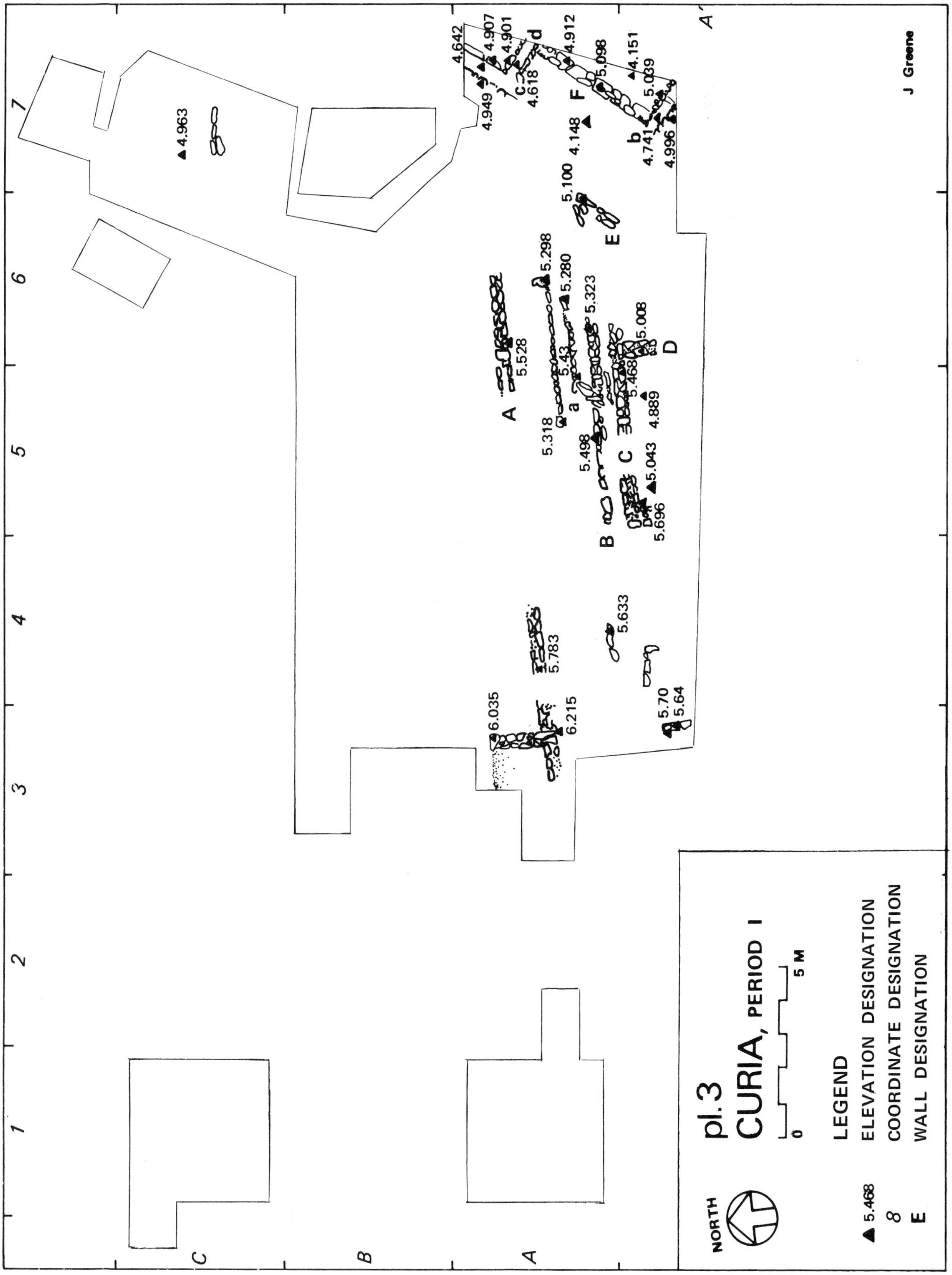

pl. 3

CURIA, PERIOD I

0 5 M

NORTH

LEGEND

▲ 5.468 ELEVATION DESIGNATION

8 COORDINATE DESIGNATION

E WALL DESIGNATION

J Greene

Plate 4

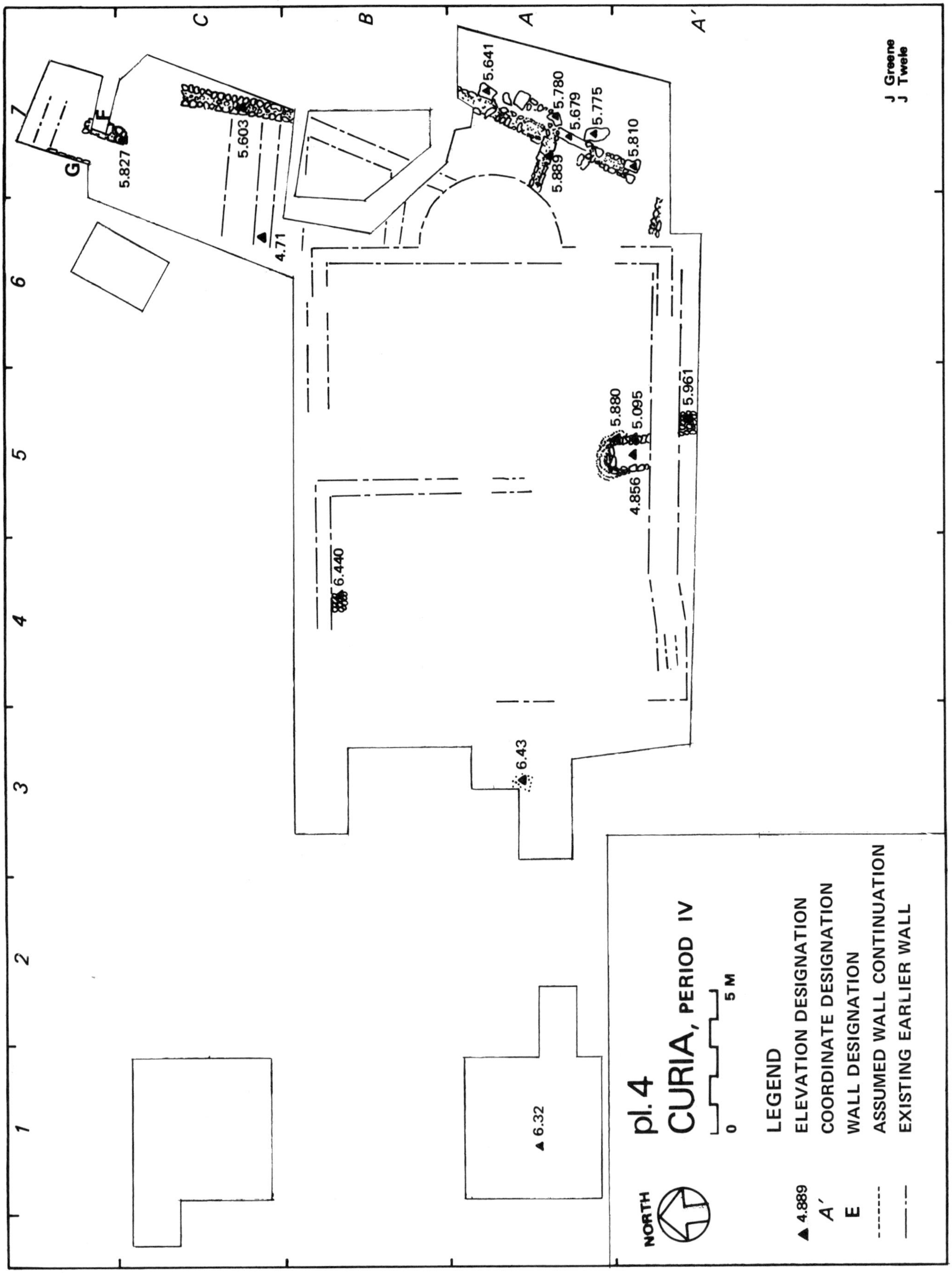

pl. 4

CURIA, PERIOD IV

0 — 5 M

NORTH

LEGEND

▲ 4.889	ELEVATION DESIGNATION
A′	COORDINATE DESIGNATION
E	WALL DESIGNATION
- - - - - -	ASSUMED WALL CONTINUATION
—·—	EXISTING EARLIER WALL

1 2 3 4 5 6 7

C B A A′

G F

5.827 5.603 4.71 6.440 6.43 6.32 5.641 5.780 5.679 5.775 5.810 5.889 5.880 5.095 4.856 5.961

J Greene
J Twele

Plate 5

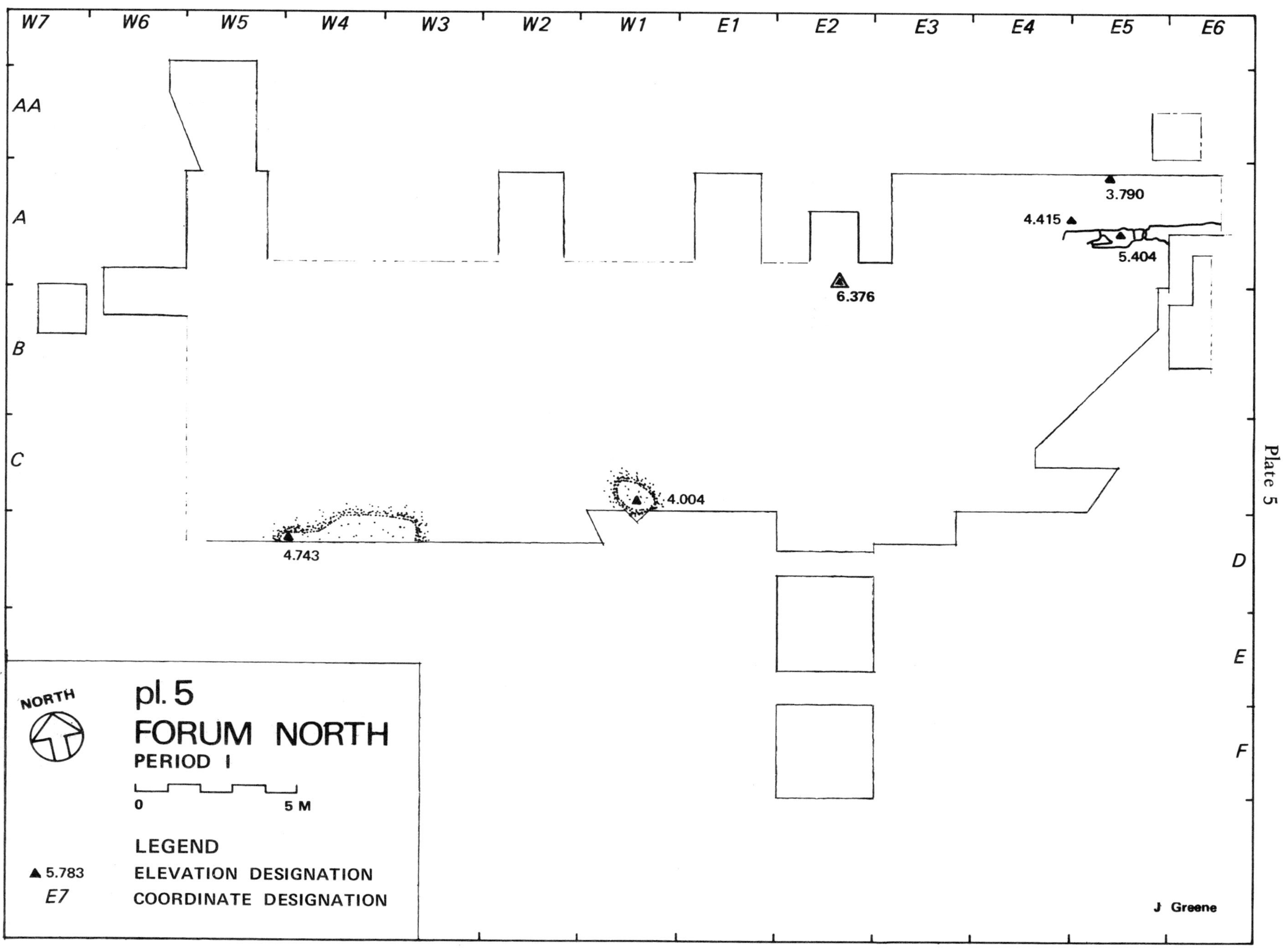

W7
W6
W5
W4
W3
W2
W1
E1
E2
E3
E4
E5
E6
AA
A
B
C
D
E
F
3.790
4.415
5.404
6.376
4.004
4.743
NORTH
pl. 5
FORUM NORTH
PERIOD I
0
5 M
LEGEND
▲ 5.783
ELEVATION DESIGNATION
E7
COORDINATE DESIGNATION
J Greene

Plate 6

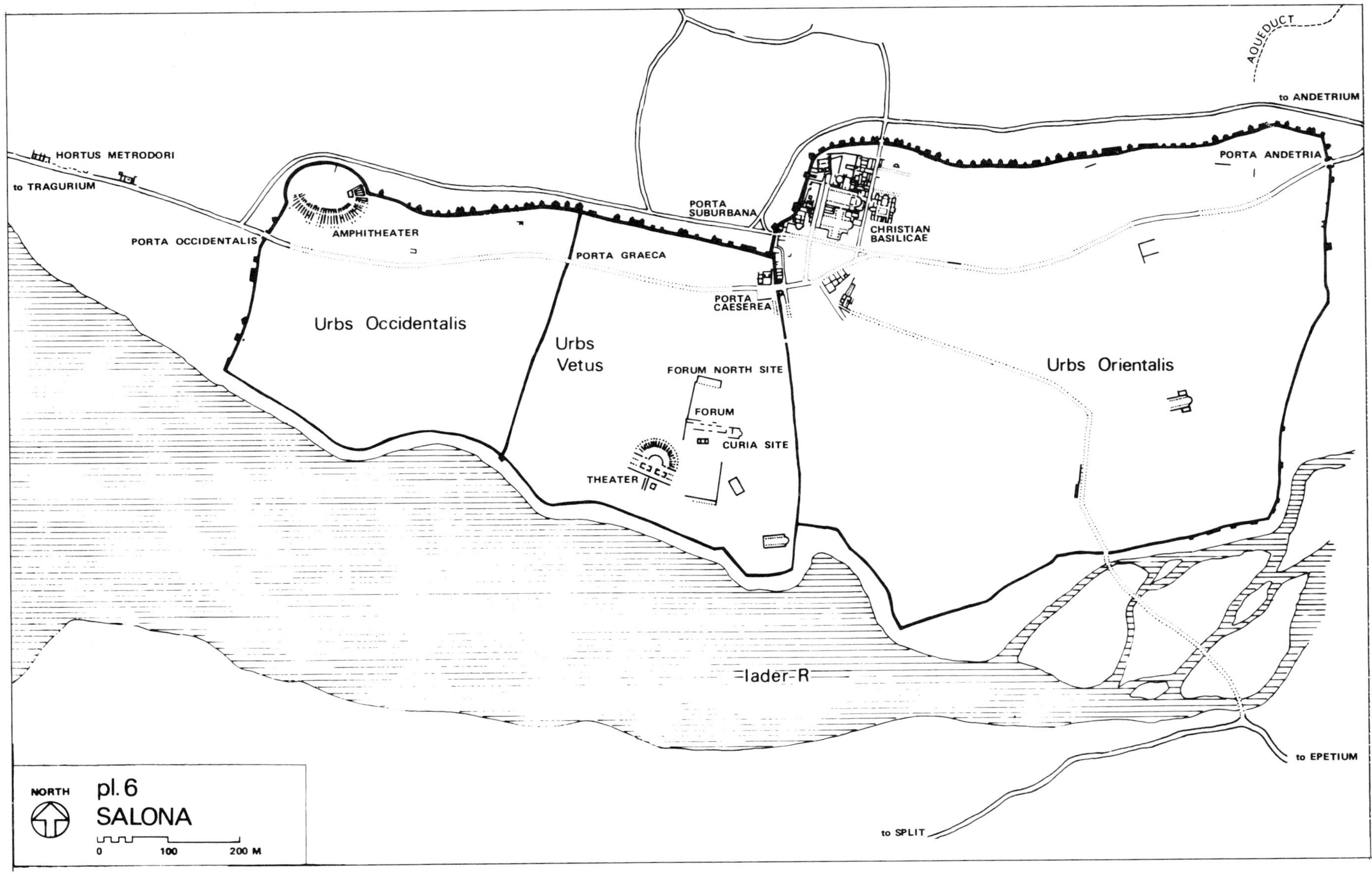
HORTUS METRODORI
to TRAGURIUM
AMPHITHEATER
PORTA OCCIDENTALIS
PORTA GRAECA
PORTA SUBURBANA
CHRISTIAN BASILICAE
PORTA CAESEREA
AQUEDUCT
to ANDETRIUM
PORTA ANDETRIA
Urbs Occidentalis
Urbs Vetus
FORUM NORTH SITE
FORUM
CURIA SITE
THEATER
Urbs Orientalis
Iader-R
to EPETIUM
to SPLIT
NORTH
pl. 6
SALONA
0
100
200 M

Plate 7

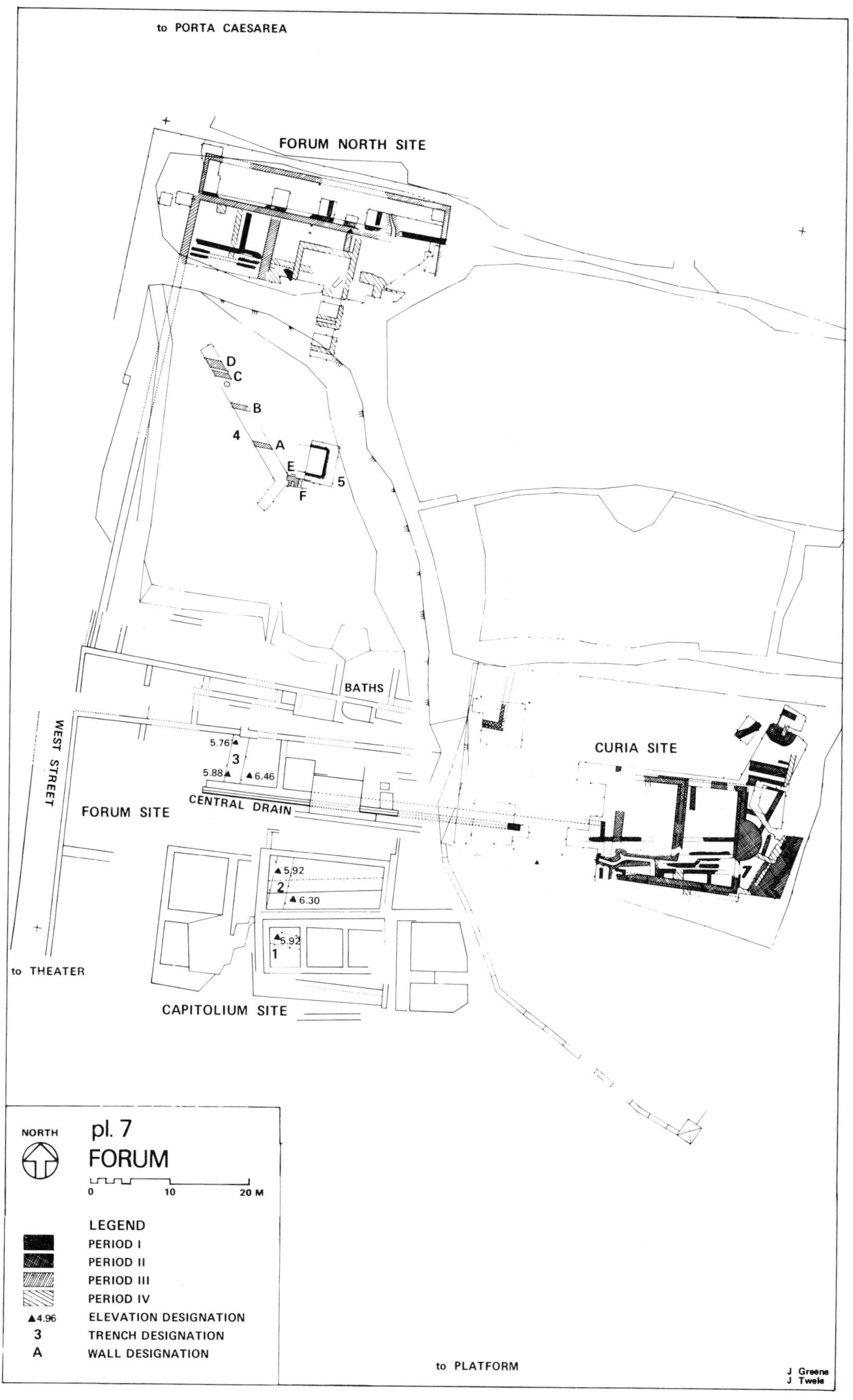
to PORTA CAESAREA
FORUM NORTH SITE
D
C
B
4
A
E
5
F
BATHS
WEST STREET
5.76
3
5.88
6.46
CENTRAL DRAIN
FORUM SITE
CURIA SITE
5.92
2
6.30
5.92
1
to THEATER
CAPITOLIUM SITE
NORTH
pl. 7
FORUM
0
10
20 M
LEGEND
PERIOD I
PERIOD II
PERIOD III
PERIOD IV
4.96
ELEVATION DESIGNATION
3
TRENCH DESIGNATION
A
WALL DESIGNATION
to PLATFORM
J Greene
J Twele

Plate 8

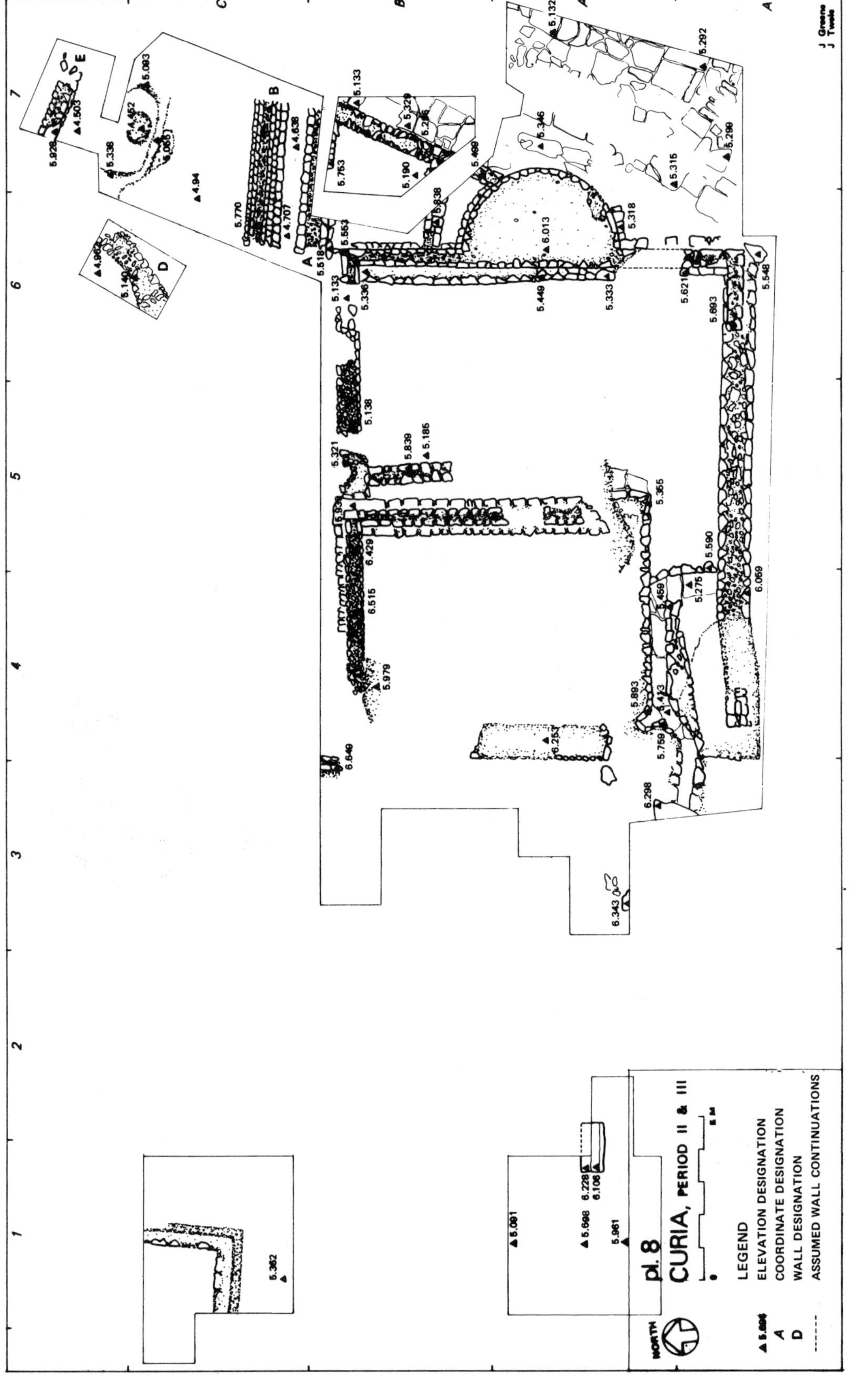
pl. 8
CURIA, PERIOD II & III
LEGEND
ELEVATION DESIGNATION
COORDINATE DESIGNATION
WALL DESIGNATION
ASSUMED WALL CONTINUATIONS
NORTH

Plate 9

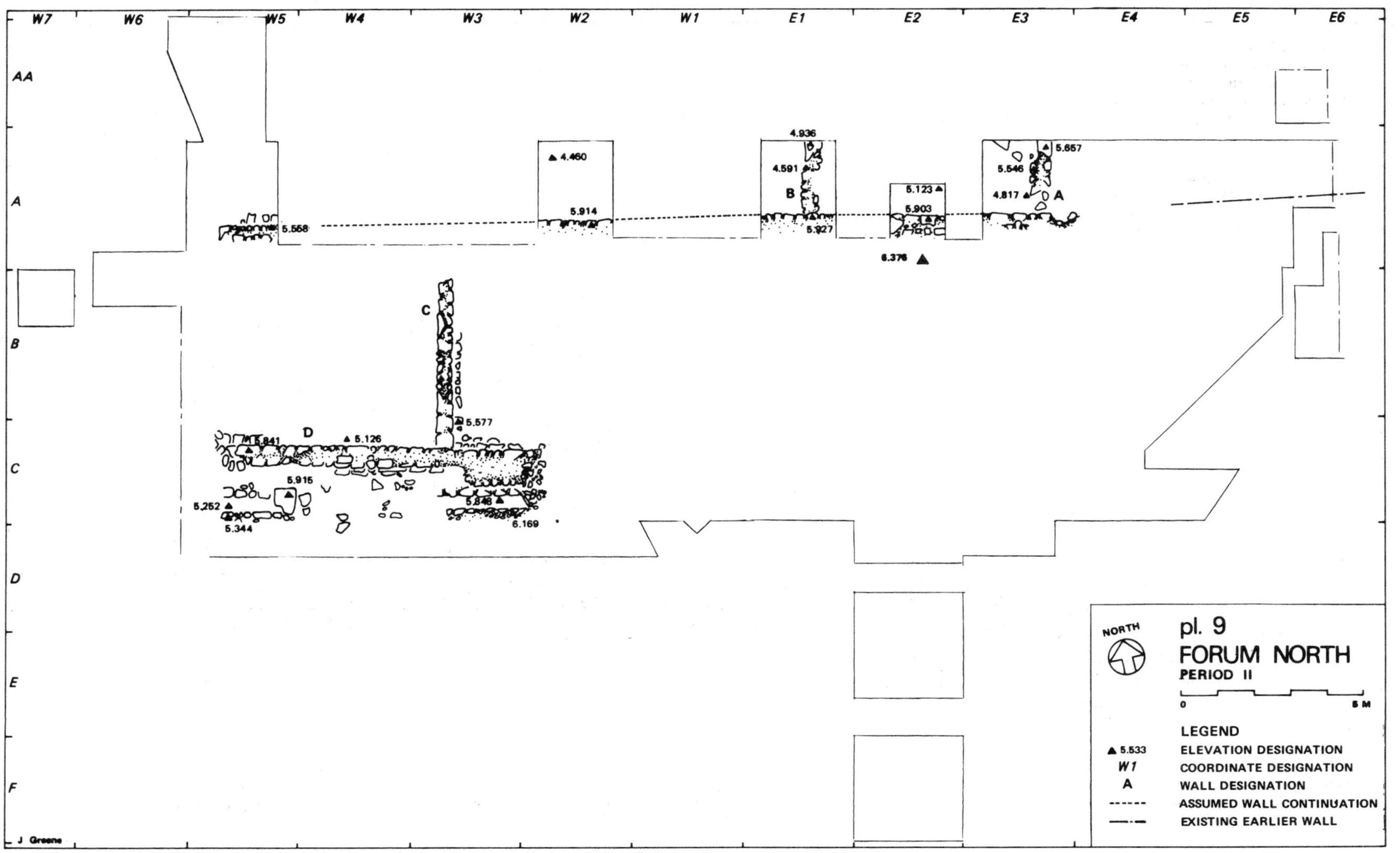

pl. 9
FORUM NORTH
PERIOD II
NORTH
0
5 M
LEGEND
5.533 ELEVATION DESIGNATION
W1 COORDINATE DESIGNATION
A WALL DESIGNATION
ASSUMED WALL CONTINUATION
EXISTING EARLIER WALL
W7
W6
W5
W4
W3
W2
W1
E1
E2
E3
E4
E5
E6
AA
A
B
C
D
E
F
J Greene

Plate 10

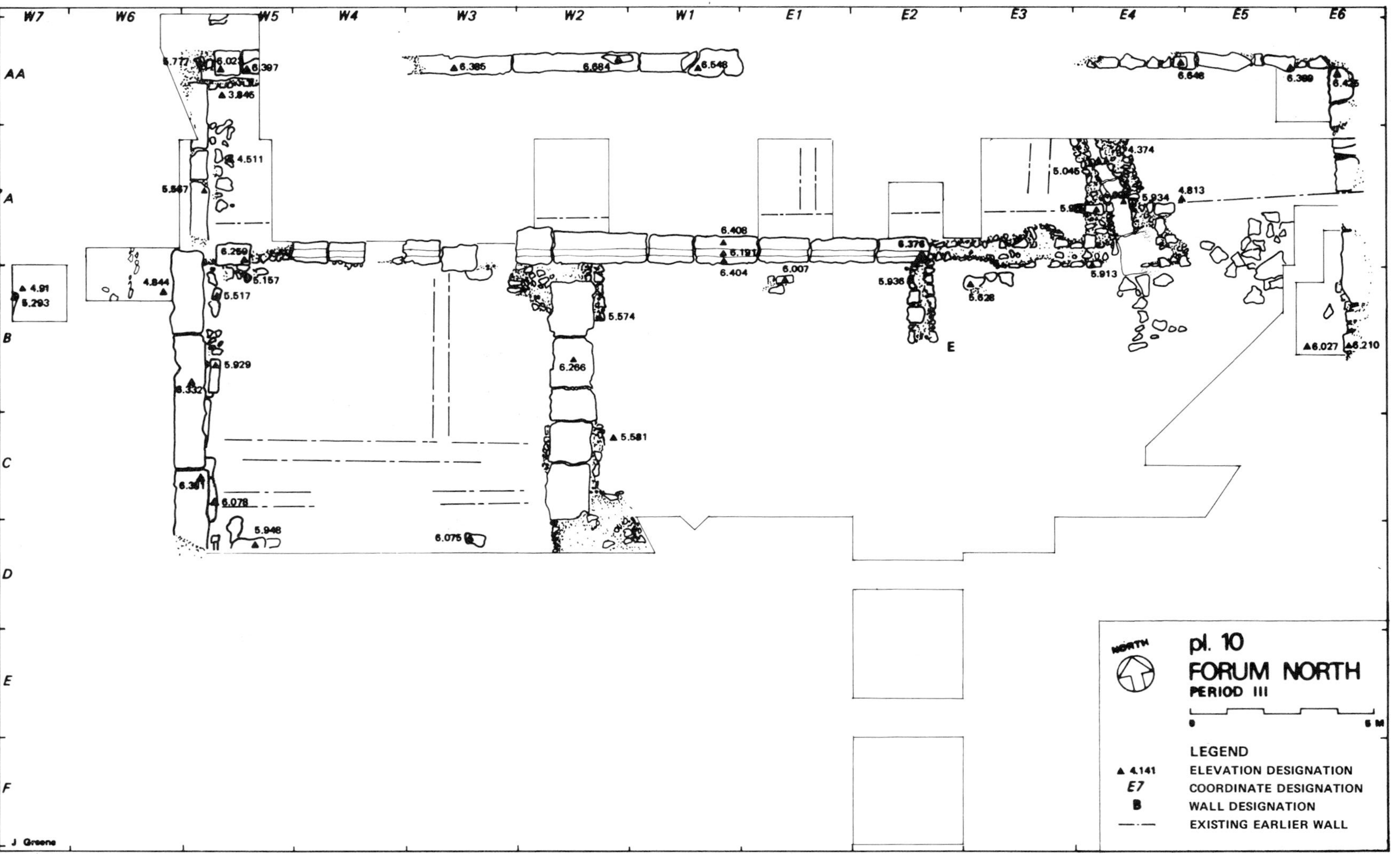
pl. 10
FORUM NORTH
PERIOD III
NORTH
0
5 M
LEGEND
▲ 4.141 ELEVATION DESIGNATION
E7 COORDINATE DESIGNATION
B WALL DESIGNATION
EXISTING EARLIER WALL
J Greene

Plate 11

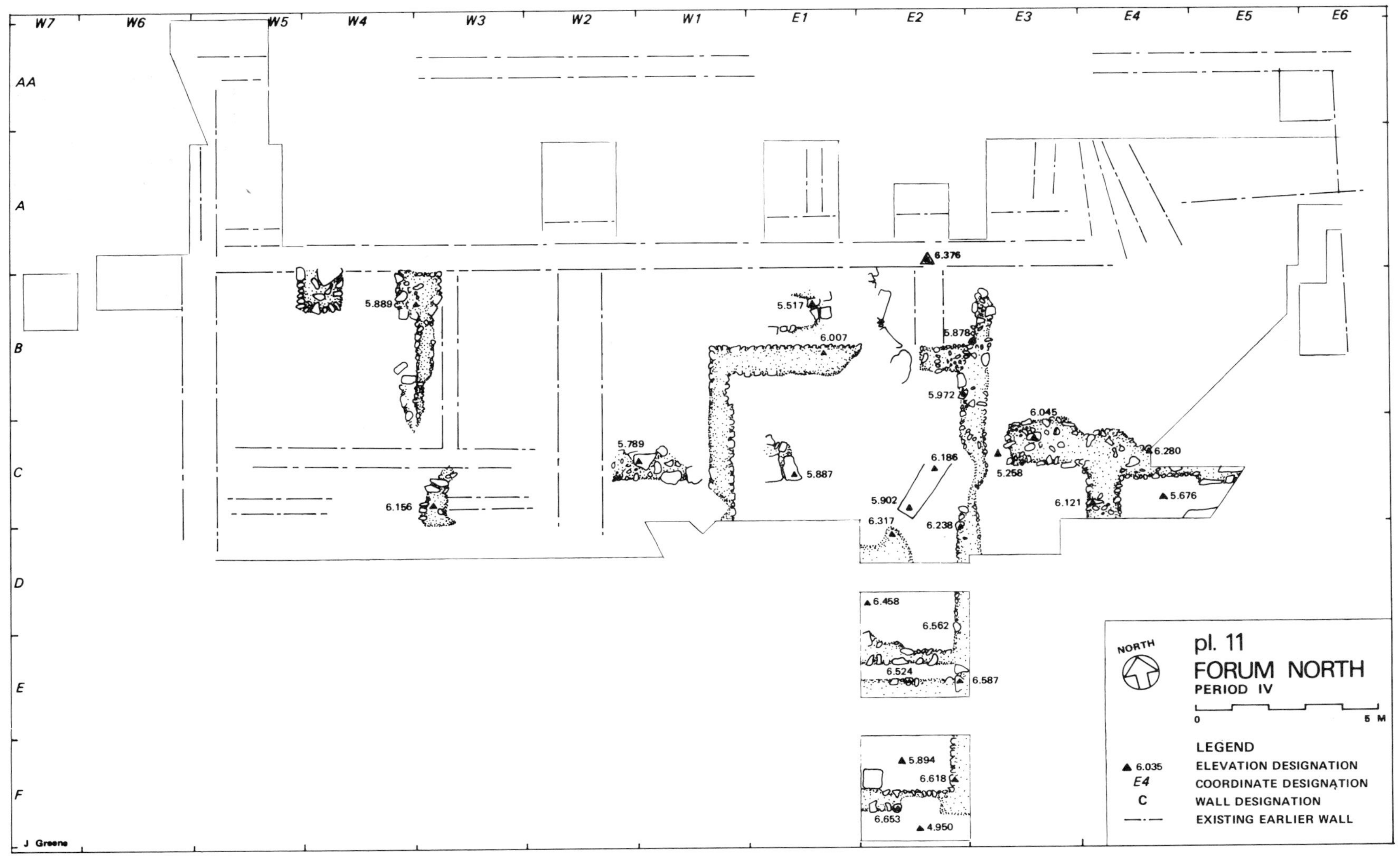
W7
W6
W5
W4
W3
W2
W1
E1
E2
E3
E4
E5
E6
AA
A
B
C
D
E
F
6.376
5.889
5.517
6.007
5.878
5.972
6.045
6.280
5.789
5.887
6.186
5.258
6.156
5.902
6.121
5.676
6.317
6.238
6.458
6.562
6.524
6.587
5.894
6.618
6.653
4.950
J Greene
NORTH
pl. 11
FORUM NORTH
PERIOD IV
0
5 M
LEGEND
6.035 ELEVATION DESIGNATION
E4 COORDINATE DESIGNATION
C WALL DESIGNATION
EXISTING EARLIER WALL

Plate 11 bis

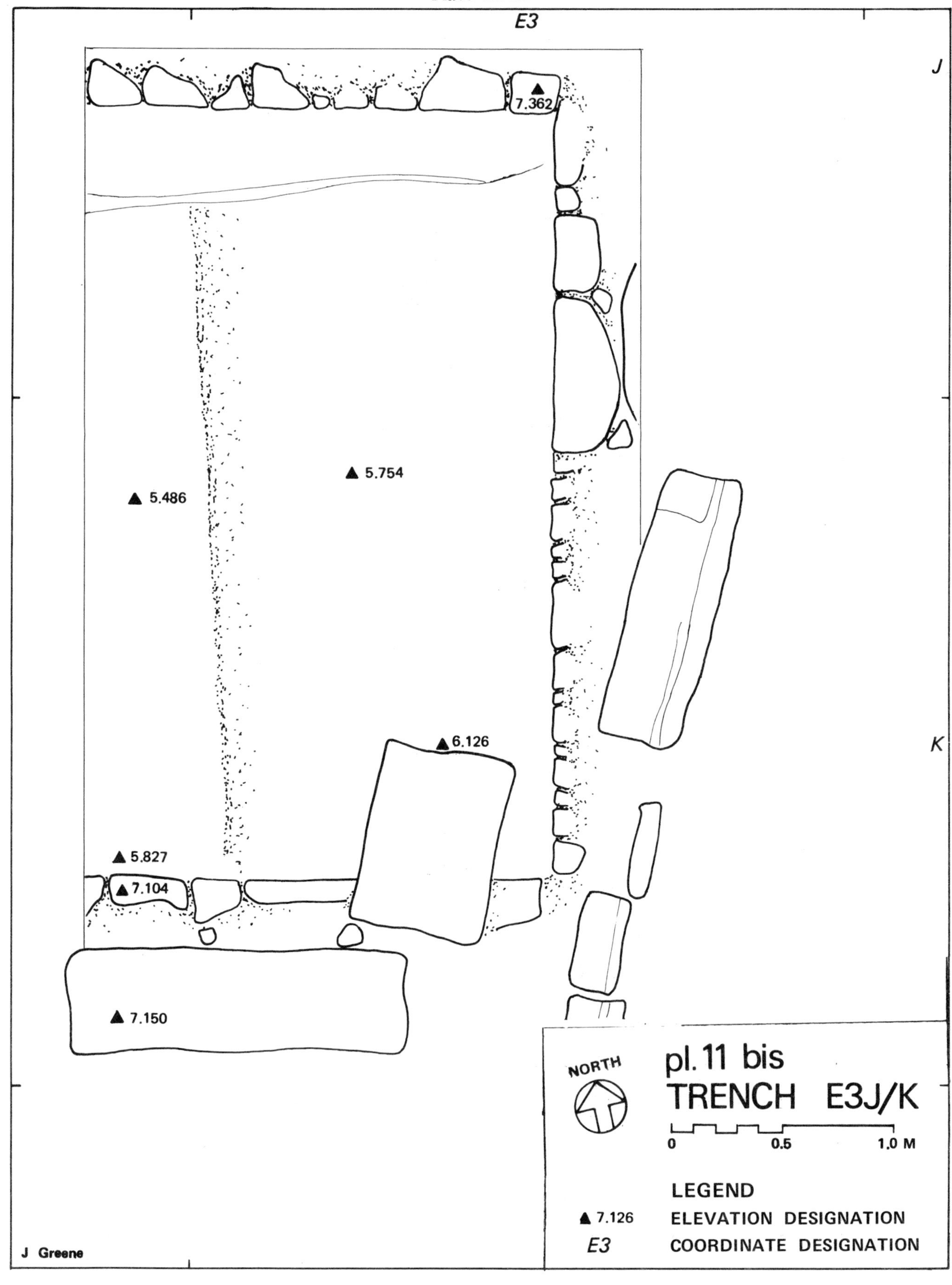
E3
J
K
7.362
5.754
5.486
6.126
5.827
7.104
7.150
NORTH
pl. 11 bis
TRENCH E3J/K
0
0.5
1.0 M
LEGEND
7.126 ELEVATION DESIGNATION
E3 COORDINATE DESIGNATION
J Greene

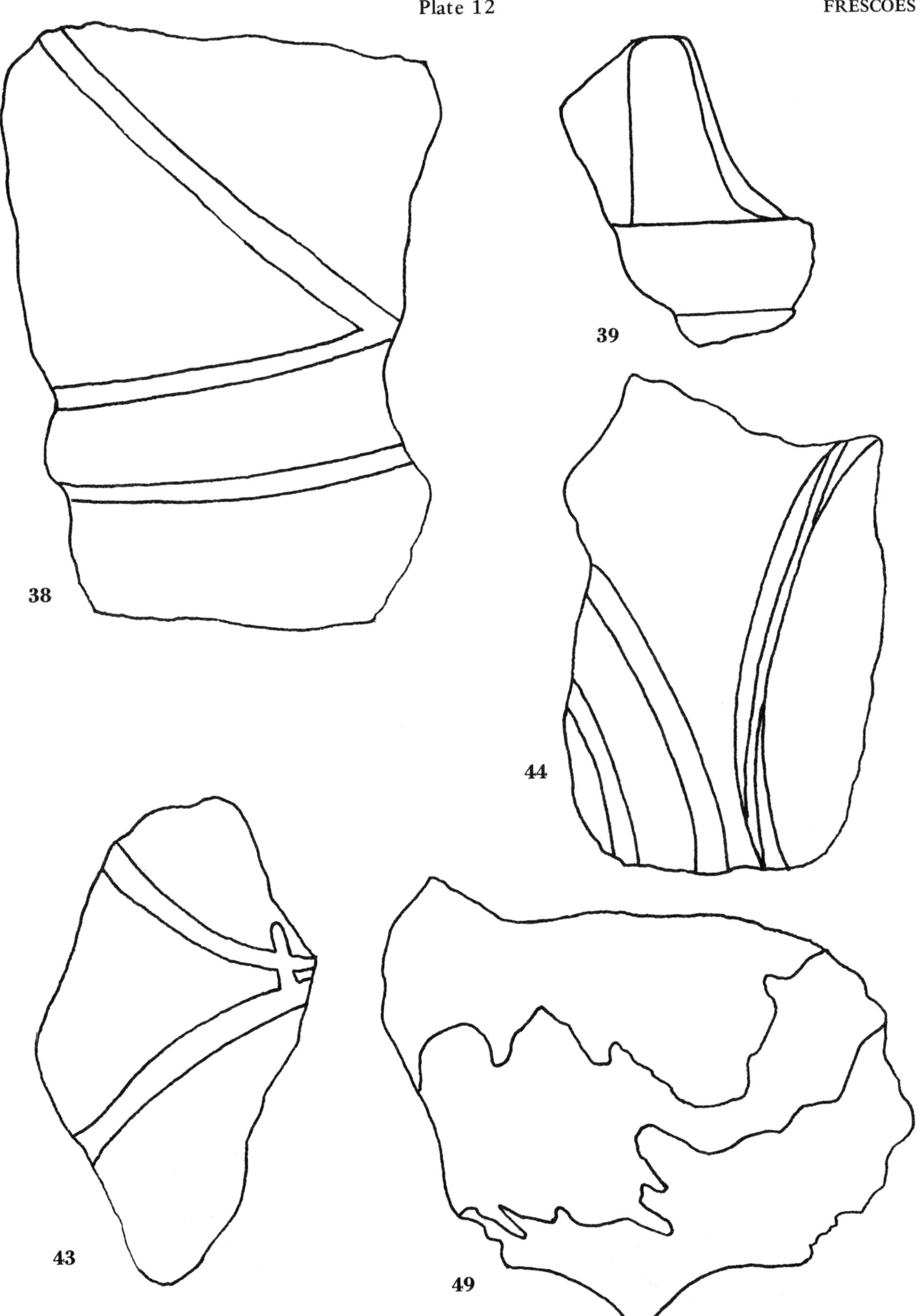
38
39
44
43
49

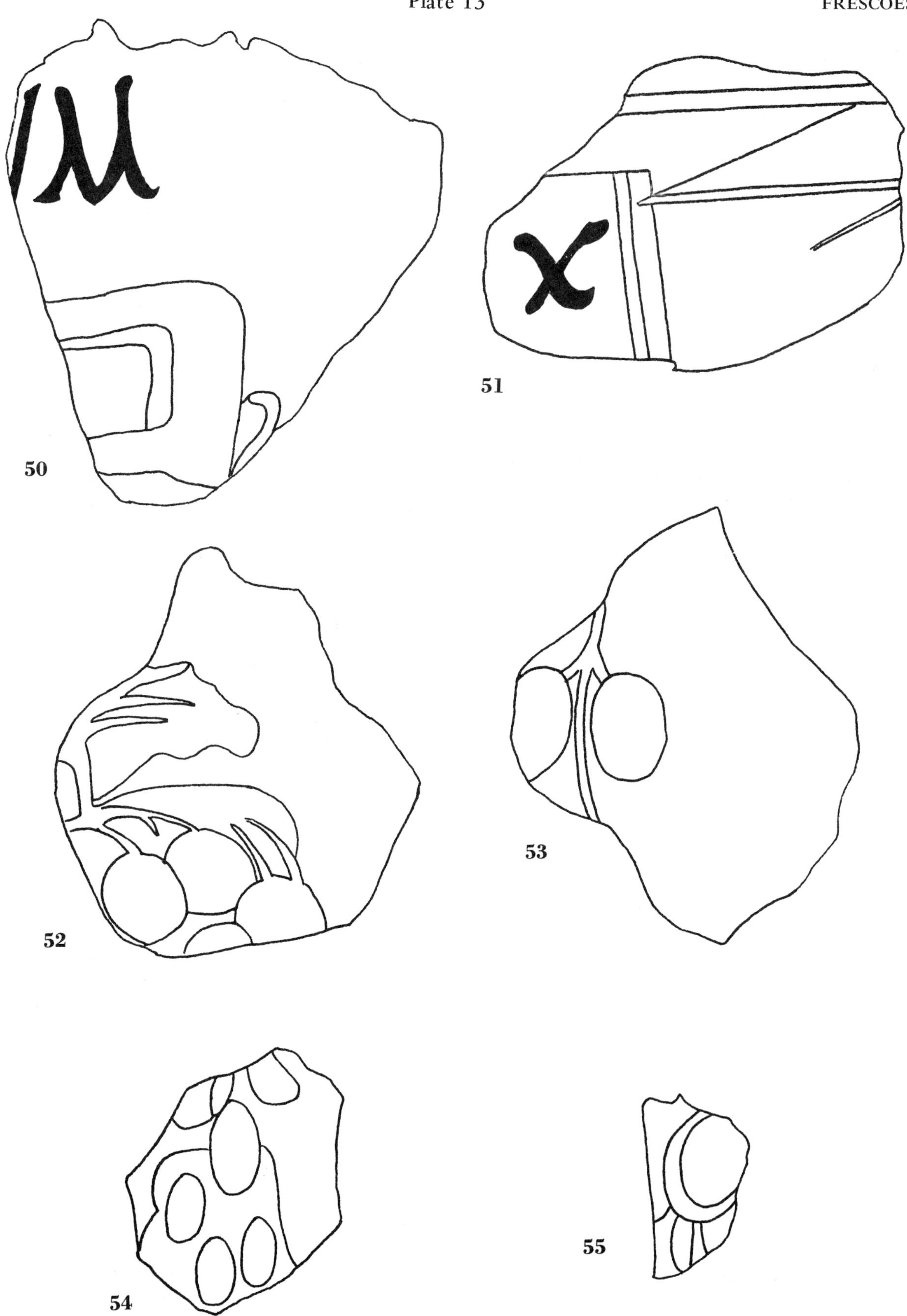
50
51
52
53
54
55

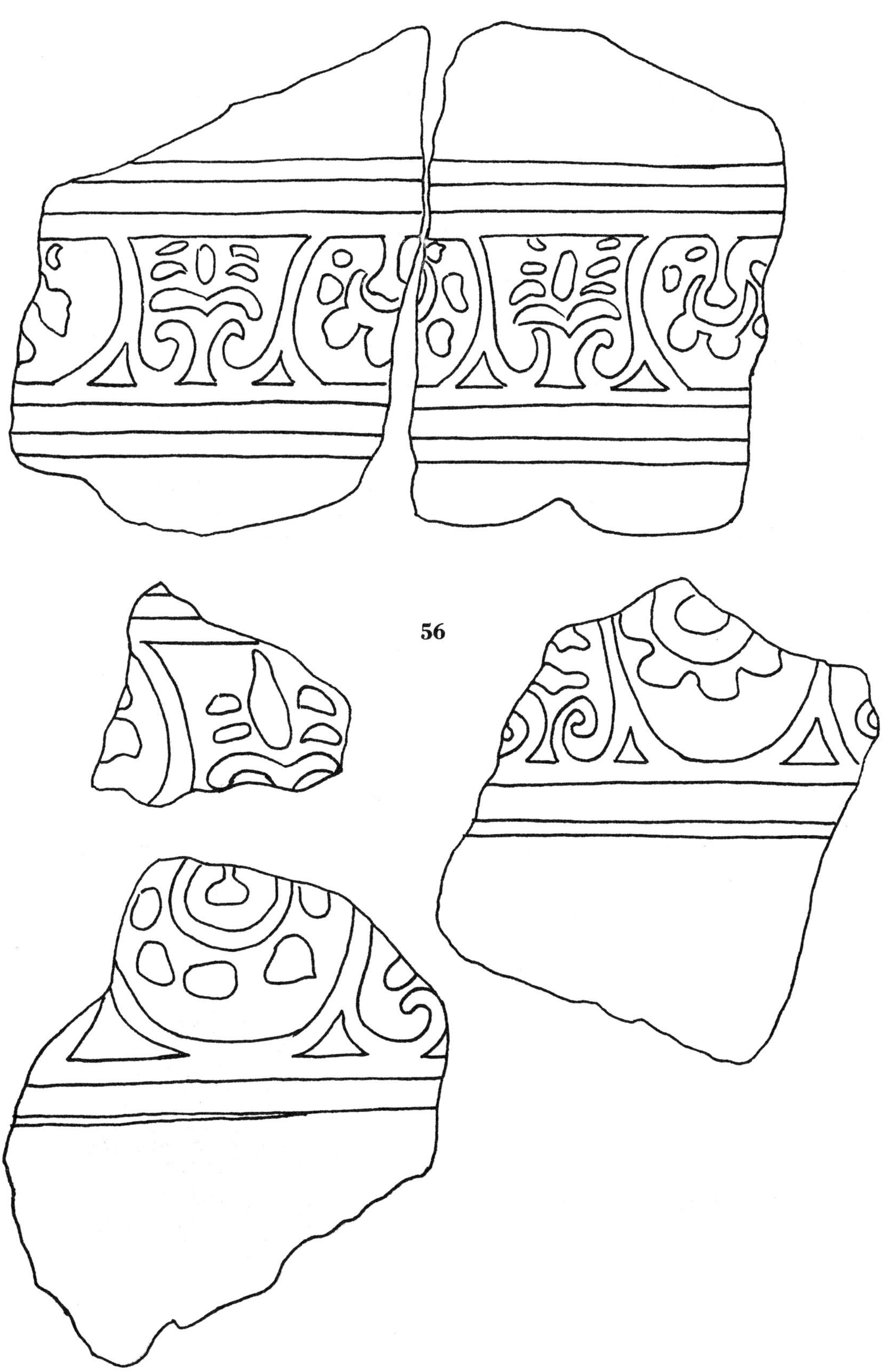

56

57
58
59
60
61
62

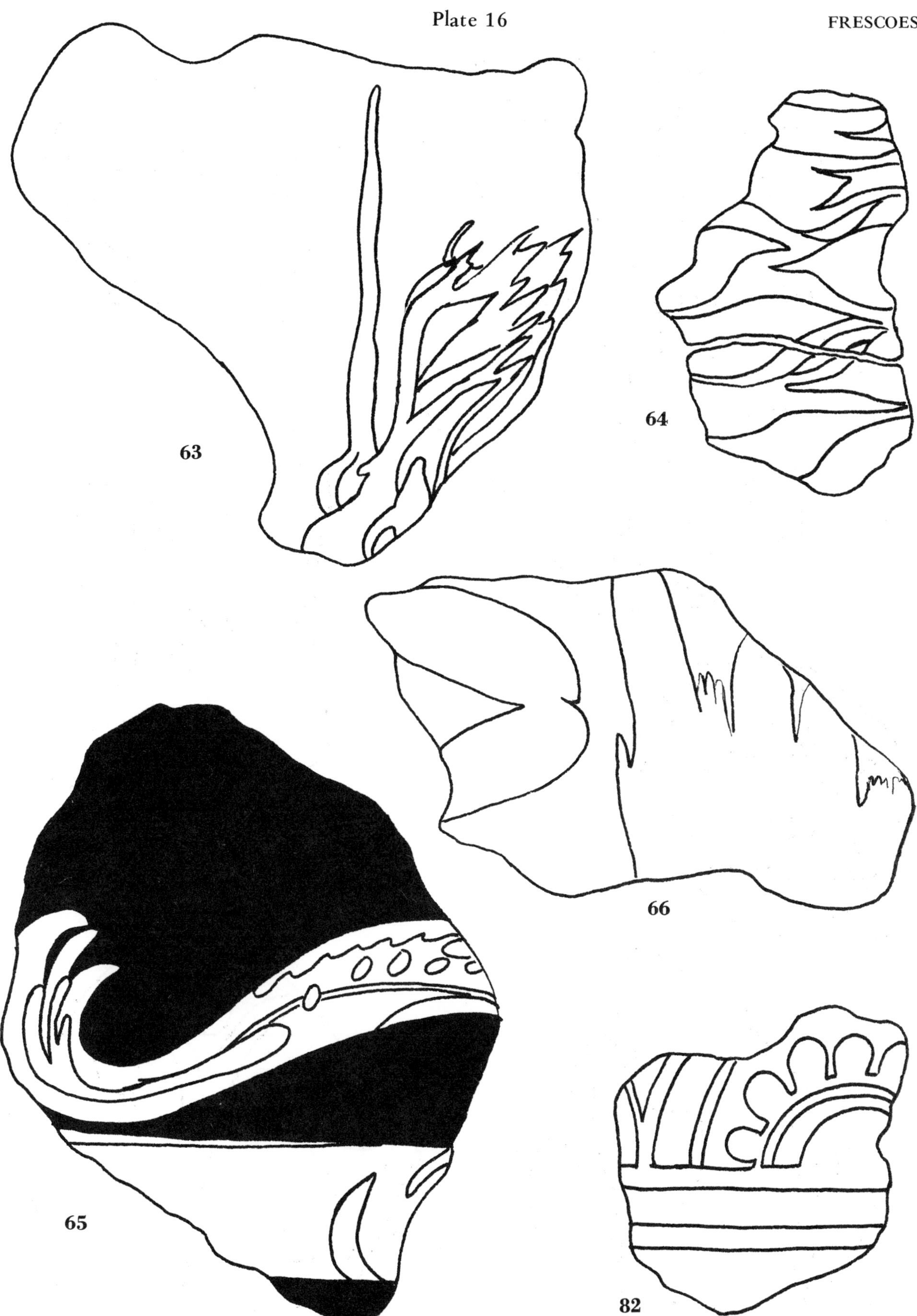
63
64
66
65
82

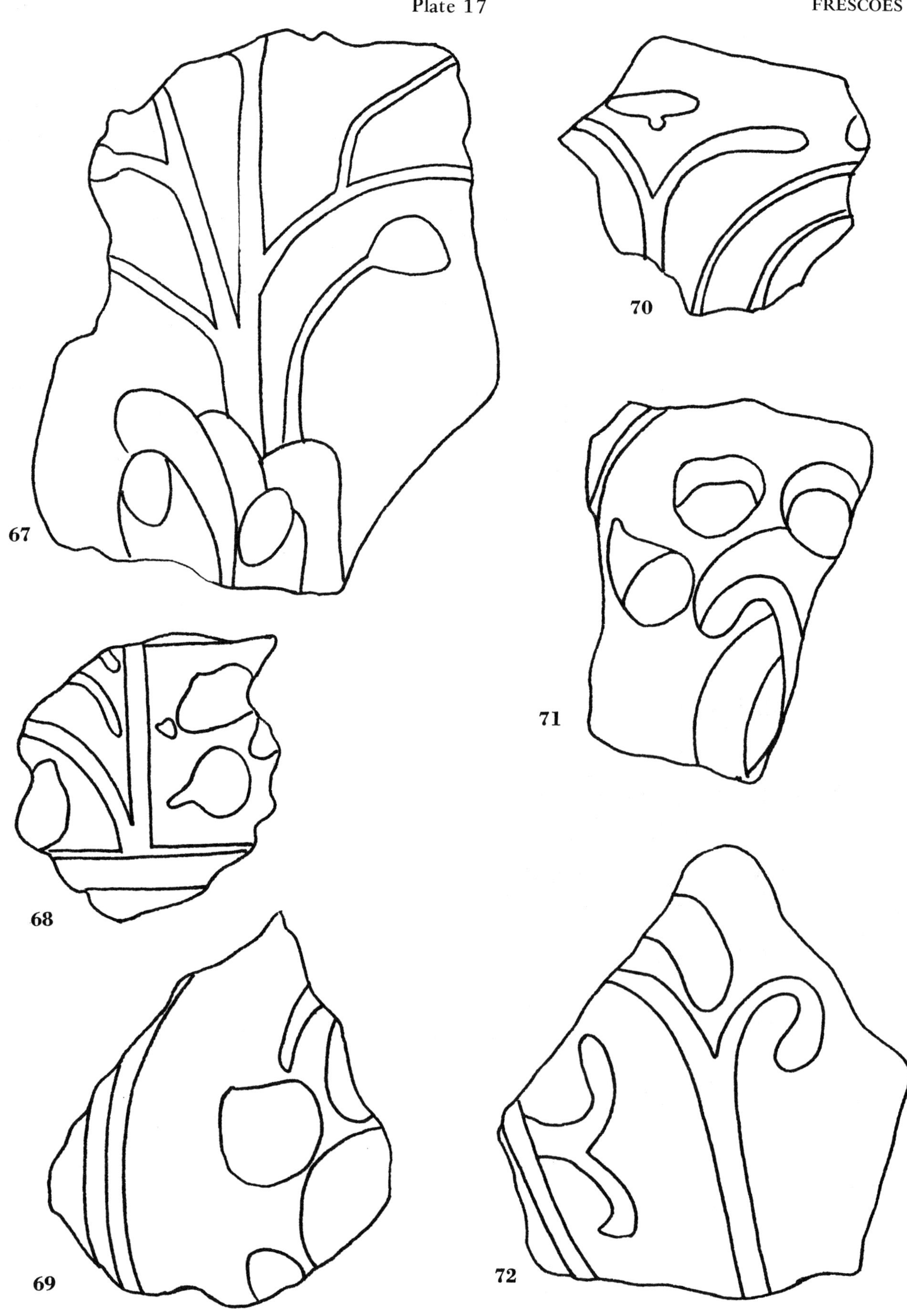
67
68
69
70
71
72

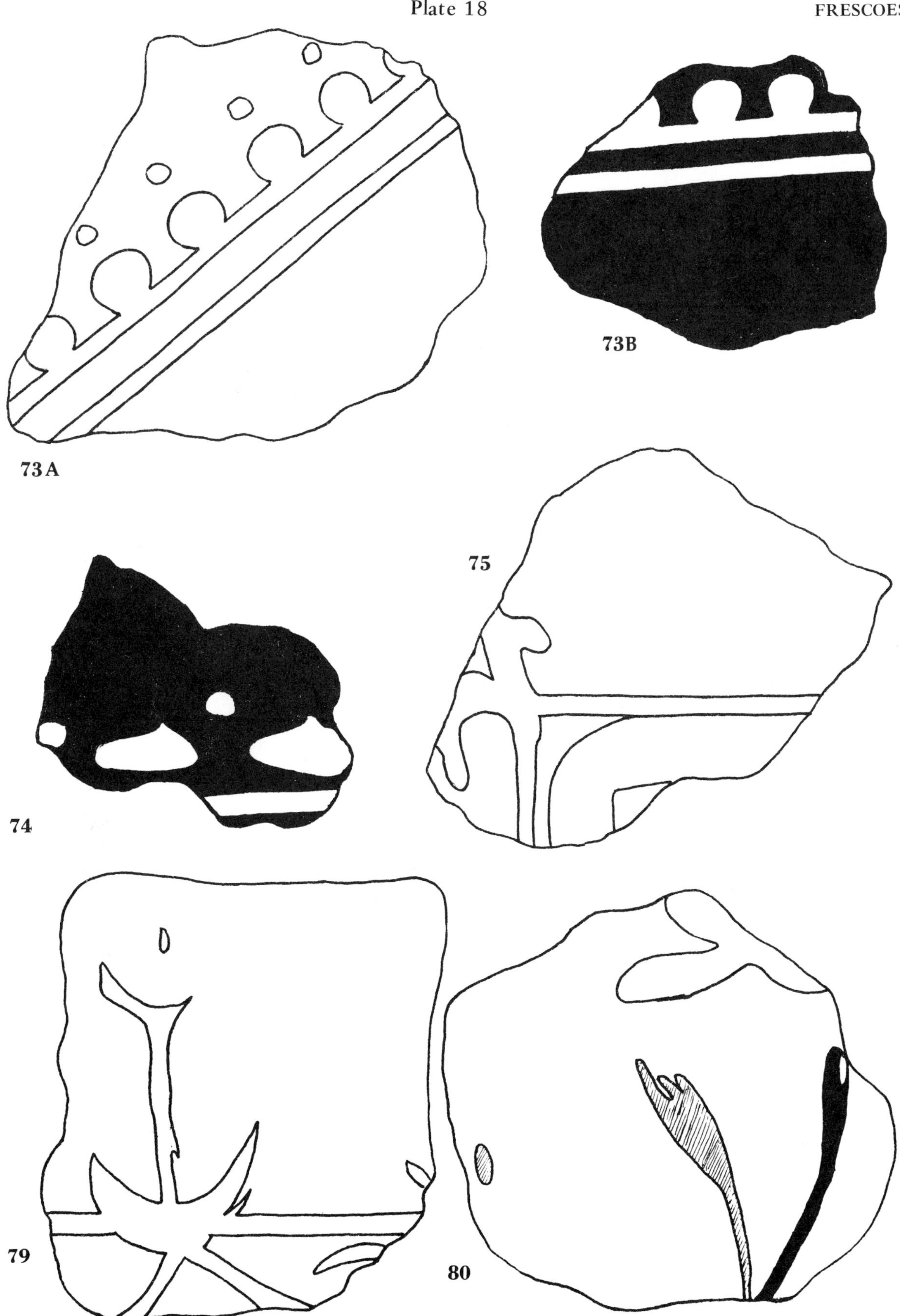
73A
73B
74
75
79
80

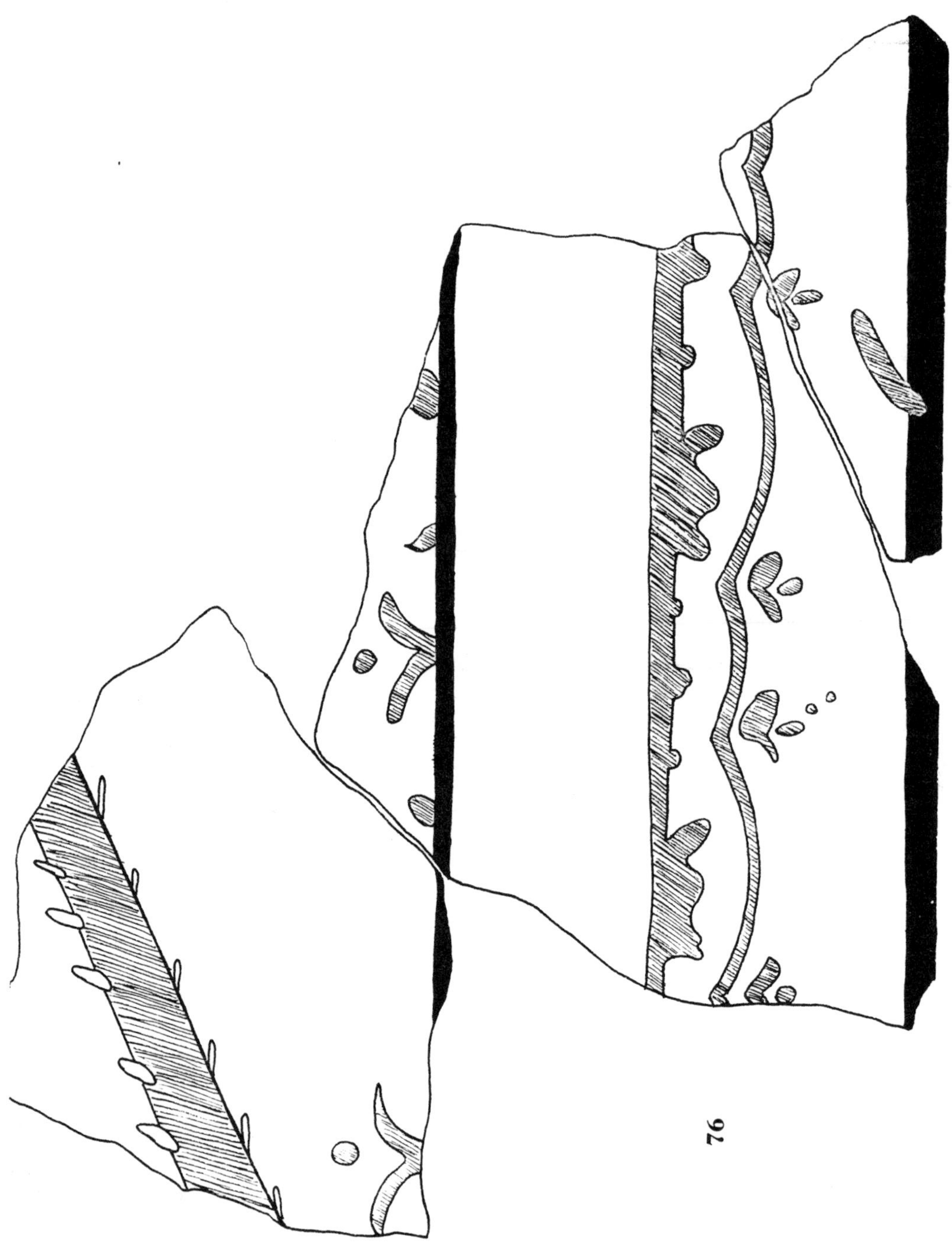

76

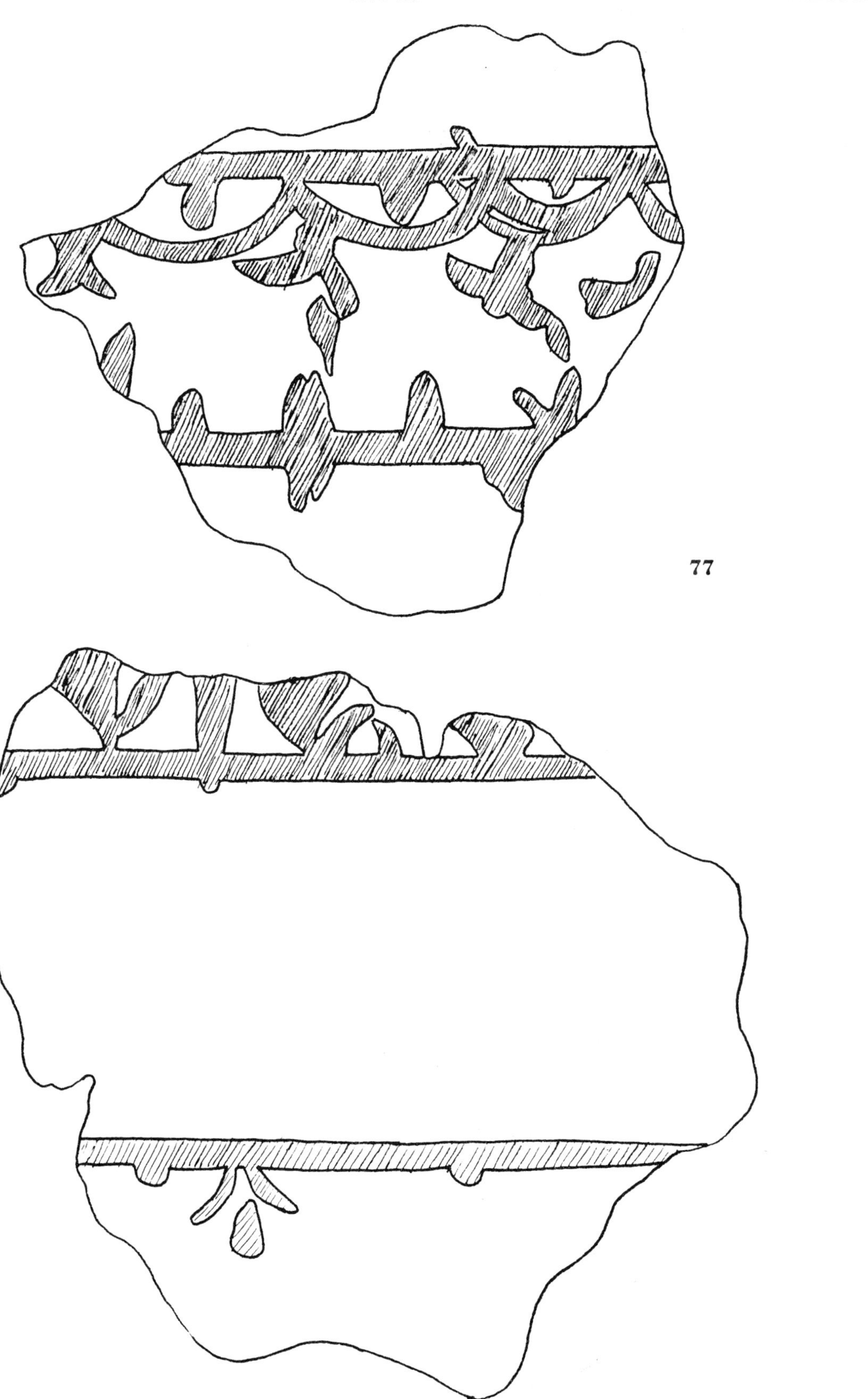

77

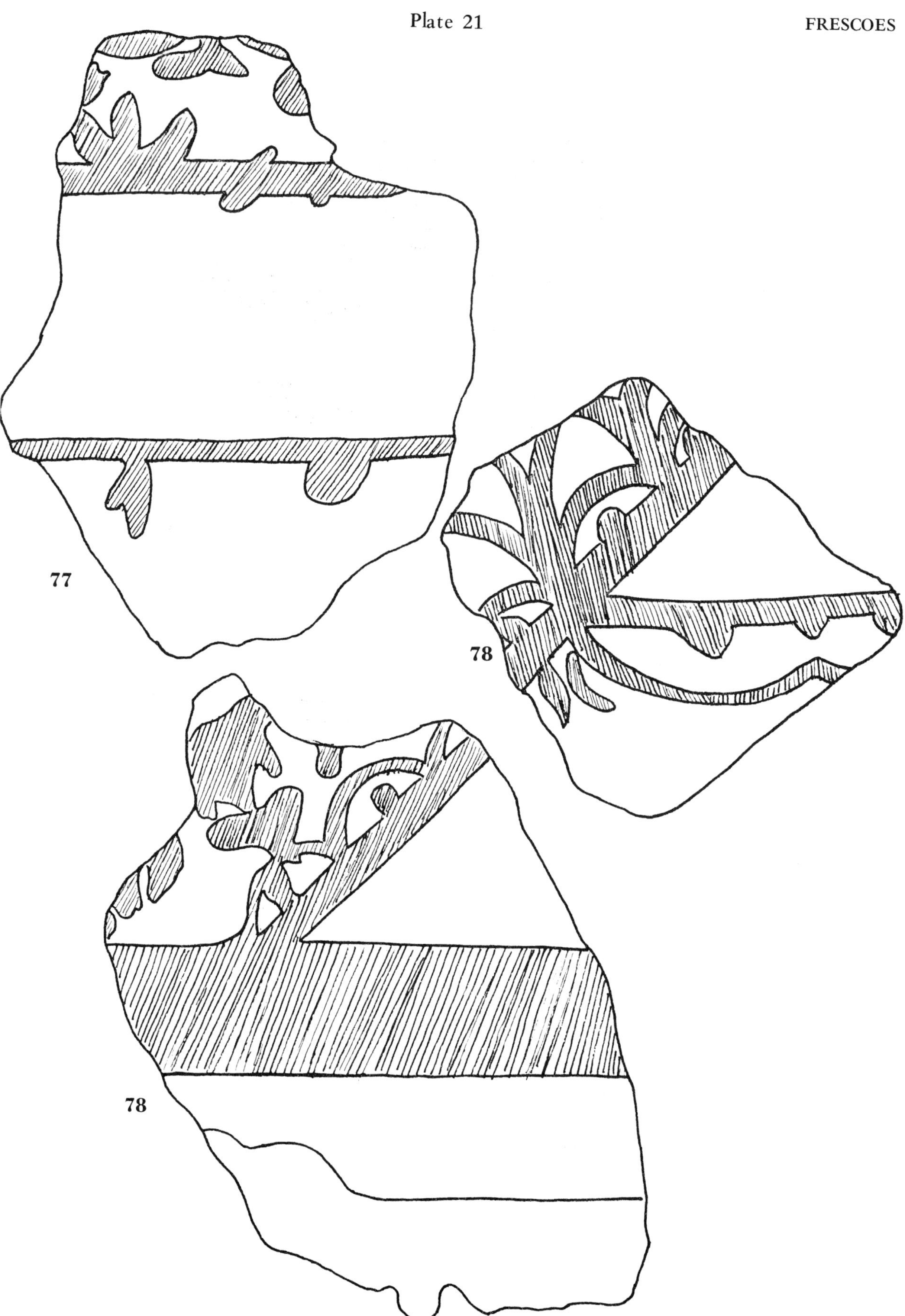
77
78
78

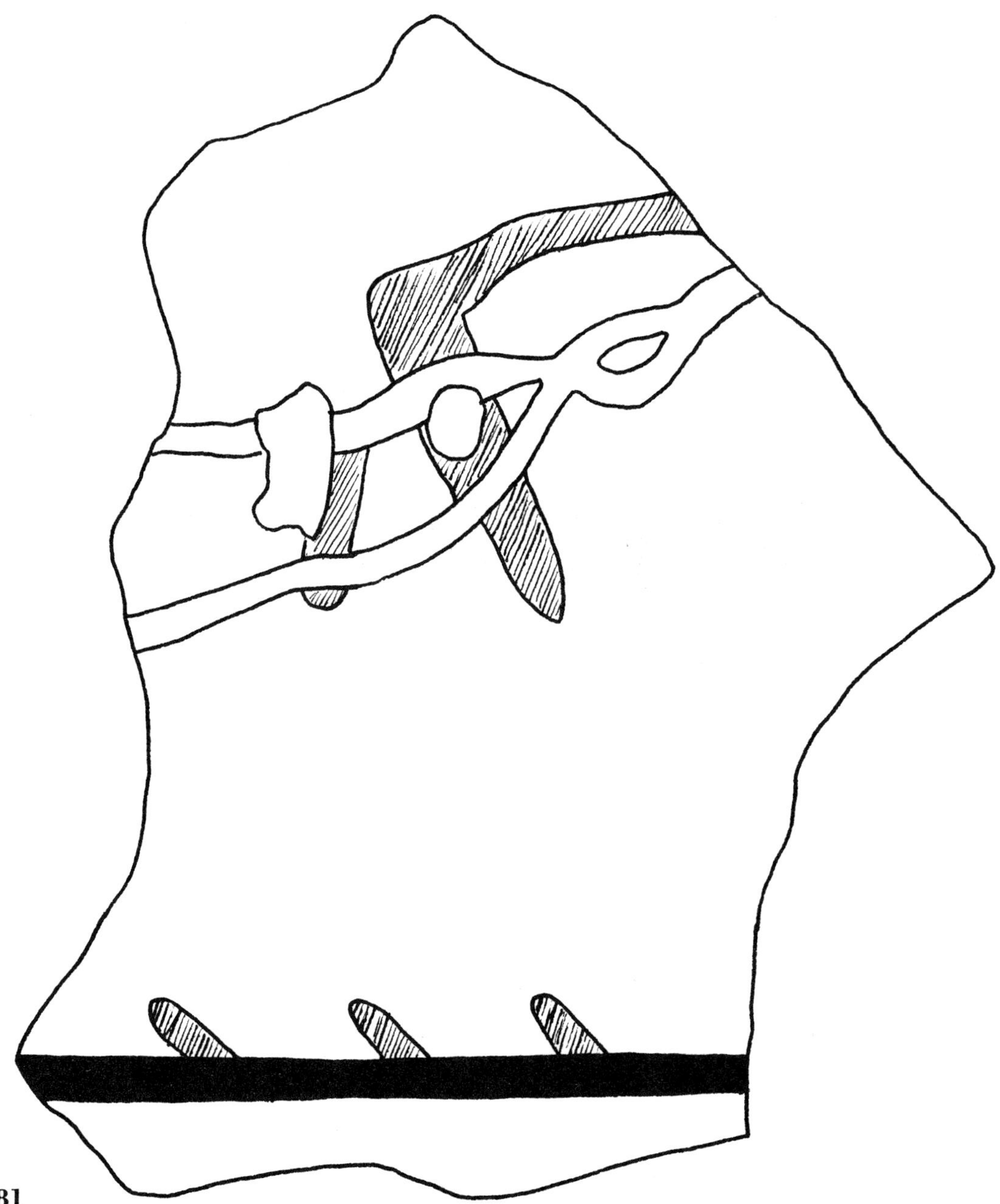

81

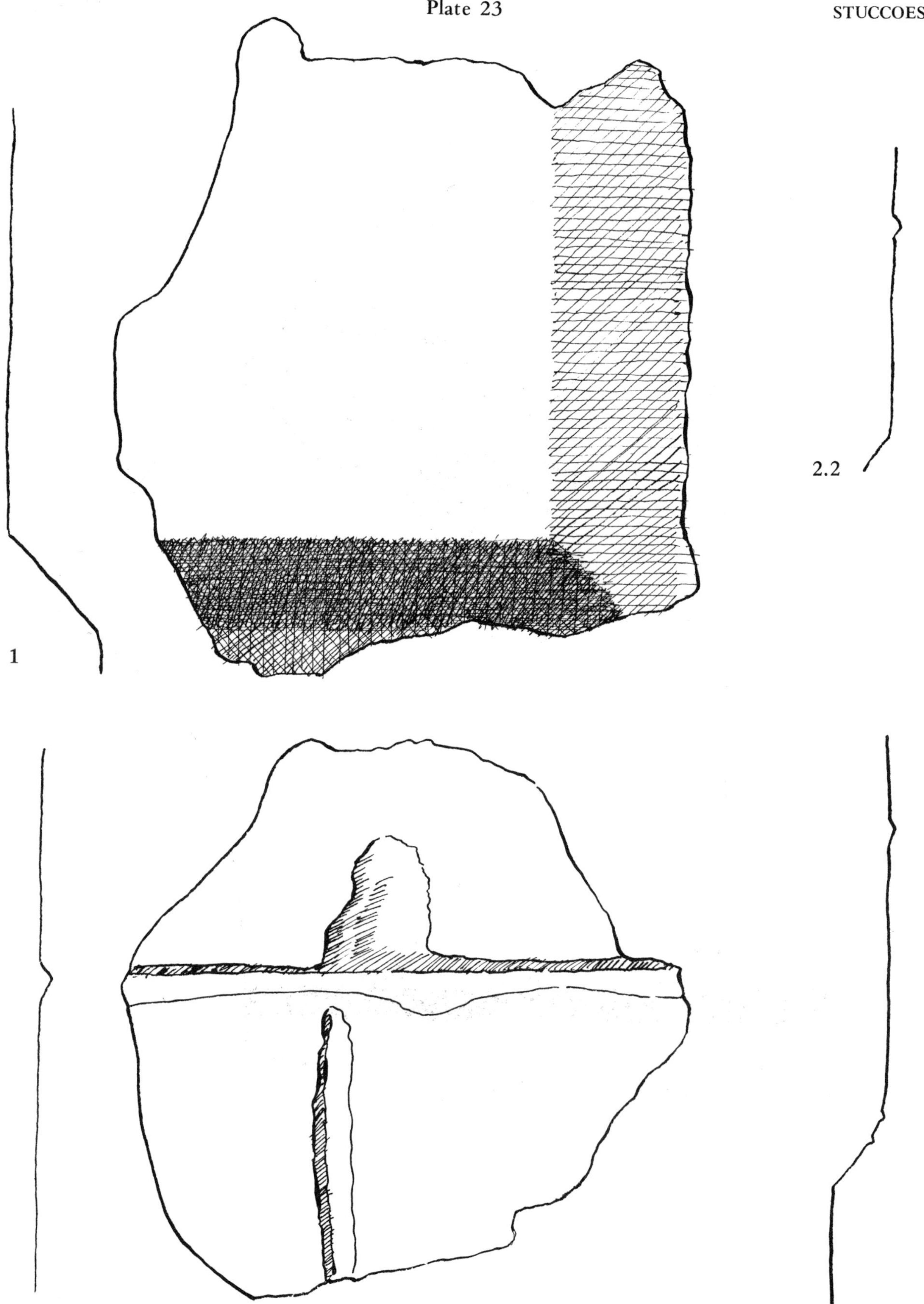
1
2.2
2.3

3.6
3.5 
3.4 
3.3 
3.2 
3.1
4.3 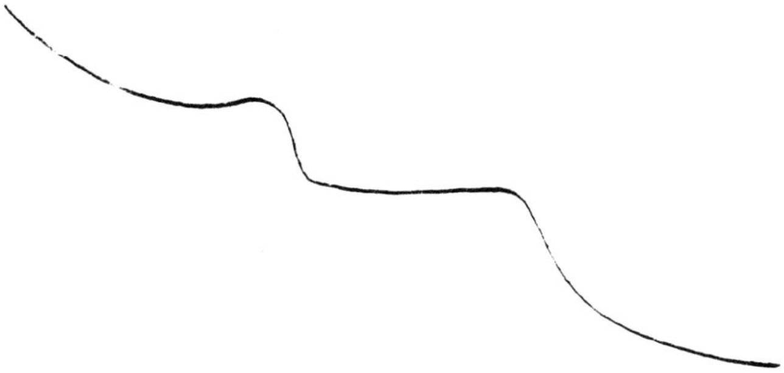
4.2 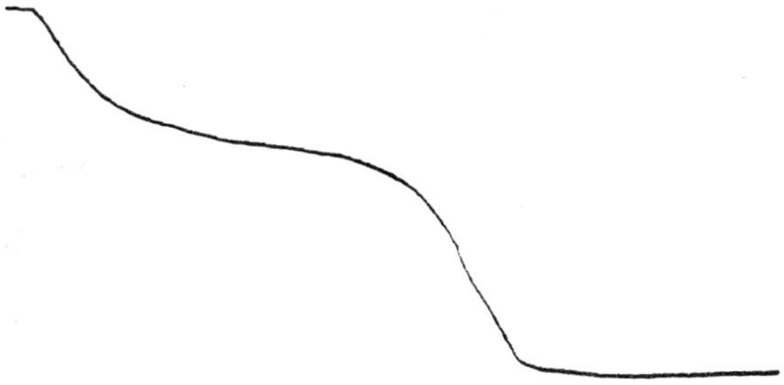
4.1 
3.8 
3.7

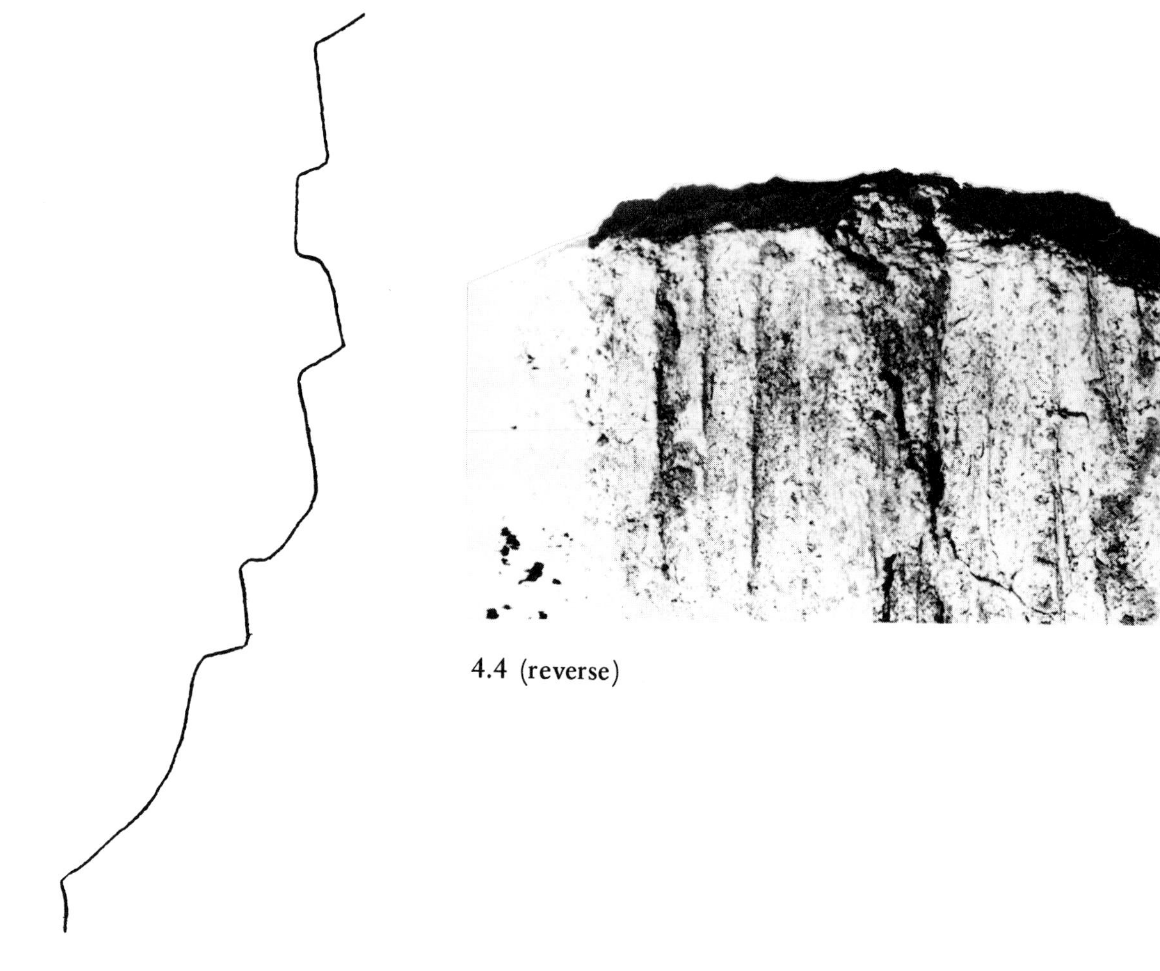

4.4 (reverse)

4.4

1

2

5

7

8

9

9

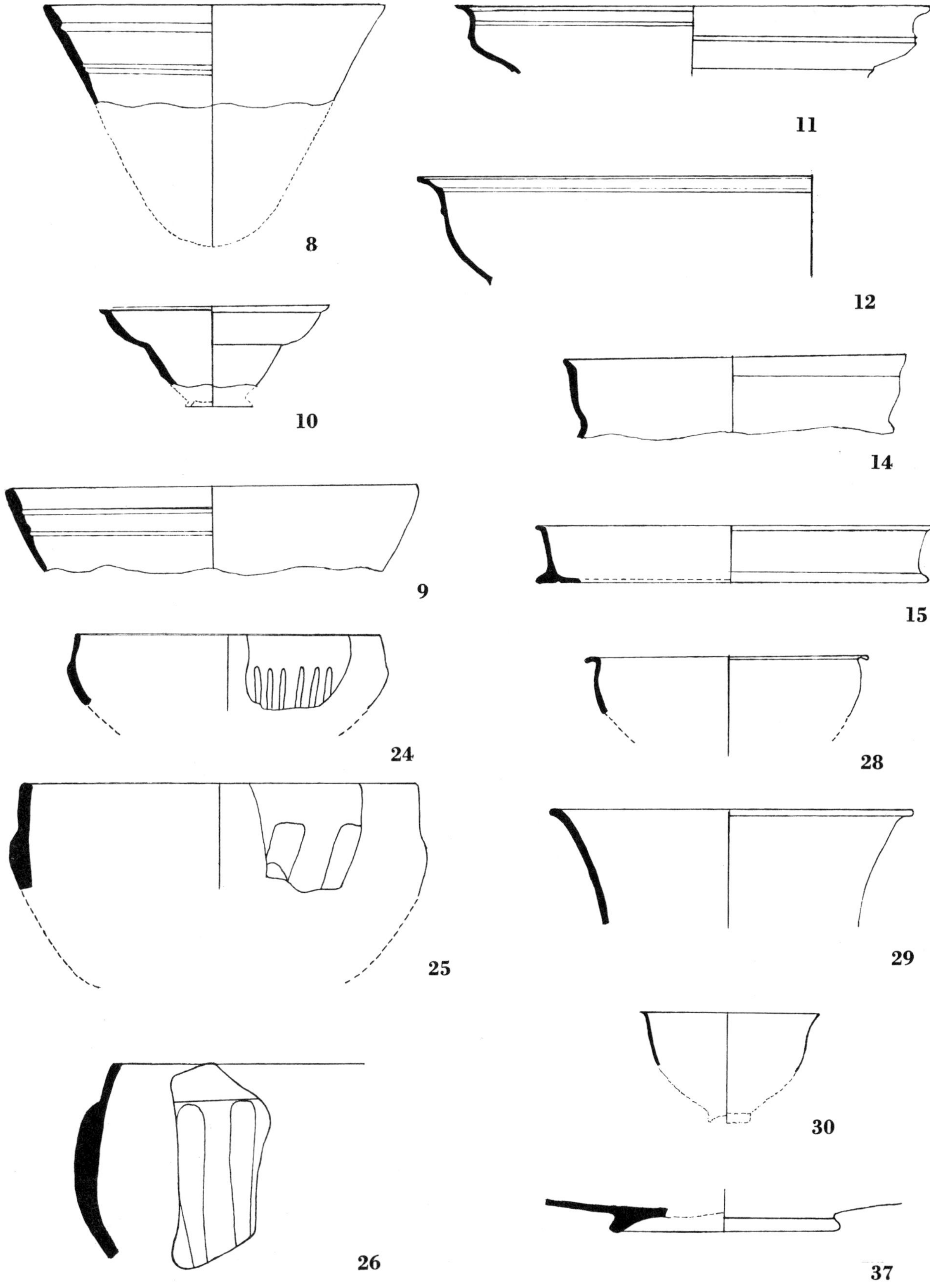
8
11
12
10
14
9
15
24
28
25
29
30
26
37

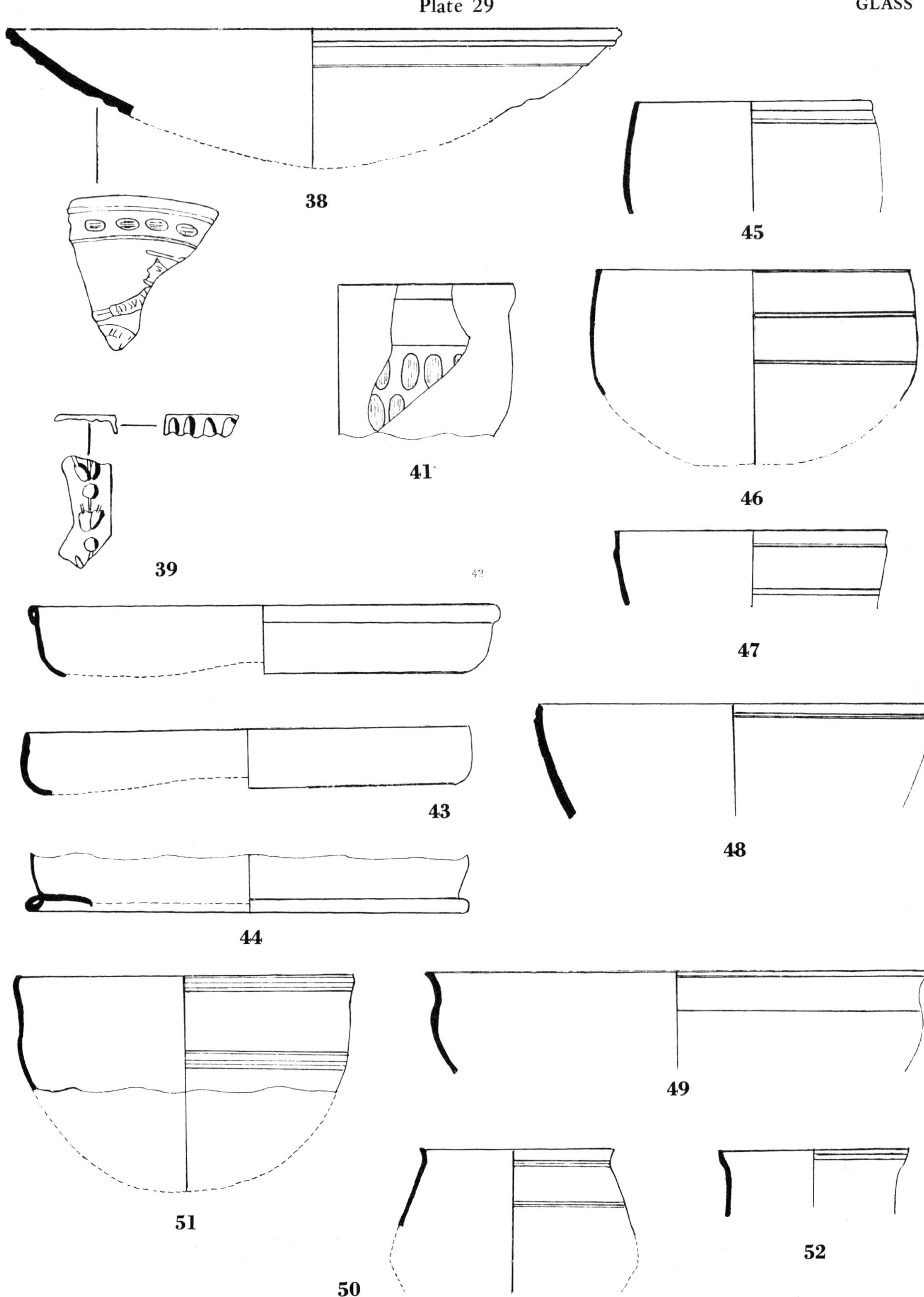
38
39
41
42
43
44
45
46
47
48
49
50
51
52

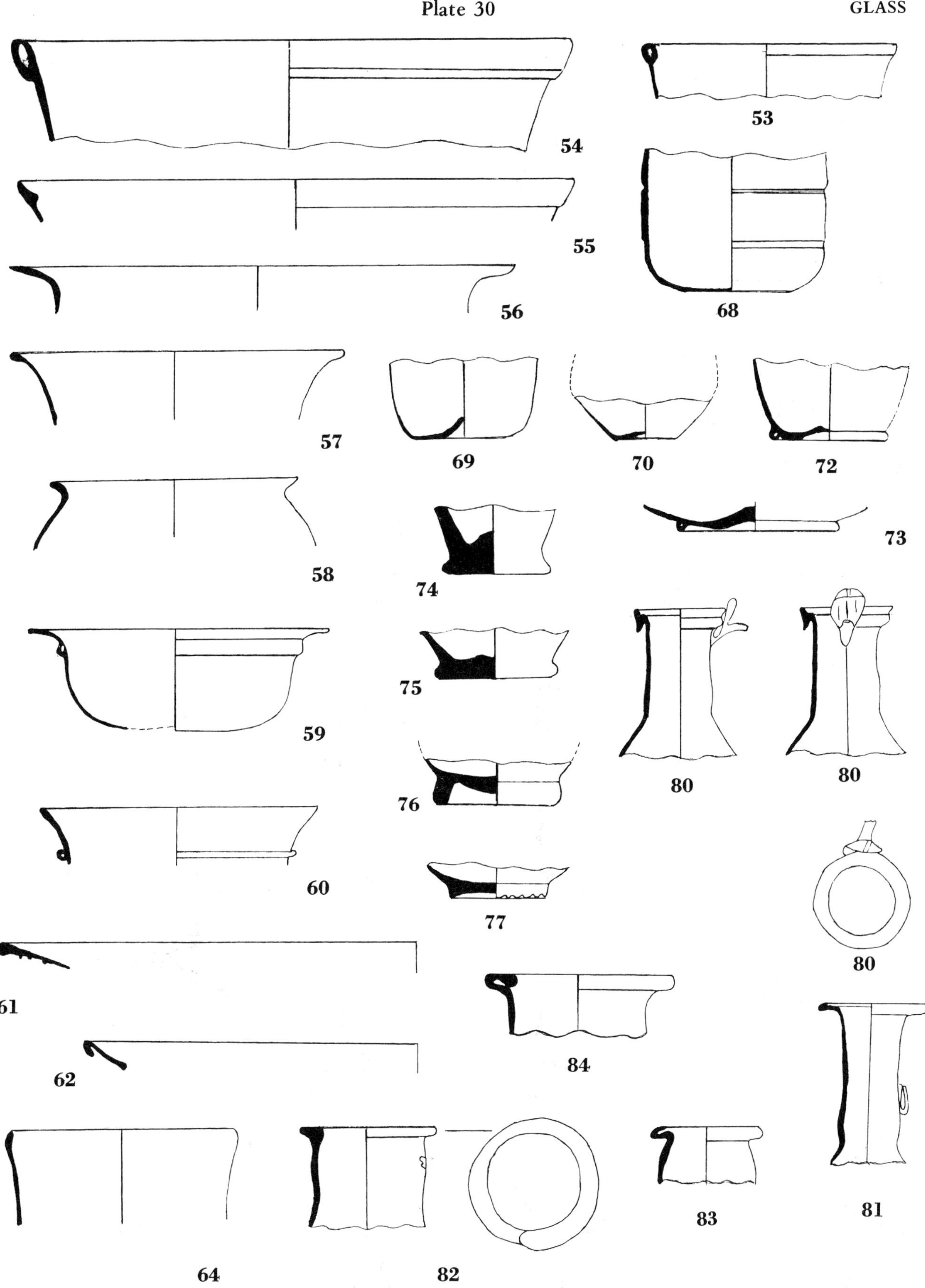
54
53
55
68
56
57
69
70
72
58
74
73
59
75
80
80
76
60
77
80
61
84
62
81
64
82
83

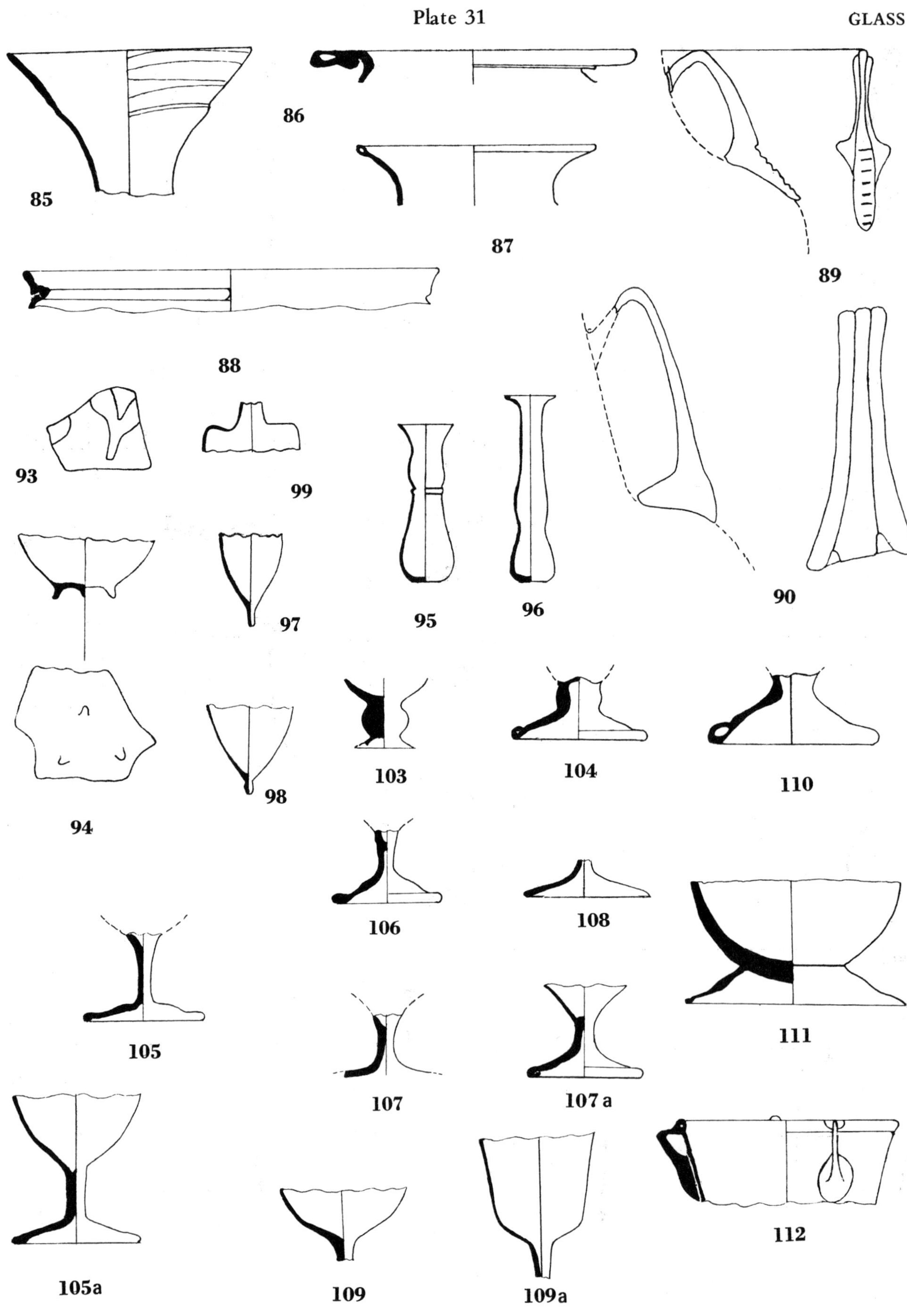
85
86
87
89
88
93
99
95
96
90
97
94
98
103
104
110
106
108
111
105
107
107 a
105a
109
109a
112

Plate 32

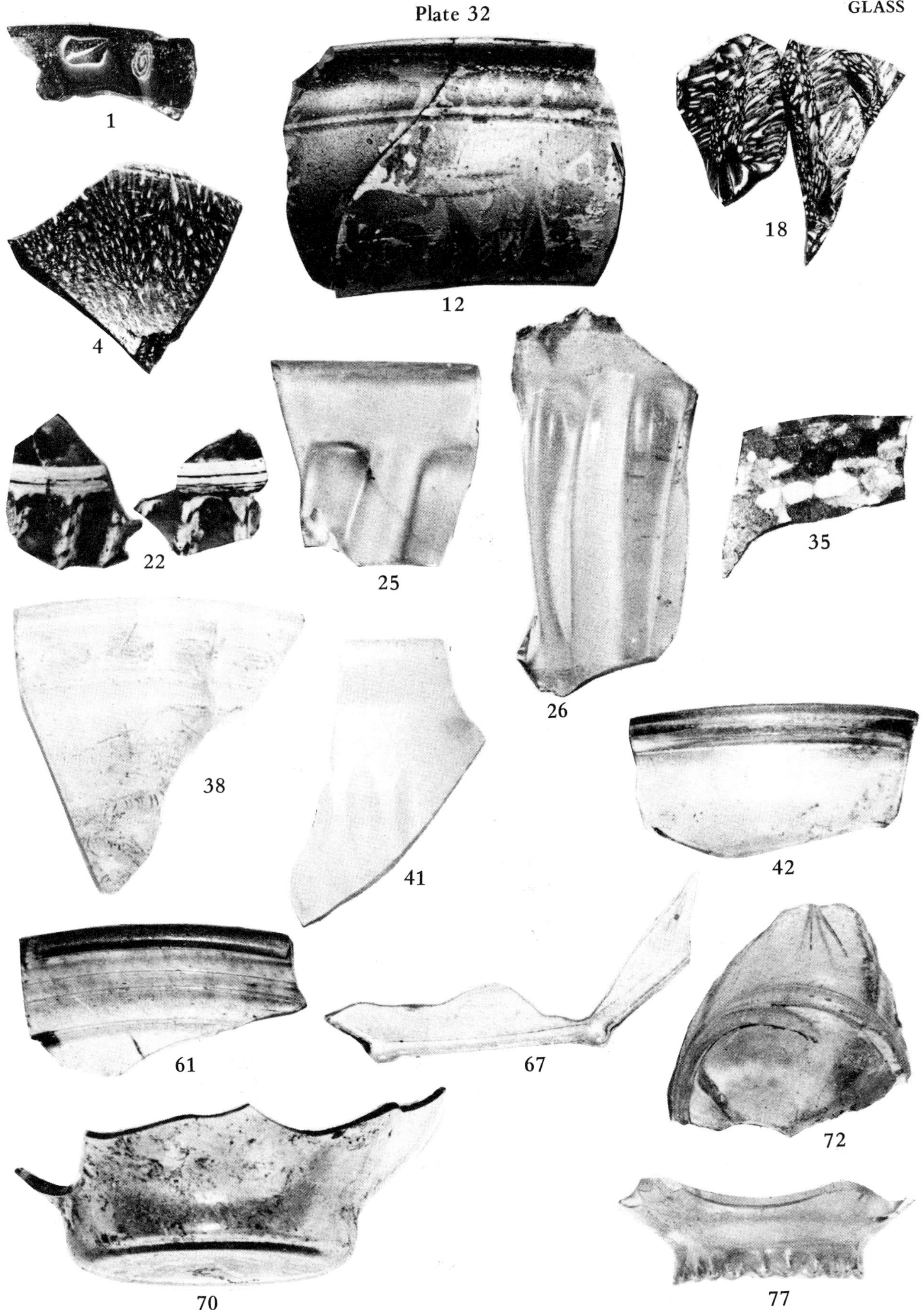

80
81
89
90
93
95
96
97
98
99
102
106
112
113
115
118
MANUFACTURING
WASTERS

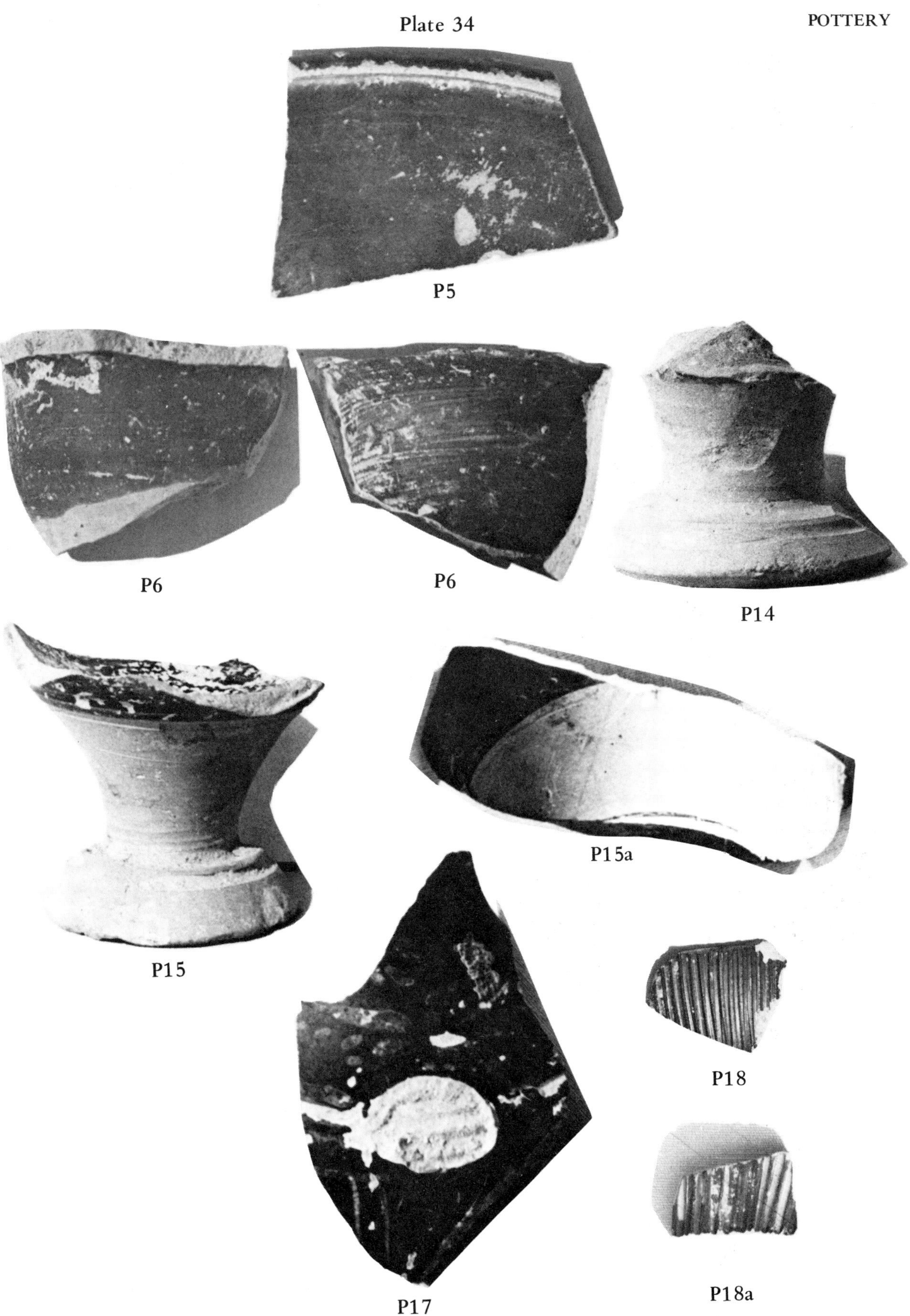

P5

P6

P6

P14

P15

P15a

P17

P18

P18a

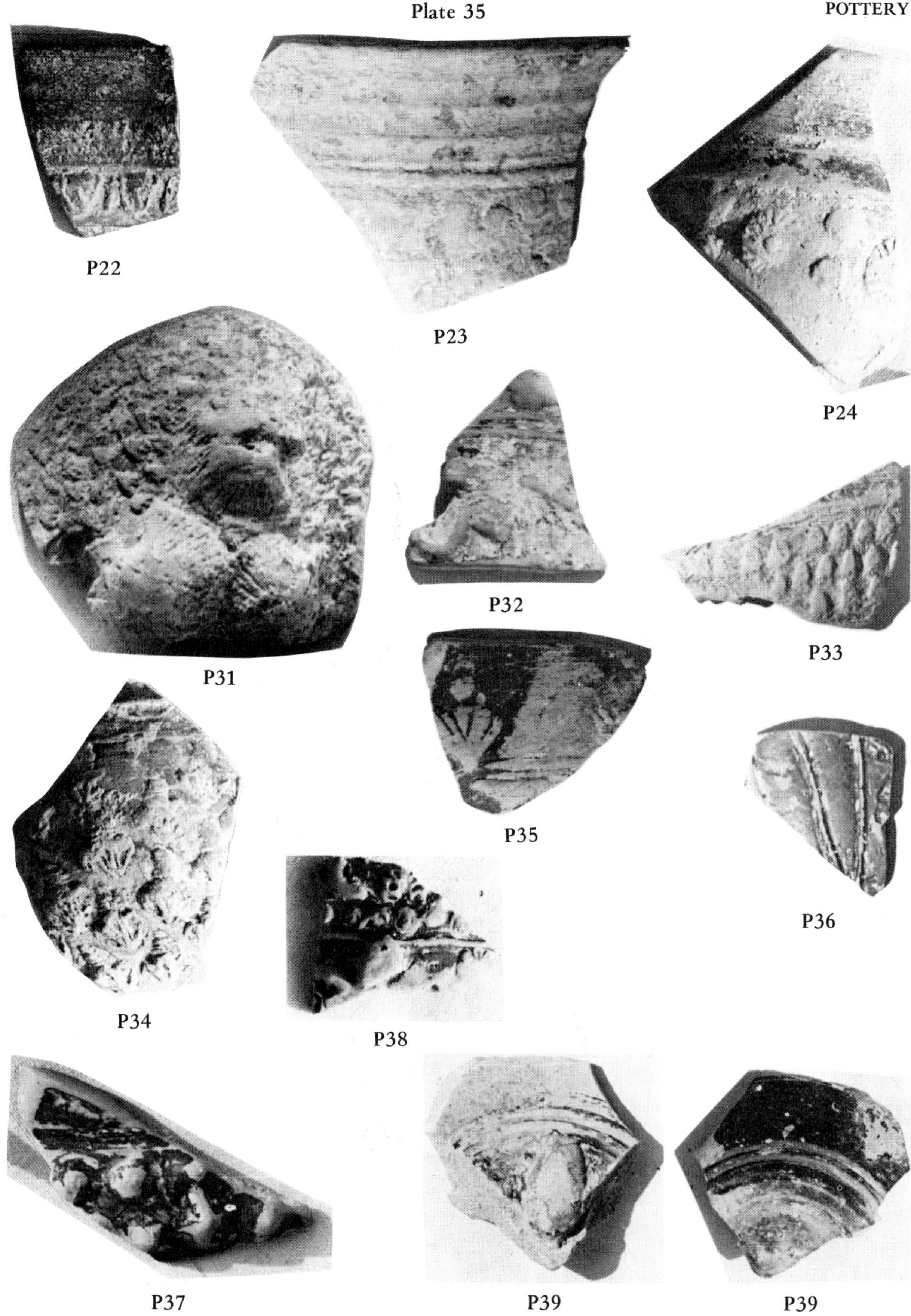

P22

P23

P24

P31

P32

P33

P35

P36

P34

P38

P37

P39

P39

P42

P53

P44 P44 P57

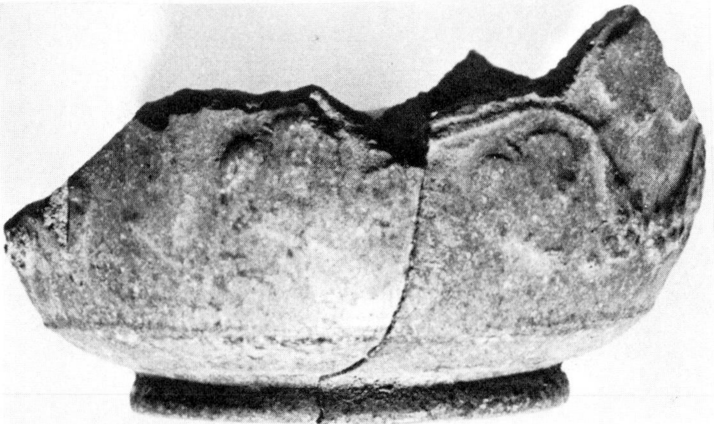

P63

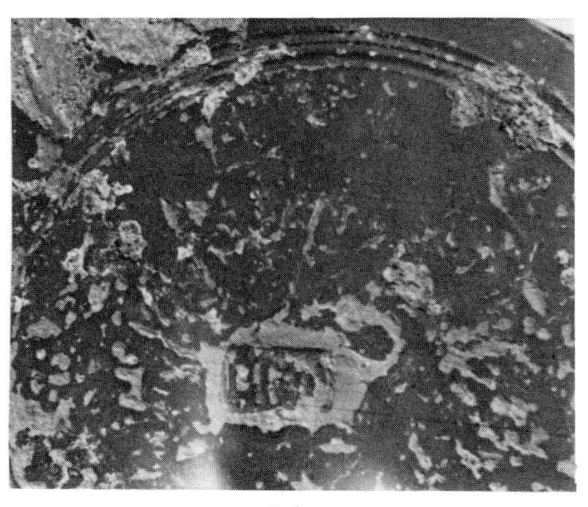

P67

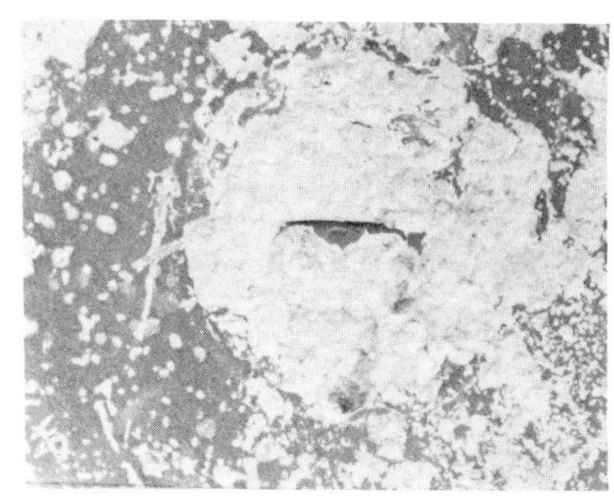

P68

*P72

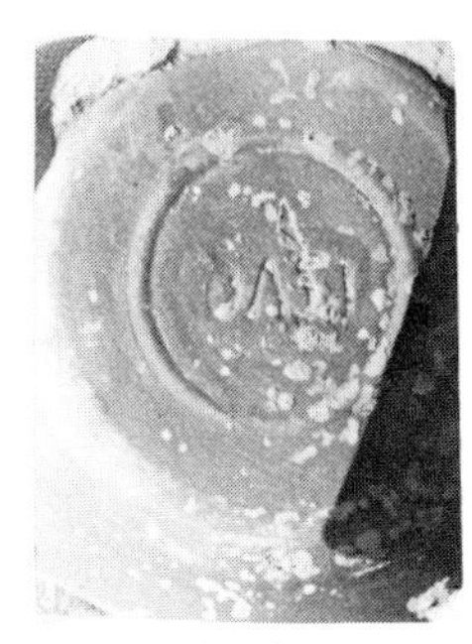

P73

P151

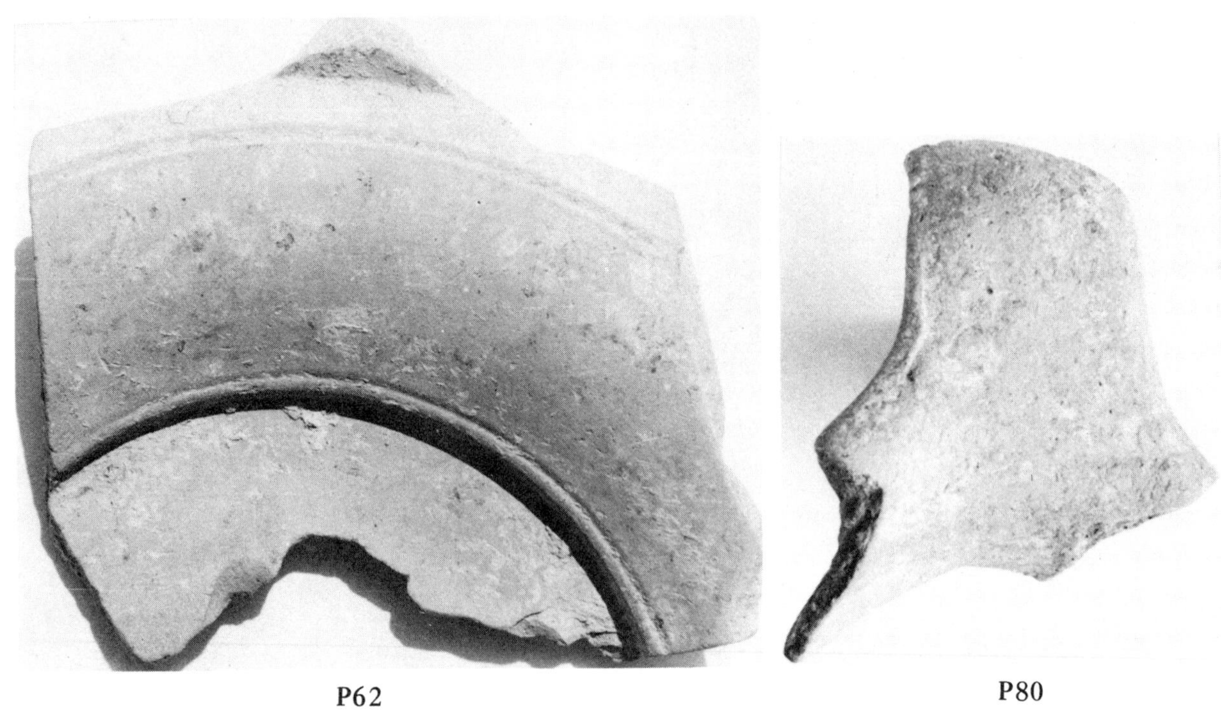

P62

P80

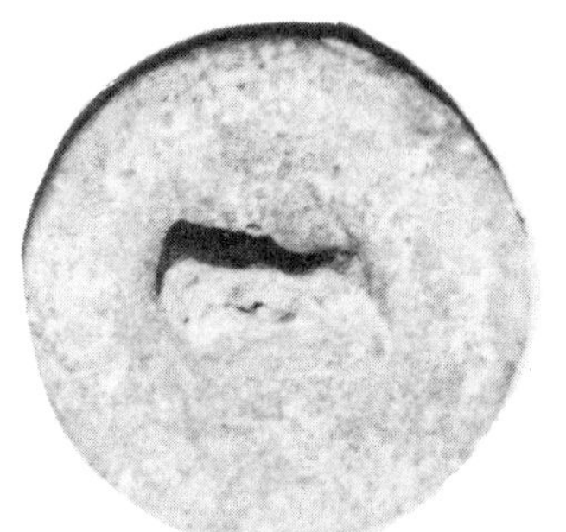

P122

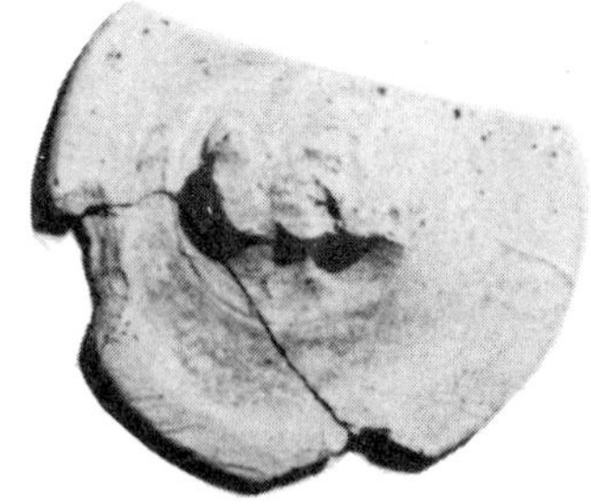

P123

P114a

1

2

1

3

4

3

13

11

14

12

15

16

17

18

19

20

21

22

23

24

26

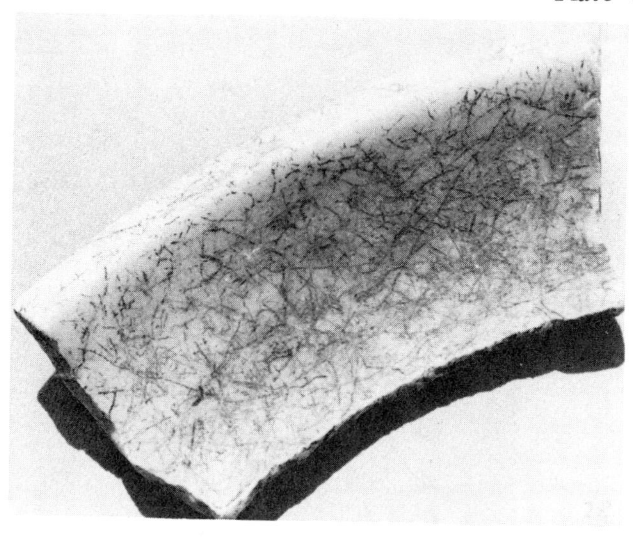
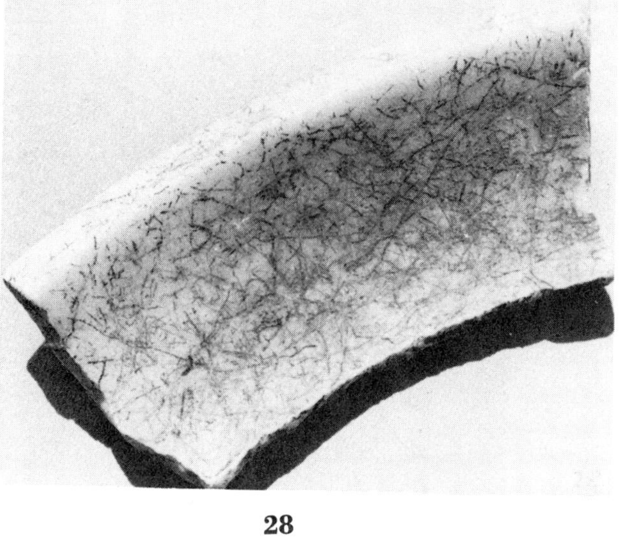

28

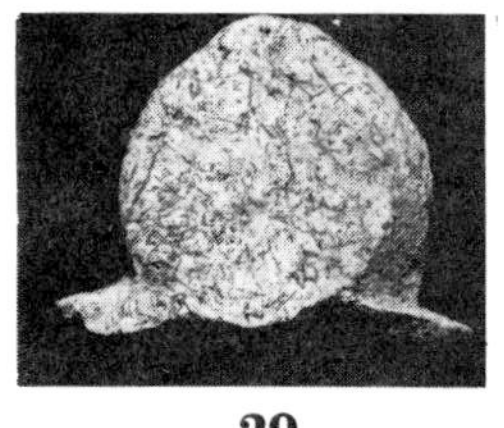

29

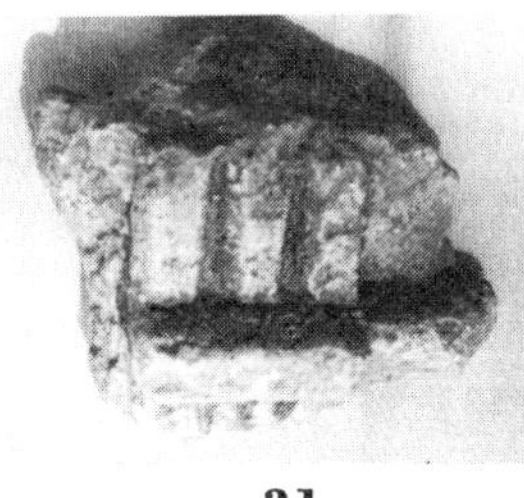

31

33

32

36

34

35

37

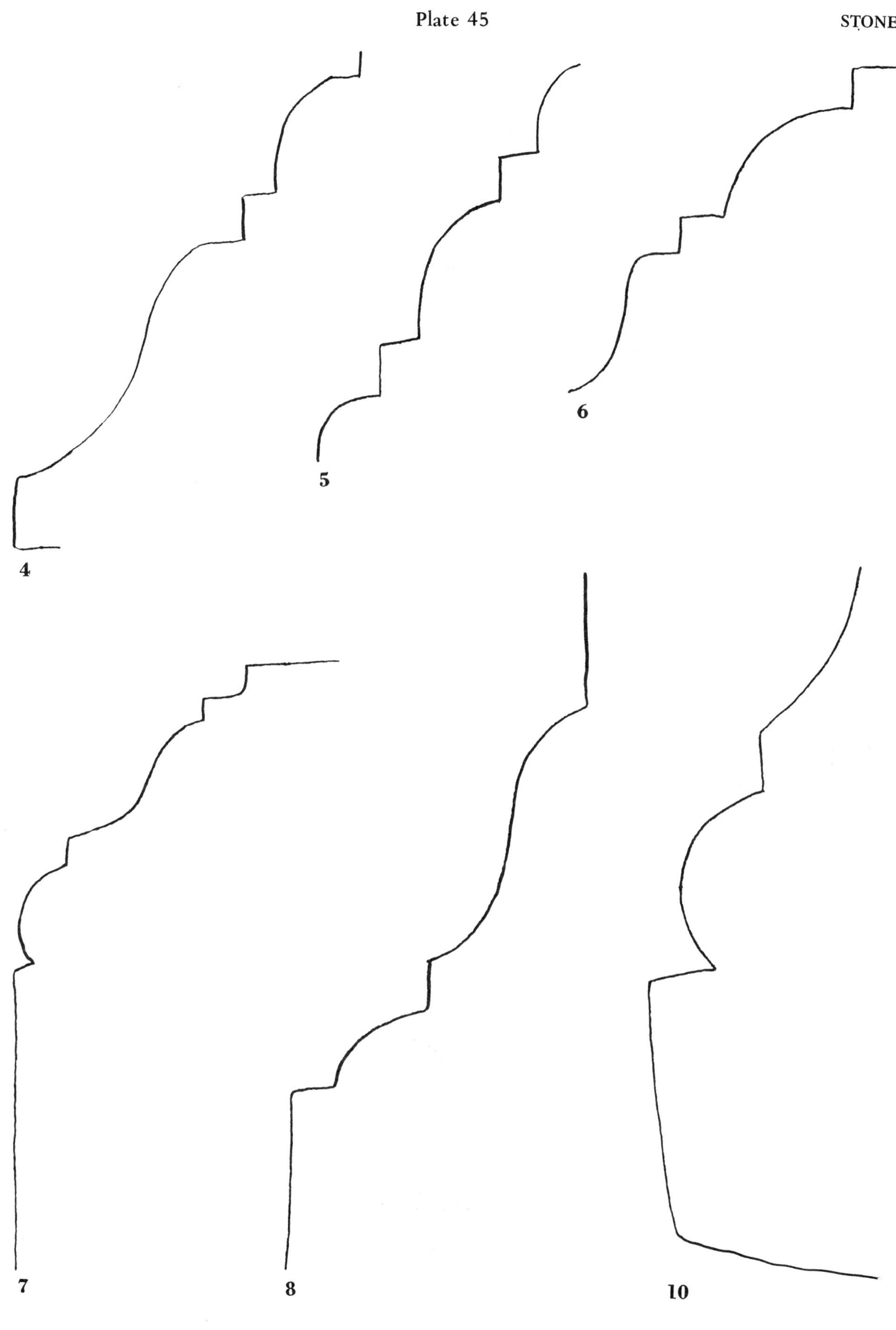
4
5
6
7
8
10

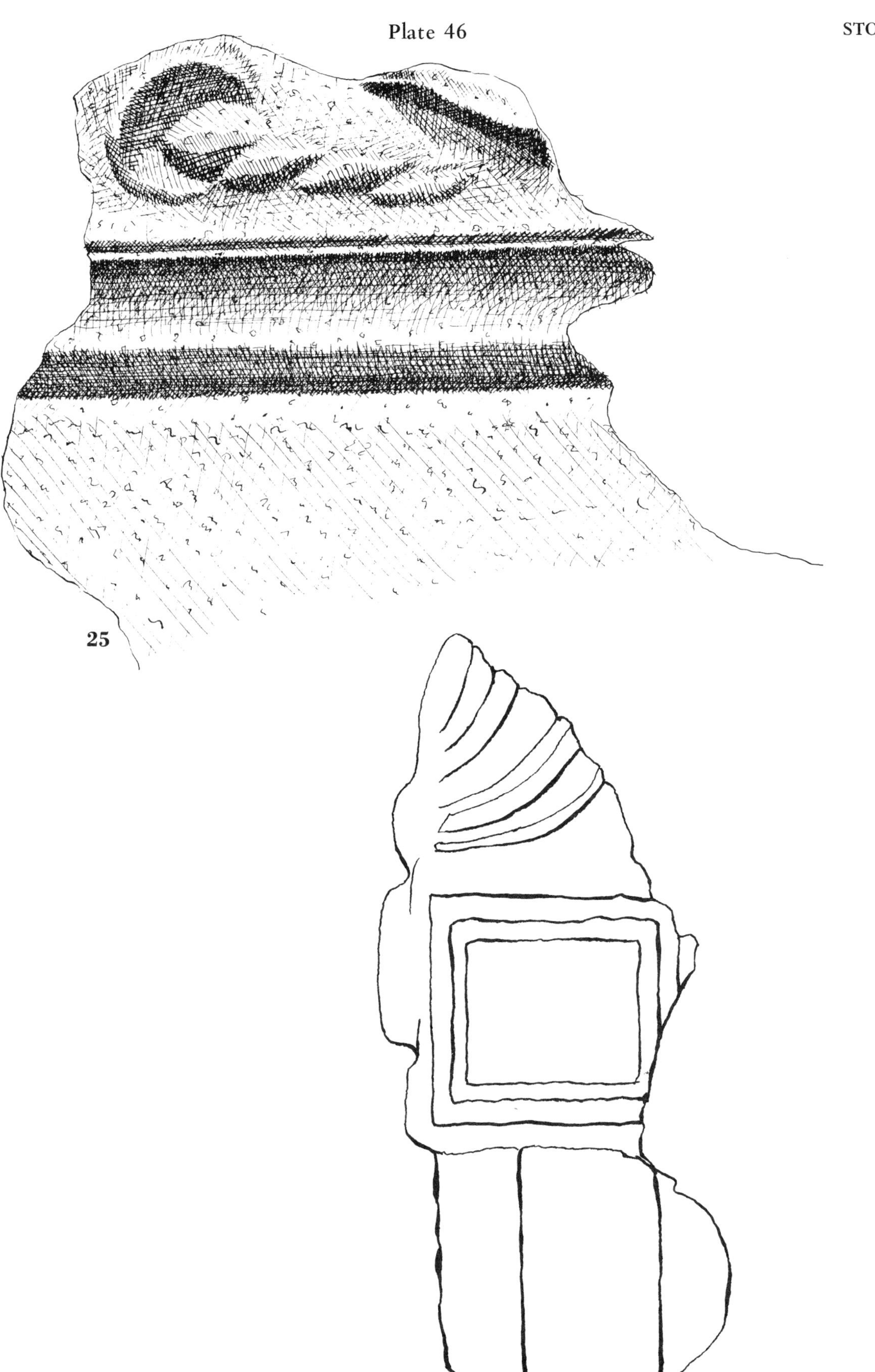
25
30

27

38

9

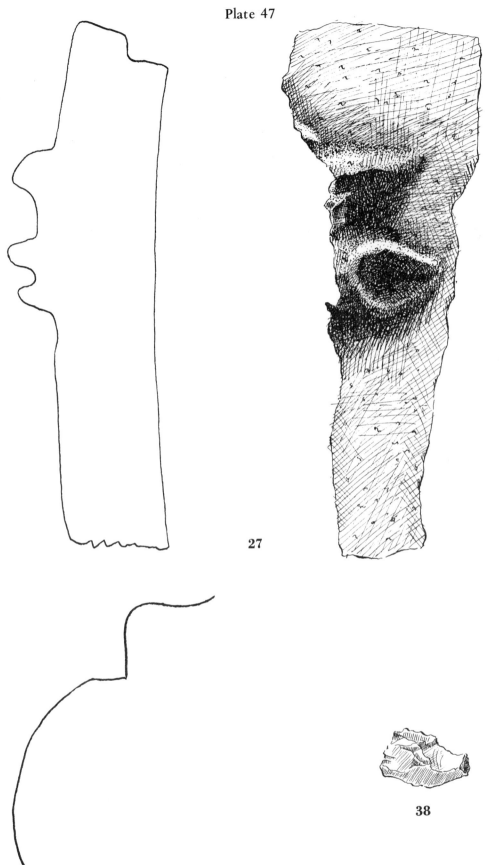

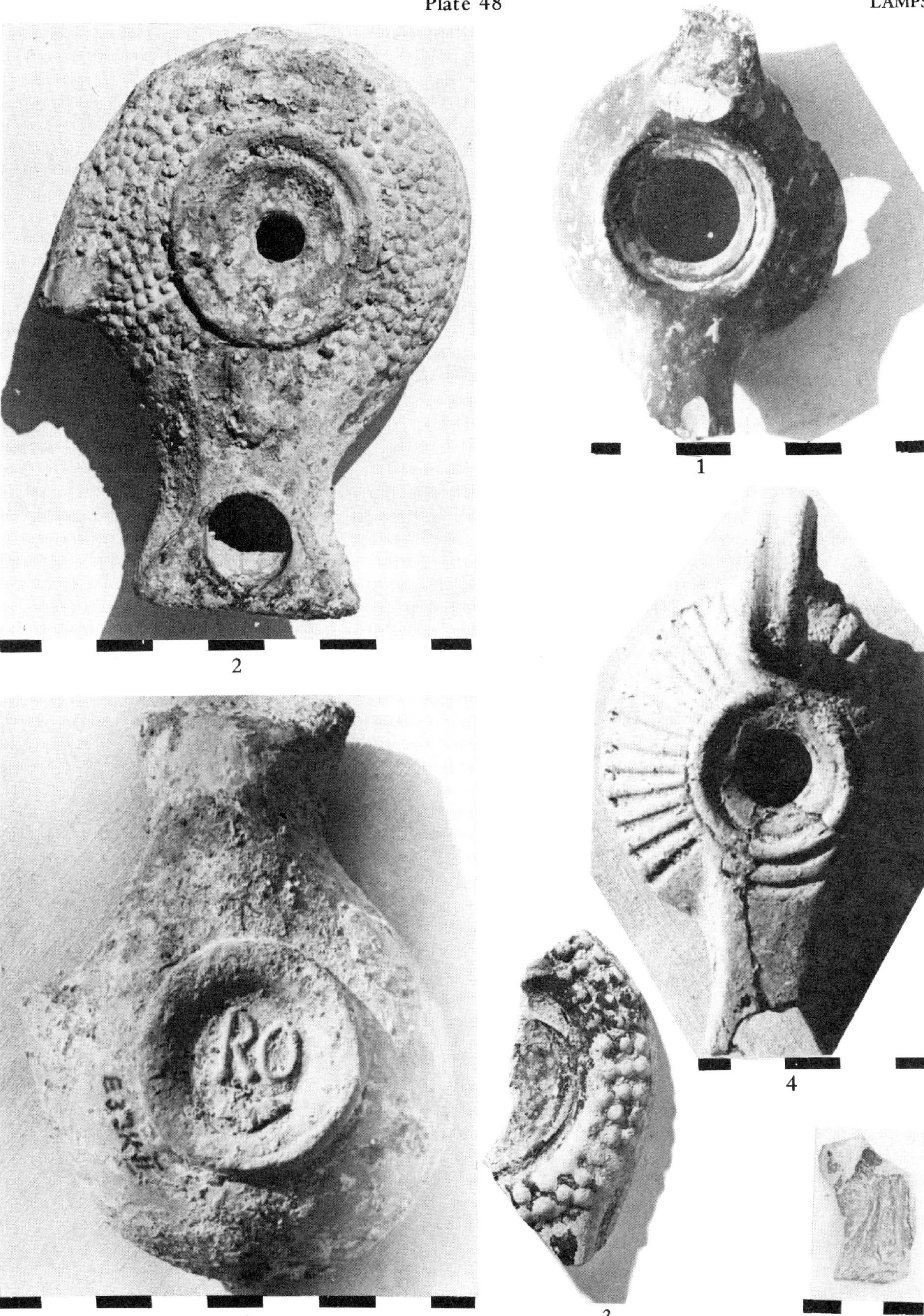

1

2

4

2

3

5

9
10
11
12
13
14
15
17
18
19
16
20
21

22

23

24

25

26

27

28

30

32

33

34

35

36

38

41

36

39

42

43

31

31

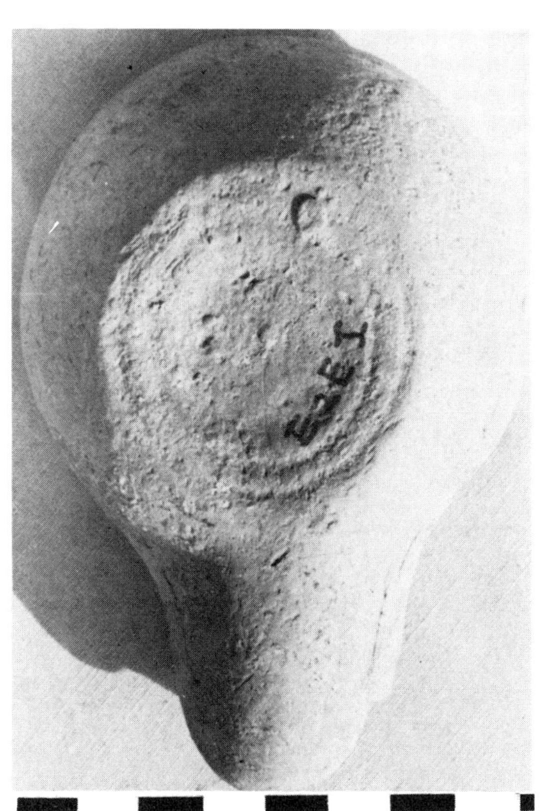
40

40

44 45 47 48 51 49 50 52

46

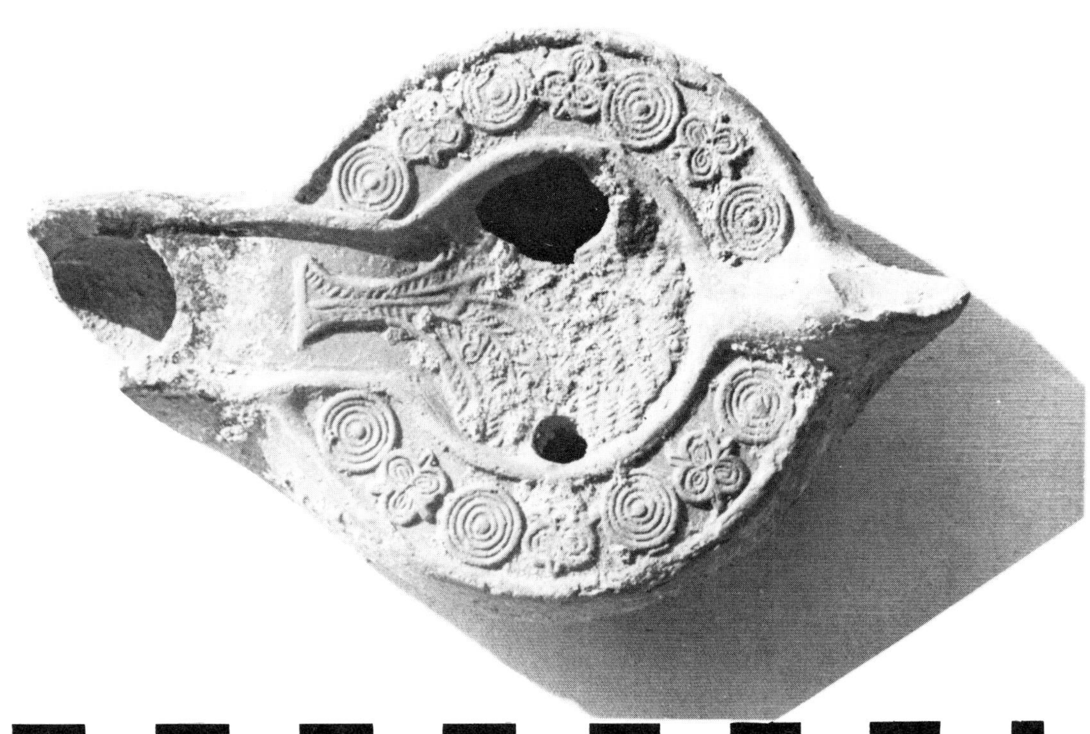

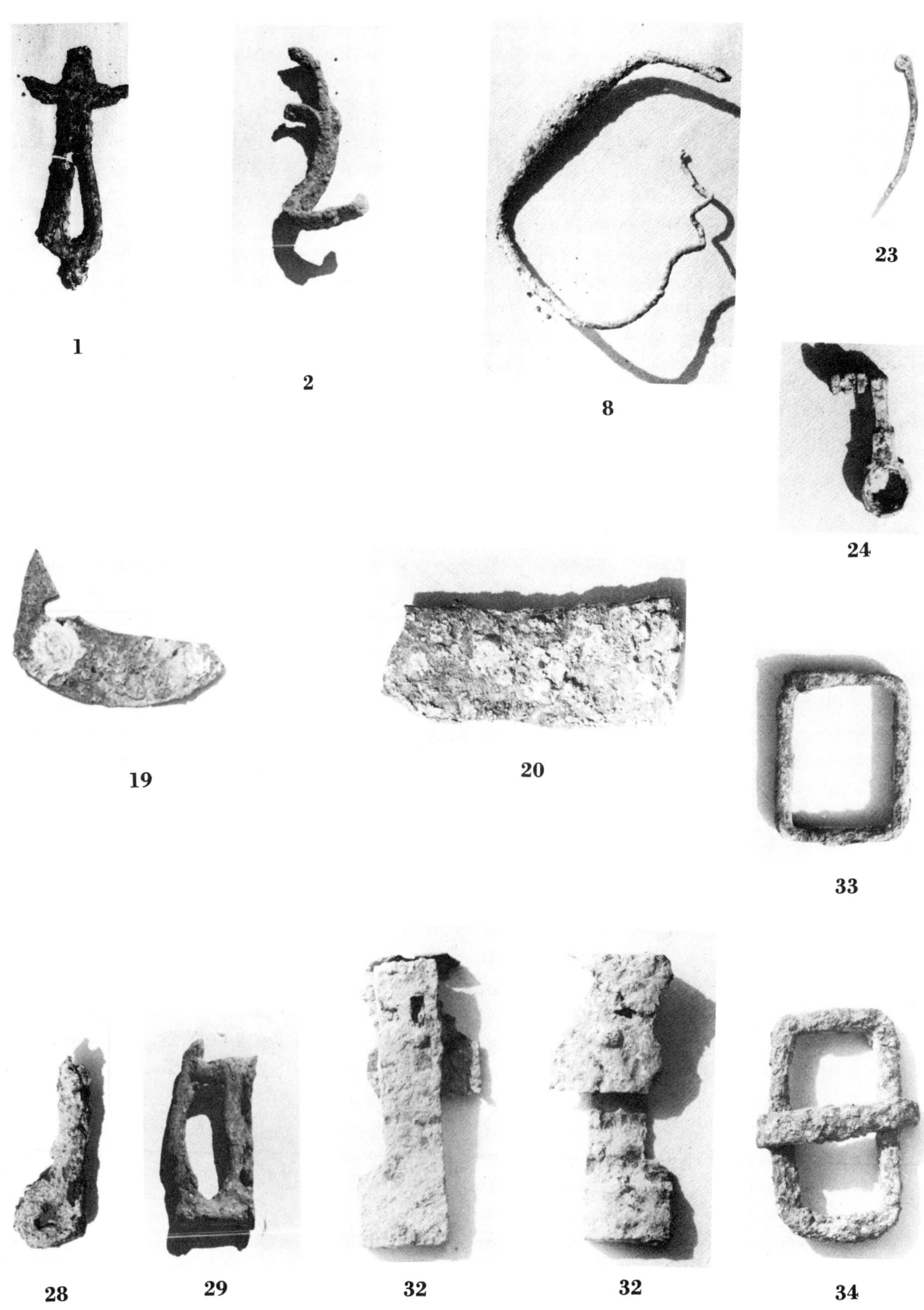
1
2
8
23
24
19
20
33
28
29
32
32
34

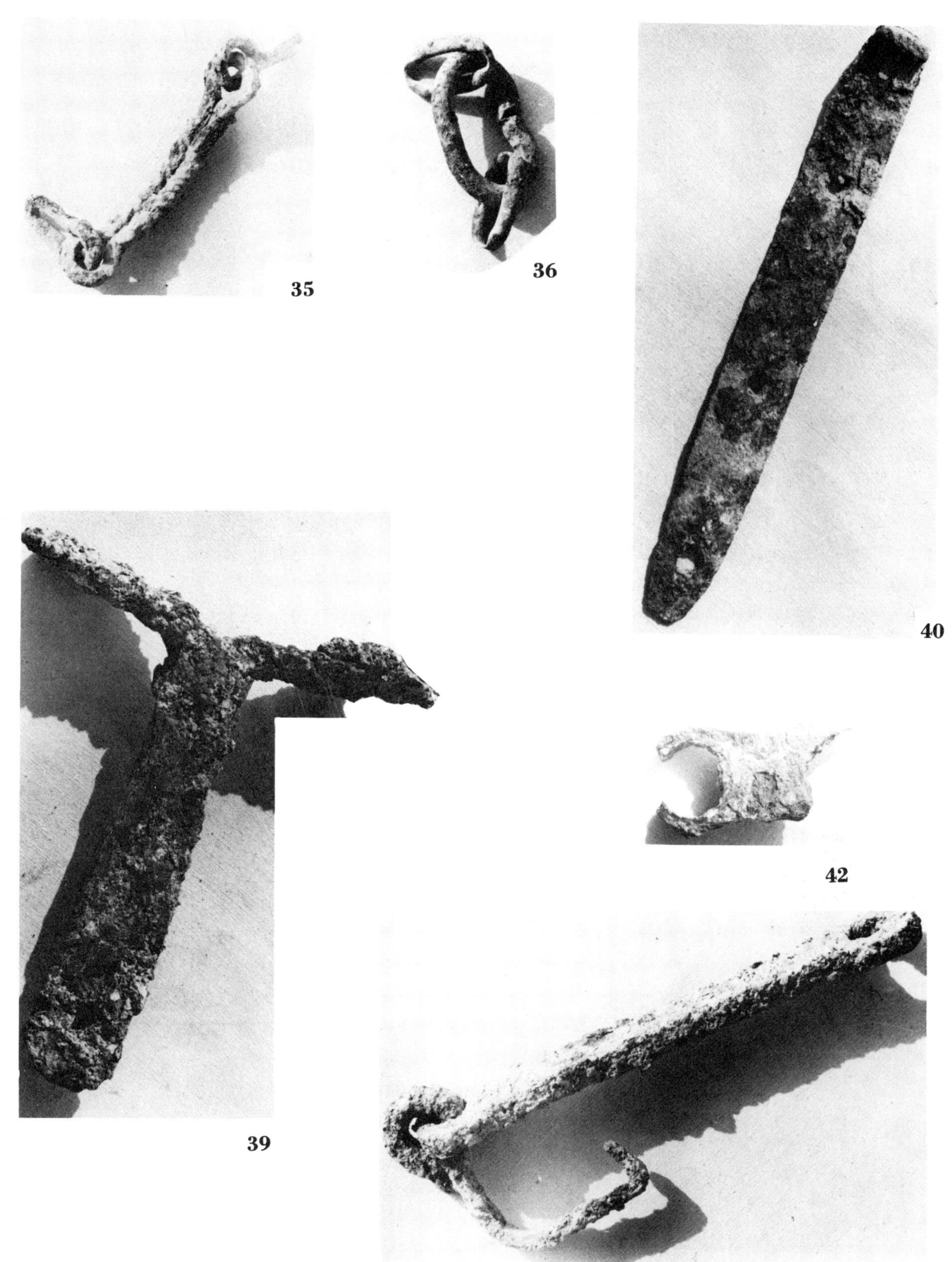
35
36
40
39
42
41

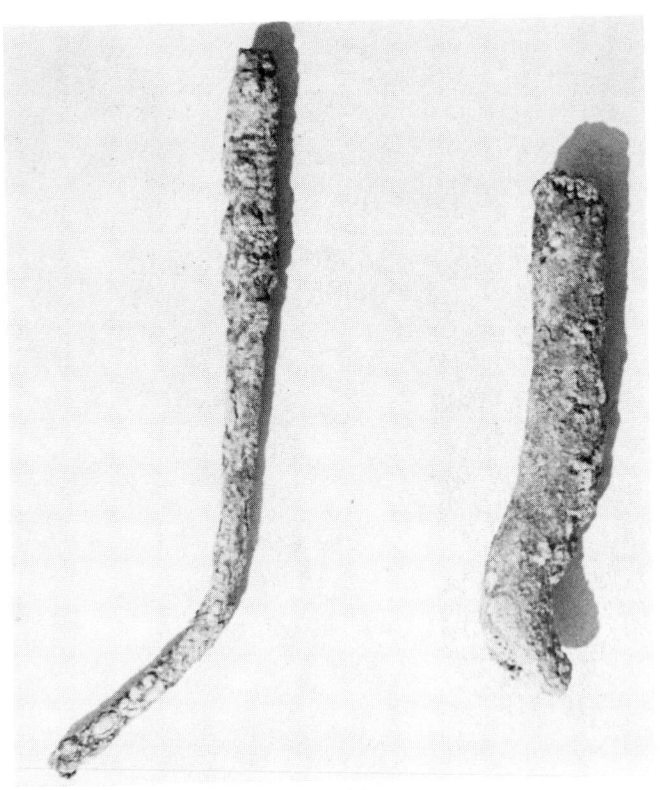

43

44

45

LEAD
(see pp. 00)

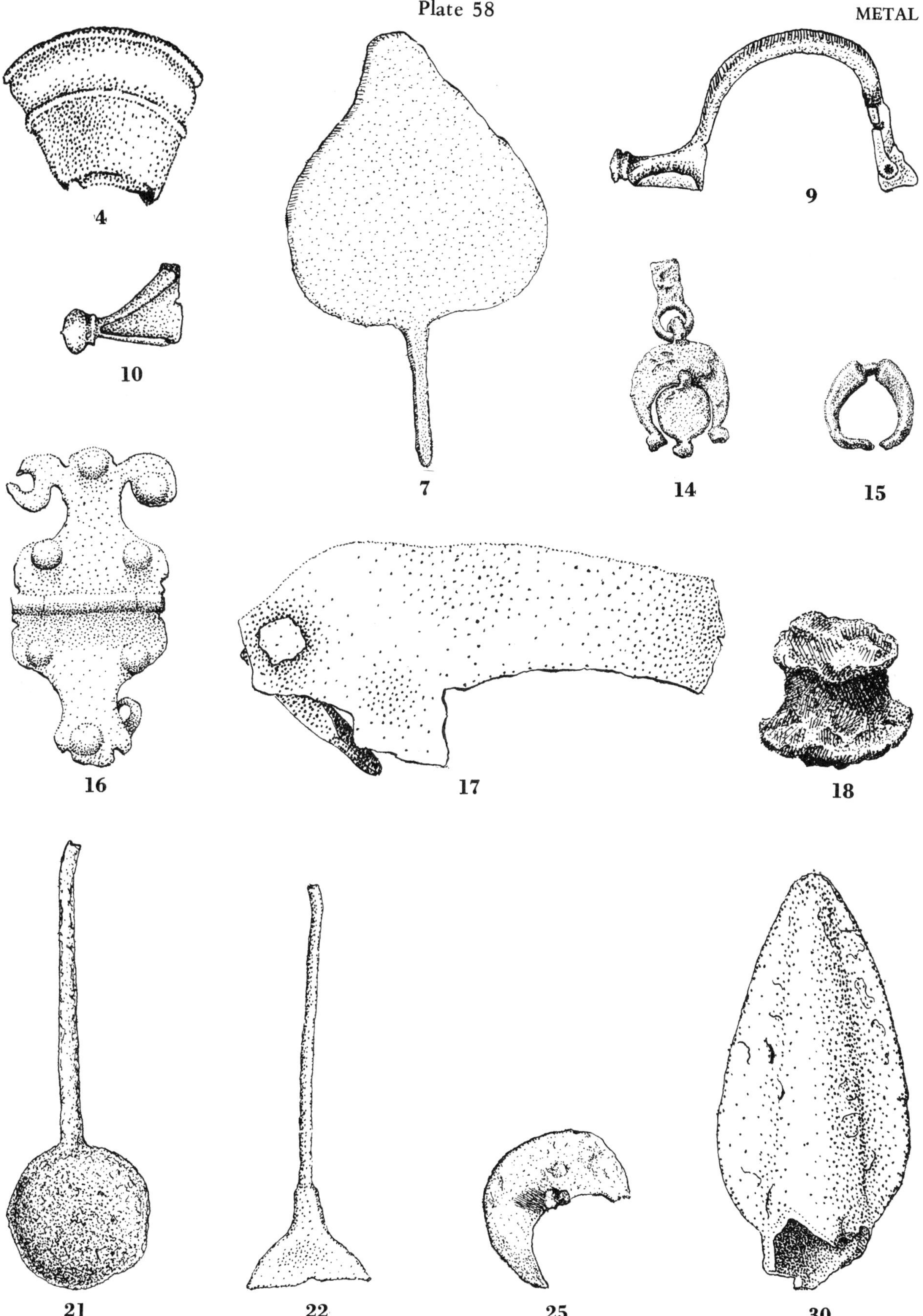
4
7
9
10
14
15
16
17
18
21
22
25
30

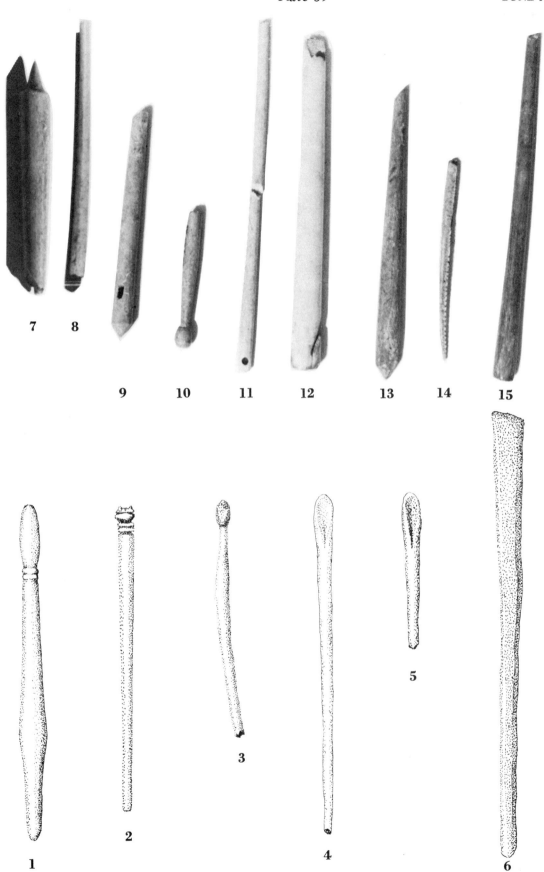

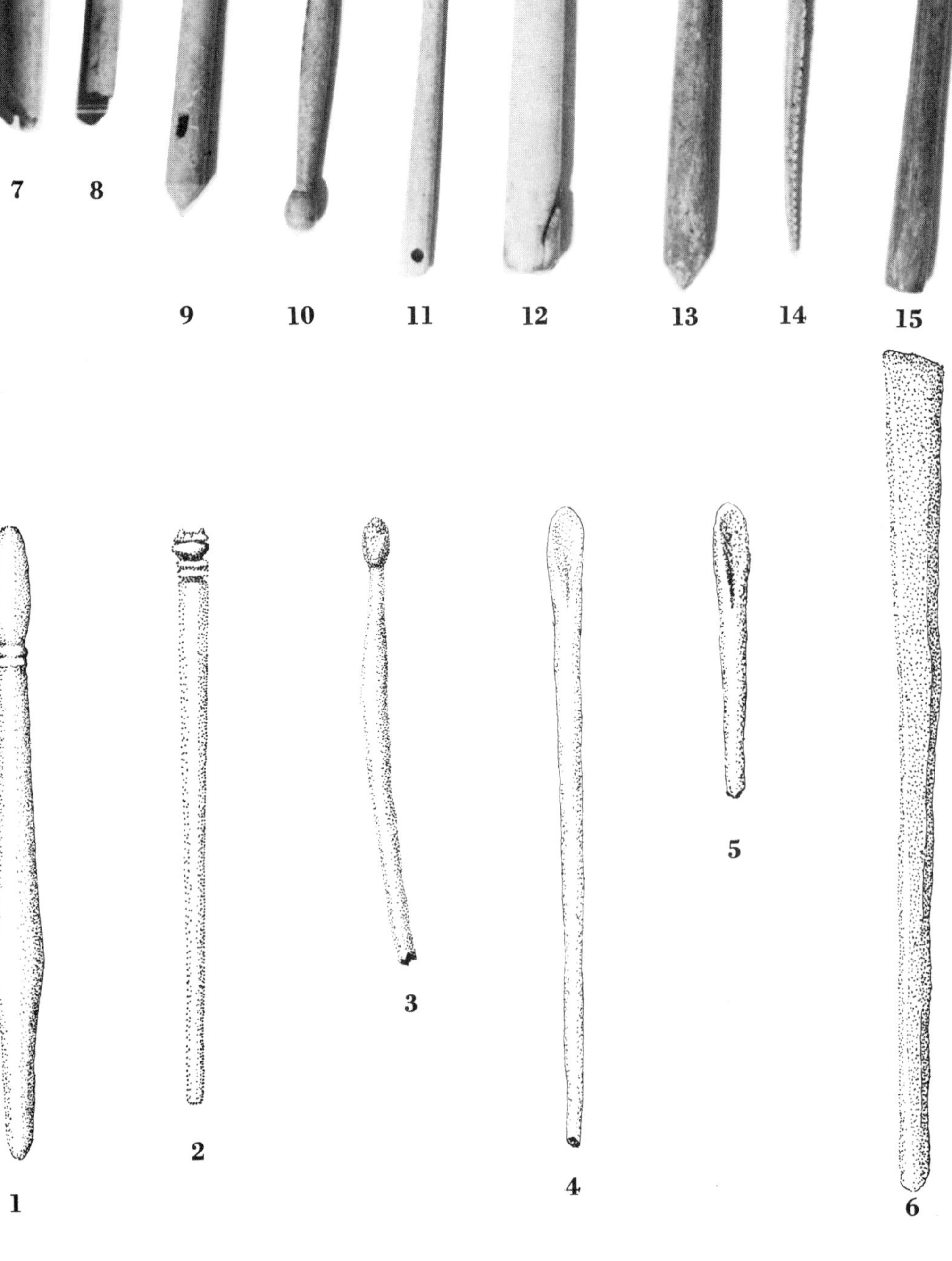
7
8
9
10
11
12
13
14
15
16
1
2
3
4
5
6

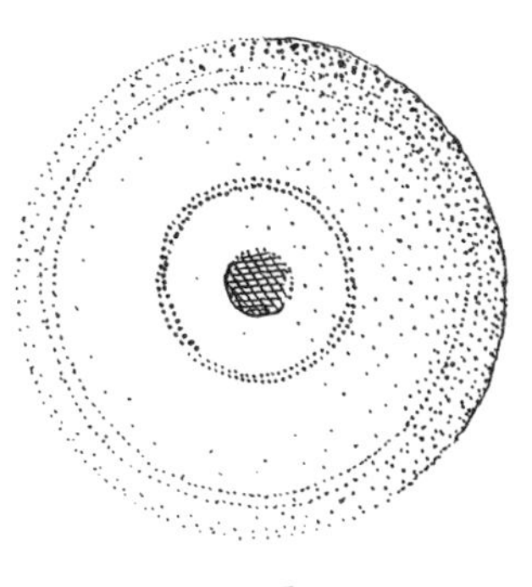

21

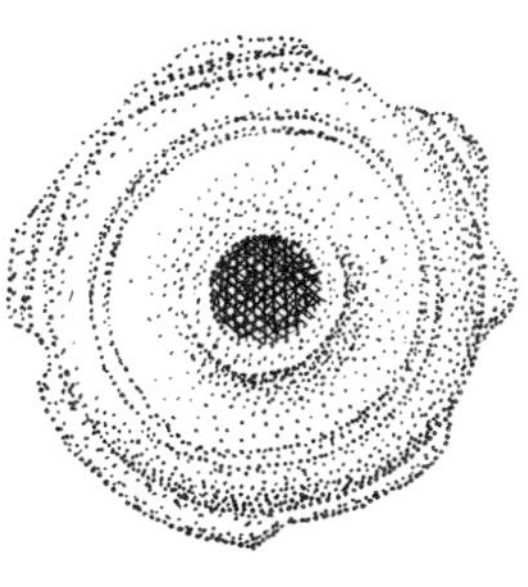

22

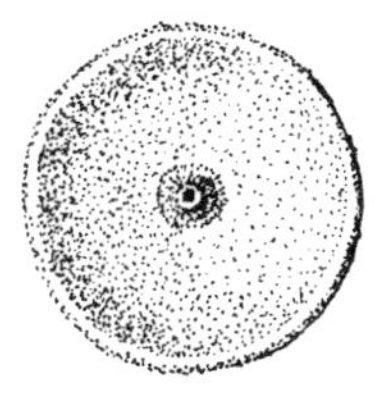

23

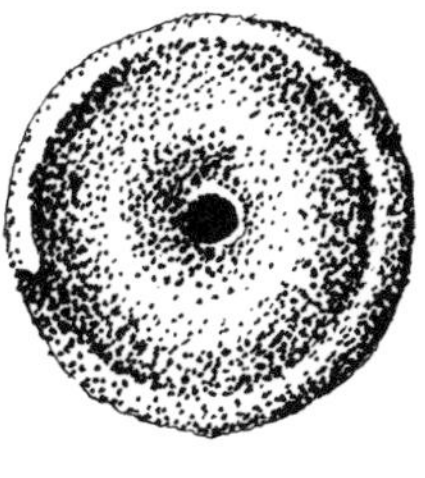

24

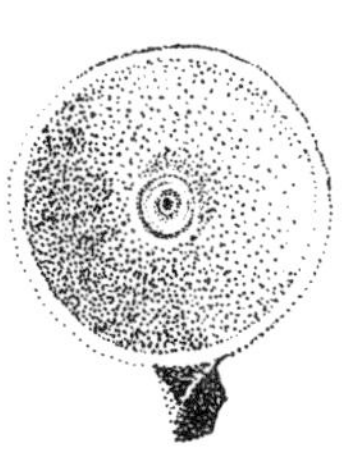

26

27

28

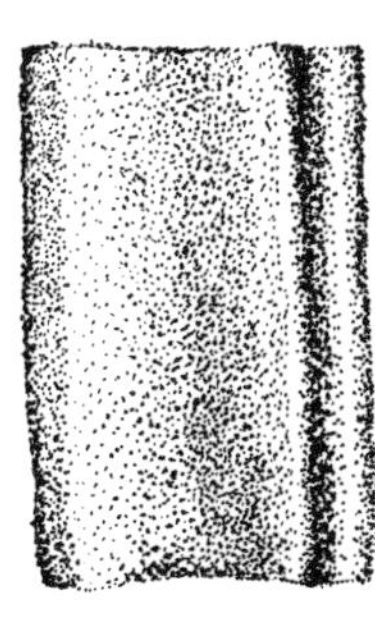

29

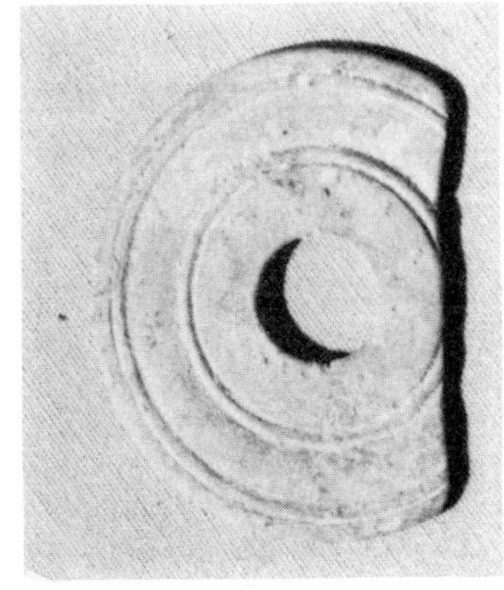

20

25

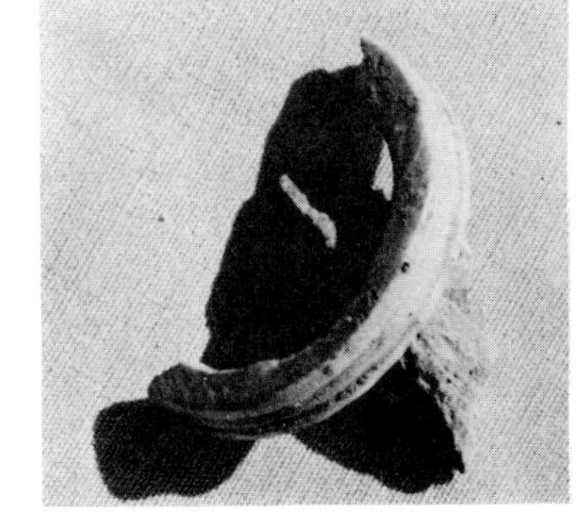

30

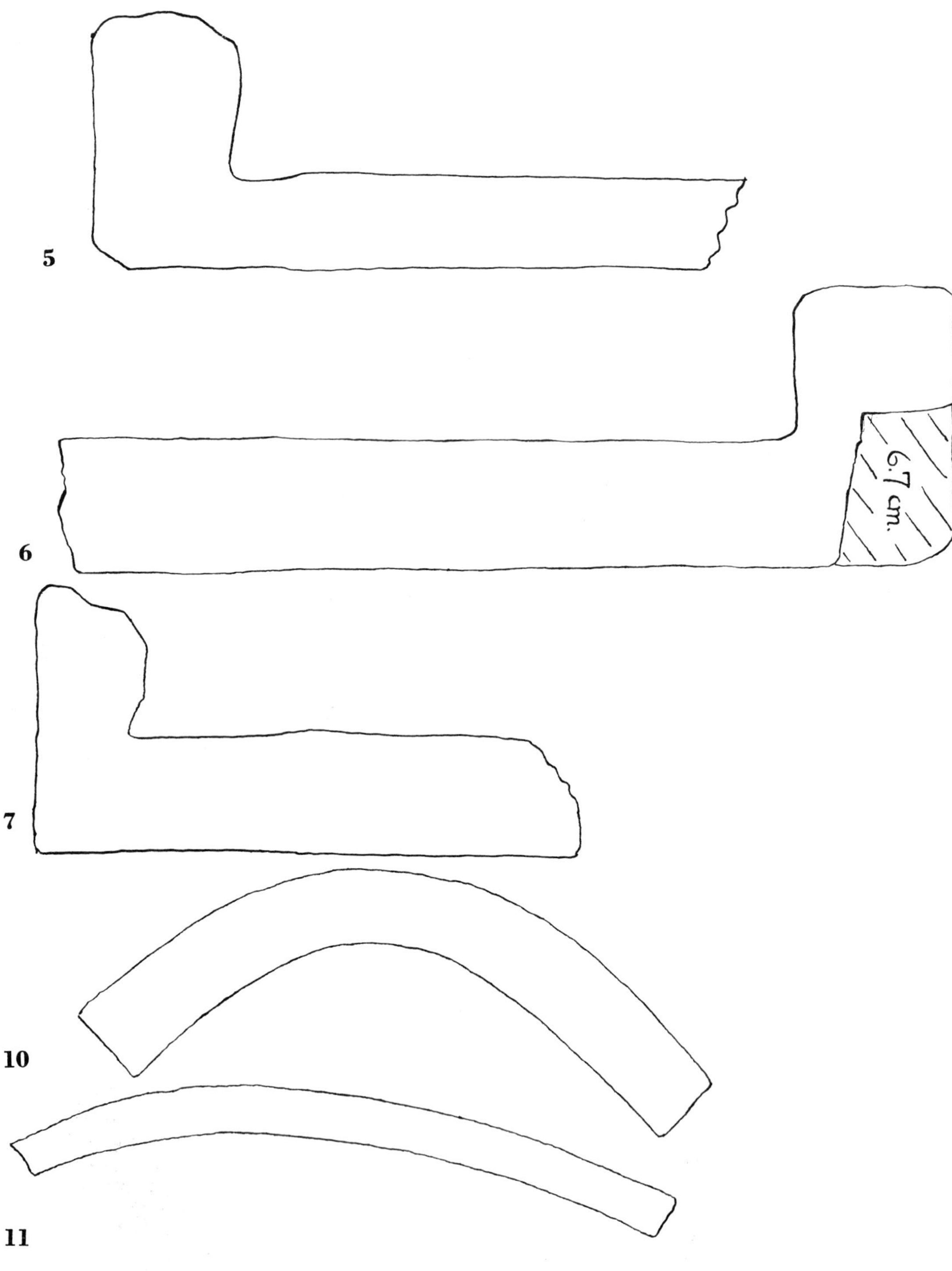
5
6
6.7 cm.
7
10
11

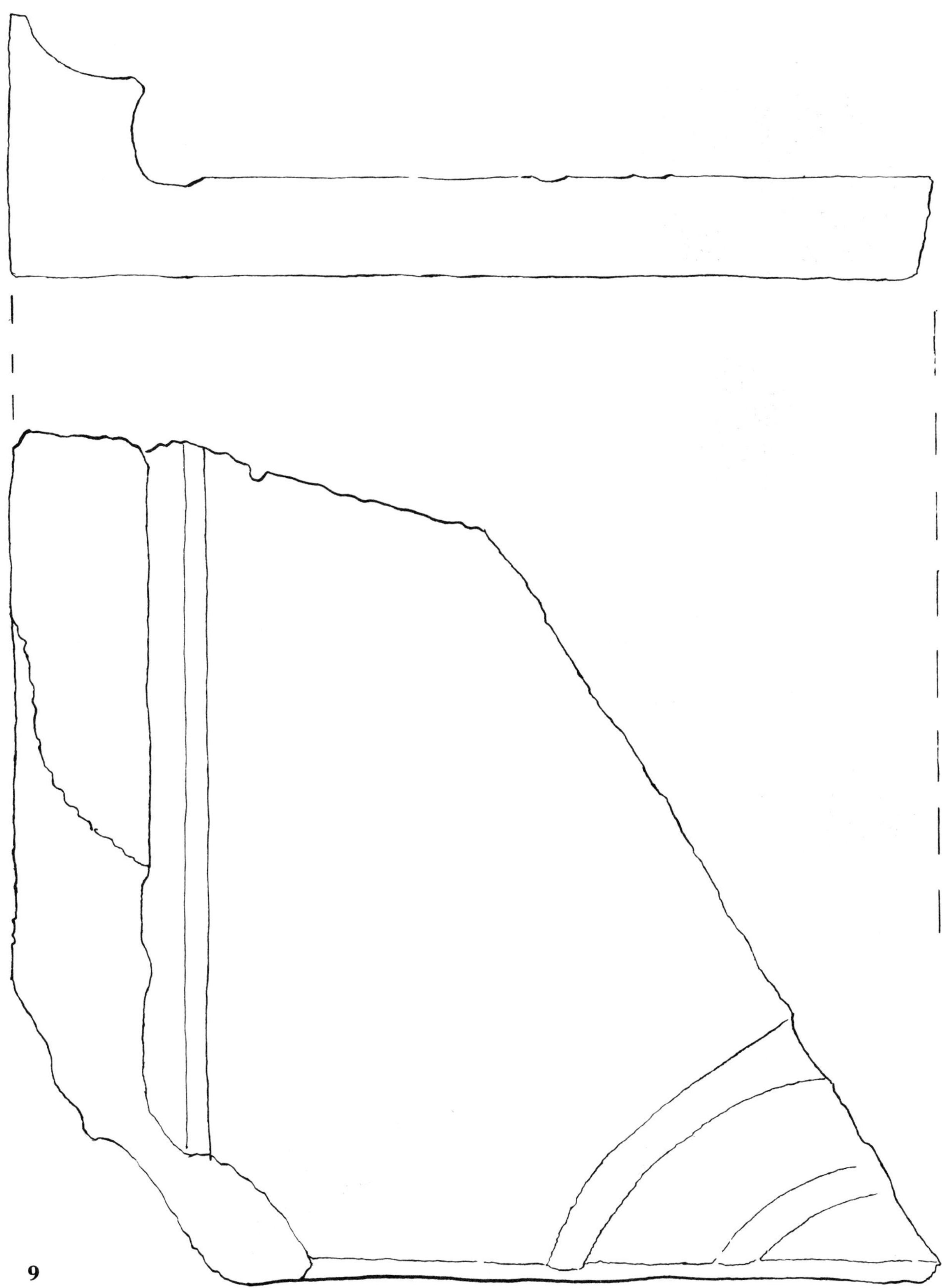

9

7 10 12 16 20 22 23 24

26 26

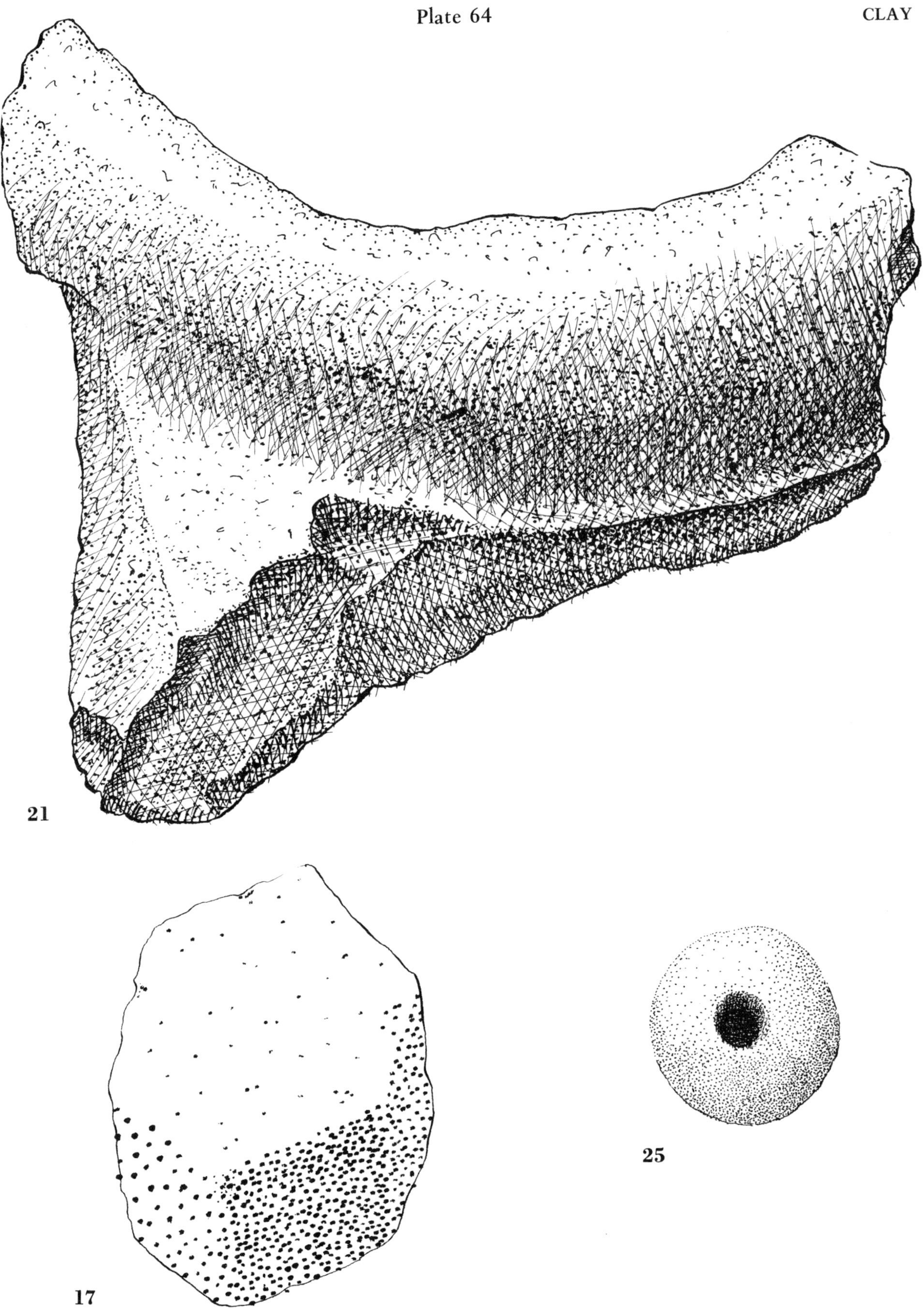
21
17
25